BECOMING ASSAMESE

This book explores the making of colonial Northeast India and offers a new perspective to the study of the Assamese identity in the nineteenth century as a distinctly nineteenth-century cultural phenomenon, not confined to linguistic parameters alone. It studies crucial markers of the self – history, customs, food, dress, new religious beliefs – and symbols considered desirable by the provincial middle class and the way these fitted in with the latter's nationalist subjectivities in the face of an emphatic Bengali cultural nationalism. The author shows how colonialism was intrinsically linked to the nationalist assertions of the middle class intelligentsia in the region and was instrumental in eroding the essential malleability of societal processes nurtured by the Ahom state.

Rich with fresh research data, this book will be useful to scholars and researchers of history, political science, area studies, and to anyone interested in understanding Northeast India.

Madhumita Sengupta is Assistant Professor of History at the Indian Institute of Technology Gandhinagar, Gujarat, India. She completed her MA in Modern History from Jawaharlal Nehru University, New Delhi, and PhD in History from the University of Calcutta. She was a Post-Doctoral Fellow at the Centre for Studies in Social Sciences, Calcutta (CSSSC), and has taught at Rani Birla Girls' College, Kolkata. Her areas of research interests include linguistic, cultural and regional identities in the nineteenth and early twentieth centuries in India, socio-economic and cultural aspects of British rule in India and the colonial history of Northeast India.

BECOMING ASSAMESE

Colonialism and new subjectivities in Northeast India

Madhumita Sengupta

Routledge
Taylor & Francis Group

LONDON AND NEW YORK

First South Asia edition 2016

First published 2016
by Routledge
2 Park Square, Milton Park, Abingdon, Oxon OX14 4RN

and by Routledge
711 Third Avenue, New York, NY 10017

Routledge is an imprint of the Taylor & Francis Group, an informa business

© 2016 Madhumita Sengupta

British Library Cataloguing-in-Publication Data
A catalogue record for this book is available from the British Library

Library of Congress Cataloging-in-Publication Data
A catalog record has been requested for this book

ISBN: 978-1-138-21960-1 (hbk)
ISBN: 978-1-315-56027-4 (ebk)

Typeset in Galliard
by Apex CoVantage, LLC

Printed in India by Replika Press Pvt. Ltd.

For sale in India, Pakistan, Nepal, Bhutan, Bangladesh and Sri Lanka only.

Dedicated to Baba, Maa, Indranath and Riju

CONTENTS

ACKNOWLEDGEMENTS

Writing this book was an opportunity for me to relive the memories of the place where I grew up and which I had to leave at a relatively young age. Unlike many others, who are not destined to go back to their places of origin, I had the opportunity to come back to Guwahati time and again since a part of my family continues to live in the city. Having grown up in a family with roots in erstwhile East Bengal, and with elderly grandparents and relatives still around to recall their *bhite bari* (ancestral house) in Poob Bangla, or East Bengal, 'migration' happened to be a much discussed phenomenon in the house. It is just that I did not quite realize how much it could hurt till I had myself made the shift from Guwahati to Calcutta. It was not easy to leave behind friends and memories, not to speak of the trauma of having to adjust in a city so large and busy that it almost seemed to engulf you – a city above all that I had never quite fancied notwithstanding my 'Bengali roots'. Interestingly enough, my very Bengali upbringing had familiarized me with the world of 'Bengali' culture although I could barely connect with my new acquaintances and felt I had always been better off with the friends I had been compelled to leave behind, even if we did not speak the same languages at home. Communication had been either in Bengali or Assamese or English since most of us, whether Bengalis or Assamese, spoke all the three languages. I am not sure whether this is how people who migrate to other places usually feel, but I will not be surprised if the sentiments come pretty close. I am very thankful to have studied history as this has equipped me with the wherewithal to make sense of my subjectivities and my constant feelings of rootlessness.

I owe an intellectual debt to some stimulating classroom lectures and interactions with teachers like Rajat Kanta Ray, Sabyasachi Bhattacharya, Tapati Guha-Thakurta, Partha Chatterjee and Lakshmi Subrahmanian, as well as to the extremely valuable suggestions from Rosinka Choudhury, Bodhisattva Kar, Prachi Deshpande and the late Prof. Anjan Ghosh which helped in moulding my research. A stimulating BA in Presidency College, Calcutta, and an MA in modern history at Jawaharlal Nehru University provided me with the basic training without which it would have been impossible to undertake this project. I thank my supervisor Prof. Suranjan Das sincerely for his constant encouragement and support. A very engaging 15 months spent as Ford Postdoctoral Fellow at CSSSC, Kolkata, during 2010–11, proved very crucial in my career. I owe a world of debt to my mentor Tapati Guha-Thakurta and my teachers and colleagues at CSSSC for their time and help. I would also like to thank Dr Sunetra Sinha, Principal, Rani Birla Girls' College, for allowing me to join CSSSC and also for her continued support for my academic projects.

The credit for providing me with sustained institutional support that enabled me to give shape to my ideas and research must go to my new institution, that is IIT Gandhinagar. I sincerely thank Dr Kumbar, our esteemed librarian at IITGN for always responding promptly to all my abrupt, frequent and urgent requests for books and articles. I thank the staff of IITGN library for their co-operation and help.

I thank the anonymous referee of Routledge who offered valuable comments to an earlier draft of the manuscript. I sincerely thank Dr Shashank Shekhar Sinha, Publishing Director, Routledge, for all his valuable publishing tips that made things so much easier for me. In this connection, I would like to thank my teacher of Presidency College, Prof. Rajat Kanta Ray, for it was he who first suggested that I should approach Routledge for publishing my manuscript. I thank Ms Antara Ray Chaudhury of Routledge for her gentle reminders at regular intervals that helped me to complete the work in time.

I thank the staff of all the archives and libraries which became my prime destinations during all those hectic months of fieldwork. For all their help in locating and photocopying records, I thank the staff and members of the National Library, Calcutta, WBSA, Kolkata, ASA and SL, Dispur, DHAS, Guwahati, District Library, NERC library, Shillong, National Archives, Delhi, NMML, New Delhi, and the OIOC, British Library, London. I would like to specifically mention the names of some of the people at these institutions, like Ashim Mukhopadhyay of the National Library, Calcutta, for the promptness with which he would procure 'missing' books; Vaishya da and Baharul of the ASA, Dispur, and its director, Dr D. Sonowal; the staff of NERC, Shillong; and Jayati di of the WBSA, Kolkata, for their sincere efforts towards the smooth functioning of these libraries and record rooms. To Anirban da and Nilanjana who welcomed me into their home during a month-long stay in London, I would like to express my sincere thanks. To my aunts and uncles-in-law in C.R. Park, New Delhi, where I usually stay during my fieldwork at the NAI, I have only sincere words of gratitude.

Baba and Maa have always been a constant source of inspiration. They brought up my son while I was busy with my work. Without this tremendous support from my parents, this book would not have seen the light of day. To my little son, who bore through my fieldwork and long absences from home as well as my usual preoccupied state of mind, I have no words to express my gratitude. For Indranath, dear husband and soulmate, and the person who stood by me steadfastly through all these years, believing more than I did in my abilities, and offering to shoulder the extra load in order to give me the time and opportunity to pursue my research, no word of gratitude would be adequate to express what I feel. I shall never be able to thank him enough for his support and innumerable acts of kindness and advice but for which this work would never have been accomplished. I would also like to thank my mother-in-law for being the wonderful person that she is.

This acknowledgement would be incomplete if I did not mention the people who have offered me intellectual stimulation, familial affection and in recent years also a warm shelter during my several field visits to Guwahati. I thank all my maternal uncles, aunts and cousins in Guwahati for making my field trips so pleasant and something to look forward to every time. Ful-mami's affectionate gestures like packing in tiffin for me so that I did not go without lunch during my archival visits and the love and affection of all members of my Boromamu's household made my stay in that house immensely enjoyable. To all the members of this household, including Bharati di, for the wonderful food and her affection, I offer my sincere thanks.

ABBREVIATIONS

ASA	Assam State Archive
ASL	Assam State Secretariat Library
BL	British Library
DHAS	Department of Historical and Antiquarian Studies
EIC	East India Company
EPW	*Economic and Political Weekly*
IESHR	*Indian Economic and Social History Review*
NAI	National Archives of India
OIOC	Oriental and India Office Collection
PHA	Political History of Assam
Progs	proceedings
WBSA	West Bengal State Archive

INTRODUCTION

I

A historian's job is far more exciting and challenging today than it was before. A plethora of new histories and debates have revolutionized our understanding of the colonial encounter. For an aspiring historian venturing to study the colonial period in India, therefore, it would no longer do to acquire a familiarity with the colonial economy or the national movement. As Sumit Sarkar observes somewhat wistfully, colonial history has long moved away from the shadow of economic contradictions and ' "material" histories' to studies of 'Western cultural domination'.[1] However, the transformation that the discipline of history has witnessed in recent years is actually far more profound – a fact that is ably reflected in Sarkar's new compendium of 'modern' Indian history called the *Modern Times*. Historians are now tested on their awareness of a whole range of concepts and tools of analysis used in disciplines across the social sciences such as literary studies, sociology, anthropology and the considerably recent domains of social and cultural anthropology. Hence, for a historian of colonial India, interested in questions of identity formations, the task usually goes beyond understanding and using as basic premises the concepts of the contingency of the nation-state and the recentness of national boundaries. Benedict Anderson's insights into 'imagined communities' and Partha Chatterjee's rejoinder about communities in the Third World as being equally original and contextual have been fundamental to a whole new range of studies into relations of affect and the myriad ways in which solidarities can be 'imagined' and subjectivities forged as well as to their heterodox and complex cultures of production.[2] Colonialism is thus no longer about the straightforward subjection, appropriation and subversion of ideas and existence. It involves an understanding of the numerous ways in which subjection is enforced and societal practices of the colonized 'understood' and

1

eventually subsumed as also about the complex negotiations between the nationalist subjectivities of the colonized elite and the other coveted attributes of an imported bourgeois modernity that is nonetheless imperfect being severely delimited by virtue of its coloniality. Thus, although Sarkar may lament that the study of modern Indian history is dominated by 'discourse analysis', the bright side to this trend is that scholars today get to examine a wide variety of discursive practices that have contributed to a better and more comprehensive interrogation of meta narratives be it that of the empire or the nation-state.

II

Given the interdisciplinary nature of modern-day historical studies, it is expected that the socially and ideologically embedded issue of 'identities' must be addressed in the light of key sociological theories that problematized the notion of belonging to non-kin groups. For a long time scholars of the social sciences sought to understand the nature of the so-called primordial attachment that members of non-kin groups claimed they felt for each other. It was not easy to examine the prehistory of groups that were too old to allow an accurate historiographical reconstruction of their antecedents. Originally a subject of philosophy, the study of identity formations became popular in the social sciences, with growing awareness of the role of socio-political factors in anchoring a particular notion of the self. Sociology's interest in how the individual is affected by and contributes to the overall social context evolved into an investigation of the notions of sameness that induce an individual to connect to others and to a particular group of people. The intensity of ethnic revival movements in Europe after the end of the Second World War, as well as the anti-colonial movements in the Third World countries, served to generate heightened interest in the study of the claims to ethnicity and nationalism within the rubric of social anthropology, as scholars strove to unpack the plethora of sentiments that accompany such claims to groupness.

Scholarly engagement with identities began first and foremost with attempts to understand kin or ethnic groups. Definitions of 'ethnic' and ethnicity varied although the common sense understanding continued to veer round biological theories of a common origin. Over the years however, there emerged two standard approaches to the question of ethnicity. One of these sought to define the concept in terms of objective attributes, while the other laid emphasis on subjective feelings. The objectivists asserted that ethnic group membership is not a matter of choice but rather an accident of birth. Clifford Geertz,[3] for instance, defined ethnic groups as those that are bound together by overt cultural forms such as dress, language or descent. The subjectivists, on the other hand, argued that an ethnic group consisted of people who 'entertain a subjective belief in their common descent. It did not matter whether an objective blood relationship existed. According to the latter school of opinion, ethnic membership differs from the kinship group precisely by being a presumed identity'.[4] This school of thought, therefore, stressed not the cultural givens of an ethnic group but the characteristics of self-ascription, triggered presumably by political manipulations and the associated myth making. The latter school came to be referred to popularly as the instrumentalist school.

Significant contribution to the field of ethnic studies was made by Fredrik Barth, who contested the ascription of permanence to ethnic ties.[5] Barth introduced the concept of ethnic boundaries as an analytical tool for understanding the ethnic phenomenon. His approach, which may be described as being broadly a subjective one, drew attention to the ethnic group as a socially constructed phenomenon that uses symbolic boundaries to mark the limits of group belonging. Barth's notion of boundaries offered a viable perspective to study ethnicity as a social phenomenon. He argued that the focal point in ethnic identities is the boundary between groups. In other words, the cultures that boundaries enclose change, but the boundaries are actually more longstanding. What Barth's theory implied was that all groups were dynamic and certain group traits would disappear eventually over time but certain features would survive, thereby contributing to the maintenance of boundaries and therefore of the group. Barth warned that it was impossible to predict which aspects of culture would anchor the identity by being important to the members. Ethnicities in Barth's approach were highly subjective entities that were formed on the basis of what was chosen and agreed by the group members. Till then, national and ethnic identities had been perceived as fixed and immutable, that once acquired could never be lost. Barth's theory encouraged scholars to view identity as a construct.

The insights generated by Barth's new research also transformed the way scholars studied the origin and growth of nationalism helping it to emerge from the shadows of conventional debates on political strategy making. Benedict Anderson restored nationalism to the level of a philosophical thought that is brought into being by the nationalist imagination which then allows a coming together of seemingly disparate peoples through the mediation of a common print vernacular. Anderson claimed that 'all communities larger than primordial villages of face-to face contact (and perhaps even these) are imagined'.[6] The professed similarities in this model are usually superficial and the discrepancies numerous. It is this characteristic that purportedly explains the disintegration of a nation and realignment round an entirely different set of issues, the form and nature of which is determined by specific historical forces. Anderson argued that what is crucial to a study of communities is not the extent of their falsity/genuineness, but the style in which they are imagined and the forces that shape this style. Anderson's notion of communities as imagined helped resolve the question of mischief in nationalist politics and accorded a healthy direction to studies of nationality formations by encouraging scholars to look for immediate and long-term contexts for specific self-images of the community.

III

The Chatterjee–Anderson debate about the impact of Western nationalism on countries in the Third World synchronized with the resurgence of interest in middle-class politics after nearly half a century of academic engagement with the politics of marginal groups.[7] Chatterjee's claim that the nationalisms of the Third World could be *sui generis* in their own context-specific ways sparked allegations that a lot of the counter-hegemonic discourses of the nationalist were actually 'mimetic'.[8] This in turn triggered a spate of studies seeking to identify the numerous ways in which the nationalist elite strove to establish itself as both 'different' from and superior to the colonizer.[9] There was no denying, however, the new elite's susceptibility to the irresistible trappings of a bourgeois modernity, however imperfect in nature. It was pointed out that the cultural response of the colonial elite in such societies could at best generate 'hybrid' patterns of thought, given the mental agony and contradictory pulls experienced by the colonized as they sought to defend their cultural universe both to themselves and to the colonial 'other'.[10] 'Hybridity' was an eminently useful frame that allowed scholars to interpret what for long was understood as mere conservativeness of the elite. Henceforth, the incompleteness of the modernistic project of the elite could be ascribed safely to the ambivalence of the nationalist position. 'Incompleteness' now has a theory which has been increasingly employed by scholars to interpret various cultures of representation, especially those that are mediated through the counter-hegemonic subjectivities of a subject population and the limitations of the latter. These limitations were taken up for close examination by scholars interested in exploring how nationalist subjectivities came in the way of critical historiography, leading to the conscious use of rhetorical devices to privilege certain kinds of pasts as more 'authentic' than others.[11] Dipesh Chakrabarty correctly points out that such counter-hegemonic projects have been crucial in resisting the challenge of a crude historicism that has permeated much of imperialist and also present-day history writing.[12] This kind of new research also offers fresh grounds that challenge polarities of interpretations between the traditional and the modern and not just between the colonizer and the colonized.[13] What this new research has achieved, therefore, is nothing less than an academic breakthrough which has revolutionized our received categories of academic judgement.

One area that has gained enormously from the new insights into the study of hegemonic practices is the domain of language 'standardization' and literary practices undertaken by both agents of colonialism and the nationalist elite. A number of studies of Hindi, Urdu, Tamil, Telugu and Assamese have thrown into focus how specific conceptualizations of the vernacular have enabled communities into being.[14] These studies not only underscored the need to interrogate colonial categories of enumeration but also indicated how the nationalist elite was complicit in reproducing colonial frameworks of representation. Above all, such studies highlighted the contingency of language boundaries opening up thereby an academic space for interrogating the presumed sacrality of notions such as those of the 'mother tongue' that helped construct varied 'languages of belonging' in the nineteenth and twentieth centuries through ideologically fraught and contrived practices of standardization. Such studies of the symbolic value of languages and literary histories for constructing subjectivities were complemented by studies of political scientists like Sudipta Kaviraj.[15] The latter's argument that the absence of enumeration in the pre-colonial world made for 'fuzzy' identities because people were not clear about the point where one's community ended and another began urged scholars to think of the presumed identities of languages in a non-linear way. These studies of the enabling role played by print and vernacular in colonial India also helped complicate Habermas's notions of a 'bourgeois public sphere' by according due weight to the varied social compositions of the literary elite as also the space created by print for articulating contrary opinions notwithstanding the limitations of the vernacular literary sphere.[16] These studies were complemented by works of other scholars who drew attention to the existence of additional forums for collective action and to the existence of other publics.[17]

IV

Studies of colonial Assam have benefitted immensely from the insights opened up by these exciting new research of the past three decades and notwithstanding the concerns flagged regarding the ultimate unknowability of the pre-colonial past,[18] new histories of Assam and the Northeast have used fresh approaches to come up with interesting new insights into 'fragments' of life and practices from the pre-colonial period. Most of these studies have called for writing 'connected' histories of the region, given the fact that networks of transactions in the pre-colonial period were seldom subject to the political constraints of rigid boundaries and restrictions on mobility.[19] Such works have been duly supplemented by others that have demonstrated how notions of space were not fixed and were mediated by and through varied ideologies of the nation or the empire.[20] Such area studies encouraged other scholars to track more broad-based loyalties and overarching patterns of thought and action which were ripped apart by hegemonic notions of space and territoriality imposed from above by colonialism.[21] Works such as these also drew from the recent academic practice to choose zones situated in between two well-demarcated regions as units of analysis. Border locations or borderlands, as these are referred to, have emerged as the most viable units of analysis on account of their ability to generate data about the prehistory of political boundaries and the impact of the latter on the inhabitants as well as the ways in which these boundaries are routinely circumvented and subverted to establish the essential inanity of enforcing rigid political demarcations. These areas are considered to be eminently suitable for affording suitable opportunities for studying how boundaries were drawn up arbitrarily and how these were disregarded in everyday life. Studying these areas is believed to be particularly productive for understanding colonial histories as they invariably yield data about the nature of colonial governance and knowledge regimes and the eventual contestation of colonial categories of dominance. The ultimate purpose behind such an exercise is to throw into focus life in places marked by older histories of shared pasts with other proximate cultural zones. Histories of borderlands have therefore become a rage, with historians and social scientists seeking to understand how people deal with each other when left alone to pursue their lives without political or cultural interferences. In their article on borderland studies, the authors, Michiel Baud and Willem Van Schendel,[22] defend their choice of border regions as units of analysis in the following terms:

> National borders are political constructs, imagined projections of territorial power. Although they appear on maps in deceptively precise forms, they reflect, at least initially, merely the mental images of politicians, lawyers, and intellectuals. Their practical consequences are often quite different. No matter how clearly borders are drawn on official maps, how many customs officials are appointed, or how many watchtowers are built, people will

ignore borders whenever it suits them. In doing so, they challenge the political status quo of which borders are the ultimate
symbol.[23]

These scholars advocate a cross-border perspective in which regions on both
sides of a political border are taken as the units of analysis. In their words,
'Our point of departure is that we can properly understand the often unin-
tended and unanticipated social consequences of national borders only by
focusing on border regions and comparing them through time and space.'[24]
It would be only pertinent to mention here that of late, even the 'border
approach' has come in for criticism for encouraging overriding generaliza-
tions that gloss over micro-experiences and fail to recognize that all boundaries including regional ones are ultimately contingent. There is therefore a
demand to write 'connected histories' that seek out trends and practices and
study their resonance across a wider and discontinuous swath of territory.[25]

Northeast India has never had it so good if the number of books on
British Assam's colonial history alone is anything to go by. This has been
matched by the growing trend to set up study centres dealing with 'North-
east India studies' in some of the country's premier academic institutions.
While one can only rejoice at the fact that the disheartening silence of so
many decades has come to an end, one does hope that the process does
not end up reinforcing the region's isolation or a fetishization of the exotic
and the exceptional. Our history demonstrates that the near obliteration of
the Northeast and its peoples from school- and college-level textbooks has
done the country more harm than good not to speak of the fact that the
void was perfectly out of sync with the nation-state's claims to the absolute
integrity of the region to the Indian nation. It is remarkable, therefore, that
the region has become a foci of interest, with a whole range of fascinating
studies addressing the obfuscation of the region's complex and dynamic
past under the impact of colonial categories of representation.

This book draws its inspiration from the philosophy that it is impossible to 'attempt a "macro history" . . . without muddying our boots in
the bogs of "micro-history"'.[26] Although the story of British Assam has
been told and re-told many times over, there are still several aspects of
the colonial encounter in Assam that seem to have slipped through the
trapdoor of historiography. This is therefore an attempt to recover those
aspects by reading the intellectual history of nineteenth-century Assam in
a new light, from the perspectives of the colonial state and the emergent
Western-educated middle-class intelligentsia so that we may recover the
micro-details of the colonization process with regard to colonial definitions
of land rights, land use and revenue-sharing mechanisms, colonial notions

of 'progress' and their implications for the province, varied ideologies of Assamese and their complex interplay and so on. In short, the present work aims at offering a micro-perspective of the nineteenth century with a view to understanding the formative years of colonialism and nationalism in the region referred to as Assam proper back in those days. The book takes a close look at policy debates in order to unpack regimes of 'knowledge' by and through which the idea of a 'frontier' was inscribed in colonial official rhetoric. Many aspects of colonialism in Assam are already known to us through previous studies of the region. The book differs in its attempts to look beyond formal decisions into the realm of the tentative in order to identify discarded and available alternatives. It follows closely official debates anticipating policy decisions so as to understand the micro-aspects of colonial administrative decision making that have a story of their own to tell. The book would examine, for instance, the notions of progress that mediated colonial denials in the domains of education and land tenure systems. It contends that the Assamese language debates contain a clue to the understanding of statist assumptions and missionary interests and ambitions. The chapter on historiography takes a fresh look at alternative frameworks of identity displaced by the hegemony of linguistic ideologies from the middle of the nineteenth century. Last but not least, the book traces the gradual chauvinistic turn in intellectual debates on Assamese identity and the emergence of an exclusivist outlook that privileged caste Hindu practices in social and devotional matters based on an increasingly narrow understanding of what it meant to be an *Assamiya*. The emergence of an Assamese identity, initially as a bond of affect towards language, and later as a sense of entitlement to 'shared' and often contested cultural symbols, was a unique feature of the nineteenth century in Assam. The nature and course of debates over meanings and attributes was stoutly contested at every step and the outcome could not be predicted. That eventually alternative ideas of nationality failed to take off was not inevitable but subject to the peculiar trajectory of Assam's tryst with colonialism.

The book revisits old debates on ideas versus traditions in the domain of land revenue settlements to show how regions like colonial Assam have a lot to offer in terms of expanding the scope of the debate. The manner in which the rights and entitlements of *ryots* in Assam were posited, violated and transformed tells a unique story of inferiorization and strategic planning that belies notions of 'paternalist protection' that previously informed scholarship on Ryotwari in India.[27] The book challenges the conventional methods of reading the colonial history of Assam through generalized tropes of interpretation that subsume Assam to the meta-history of colonialism in the subcontinent. It contends that conclusions may be similar but need

8

not always be so as a matter of course. For instance, the language debate was inflected alternately by strategic calculations and sheer ideology. The same agglomeration of influences may be perceived in the realm of education policies although in the end imperialist choices tended to predominate. However, education in Assam represented a unique case of denial in the name of intellectual progress that had no parallel in other parts of the British Indian Empire. Likewise, the domain of middle-class politics in Assam did not always follow the standard trajectory of middle-class nationalism in India. This was because of the presence in colonial Assam of the Bengali immigrant as a significant other that could deflect the thrust and orientation of anti-colonial sentiments. The nineteenth century offers the perfect backdrop for studying these and a host of other aspects of the colonial encounter that have received far less attention than they deserve. The book contends that Assam was made into a frontier through a series of acts of trivializations long before policies actually began to override its material culture and convert the region into a 'land frontier'. We contend that the idea of a frontier was intrinsic to the manner in which Assam was imagined long before the actual acquisition of the region. The idea of Assam was forged and nurtured long before Scott assumed charge of the administration of the region. It may be traced to Captain Welsh's early impressions of the region and to Francis Buchanan's reports. These impressions were reinforced by the administrative experiences of the early officials like Scott and Jenkins, but the former predated the later notions by a good many years. It is in these impressions that the scholar may find an answer to the riddle of a 'frontier' and its possible remedies as envisaged in official discourse. Assam was written off at the very moment when it was imagined, which made it possible for the state to treat it as a land frontier. This book argues that this dismissal was subsequently reinforced through policies in key domains such as land rights and revenue settlements, language and education and religion. The subtle means, through which dismissal was reinforced and then legitimized by means of a rhetoric of progress, may be understood if we consider the policy debates within the bureaucratic circles anticipatory to policy formulations. This is precisely the method undertaken by this work to place otherwise known aspects of colonial policy decisions in their appropriate perspective. Such an account also serves the purpose of explaining why adverse decisions failed to attract suitable responses for the better part of the nineteenth century, and here the book shows how the colonial rhetoric served to mask the true intent of colonial administration which almost always presented its choices under the garb of 'benefits' or 'advancement'. The cultural thrust of Assamese middle-class politics, as also its impact for the consolidation of a community identity, constitutes the other important aspects that the book seeks to throw into focus. The book takes issues with some of the common tropes in terms of which the British imagined Assam. This includes notions of vast 'empty' spaces, of the king as the ultimate owner of land and subjects, of a degenerate monarchy incapable of holding its own against external assault, of a people lazy and indolent and possessing strong superstitious beliefs and a narrow outlook and questionable intellectual abilities. The book shows how the model of progress desired by the nationalist also did not succeed in breaking free from the colonialist mould and how this produced instead the counter-trope of the Bengali other to justify the non-realization of development projects. The resultant lack of effective antagonism against the East India Company policies forms an effective backdrop to study the many levels of Assamese intellectual negotiations with the colonial rhetoric of progress. Assam, this section has argued, was deemed to be a cultural backwater of India long before specific policies were put in place to reinforce this status. The contestation of this marginality consequently becomes a remarkable episode that deployed innovative and subtle counter-hegemonic methods of contestation and subversion of dominant tropes of colonial imagination. Colonization ripped apart the delicate fabric of social and cultural life in the region apart from inflicting a terrible blow to the province's economy. The liberal and adaptive spirit of pre-colonial rule had enabled much intermixture of modes of living giving rise to what may be loosely termed as a 'liminal' culture that sustained interpenetration and exchange. The highly diversified nature of the caste system in Assam that often confounded the British, and described in the book, bears testimony to this. Yet another interesting evidence of this is afforded by seemingly anomalous traits such as the absence of any aversion to non-vegetarian diet among followers of the Vaishnava faith in Assam, which is out of sync with Vaishnavism's known aversion to the same across the country. The book foregrounds these aspects of pre-colonial society in Assam to argue that the pre-colonial world was characterized by any felt need to either conform to or differ from rest of India's peoples. Consequently, socio-cultural practices could evolve in a way that was in sync with the region's diversity. Under colonial rule, faced with the threat of being relegated to the margins, the middle class in Assam perceived that they stood a chance to survive with dignity in the emergent nation only by merging their identities with the more acceptable forms of Indic culture or by asserting their 'difference' from 'Bengali' cultural norms. This rush to forsake ambiguity may be regarded as the principal characteristic of Assamese middle-class politics in the nineteenth century. The elite rushed to order a new history for itself without caring to defend the one that could have made for a more sustainable way of life in the region.

Notes

1 Sumit Sarkar, *Writing Social History*, New Delhi: Oxford University Press, 1997, p. 4.
2 See Benedict Anderson, *Imagined Communities: Reflections on the Origin and Spread of Nationalism*, London: Verso, 1983; and Partha Chatterjee, *The Nation and Its Fragments, Colonial and Postcolonial Histories*, Princeton, NJ: Princeton University Press, 1993.
3 Clifford Geertz, ed., *Old Societies and New States*, The Quest for Modernity in Asia and Africa, ed. Clifford Geertz, Glencoe: Free Press of Glencoe, 1968.
4 Weber (1968), cited in John Edwards, *Language, Society and Identity*, Oxford: Basil Blackwell, 1985, p. 8.
5 Fredrik Barth, *Ethnic Groups and Boundaries: The Social Organization of Cultural Difference*, Illinois: Waveland Press, 1969.
6 Anderson, *Imagined Communities*, p. 7.
7 See Chatterjee, *The Nation and Its Fragments*.
8 See H.K. Bhabha, 'Of Mimicry and Man: The Ambivalence of Colonial Discourse', October 28, Spring, pp. 125–133.
9 See Dipesh Chakrabarty, 'Postcoloniality and the Artifice of History: Who Speaks for "Indian" Pasts?', *Representations*, No. 37, *Special Issue: Imperial Fantasies and Postcolonial Histories*, Winter, 1992, pp. 1–26.
10 Bhabha, 'Of Mimicry and Man'.
11 Ranajit Guha, *An Indian Historiography for India in Dominance without Hegemony History and Power in Colonial India*, Cambridge: Harvard University Press, 1997; see also Chatterjee, *The Nation and Its Fragments*.
12 Dipesh Chakrabarty, *Provincializing Europe*, Princeton, NJ: Princeton University Press, 2007.
13 Sumit Sarkar, *Modern Times India 1880s–1950s Environment, Economy, Culture*, Ranikhet: Permanent Black, 2014.
14 See the following for the status of research in this field: Christopher King, *One Language, Two Scripts: The Hindi Movement in Nineteenth Century North India*, New Delhi: Oxford University Press, 1994; Richard Burghart, 'A Quarrel in the Language Family: Agency and Representations of Speech in Mithila', *Modern Asian Studies*, Vol. 27, No. 4, 1993, pp. 761–804; Sumathi Ramaswami, *Passions of the Tongue: Language Devotion in Tamil India 1891–1970*, New Delhi: Munshiram Manoharlal, 1998; and Lisa Mitchell, *Language, Emotion, Politics in South India: The Making of a Mother Tongue*, Ranikhet: Permanent Black, 2009.
15 Sudipta Kaviraj, 'The Imaginary Institution of India', in Partha Chatterjee and David Arnold (eds), *Subaltern Studies*, Vol. VII, New Delhi: Oxford University Press, 1993.
16 See Anindita Ghosh, *Power in Print Popular Publishing and the Politics of Language and Culture in a Colonial Society 1778–1905*, New Delhi: Oxford University Press, 2006; Vasudha Dalmia, *The Nationalization of Hindu Traditions Bharatendu Harishchandra and Nineteenth-Century Banaras*, New Delhi: Oxford University Press, 1997; Ulrike Stark, *An Empire of Books: The Naval Kishore Press and the Diffusion of the Printed in Colonial*, New Delhi: Orient Blackswan, 2009; and Francesca Orsini, *The*

Hindi Public Sphere (1920–1940): Language and Literature in the Age of Nationalism, New Delhi: Oxford University Press, 2009.

17 See Sandria B. Frietag, *Collective Action and Community: Public Arenas and the Emergence of Communalism in North India*, Berkeley and Los Angeles: University of California Press, 1989.

18 G.C. Spivak, 'Can the Subaltern Speak?', in C. Nelson and L. Grossberg (eds), *Marxism and the Interpretation of Culture*, Basingstoke: Macmillan Education, 1988, pp. 271–313.

19 See Sanjib Baruah, *India against Itself: Assam and the Politics of Identity*, New Delhi: OUP, 2001; Sanghamitra Misra, *Becoming a Borderland: The Politics of Space and Identity in Colonial Northeastern India*, New Delhi: Routledge, 2011; Bodhisattva Kar, '"Tongue Has No Bone": Fixing the Assamese Language, c. 1800–c. 1930', *Studies in History*, Vol. 24, No. 1, n.s. 2008, 27–76; and Indrani Chatterjee, *Forgotten Friends Monks, Marriages and Memories of Northeast India*, New Delhi: Oxford University Press, 2013.

20 See David Ludden, 'Spatial Inequity and National Territory: Remapping 1905 in Bengal and Assam', *Modern Asian Studies*, Vol. 46, No. 03, May 2012, pp 483–525; and David Ludden, 'Where Is Assam? Using Geographical History to Locate Current Social Realities', in *CNISEAS Papers*, Guwahati: OKD Institute of Social Change, 2004; see also Gunnel Cederlof, *Founding an Empire on India's North-Eastern Frontiers 1790–1840 Climate, Commerce, Polity*, New Delhi: Oxford University Press, 2014.

21 See Misra, *Becoming a Borderland*; and Chatterjee, *Forgotten Friends Monks*.

22 Michiel Baud and Willem Van Schendel, 'Toward a Comparative History of Borderlands', *Journal of World History*, Vol. 8, No. 2, Fall, 1997, pp. 211–242.

23 Ibid., p. 211.

24 Ibid., p. 212.

25 Sanjay Subrahmanyam, 'Connected Histories: Notes towards a Reconfiguration of Early Modern Eurasia', *Modern Asian Studies*, Vol. 31, No. 3, July 1997, pp. 735–762.

26 Ibid., p. 750.

27 Eric Stokes, *The English Utilitarians in India*, London: Clarendon Press, 1969.

Part I

1

THE POLITICAL ECONOMY
OF A FRONTIER

In his eponymous work *History of the Relations of the Government with the Hill Tribes of the North-East Frontier of Bengal*, Sir Alexander Mackenzie deliberates on the meaning of the term 'frontier' as implying alternately a boundary line or an entire tract or zone. Mackenzie wrote:

> The north-east frontier of Bengal is a term used sometimes to denote a boundary line and sometimes more generally to describe a tract. In the latter sense, it embraces the whole of the hill ranges north, east, and south of the Assam valley, as well as the western slopes of the great mountain system lying between Bengal and independent Burma, with its outlying spurs and ridges.[1]

Although this passage gives the impression that Mackenzie was deploying the term 'frontier' to refer to the tract lying beyond the Assam valley, in reality, 'frontier' as an appellate became intimately associated with the whole of British Assam, with serious policy implications for the plain regions comprising the Brahmaputra valley and its adjoining territories that had once formed the core of the pre-colonial Ahom kingdom. Mackenzie's observation highlighted two key aspects of British colonial policy that had become by then the cornerstone of the East India Company's (EIC) strategic understanding of the region. First and foremost, the entire region to the north-east of Bengal was visualized in the context of the security of the lucrative Bengal province of the EIC. Second, in the colonial administrative framework, the entire region to the north-east of Bengal was treated as an undifferentiated land mass to be dealt with in terms of a unified and uniform policy perspective. Mackenzie's work thus provides a crucial window to how the region was conceptualized in dominant official discourses of the colonial state in the nineteenth century. This book argues that the discursive label of a frontier was not retrospectively thrust on the plains of

British Assam but constituted a truthful rendering of the way in which the region was perceived right from the inception of colonial rule in Assam although policies were gradually drawn up to reinforce the status. In other words, in the official imagination of the colonial state, Assam was a frontier right from the beginning although the latter's status was gradually confirmed and shored up through a series of highly discriminatory and inhibitive policies. The latter formed the means of putting in place a mechanism of rule that was highly debilitating from an intellectual, economic, social and cultural standpoint. This book explores the various dimensions and implications of frontier-hood that would unfold over the course of the next few decades as the plains of Assam were subsumed under a comprehensive framework of governance. The book argues that 'frontier' was something more than a mere label. It translated into a specific approach towards the entire region to the north-east of Bengal – be it the hills or the plains – an approach that was constituted by and large through a unique framework of governance informed by highly biased assumptions and prejudices. Such an approach was underpinned above all by an overweening concern for security and strategic calculations, and demonstrated in the long run a resolute tendency to avoid an affective engagement with issues of concern involving the people and their claims and entitlements at a time when many of these entitlements were being addressed elsewhere in the country. This book seeks to bring into focus the underlying principles informing what may be dubbed as a frontier approach with regard to the colonial history of modern-day Assam which coincided with the plain regions of the pre-colonial kingdom of the Ahom rulers.

I

Taming the wild

On 20 May 1784, the *Calcutta Gazette* carried an advertisement asking the merchants of Bengal to travel to Tibet, with the assurance that as per an agreement with authorities in Bhutan, the former would receive all kinds of assistance along the way once they had crossed the frontiers of Bhutan. To encourage the merchants to undertake the travel, the Governor General in Council promised that 'there shall be an exemption of all duties upon such articles as shall be taken out of Bengal to compose their first adventure to Tibet', the idea being to secure the prosperity of both the territories by opening an intercourse of trade between Bengal and Tibet.[2] The notification envisaged returns from the trade in the form of gold dust, talents of silver, musk, cow tails and goat's wool. The EIC's commercial vision was an expansive one as a recent book called *Founding an Empire on India's North-Eastern Frontiers 1790–1840*, by Gunnel Cederlof ably demonstrates. Cederlof has shown how at the turn of the eighteenth century, the British government's attempts to settle land tenure and revenue-related matters brought it into close contact with Sylhet and subsequently to the Cachar and Jaintia kingdoms beyond. During the first two decades of the nineteenth century, the EIC was also forced to confront groups of Garo settlers inhabiting the hill ranges separating the Khasi hills bordering Bengal. Cederlof argues that the British encounters with other dwellers of the various hill ranges that separated Bengal from the kingdom of Ava was part accidental and part voluntary.[3] The EIC was driven by an urge to establish direct trade relations with both Ava and China. After all, the region designated as the Northeast had always enjoyed vibrant commercial exchanges with Tibet and Burma, and several trade routes crisscrossed the hills.[4] The EIC's officials were aware of this and hoped to tap into this commercial world. Cederlof refers to the numerous cartographic and medical expeditions undertaken by EIC officials in these early years to gather information and explore the feasibility of reviving the traditional trade routes. For a fairly long time, as company officials explored the possibility of safe and secure transit across the hills, there was a simmering hope that this was something that could be fulfilled with a degree of success. This was before the beginning of hostilities between Ava and the EIC in the valley in connection with the subjugation of the Ahom kingdom by Burmese forces and the subsequent threat posed by the latter to EIC territories in Bengal.[5] Till then perhaps, the British had not contemplated seriously any scheme of routing this trade through the territories held by the Ahom monarch. This was only natural since there existed serious travel restrictions for outsiders seeking an entry into the Ahom kingdom.

By the second decade of the nineteenth century, the EIC dreams had begun to turn sour, as reports streamed in about the 'unpredictability' and 'wildness' of the hill dwellers such as the Singphos, the Akas, the Abors, the Kukis and the Nagas.[6] Interestingly enough, although it is usual to hold colonial ethnological reports as the culprit for generating tags of wildness and savagery with which these peoples came to be invested, many of these reports actually highlighted interesting aspects of life in the hills, which failed to strike a chord with the supreme authorities in Calcutta. It was the more exotic rites of head-hunting purportedly practised by many of these peoples, their 'queer' diet and their predilections for violence that were selectively adopted for repeated discussion and circulation by officials and ethnographers alike constituting eventually the dominant public image of the hill dwellers.[7] Ajay Skaria correctly points out that it was the manner

in which individual traits were seized and magnified that enabled the colonizers to come up with typologies that essentialized life and practices in
the hills. Through a series of selections and omissions, these people would
be soon subsumed under a broad classificatory schema that would label
them 'tribes' and invest them with a position inferior in scale to the more
civilized castes. Thus, the caste–tribe dichotomy decontextualized cultural
traits and social behaviour practised by people living in forests and hills
in order to construct essences of tribalness, which distinguished members
of a tribe from those belonging to a caste society following a purportedly
more sophisticated mode of living. This is, of course, not to ignore that
these early ethnographic reports paved the way for the official constitution
of something like a public repertoire of 'knowledge' that facilitated their
subsequent notification as tribes. However, this was not all there was to
these reports, and many of these threw light on properties and practices
that would today be regarded with admiration, such as participatory governance, the central role of women in many households and clever tech-
nologies of building dwelling units that could withstand inclement weather
at high altitudes. These reports also noted with gratitude the numerous
friendly gestures with which European visitors were greeted in the hills and
the offers of food, shelter and navigational assistance without which their
journeys would have been rendered impossible. Let us take the example
of the earliest report on the Garos written by John Eliot in 1789.[8] Eliot
observed:

> The mountaineers, who inhabit different parts of India, have been
> generally considered savages, equally unrestrained by law and
> morality, and watchful to take every opportunity of committing
> depredations on the low country. . . . Their burly looks seem to
> indicate ill temper, but this is far from being the case, as they are
> of a mild disposition. They are, moreover, honest in their dealings,
> and sure to perform what they promise.[9]

Eliot's report also referred to the sturdy dwelling units constructed by the
Garos, their easy-going nature as also to their habit of deliberation on all
important issues during which all members of the clan or village assembled
with the wives of the chief enjoying as much authority as the chief on
such occasions. Such admittedly progressive practices, wherein women
were accorded respect and an equal say in matters concerning the entire
village, were blatantly passed over by policy makers, who had eyes only
for exotic rituals and gory details such as the ones about head-hunting.[10]
However, even a seemingly unbiased report as the one by Eliot did not fail

18

to observe, with barely concealed disgust, the food habits of the Garos. The report observed:

> These people eat all manner of food, even dogs, frogs, snakes, and the blood of all animals. The last is baked over a slow fire . . . till it becomes a nasty green colour. They are fond of drinking to an excess. Liquor is put into the mouths of infants, almost as soon as they are able to swallow.[11]

In course of a survey of Assam and the neighbouring countries conducted in 1825–26–27–28, Lieutenant R. Wilcox noted that the Abors 'though obstinate on the score of a further advance and troublesome, from their rude habits and childish curiosity, were on the whole, amicable and communicative'.[12] Wilcox's account contained details of the numerous friendly gestures shown by the hill peoples who not only offered him food and shelter on his journey but also provided navigational assistance on the way. However, the same report also noted the predatory raids carried out by the Abors on the plains peoples in the following terms:

> The Abors seem to have been in the habit of levying contribution on their low-land and less martial neighbours of Assam, and to have resented any irregularity in their payment, by predatory incursions, carrying off the people prisoners. Several Assamese captives were found amongst them, as to have become completely reconciled to their condition.[13]

Another report written in 1826 by Captain Bedford referred to the Mishmis as a people who 'evinced more apprehension than hostility, and suffered the land operations of the survey to proceed without interruption'.[14] Like Bedford, there were other travellers who noted that the hill dwellers were more apprehensive than hostile in their interactions with the Europeans. A letter written by the missionary, Cutter in 1837, referred to the Nagas as 'more frightened at seeing me than I at seeing them'.[15] Cutter was modest enough to confess that it was the appearance of his Naga visitors, 'armed with das, spears, shields, &c., and tattoed from head to foot, which gave them a more savage and wild appearance than they otherwise would have had'.[16] Yet it was the tag of violence and savagery that invariably endured instead of the many endearing aspects of their behaviour and living duly recorded in many of these early reports. A complex set of factors such as imperialism's justifying mechanisms, strategic concerns and eighteenth- and nineteenth-century European 'modernistic' beliefs as much as plain racist disdain for the vanquished came together to create the colonial 'savage'.[17]

By the second decade of the nineteenth century, for various reasons and in various ways, the entire Northeast had degenerated into a veritable *terra incognita* in colonial official discourse as much as in the imagination of the average European and the nascent English reading 'public'. It was to be henceforth a region that had to be suitably 'tamed' and disciplined before anything fruitful could be aspired for in terms of interaction or even communication. Knowingly or unknowingly, the early ethnographic reports, by no means detailed or meticulous or even deterministic, had, by virtue of their curiosity and sheer power of the colonial gaze, sprouted the germs of a frontier policy. That, however, the primary fear arose from the possible consequences of an impending assault from the hills on the revenue-rich and fertile Bengal province located in close geographical contiguity with the former region is clear from many overt and not-so-overt remarks made by officials. What became subsequently a source of alarm was the military presence of the Burmese in the region. Once Burmese troops actually threatened to intrude into EIC territories, the urgency became palpable, especially after news reached that both the Jaintia and Manipur kingdoms had already fallen to Burmese encroachments. The following passage from one of the earliest ethnographic works on Assam to be written provides valuable insights into the motives underpinning a frontier policy in the Northeast. Justifying the amount of money spent on the upkeep of the Assam administration, Major John Butler, author of one of the earliest accounts of Assam to be written, observed:

> The sum yearly expended in excess of the rent revenue for the management of Assam, it must be borne in mind, is not thrown away, for Assam forms the best frontier protection for Bengal that could be desired, and if troops were not located in that province, a force would be required on the north eastern frontier, involving much heavy expense than the local corps of Assam.[18]

The best exposition of the logic of treating the Northeast as a frontier is, however, provided by Alexander Mackenzie. The latter writes:

> Year may elapse, ere the full value of the controlling influence we have established in these hills becomes generally appreciated . . . but we already begin to reap the advantages of our position, in the cessation of those murderous visitations, which for years kept the border villages of Sylhet, and Assam, in a state of constant anxiety

and alarm; and from which, we were liable to the irruptions of a horde of unknown barbarians, at moments when, struggling against the invasion of a formidable foe, from a remote quarter, we might have been able to guard our defenceless frontier and its timid inhabitants. . . . When we contrast our present advanced position on the eastern frontier, with that which we occupied before the Burmese war, it is impossible not to perceive, that the acquisition of the several countries in that quarter, has given a degree of security to our more ancient possessions, which they never before enjoyed; and has placed in our hands, all those avenues of admission to the fertile districts of Bengal, through which they were invaded, by the forces of an arrogant and unfriendly power. A consolidation of territory, embracing the several states of Assam, Cachar, Jynteeah, Cossyah, and Arracan, has given additional strength to a frontier, which as long as they remained subject to the weak and imbecile rule of their native princes, constantly exposed us to the danger of collision with the ambitious power beyond them.[19]

Mackenzie's report provided the ultimate logic for policies that were to mediate the EIC's subsequent relation with the Northeast at least for the nineteenth century. The Northeast for the EIC would henceforth be a high-security zone to be guarded zealously and held earnestly against all perceived threats. It would soon become a case study for the application of military solutions and authoritative modes of governance. In short, the Northeast had become a strategic frontier separating Bengal from the unruly east beyond which lay 'unfriendly' powers such as the kingdom of Ava about whose intentions the British would remain ever wary. As a frontier, the Northeast would be progressively denuded of its history, agency and meanings, which would be selectively adapted and even more restrictively interpreted in order to manage effectively the people, the resources and the geographies of the region. The region would soon be rendered fit exclusively for the exercise of 'transformative visions' imposed from above, as Gunnel Cederlof so aptly states.[20] What such an understanding implied in terms of policy decisions can be seen in the creation of the Non-Regulation measures proposed originally for the Garo hills and subsequently extended to the entire region.[21] Scholars have highlighted the manner in which the Inner Line Regulations were drawn up separating the hills from the plains. In addition to this, the frontier approach dictated a military solution to most conflicts supplemented by a free license to the Christian missionaries to discipline through evangelization.[22] Our concern in this chapter is to show how territories hitherto belonging to the regime of the Ahom kings met with a similar fate as that which besieged its hill neighbours. The chapter goes on to discuss how such a policy was epitomized in the first phase by a summary refusal to honour pre-colonial entitlements, while the subsequent chapters show how the British rule was imbricated in a progressive emasculation of indigenous society and the envisioning of an inherently biased and intrinsically racist framework for interpreting and mediating the social and cultural domains in this region. Clinching the EIC's framework of mediation in the Northeast was the growing awareness of the immense potential of the region in terms of natural resources such as limestone and semi-precious stones, which could be effectively tapped through a more authoritative regime. The exact mechanism of control was to be worked out in due course, but a strong military presence in the region was identified as a facilitator. Gunnel Cederlof correctly identifies that 'frontier' soon metamorphosed into an 'expansion zone' for the fulfilment of the colonial state's economic aspirations vis-à-vis the region.[23] The safety and security of a proposed commercial venture with the far east could be ensured solely through a strict regulatory mechanism that would allow the colonial state to curb the perceived violent tendencies of Singphos and other groups deemed 'predatory' in their habits. Cederlof correctly points out that in these early days of colonial geographical enquiries, the Northeast was by no means a peripheral region in the spatial imagination of the EIC.[24] Through a subtle interplay of the ideological and the pragmatic, the plains of Assam were progressively denuded of their past and subjected to a present that left much to be desired although the germs of this denial were there right from the beginning.

II

Why Assam?

Assam's trajectory as a 'Northeast Frontier' territory was by no means a predetermined affair. There is little indication that the EIC possessed a clear idea of the resources of the Assam valley prior to its annexation. Whatever familiarity it had with the region was acquired through the reports of Welsh and Buchanan Hamilton, both of which were rather perfunctory in their assessments of the economic potentials of the region. The EIC's instructions to Dr Buchanan Hamilton to avoid entering into the territories of the Assam Raja, as it lay outside the jurisdiction of the EIC, bear testimony to a vision that did not envisage immediate subjugation. It was the Burmese threat in the second decade of the nineteenth century that for the first time foregrounded territorial security as an imminent goal for the colonial government of Bengal. It materialized an ideological shift towards the entire region that gradually relegated hopes of a long-term commercial intercourse with the far east, a remote possibility although for some time after the Burmese invasion, the British would continue to hope for some renewal of relations. Thus, in the coming years, as the British were drawn into a more direct relation with the region, it was the issue of territorial security from impending Burmese strikes that made for an increasingly paranoid policy vis-à-vis the region. Instead of devising mechanisms of rule suited to the needs of the region, the British government began adopting decisions that would secure its lucrative territorial possessions in Bengal. This resulted in policy choices that began to treat Assam as merely a frontier outpost requiring constant vigilance and regimentation rather than flexibility, empathy and understanding. The special ecological and cultural landscape of the region was subsumed under a mechanism that prioritized the needs of the empire and its security. This and the universal colonial logic of economic gains decided the region's future trajectory within the geo-body of the empire. This aspect of the colonial state's shifting perspective vis-à-vis the region has been highlighted by many officers who played a crucial role in the formative years of Assam's integration into the company's empire. Once again, Mackenzie's observations throw light on the rationale for a frontier approach:

> So much as has been stated it was desirable to bring into prominence, that there might be a clear understanding of the circumstances under which a frontier policy first became necessary for us in the north-east. These will be made more apparent as we deal with the history of each tribe. But I may here remark, by way of general preface, that we found the Assam valley surrounded northeast, and south by numerous savage and warlike tribes whom the decaying authority of the Assam dynasty had failed of late years to control, and whom the disturbed conditions of the province had incited to encroachment.[25]

Mackenzie's statement offers valuable insights into what was surely a major concern at the higher level of the EIC. The passage draws out the apprehensions about an impending threat from savage hordes at the core of the fashioning of a frontier policy. It also at the same time brings out the assumptions underlying the annexation of Assam and its subsequent inclusion into the high-security zone, which was the Northeast Frontier. Assam's geographical proximity to the hills ruled by the 'rude tribes' was its principal drawback as also the perceived inability of its rulers to 'discipline' the former. Assam's tryst with the frontier discourse of the colonial state had also to do with dominant notions that its monarchy and nobility had both become defunct, corrupt and decadent. Virtually each and every account of this period iterated the complete failure of the monarchy to afford protection to the people and the unhealthy bickerings and selfishness of the nobility. This was a cause for concern on account of the geo-political proximity of the valley to the hills. The Assam government would eventually send out an invitation to the Baptist missionaries to come and preach among these untamed people was underwritten by the imperialist concern for an ordered landscape of human habitation. In this way, evangelism and imperialism worked together to an extent to create the empire. Mackenzie would conclude his deliberation by reflecting that had there been a 'strong, systematizing, aggressive despotism' in the past, the British would not have had to deal with the issue of the desirability or not of a 'definite policy on this frontier'.[26] He added that 'the security of our eastern districts made it necessary to retain strong military control of this part of the frontier'.[27] Dr Bayfield's summary of British relations with Ava, compiled soon after the war with Burma, indicates that the British were provoked to retaliate against Ava out of fear that the Burmese would eventually reach Rangpur and Dhaka, which, it was believed, the latter had been eyeing for some time.[28] Assam's trajectory was thus made a function of concerns governing the security of her western neighbours.

Contemporary accounts indicate a growing concern with the raids of these tribes, especially the carrying off of Assamese men and women as slaves by the Singphos as well as the concessions made by the Ahom rulers to these peoples to buy peace – a habit that was perceived as cowardly. Cartographic survey reports repeatedly emphasized the unpleasantness of these raids and the inability of the Assamese to resist. Observations such as the one made by Captain Neufville were sufficiently provocative:

> They (Khamptis of Sadiya) took possession of Sadiya, ejecting the then Sadiya Khawa Gohein, and reducing the Assamese inhabitants to slavery – they have maintained it, uniting with the Burmese interest, during their invasion and occupation.[29]

In his 'Memoir of a Survey of Assam and the Neighbouring Countries Executed in 1825–6–7–8', Lieutenant Wilcox also noted that he was asked to accompany a regiment sent to 'to protect the Assamese of the intermediate district in advance of Rangpur, from incursions of Singfos, who had lately, in considerable strength, made a very daring and successful incursion close in the neighbourhood of the force'.[30] He made a similar observation about the Abors. It is a different matter that many of the demands made by the hill peoples on the plains or paid by the latter to the former as *posa* had originated in pre-colonial agreements and shared kinship and religious ties between the peoples of the hills and those of the plains across the trans-Himalayan region as Indrani Chatterjee argues in her recent work.[31] Many of these concessions had also been conceded voluntarily to these peoples by the Ahoms for strategic considerations to purchase their neutrality during the Mughal wars.[32] The Ahoms had also known precisely how to bring the offending hill men to task by sealing off the mountain passes or *duars*, which comprised something like a lifeline for people such as the Daflas, the Miris, the Abors and the Nagas, who were also inveterate traders, exchanging clothes and other commodities for their essentials with the plains peoples.[33] To the colonial observers, unwilling or unable to comprehend the cultural universe of exchange and reciprocity that animated Himalayan politics, such interfaces symbolized violent and unjust intrusions that disturbed the peace and stability of the plains and, consequently, had to be arrested. There was a general consensus that left alone the valley would not be able to hold its own against these hordes as well as against a possibly resurgent Burma. The *East India Gazetteer* echoed what seems to have been a general consensus – that the indigenous rulers of Assam were incapable of shoring up the defences of the region from accosting hill tribes.

> Indeed without population and with an unknown frontier, this phantom of a kingdom could not for a year exist on its own resources, it must consequently be supported by its conquerors: a civil and military establishment appointed; a fleet of boats maintained on the Brahmaputra, and many other expensive drains created on the Bengal treasury.[34]

Thus, a more persuasive and aggressive policy was felt to be the need of the hour, and this was what the British set out to fashion in the coming years that gradually endowed the valley with a new set of meanings and an entirely new framework of understanding. Cederlof's argument that the colonial state's Northeastern Frontier was 'an open-ended affair' in the initial years at least does not hold ground in the light of fairly common assertions made vis-à-vis the region both by officials in charge of affairs at the local level and those at the top – a disjuncture that she has noted in her study of Bengal. There was clearly a hierarchy that governed EIC relations with regard to different regions and, as the book shows, with regard to different issues within the same region depending on the latter's strategic significance for imperialist designs.

Although the image of the Ahom monarch as an incompetent and unworthy figurehead was reinforced by the victory of the Burmese troops and the consequent flight of the monarch to British territories, leaving his subjects to their fate, the image of the old regime as a decadent institution had stuck since the expedition of Captain Welsh in 1792. Welsh's encounters with the court of Gaurinath Singha and with the monarch himself had led him to draw up a fairly sad picture of the shape of things in the old kingdom. Such images resurfaced once the Burmese threat loomed large on the horizon. The memorandum circulated by the British at the outbreak of their hostilities with the Burmese gives the indication that they had no intention to quit even after matters had cooled down between the warring parties and the Burmese had been driven out of Assam. There appears to be very little truth in Alexander Mackenzie's statement that 'the Government in Calcutta was strongly averse to taking absolute possession of the province' and that 'had any of the Native Royal house shown real capacity or ability to govern with acceptance to the people, there can be no doubt, from the tenor of the Secret Consultations in the foreign office, that he would have been forthwith installed as Raja'.[35] There was a palpable sense of distrust towards the ruler and the ruled, which eventually stalled tentative attempts, if any, to install a native prince of the ruling house in the region. David Scott, the man of the hour and the subsequent first Agent to the Governor General in the Northeast, was not too keen to restore the previous rulers. The latter had no faith in the ruling house and especially in the nobility. He described the pre-colonial elite as 'much divided among themselves, and . . . generally obnoxious to the body of the people'.[36] The people, he believed, had lost all faith in their princes. According to Scott, 'their imbecility, cowardice and treacherous principles having been so fully developed in the last contest so as to remain no longer concealed even to the meanest peasant'.[37] It is telling that Scott did not hesitate to recommend the agency of a protected 'native rule' in neighbouring Manipur, the reason offered being that while the Assamese were 'timid and effeminate' and hence must be protected, the Manipuris were 'imbued with all military spirit, that distinguishes the Rajput tribes Northern of Hindustan'.[38] Although later he proposed the restoration of the old monarchy in Assam, this was purely on strategic considerations in order to conciliate the disgruntled and dispossessed nobility – the *dangariyas*. He later revised his proposal to one recommending restoration of Upper Assam to a prince of the royal family, in which form his advice was executed by the EIC after his death. For the time being, however, the officials in Calcutta were not too keen to take up either of the proposals, and this was owing to the strong climate of distrust that prevailed about the monarchy. It is telling that neither Scott nor the EIC as a body entered into any sort of negotiation with members of the royal family at this stage. The authorities in Calcutta felt that the proposed monarchy would not be able to command the respect of its subjects and would be completely unequal to the task of managing the hill tribes.[39] There was, thus, little difference in perception within the EIC with regard to Assam. Subsequently, in 1833, *swargadeo* Purander Singha was given charge of the Upper Assam districts of Sibsagar and Lakhimpur on his agreement to pay an annual tribute of Rs 50,000 to the East India Company. Purander Singha had to sign an agreement with the East India Company. The latter laid down in clear terms that the prince could continue to reign only so long as he abided by the provisions of the treaty. The terms of the treaty left no doubt about the status of the monarch. It stated:

> In the event of the Rajah's continuing faithful to the articles of the Treaty, the British government engages to protect him from the aggressions of any foreign force, but if, he should in any way depart from a faithful adherence to the same, and be guilty of oppressing the people of the country entrusted to his charge then the right is reserved to the Government of Honourable Company either to transfer the said country to another ruler, or take it into its own immediate occupation.[40]

The terms of the grant were thus fairly comprehensive and provided against all kinds of failures, big or small, while leaving room for grey areas of nonconformity. The king bound himself by virtue of this treaty not to indulge in mutilations and other torturous forms of punishments such as were practised by his ancestors, to listen to the advice of the political agent stationed in Upper Assam with regard to the conduct of the affairs of the country entrusted to him and not to carry on any correspondence with any foreign states. This system of dual government continued till 1838 when the whole of Assam was annexed to the British Empire as part of the Bengal province on the grounds that the Purander Singha had failed to pay the stipulated amount to the company apart from his inability to provide effective administration.[41] By 1838, the commissioner of Assam, Francis Jenkins, was convinced of the futility of the enterprise. Despite the fact that the Governor General in Council was opposed to the idea of a dismissal of the government of Purander Singha, and despite the fact that the political agent of Upper Assam Adam White observed in his report that the government did not have a fair trial and that 'it worked as well as could have been expected',

Jenkins was not convinced. His repeated overtures eventually persuaded the authorities in Calcutta to resume Upper Assam in 1838.[42] Jenkins had long made up his mind as to the futility of the venture when in course of his tour of Upper Assam he had noted that 'his (Purander Singha's) courts were ill regulated and had been the cause of great grievance to the people' without bothering to cite his sources of information.[43] Jenkins observed that he 'found a great difficulty in communicating with the Rajah from his having apparently no respectable man in his confidence'.[44] It is a different matter that it was the same monarch who had been commended earlier by Jenkins himself for the latter's progressive response to a proposal for government funding to instruct young Assamese boys.[45] The security of the empire is once again writ large in Jenkins's apprehensions that the monarch would fail to arrest the incursions of the Dafflas. He observed:

> If something is not done to arrest the progress of the Dafflas this bank stands a chance of being totally abandoned to these barbarians. I have little hope the Rajah will be capable of making any exertion to save the country, his management appears to be solely intent upon raising the largest possible present Revenue without any advertence to future consequences.[46]

Thus, Purander Singha's fate was foretold although Jenkins's portrayal of the monarch could barely conceal his admiration for the physical fitness of the latter – an indication of the British obsession with sheer male physicality, which often led them to feminize the colonized.[47] Jenkins observed wryly,

> This gentleman is young but very large of stature and to judge from his physiognomy he is one that could act well again the bloody scenes which distinguished his grandfather's supremacy. He is most morose in appearance and I learnt that his sole amusement was in hunting the great beasts of the Forests. This is a very uncommon pursuit for the Assamese gentlemen of the present day and shows that the spirit of the family is not extinguished though now divested to a very harmless pastime.[48]

It is clear that Purander Singha had to go for Jenkins's schemes for Assam to materialize. Hence, despite the former's repeated attempts to address key revenue and administrative concerns and despite the fact that his pleas to the British for revising their revenue demands as well as their leniency towards the Muttock territory, his efforts were undermined by Major

Francis Jenkins, who saw no reason to take the practical problems faced by the unfortunate ruler into account in deciding the latter's fate. His rejoinder to the report submitted by Adam White, the official sent to survey the conditions of Upper Assam under Purander Singha, made it impossible for the company to prolong the existing arrangement.[49] By the time Jenkins assumed his office, the economic potentials of Assam had become fairly well known. In addition to tea, the rich mineral resources of the region had become a significant factor that inflected official decisions and administrative arrangements vis-à-vis Assam. Already on his tours of Upper Assam, Jenkins had found 'traces of coal on either side to the distance of about a mile the beds running into the low hills of the first range which attain a height of 300–400ft'.[50]

III

The new dispensation

It is far too simplistic to regard David Scott's early revenue and administrative measures in the Assam valley as indications of the legendary British paternalism as scholars like Nirode K. Barooah have done, even though scholarship on colonial India has done much to divest the latter ideology of much of its endearing qualities. David Scott's initial revenue measures after assuming charge in Assam reflected the resolve of the EIC to rule unambiguously and with firmness. Although Scott provided employment to some members of the erstwhile nobility, in the newly set up revenue administration, his measures spelt decided ruin for the old aristocracy. Scott has received considerable adulation among scholars for his paternalistic mode of functioning. His contemporaries described him as a man known for his tolerance and his lenient handling of the people. He was also immensely popular among the latter. For the colonial state too, Scott would remain the officer who displayed exemplary judgement and keen administrative acumen in devising a scheme for the effective integration of Assam into the British Empire. Scott was instrumental in instituting a system of revenue appropriation that proved to be the most abiding feature of the colonial revenue regime in the region and one that lasted with minor modifications till the end of colonial rule. Our assessment of Scott's contribution to the local community, however, should take into account the immense distress caused by Scott's decision to introduce the seeds of a Ryotwari system in Assam even if we acknowledge that the final contours of such a system were deliberated upon and decided by his successors. Crucial to any assessment of Scott should be his choice of mechanism for revenue assessment in Assam which was a far cry from that which was practised in the rest of Bengal of which Assam was a part. The frontier policy with regard to Assam panned out in the form of an outright denial from the outset of pre-colonial entitlements and a persistent refusal to concede the demands of the pre-colonial ruling class. It was also, above all, characterized by weak attempts and frequent refusals to grant pensionary benefits and other reliefs to ruined families, including members of the royal family.[51]

The company's Supreme Government in Calcutta had decided that the administration of Upper Assam should adhere to the old native system since there was a possibility that it might be restored to an heir from the erstwhile ruling house. Lower Assam, on the other hand, was fully integrated with the British Empire, and a proper mechanism was devised for the collection of land revenue from the region. Curiously enough, Scott's model for Assam constituted a significant departure from the Bengal model. In Bengal in 1793, Lord Cornwallis had executed a permanent settlement with superior land holders, who henceforth came to be designated collectively as *zamindars*.[52] This settlement held several advantages for the superior land holders, for it fixed the claims of the state in perpetuity while granting the *zamindars* alienable and hereditary rights to their estates. Perhaps the most significant outcome of the colonial land revenue settlement in Bengal was the institution of the rule of property in land. While there were a host of factors that clinched matters in favour of the Bengal *zamindars*, a crucial determinant was surely the hope that the beneficiaries of the new *bandobast* (arrangement) would emerge as modernizing agents of economic growth in rural Bengal as well as potential allies of the colonial state.[53] Scott's model of land tenure for Assam was not crafted on the Cornwallis system. The government in Assam did not deem it expedient to allow any intermediate class of superior land holders to mediate between the state and the ordinary peasants. Instead individual peasants were directly brought under the ambit of assessment subject to periodic revision of revenue rates. Scott introduced an area-specific land tax payable by individual peasants directly to the state through revenue collectors appointed by the government for the purpose.

It would have been perfectly alright had Assam not possessed a sizeable class of landed intermediaries at the time of the British takeover.[54] Scott was well aware of the presence in Assam of a nobility of rank claiming possession of vast stretches of land granted to them as service tenures by the previous regime.

In order not to appear arbitrary in his treatment of the erstwhile nobility, Scott went to the extent of demanding some sort of an authentication of these land claims. Those who could produce deeds in favour of their entitlements were allowed to retain holdings after paying the assessed rent to the state. Scott further brought within the ambit of assessment those privileged tenure holders who had hitherto enjoyed rent-free holdings. Thus, Scott did not spare lands granted free of rent to religious persons by the pre-colonial rulers of Assam. These were assessed, albeit at a milder rate. There was a strong rumour at the time that Scott intended to relinquish this source of revenue in the future, but this possibility was not redeemed in the lifetime of the former. The only tracts that were not assessed were land attached to Hindu temples and Vaishnavite monasteries locally known as *sattras*.[55]

There are clear indications that Scott's principal objective in devising a Ryotwari style settlement in the Assam valley was to maximize the revenues of the state. Soon after the acquisition of Assam, Scott had begun to explore the revenue potential of the region. Early in his tenure, he had ordered comprehensive land surveys to determine the potential sources of revenue for the colonial state in Assam. He sought Ahom-era documents that could offer valuable insights into the possible sources of revenue. He finally acquired these documents from the Majumdar Barua or the head *qanungo* of Kamrup. When these documents proved difficult to interpret, Scott made a rough estimate of the expected revenue by enquiring with the three Majumdar Baruas, functionaries of the previous regime. The latter were appointed in the revenue department to assist in the process of revenue assessment and appropriation. On the strength of his sources of information, Scott estimated that Lower Assam was capable of yielding an annual revenue of 4 to 6 lakhs, given the fertility of the soil and the abundant availability of cultivable waste land. He proposed a survey of Lower Assam as early as 1825, which was finally made in 1825–26 on the basis of which land revenue demand was raised.[56] This survey revealed that a large part of the territory was under rent-free grants or exempted from the payment of revenue.[57] A direct settlement with the service class designated as *paiks* by the pre-colonial regime was bound to be economically more fulfilling for the Raj. Such an astute administrator as he was, Scott could not possibly have lost sight of this aspect. His decision to tax the religious land grants was also aimed at widening the tax base by bringing the most substantial category of rent-free religious tenures under assessment. Shortly into his tenure, he even sanctioned enhancement of revenue demand on the grounds that land in Assam was fertile and capable of producing far more luxuriant crops than any part of Bengal.[58] Scott was in immediate need of money to cover his military costs and could not afford to allow any tract to go rent-free. So he tapped every possible source of revenue, including rent-free religious holdings. Despite launching such precise steps to gather information about the financial worth of the acquired territory and the adoption of prompt measures for ensuring appropriation of surplus, Scott is labelled as a paternalist and given benefit of doubt on the grounds of his alleged sympathies for the ruled.

Behind Scott's purported measures to empower the peasant lay a deep distrust for the erstwhile nobility rather than the weight of opinion of such powerful ideologues of the paternalist philosophy such as Munro and Malcolm. This is not to suggest that permanent settlement as a mechanism of rule had not been discredited in the preceding decades when aristocrats of Bengal failed to usher in an agrarian revolution. Moreover, officials like Scott who were prone to support settled cultivation in the spirit of eighteenth- and nineteenth-century agrarian philosophy were bound to be disappointed at the sight of bare fields such as the ones that greeted the British on their first forays into Assam. Field reports sent by the district officials to the headquarters also indicate that the upper class was dismissed as having been both degenerate and intellectually unsuitable for administrative functions. The landholding elite in Assam may have failed to pass muster as potential agents of modernization, on account of their failure so far to herald an expansion of cultivation in the region. Scott may, therefore, have deliberately decided not to conciliate the aristocracy. Instead, he recommended the restoration of the monarchy in Upper Assam to conciliate local sentiments. Scott's treatment of the aristocracy was, thus, far from being paternalistic. However, having robbed the latter of some of their privileges, he sought to salvage their position by advocating the retention of their slaves. His role in this respect deserves to be mentioned in view of the fact that this helped project a benevolent image of the man in the eyes of the people. When called upon by the directors to explain his support of slavery, so obnoxious to the Christian religious ethos of the eighteenth and the nineteenth centuries, Scott claimed that the slaves were well treated by their masters who would be rendered helpless in the latter's absence.[59] He recommended a gradual abolition of slavery in view of its immense significance to the emasculated aristocracy. What remained unspoken in his rhetoric was his concern for gaining acceptance for the new regime. Scott's benevolent rhetoric concealed his growing concern at the sudden spurt in conspiracies by royalist supporters desirous of restoring the Ahom rule.[60]

Jenkins later could not afford to take any chances when he confirmed Scott's measures of revenue collection. British revenue reports pertaining to this era, as well as some of Jenkins's own correspondences, reveal that the vast stretches of uncultivated land in the region and the popular practices of shifting and itinerant cultivation tended to confound the officers of the revenue department.[61] Products of an age when sedentary agriculture was prized for its obvious economic advantages, Jenkins and his colleagues found it hard to explain the magnitude of uncultivated land in the region. Mills expressed his surprise at the phenomenon attributing it to the indolence of the Assamese *ryot*. There was also thus a strong belief that the Assamese *ryot* was lazy, indolent and unwilling to exert himself, which took firm roots in official circles. This perception generated by the low level of cultivation in Assam was articulated by Mills in his report,

> It is the generally conceived opinion that the present stagnant state of the Province arises from the minute sub-division of land, and the population having cultivated as much land as it requires to meet its very limited wants. It is contended that the Assamese peasant is apathetic and indolent, that he is satisfied with an easily attained competency, and that without a large increase of population, which is at present checked by the ravages of cholera and epidemic disease, by the inordinate use of opium, and the licentious habits of the people, there is no prospect of extending cultivation in any considerable degree.[62]

The apathy of the Assamese peasants for hard work was also believed to be a principal cause behind their reluctance to work in the plantations.[63] The plantation economy was facing a crisis in the form of the scarcity of labour. Jenkins's correspondences indicate that granting clear-cut proprietary rights to the *ryots* in land was meant to induce them to take an active interest in cultivation. Jenkins had all along held that security of tenures would induce the *ryot* to take up land for cultivation. Ryotwari, thus, was expected to tackle the perceived lethargy of the Assamese *ryot*, inducing him to work in order to preserve his holding. It was also expected to resolve the perennial problem of resignation of land or *istifas* that became a huge concern for the administration.[64] Further, Jenkins was also keen to check the migratory habits of the Assamese peasants at all cost. Ryotwari appeared to promise a solution to all such perceived evils believed to be plaguing peasant economy in Assam. This is confirmed by a letter written by Jenkins to the Board of Revenue in 1838,

> All the officers are agreed in considering the ryots the actual proprietors of the lands they severally occupy and I have already frequently submitted to the Board and Government my opinions declaring them such. This would greatly tend to fix our villagers to the paternal abodes and would go far to remove the difficulties some of the collectors apprehend in making settlements for long periods of years.[65]

Amalendu Guha has highlighted yet another dimension to the history of Ryotwari in Assam. Guha feels that the decision to liquidate all forms of property in Assam was a political one taken to facilitate the burgeoning plantation economy, which needed both land and labour for its growth.[66] It was equally imperative to establish the planters as the only elite by eliminating the erstwhile aristocracy. Ryotwari was thus meant to bring pressure directly to bear on the peasants so that labour could be flushed out through excess pressure into the plantation sector.[67] This perhaps explains the frequent enhancement of taxes irrespective of the unrest among the peasantry over the issue.[68]

Scott's decision to bring the erstwhile nobility under assessment hit the latter hard, especially since Scott had also abolished the practice of unpaid labour service that the former had been entitled to. One of the earliest measures taken by Scott was to abolish compulsory personal services rendered by a class of hereditary service providers called *paiks* and to free the latter from the bond that connected them with the aristocracy. This measure prompted a large number of the *paiks* to promptly abandon labour services to their masters and to seek their fortunes in the other avenues opened up by colonial rule in Assam and elsewhere. Some reportedly migrated to neighbouring countries like Bhutan in search of a better life.[69] This deprived the aristocracy of the labour required to cultivate their agricultural estates. Consequently, soon after the settlement measures were enforced, many members of the erstwhile aristocracy, who were allowed by Scott to hold onto their estates, lost the estates for non-payment of revenue.[70] Scott's measures were, however, immensely beneficial to the new regime for this brought the largest section of the *swargadeo*'s subjects, that is the *paiks*, within the ambit of revenue assessment. Conversely, these measures spelled ruin for the erstwhile nobility whose *khats* were worked by the *paiks* and the slaves. The list included both the higher, middle and lesser nobility of the previous regime, all of whom had got used to a life of comfort. The imposition of a levy on their tracts, however mild, and the sequestration of claims to unpaid labour services reduced these men to utter penury and forced many to throw up their tracts. The maximum blow was certainly taken by the revered *dangariyas* or the highest nobles of the reign, but the new rules had a deleterious effect on all categories of nobles – high or low.

Reports sent by field officers of the new regime testify to the severity of the impact on the erstwhile nobility. Scott was clearly not unaware of the plight of this class. He tried to soften the blow on the latter by pleading that they be allowed to retain their slaves, but his plea was overruled by the Supreme Government on the grounds that this was against the ethos of civilized existence. At a subsequent period, we have statements by officers like Captain Brodie, the commissioner of Nowgong, who recommended some form of favourable treatment to the incumbents at least during the latter's lifetime. After the resumption of Upper Assam, Lieutenant Brodie was made the principal assistant of Upper Assam, with his office at Jorhat. Brodie tried to provide relief to the distressed aristocracy by effecting a liberal assessment of land. In his report on the district of Sibsagar, the seat of the Ahom monarchy, Captain Brodie wrote,

> I beg at the same time to state that the circumstances of this division are somewhat peculiar, inasmuch as the bulk of the old Assam nobility are located here, and notwithstanding the number of this class who either hold office or have received pensions from the liberality of Government, there are still very large numbers out of employ and who find the utmost difficulty in meeting the present demands upon them. In recommending therefore a general increase on the rate (of rent), I would couple this with some relief.[71]

Captain Brodie proposed that the higher classes who paid Rs 20 and upwards of rent should pay a moiety of the assessment, and those who paid Rs 10 but did not pay Rs 20 should have a deduction for the excess over Rs 10. This proposition was approved by commissioner, Jenkins.[72] It was soon found, however, that the benefits were being misused in as much as ordinary *ryots* were throwing their several lands together so as to make up the quantity of holdings entitling them to indulgence reserved only for the better classes whose lands were thrown out of cultivation by the loss of *lickchous* (a class of servants usually owned by the master and who stayed in the household of the master usually for their entire life time) and slaves. As a result, the government was being defrauded of large amounts of revenue. Jenkins therefore asked Captain Holroyd, the principal assistant, to submit a report on the matter, which the latter furnished on 10 June 1852. In his letter to Jenkins, Holroyd recommended that the indulgence be continued during the lifetime of the incumbents to the extent of their holdings in 1844–45 to the *Gohains, Phookuns, Rajkahwahs* and *Burooahs* and that the remission made to all other holders to be resumed immediately. He further suggested that no new claims for remission on similar grounds should be entertained. He also proposed that the number of beneficiaries be reduced by excluding from the list lesser nobles like the *Saikias, Borahs* and *Hazaries*.[73] Brodie also addressed requests for loans and aids, albeit on a reduced scale.[74] Revenue divisions were increased in number in order to increase avenues of employment for the latter. Despite the affective solution suggested by these officers for providing relief to the erstwhile nobility, and irrespective of the remissions in rent collection subsequently granted to them by the state, the situation of the latter did not improve. This was so because these relief measures came too late. Already many families were impoverished under the impact of colonization. Men of dignity, not used to manual labour, often declined to accept mouzadarship (mauzadars were officially appointed revenue collectors and were usually selected from the eminent men of the locality depending on their economic and social status) in distant villages, hoping that there would be eventually better opportunities at the headquarters. Jenkins's note to Mills summed up the hapless state to which the nobility had been reduced:

> It (Assam) has had to labour . . . under other difficulties in its progress, the greatest perhaps of which has been the utter impoverishment of every man of rank in the country, first by the sequestration of their Pykes and next by the emancipation of their slaves. These formed the estates of the native gentry, who were not generally land proprietors, and though they had in many instances small patrimonial farms, that is, estates which they had originally cleared from jungle, called khats, they were unable to cultivate these when their slaves were liberated, and they have with small exception either thrown them up or allowed them to be sold for arears of revenue and debts.[75]

There was little however that the state would do to mitigate their plight. Moneeram's petition to Mills articulated the frustrations of a class used to privileges and protection:

> Those classes who had been exempted from the payment of revenue for 600 years are now brought under the assessment. Those again whose ancestors never lived by digging, ploughing or carrying burdens, are now nearly reduced to such degrading employments.[76]

There was thus nothing paternalistic about Scott's decision to rule out mediators between the state and the cultivators. He was acting in the best interests of the colonial state. Moreover, Scott's decision was totally in sync with the general climate of opinion in higher British bureaucratic circles. One of the earliest injunctions passed by the colonial state was to declare that the manner of acquisition of Assam had nullified all previous entitlements enjoyed by the people of the realm. On examination, the land revenue measures of the colonial state appear quite consistent from the earliest days of the establishment of British rule in Assam. The seeds of a gross violation of the pre-colonial entitlements were already there in the earliest policy statements issued by the functionaries of the new regime if we overlook one single attempt to project a somewhat reassuring self-image to the subject people. Just before undertaking the Burmese expedition, in 1824, the Supreme Government of India issued a proclamation addressed to the people of Assam, suffering from a prolonged Burmese occupation of the country. The proclamation read:

> We are not led into your country by the thirst of conquest: but are forced, in our own defence, to deprive our enemy of the means of annoying us. You may, therefore, rest assured, that we will . . . re-establish . . . a Government adapted to your wants and calculated to promote the happiness of all classes.[77]

It was soon apparent, however, that the company's government was far from willing to fulfil its promise to the people of Assam. Soon after the acquisition of Assam, which was added to the existing British province of Bengal, the government revealed its intentions vis-à-vis the newly acquired territory. The latter came out with a statement that the manner of acquisition of Assam had absolved the government of the responsibility to honour any pre-colonial entitlements. Unlike in Bengal where Lord Cornwallis was directed to consider the laws and customs of India and the local systems of land rights in Bengal, in Assam it was declared that 'with the exception of Sylhet Proper and the permanently-settled tracts of the district of Goalpara, the successive conquest of districts or portions of districts, including the hill districts, has been held to have extinguished all private rights in land previously existing, unless expressly recognized by the British Government'.[78] Thus, the government made it amply clear to all concerned that all pre-colonial rights had been extinguished by the Burmese and that it was totally up to the discretion of the British government whether to restore these rights once again. This statement set the tone and tenor for future land settlement policies in the region as the state arrogated to itself the right to decide the future of pre-colonial revenue entitlements of the inhabitants of Assam.

Scott's successors tried to salvage the pride of the deposed aristocracy by incorporating the latter into the new administrative system by granting them *mauzadari* rights or the right to collect revenue over designated areas. However, the condition of the elites deteriorated further when towards the end of the nineteenth century the government raised revenue assessments after 1893. While the landlords had to pay the enhanced rates, they were debarred from exercising pressure on the tenant cultivators to realize the money on account of various preventive measures undertaken by the state. The plight of the superior land holders has been highlighted by Arup Jyoti Saikia in his works on the Patharughat revolt of 1893–94.[79]

IV

Invoking traditions

If posterity has been soft to Scott and full of admiration for the affective nature of his rule, Scott himself deserves credit for the same. Through a smoothly crafted rhetoric Scott was able to establish his revenue measures as having been modelled on the pre-colonial system of land tenure and consequently in sync with pre-colonial traditions. By a sleight of hand he was able to convert the service class in pre-colonial Assam into a class of ordinary *ryots*, as cultivators in British India were referred to. In a note on Captain Welsh's Report on Assam, Scott wrote:

> With exception to Royal grants and the Khats or farms of individual usually of small extent, there is no division of the land in Assam amongst a comparatively small number of individuals such as seen in the feudal countries of Europe and in Bengal, and the cultivated soil may be considered as the property of the pykes or peasants owing service to the state to whom it is allotted. Waste land might be reclaimed by anyone who had the means of bringing it into cultivation, and a property in the soil might be acquired, subject, however, if held without a grant from the king, to an agrarian law which rendered the whole of the transplanted rice lands (roopeet) liable to division amongst the pykes, on a new census taking place, in case there should be an insufficiency of waste land for their support. . . . It is believed that no estate of this kind exists exceeding in extent 2000 Bengal beeghas, and that no individual in the country possessed altogether of 900 beeghas of such land of roopeet quality.[80]

Scott's views regarding the essential similarity between the two regimes of land revenue regulations were echoed by subsequent commissioners, who claimed that the revenue measures of the new regime were nothing but a slightly modified version of the pre-colonial mechanism of surplus appropriation. Writing in 1853, A.J. Moffat Mills, a judge of the Sadar Dewani Adalat, deputed to enquire into the condition of administration in Assam, echoed Scott's line of argument that the revenue system introduced by the British was a modification of that which had previously existed.[81] Mills added,

> The Ryot had no right of property in the land saving his Bari land. . . . There was no middleman with any like pretensions; the country was depopulated and laid waste, and there was not even the trace of a village community. Under such circumstances I think the authorities acted rightly in not transferring the Government right in the land to the Chowdrees and heads of clans, and creating a zemindaree system like that of Bengal.[82]

Official rhetoric in this regard drew on the fundamental premise that land under the Ahoms constituted the property of the state to be given away or retrieved at will. Colonial officials further argued that under the erstwhile rulers the bulk of the land was parcelled out among a host of small holders as service tenures. British officials strove hard to convey the impression that the new revenue regulations were in consonance with the pre-colonial system of land tenure characterized by state ownership of land and the absence of a class of substantial landholding rural gentry. Francis Jenkins, the commissioner of Assam from 1834, asserted in one of his letters to Mills,

> There was then left no class of people in the country who could be called landholders above the mere Ryot and actual cultivator, holding the merest plot of land on which he could subsist, and that liable to sub-division amongst all his heirs.[83]

The intention behind all this rhetoric was a purely political one designed to gain legitimacy for British rule in Assam and to generate in public perception an image of the British as the legitimate and ideal successors to the Ahom legacy.

The institution cited as the model for the new revenue regulations was none other than the *Khelwari* system believed to have constituted the institutional basis for the erstwhile administration.[84] British official discourse understood the *Khelwari* system as being premised on the idea that soil and people alike were the absolute property of the king or the *swargadeo*. British official documents claimed that under the previous regime, the whole population was divided into some groups called *khels*, 1,000 to 5,000 persons, who were subdivided into *gots* consisting of four *paiks*. The entire male population of the *swargadeo*'s domain above a certain age, excepting the nobles or *dangariyas*, was designated as *paiks* and required to render personal service throughout the year either to the *swargadeo* or the king or to one of the *dangariyas*. In return, each member of the *got* was allowed two *puras* (nearly three acres) of rice land termed *ga mati*, free of rent, and a piece of land for his house and garden (*bari* or *bustee*). On the basis of an enquiry into the question of land rights at the close of the Ahom regime, the early British administrators of Assam concluded that traditionally the individual *ryot* had permanent rights only to his *bari* land.[85] The part of his land termed *ga mati* was separate from the rest of his holding and revocable at will by the state. If a *paik* cultivated any rice land in excess of his two *puras*, he was assessed on it at the rate of Rs 1 per *pura*. When a *paik* was away from his land on state service, the other members of his *got* cultivated his land on his behalf. Scott's enquiries into the pre-colonial system of landholding convinced him that land in pre-colonial Assam actually belonged to the king but was held by *paiks* who were, therefore, comparable to the class deemed as *ryots* in the rest of the company's dominions in India. Scott therefore wasted no time in abolishing compulsory labour services rendered by the *paiks* and entered into settlements with each individual *paik* on the basis of the latter's proven holding. Each *paik* was, according to this system, assessed at the rate of Rs 3 on his holding, which was calculated as the amalgam of the homestead, garden and rice land held by him. The revenue rhetoric of the colonial state in Assam rested on the fundamental assumption that the *paiks* of Assam were nothing but peasants or *ryots* found in the rest of colonial India. Seen from this perspective, the British had merely confirmed the latter's status as surplus creators, and since the *paik* system represented the functional aspect of the erstwhile administration, the revenue measures of the colonial state had merely given legal sanction to an already established institution. The translation of *paiks* into *ryots* was arrived at through a clever mechanism of translation that was simultaneously devious and irreverent.

Scott's claims that he had preserved intact the spirit of the earlier mode of land tenure in Assam was far from correct. The *paik* system, as understood by the British, elided several crucial aspects of the institution as it had functioned under the previous regime. To begin with, entitlements in pre-colonial Assam were characterized at times by overlapping prerogatives. These were also often not fixed in nature either in a territorial or a more substantial sense. Finally, claims were not always backed by written documents and could very well be verbal grants customarily honoured and therefore more easily ascertained by engaging the local people. Thus, the British often encountered multiple claims on the same piece of land

and had to resolve on the basis of hearsay and impressions. Such a system was not foolproof, and therefore, decisions often caused much heartburn. Again, in Assam's pre-colonial economy, the *paik* was granted rice land in the wet land zone suitable for cultivation, while his garden and homestead could be located in compact blocks away from his cultivable plot. The British officials, used to clear-cut demarcations and compact holdings, found it impossible to manage such scattered holdings. Consequently, efforts were made to integrate these scattered tracts into more compact blocks. The process proved to be quite tortuous, involving numerous adjustments with multiple holders, and the outcome was far from pleasant to many. There were numerous occasions when the process of demarcation of holdings failed to meet with the expectations of claimants. In his report on Assam in 1853, Mills stated:

> Numerous petitions are presented to the collector and the Commissioner, after the settlement has been completed, complaining of false measurement, and incorrect of classification.[86]

Again, under the previous mechanism, although some of the *paiks* had continued to be members of their respective *khels* or groups, and held their rice and garden land, some had become detached eventually from their *khels* and lived on the *khats* and *chamuas* of the religious and secular aristocracy, entering into some sort of share-cropping arrangement with their masters. Although they were entitled to land for their homestead, they often lost track of their rice land in the process. This did not affect them earlier because they were allowed to retain a share of the crops they grew on the land of their masters. The number of such *paiks* was presumably substantial, given the huge number of *paik* population. According to a list provided by Moneeram Dewan, the *Boorah Gohain* had nearly 80,000 *paiks* under him, which was reduced to 43,000 at the time of the British takeover of Assam.[87] *Paiks* assigned to temples or the *sattras* for providing specific services also often became detached from their respective *khels* and attached to grants of land devoted to the service of the gods or to the maintenance of priests. They were known as *bhakats* when attached to a *sattra* and *dewalia* (temple), or *paik* when attached to a temple. These temple *paiks* were just entitled to some land for their homesteads.[88] Again some *paiks* at times took refuge on the *khats* or landed estates of the nobles in order to save themselves from service to the state. They then passed themselves off as slaves since slaves were immune both from state services and from the payment of taxes. These *paiks* presumably had to give up claims to their *ga mati* eventually in order to protect their new-found identity.

Again, *paiks* constantly migrated to distant parts of the province outside their *khel* boundaries in order to avoid taxation or oppressive officers or for other reasons. This was permitted by the authorities, but the migrating *paiks* were obliged to account for their revenue to their respective *kheldars*. Such migrations increased during the period of Burmese occupation during which time the *khel* system could not be properly maintained. While the colonial regulations benefitted those *paiks* who could produce evidence of their membership of *khels*, the others who could not produce any such evidence suffered when the government made it mandatory to produce *sunnuds* or at least the oral evidence of the *khel* officers for authentication of claims. In the absence of documents, it is impossible to trace the fate of thousands of these freed *paiks*, who were released during the tenure of David Scott. The number of men rendered landless swelled further on account of the annulment of slavery in 1843. It has already been pointed out that many of these so-called slaves were actually *paiks*, who were now robbed of their means of sustenance for failure to produce documentary evidence of their *paikan* status. Without the protection afforded by their masters, these freed men must have found it difficult to survive and joined the growing number of landless labourers in the province. It has already been stated that the process of demarcation of rights to holdings was far from smooth. It was difficult to ascertain holdings not only on account of the absence of compact holdings but also because many documents had been lost during the prolonged occupation of the country by the Burmese. The Burmese incursions had led to the redistribution of population and the loss of rights held hereditarily. The British attempt to ascertain these rights therefore met with numerous resistance and counterclaims. Numerous petitions were addressed to the colonial officers alleging violation of customary rights. Many such claims had to be settled through the personal intervention of the commissioners.

The fixation of the size of the *ryot*'s holding was once again based on the rigid understanding of the notion of the *ga mati*, literally meaning body land purportedly held by the *paiks*. Colonial accounts cited pre-colonial references to determine the latter's extent as two *puras* of rice land. This together with some additional land for homestead and garden became the basis of the colonial state's settlement with the *ryots*. Such a rigid notion of *ga mati* belied the fact that under the previous regime the *paik* was allowed to supplement his quota of wet paddy land and that such reclaimed waste land was exempted from the payment of taxes for the greater part of the Ahom rule. Nominal taxes on additional landholding were introduced only in the later Ahom period.[89] The *paik* could also acquire any amount of inferior land for his homestead and garden, and this was initially free of tax. Further, *paiks* had free access to unoccupied dry lands for fuel wood and building materials or for grazing and temporary cultivation. Thus, the extent of holding of the *paik* was not as rigid as has been portrayed by the colonial authors. Under the new regime, however, the *paik* was compelled to accept a rigid limit to the amount of land held by him. Both Amalendu Guha and Sanjib Baruah argue that in the land-surplus situation of pre-colonial Assam, the peasants supplemented their primary holdings with additional land for occasional cultivation. The latter could occupy any amount of cultivable wastes for rent-free seasonal cultivation. Guha points out that such practices were not restricted to 'tribal' peasants commonly perceived as the only practitioners of shifting cultivation in India.[90] Guha shows how transplanted rice cultivators who comprised the bulk of the *paik* population also practised shifting cultivation occasionally in other regions. Baruah further highlights that peasants utilized land apart from their *ga mati* for a variety of non-agricultural uses, such as collecting house-building material and raw material for basket-weaving and raising silkworms, which were now severely curtailed on account of a strict demarcation of the size of holdings as well as due to the assertion of state rights over waste land.[91] Baruah argues that the new rules of property resulted in enormous dispossession of the Assamese peasantry.[92] Further, the colonial state increased the burden on the erstwhile *paiks* by bringing the *bari* and *bustee* land which were not liable to taxation or distribution earlier, under the ambit of taxation. Colonial understanding of the *paik* system in pre-colonial Assam also projected the same as an unchanging and homogenous structure immune to abuses and changes. In reality the system allowed arbitrary exercise of power to the *kheldars* or officers administering the *khels*. Many *paiks* were arbitrarily deprived of their legitimate share of the village land under oppressive officers. Again, given the sparse population of the region, the system at times also allowed *paiks* access to surplus land for cultivation in excess of their legitimate share of rice land.

There were many other ways in which the erstwhile *paiks* stood to lose from the new dispensation. Under the previous regime, the *paik* was allotted rice land as per availability of cultivable tracts, allowing him to enjoy holdings in areas not always contiguous to his residence. This often gave him access to fertile tracts outside his immediate locality. This is illustrated by the *Perah Kaguz*, which Scott made the basis of his land revenue measures. One of the first things that Scott did on assuming office was to obtain a copy of a document called the *Perah Kaguz*, from one of the old Assamese authorities. After the death of the first agent, his one-time colleague, James Matthie, was to exult over what he held out as the remarkable astuteness demonstrated by the former in acquiring the said document. Matthie wrote:

> The Perah Kaguz is simply the ancient Assamese Government measurement registers and which also record the extent and nature of the Lakheraj grants made by the Assam kings to their spiritual advisors/Gossains, Brahmins and other holy men as also to individuals for any particular services to the state. This document was obtained by Mr. Scott on our conquest of Assam from some of the old Assamese authorities and is now an official record of reference at Gowhatty and which will be the guide in deciding on the cases now pending of Lakheraj claims. It is perhaps scarcely necessary my stating how necessary it was to obtain a fair legible copy of such a document.[93]

It was not easy, however, to interpret the provisions of this document. Scott did not live long enough to witness the practical problems encountered by his colleagues in deciding the boundaries of revenue units on the basis of the information culled from the *Perah Kaguz*. In 1834, Captain Bogle, as the officiating collector of Lower Assam, complained about the 'scattered and disunited nature of the Pergunnahs and even Mauzahs of lower Assam, rendering it utterly impossible to maintain either an efficient police control or a systematic and accurate Khas Tuhseel'.[94] Bogle wrote,

> In former times the government demand being chiefly confined to the personal labour of the pykes, and no part of it being reckoned with reference to land, whenever a pyke of one Pergunnah migrated to another part of the country, the lands he occupied assumed the name of his pergunnah this is one cause of the present confusion; another is to be attributed to the desire which generally pervaded the upper classes to get small grants in various parts, that they might the more easily be able to usurp a large tract near to each. These grants were often designated by the name of the Pergunnah in which the owner originally resided – other causes may also be adduced. . . .
>
> As instances of this I beg to draw attention to the case of Bar. . . . The chief part of this Pergunnah lies near Gowalparah but every bit of it are to be seen in every quarter from the Pohoomarrah River to the Bur Nuddee, the boundary of Durrung.[95]

Thus, *purganas* under the previous system did not form integral lots. They were scattered in small portions all over the province, which added to the bewilderment of the British officials. The colonial state, on its part, did not consider it in its interest to honour the spirit of the pre-colonial distribution of land grants. Bogle, therefore, decided to mould the boundaries of each division by cutting off the outlaying dependencies and incorporating these with the *pergunnahs* in which they were situated. Bogle's measure, which received the whole-hearted support of his superiors, constituted one of the numerous such steps that Jenkins undertook in order to draw immediate and manageable boundaries. Needless to say, these measures constituted a gross violation of the very ethos of pre-colonial land grants. Bogle's measure constituted one of the numerous such steps that the colonial state would be required to undertake in the near future in order to translate an unfamiliar world of indeterminacy into a familiar one of determinate boundaries. The administration's demarcation of tenurial boundaries, on the basis of the *Perah Kaguz*, was as flawed as it could get, apart from being a gross violation of the very ethos of pre-colonial land grants. Thus, the colonial state was forced to reorder these holdings in favour of more proximate and manageable units. There was an unavoidable reduction in the size of these holdings as a result of this reordering, not to mention the loss of fertile tracts which had to be exchanged henceforth with land of questionable fertility for the sake of contiguity. The *ryot* in British revenue records was thus a far cry from the pre-colonial *paik*, and although the latter's lot may not have been necessarily better, he was at least capable of shifting his position if the situation got too tight – a flexibility denied to him under the present circumstances.

V

How did the ryot *fare?*

Following Scott's death in 1831, T.C Robertson was appointed as the next agent in the Northeast. In 1832, the latter directed that each district should be divided into *mahals* (divisions) and that all land would be settled annually until 1835.[96] Subsequently during his tenure, the commissioners of the three districts, namely Kamrup, Durrang and Nowgong, divided the entire cultivable land in their respective divisions into circles called *mauza*. The task of collection of the land revenue was assigned to commissioning agents called *chaudharis, mauzadars* and *kagotis.* Those selected for the purpose were usually men of substance in their respective localities, and they were assisted in their task by village accountants called *Patwari, Thakuria* or

Kakati. The officer in charge of a fiscal division was made accountable for the revenue in his division and had to make good any shortfall in collection, just as he was permitted to appropriate any increase in the amount collected arising out of extended cultivation. He was remunerated through a percentage share on the total amount collected. In 1854, all lands were further divided into three main classes: *basti or bari* or homestead, *rupit* or low rice land and *faringhati* or high lands. There were primarily two types of cultivation in Assam: permanent and fluctuating. The first was carried on in both *rupit* and *basti/bari* land, while the *faringati* land comprising flood-prone or sub-montane grassy tracts was used predominantly for shifting cultivation.[97] The rates assessed on these three classes were made different for each district. The economy of Assam on the eve of the annexation was not sufficiently monetized, and consequently, the peasants were hard-pressed to pay these taxes.[98] Their liability for taxation also increased because they were now assessed on their entire holding unlike in the past. No part thereof was exempt from taxation. The revenue measures of the British thus constituted a serious violation of the pre-colonial system of assessment. The short tenure of the revenue-collecting officers, coupled with the short leases granted to the *ryots*, caused tremendous instability in the revenue administration, and led to increasing pressures on the *ryots*.[99]

The most crucial decision taken after 1861 was to grant proprietary rights to the *ryots*. Between 1861 and 1867, the issue of providing the cultivators with a permanent, heritable and transferable property in their lands formed the subject of considerable discussion between the Bengal government, the Board of Revenue and the commissioner of Assam.[100] The Board of Revenue advocated long-term settlements with the *mauzadars* and the creation of a class of landed proprietors 'by the assignment of leases for longer periods, to be eventually converted into permanent holdings'.[101] The commissioner of Assam drew up a set of rules based on these principles, and in 1870 these rules came into force. The Settlement Rules of 1870 remained in force till 1887 when they were superseded by rules made under the Land and Revenue Regulation. The Settlement Rules of 1870 for the first time clarified the rights in land possessed by the cultivators of the soil. They recognized a permanent heritable and transferable right in land (subject to registration of all transfers and successions) as attaching to all persons who took periodic leases from the government for lands held permanently. In the case of this land, the cultivator was allowed the option of taking a lease for any period not exceeding ten years, and the lease so given guaranteed him against enhancement of assessment for the term of the lease. The lessee was allowed the option of relinquishing his land whenever he pleased, provided he gave three months' notice. The rules allowed a form of annual lease, with the addendum that if the government required such land for a public purpose, it could take it away from the lessee without paying him any compensation for the land itself, compensation being paid only for the loss of any crops or houses that might be standing upon it. Such holders were not permitted any permanent heritable and transferable rights in land. The rules divided all cultivable land in Assam into 'fixed cultivation' and 'fluctuating cultivation'.[102] The former included *rupit* and homestead lands, held for the most part permanently, while fluctuating cultivation included all high paddy lands and lands where mustard seed and the different descriptions of pulses were grown. In the case of fluctuating cultivation, the Settlement Rules allowed only annual leases.[103] That the British regime of taxation was more comprehensive is clear from the fact that under the previous regime fluctuating cultivation was not always subject to taxation owing to the uncertainties of production and therefore yields.[104]

In 1886, the first comprehensive proposal outlined the colonial state's revenue claims on the people and resources of the region. It was proposed by Chief Commissioner Henry Hopkinson, who had always opposed longer settlements with the peasants. Like his predecessors, however, he favoured throughout Assam 'a raiyatwari settlement of the simplest and purest character', the collections being made directly from the *ryots* by government officials.[105] His draft Land and Revenue Regulation consisted of nine chapters dealing with matters such as the definition of the rights of the different classes of owners of land in the province, the settlement rules to be followed by the Assam government and the rules for the allotment of grazing grounds and of land for hill tribes practising *jhum* or migratory cultivation, as well as the general principles to be followed in effecting land settlements and the survey of land prior to settlements. It provided for a record of rights and prescribed the procedure for resuming land held revenue-free under invalid titles. The regulation further defined the powers of revenue officers of the province from the chief commissioner downwards, and laid down the procedure to be followed for realizing arrears of revenue. After the Land and Revenue Regulation was passed, steps were taken to frame and issue rules under that enactment, prescribing in detail the procedure to be observed in the various categories listed by the latter. The proposals were highly comprehensive and meant to expand the revenue base of the state.

Following the adoption of the new regulations, the government soon classified landed interests in Assam into the following categories:

(i) *Lakhiraj* estates and certain similar estates for which the holder paid minimal rates and which were dubbed as 'fee-simple' estates, along with estates held under the Special Waste Land Rules

(ii) Permanently settled estates of Sylhet and Goalpara
(iii) Temporarily settled estates other than town lands, held direct from
       government on periodic lease.

Despite Henry Hopkinson's reluctance to make long-term settlements, the
government of India decided to go ahead with the latter on the grounds
that it was 'in every way a preferable course to give the actual occupant of
the soil as secure a tenure as can be conferred upon him, subject to the
payment of revenue to the Government at rates fixed for long periods,
and to preserve a clear distinction between the rights and obligations of
proprietorship and the duties of fiscal and official administration'.[106] It was
decided that the term of settlement of lands held permanently was to be
ordinarily 10 years, with discretion to the commissioner to make settlement
for 15 years. The settlement was to be made with the occupant cultivators.
The rates of assessment were to be fixed for the term of settlement but to
be liable to alteration in future settlements. Further, permanent holdings
were to be heritable and transferable on condition that transfers were registered. The revenue was to be collected by the *mauzadars* placed in charge
of fiscal circles, and the latter were to be allowed no interest in land but
were to get a commission on the revenue they might collect. The new rules
brought all extant areas within the ambit of taxation. This automatically
restricted the mobility of the peasants hitherto accustomed to a wider variety of agricultural practices involving movements supplemented by a more
liberal and flexible tax regime.[107]

   In the years that followed, the official assessment policy became even more
stringent, as care was taken to bring every inch of land under assessment.
This rigour was the outcome of the belief in some circles that the government was depriving itself of a large amount of revenue by imposing a flat
rate of taxation for all categories of land, whereas land of superior category
ought to be priced higher. This debate induced the government to undertake a cadastral survey of land in Assam in 1882. This survey was carried
out in Kamrup and select areas in each district of Assam Proper, which were
believed to be held more or less permanently. The purpose of the survey was
to identify and rectify errors in measurement and classification of land carried out under the Settlement Rules of 1870. The survey aimed at drawing
up accurate village cadastral maps, with fixed location boundaries of every
cultivator's holding. Another purpose was to discover concealed cultivation,
if any, in any of these tracts liable to assessment.[108] The survey fulfilled its
purpose as it revealed that 'in every district, the measurements reported by
the mauzadars were more or less incorrect, and that the lands had generally been under-classified, much *basti* and *rupit* land having been classified

48

by the mauzadars as *faringhati*.[109] The survey extended over a period of nine years from 1883–84 to 1892–93 and resulted in an annual increase of Rs 2 lakhs in revenue.[110] The outcome of the survey was to identify the basis for re-settlement of land in the districts of Assam Proper since the previous decennial settlement made in 1883 was due to expire. Accordingly, in December 1892 a new set of settlement rules were published, which stated that the main principle for re-assessment and re-settlement was the value of the land as indicated by the demand for land.[111] The valuation was to be decided on the basis of the following criteria:

(i) The proportion of cultivable waste to cultivated land
(ii) The proportion of fluctuating to permanent cultivation
(iii) The density of population

Needless to say, these were highly inadequate factors wherewith to adjudge the value of the land, not to speak of the rates of assessment.

The new rules retained the old division of cultivable land into *basti* or homestead and garden land, *rupit* or transplanted rice land and *faringhati* or high land but recognized that there were disparities in value and productiveness within each of these categories of land in different and sometimes even in the same districts. Hence, each of these categories of land were sub-classified into first, second and third classes, and the district officers were given the option to propose a fourth sub-class. With regard to land that had not been surveyed, it was decided that these should be ordinarily placed in the lowest sub-class adopted for the district although once again, the settlement officer was given the power to place them in a higher sub-class if he so felt.[112]

Jenkins and his colleagues had been highly confident that the new dispensation had immensely benefitted the *ryots* by releasing them from the obligation of rendering compulsory labour services and by granting them occupancy rights in land. In a self-satisfactory manner, he remarked:

> Notwithstanding its greatly impoverished and depopulated state . . . Assam has greatly recovered its cultivation and much of its internal prosperity. . . . The Assamese are now, I may safely affirm, I believe, as well off in all respects as any Ryots in India.[113]

Mills was equally pleased at the impact of the new revenue administration on peasant society in Assam and noted, 'Under the Assam rule the Ryot could not dispose of his cultivated land by sale, gift, or even mortgage; he has under us been permitted to exercise that power, and to possess all but the name of the proprietor'.[114] The actual condition of the peasantry under the new regime belied the self-congratulatory statements of Scott, Jenkins and their colleagues in the administration. In contradistinction to the British claims that land under the pre-colonial state was the principal owner of the soil, in principle, it was the former who exercised this prerogative more effectively than their predecessors. To begin with, under the colonial state all waste land became the property of the state and hence amenable to allocation as and how it suited their interests. Initially, the British encouraged the peasants to take up additional land for cultivation, but later they denied such rights to the latter and reserved such tracts exclusively for European investors who were given grants of huge amounts of land on liberal terms. The Ahoms, on the other hand, had been non-discriminatory and had conceded revenue remissions to all those who brought fresh land under cultivation, be it the nobles or the *pykes*. The British government, however, denied such rights to the local people, reserving the same initially for the European planters and later for East Bengali migrants. The peasant, therefore, lost his earlier rights to supplement his income by occasionally cultivating additional land for which he did not have to pay taxes.

The *mauzadari* system also did not work in favour of the peasants. In his work on the impact of Ryotwari on the Assamese peasants, Amalendu Guha has highlighted the plight of the *ryots* under the *mauzadari* system of revenue collection.[115] The brief and uncertain nature of tenure of the *mauzadars* and other revenue officers, coupled with the proviso that the latter had to make good any shortfall in the estimated revenue from their respective circles, led to a strict and often harsh regime of revenue collection. It also hampered cultivation as the *mauzadar* had no interest whatsoever in improving the land since he could never be sure that his tenure would be renewed. Given the lack of any improvements in cropping patterns (double cropping and crop rotation were practised on a limited level), the level of production remained very low and there was no improvement in cultivation whatsoever.[116] It was thus difficult for the *ryot* to pay the revenue as the surplus generated was hardly sufficient after meeting his household consumption levels. This naturally exacerbated the incidence of rural indebtedness although details are not forthcoming for the greater part of our period. One is, however, sceptical about Arup Jyoti Saikia's claim that rural indebtedness was not a cause for concern for this period.[117] It is possible that rural indebtedness increased in the later half of colonial rule in Assam, but there can be no doubt that the basis for the former was laid in this period itself with the monetization of rent payment and the simultaneous impoverishment of the peasantry. The Marwari merchants, who doubled as money lenders, had already entrenched themselves in the rural society through their near absolute control of internal trade. The latter were only too eager to lend money to the *ryot*, which they did against the security of the latter's crop rather than his holding.

The best illustration of peasant dissatisfaction comes from the incidence of resignation of land or *istifas*, which became a serious concern for the revenue administration in the nineteenth century.[118] A good amount of land was resigned every year by the *ryots* despite initial agreement to the terms of the settlement in the form of submission of *kabooliyats*. The British administration regarded this as a problem although it had no option but to allow such practices in order to prevent the peasants from emigrating from the land altogether. The practice itself was, however, considered a serious menace, not only because it affected the profits of the *mauzadars* or revenue collectors of the new regime but also because it hindered the progress of cultivation. Contemporary colonial documents reveal that the matter formed the subject of much animated discussion in official circles as officers tried to devise suitable means of inducing the *ryots* to stick to the original agreement. It seemed to many officers that the best possible way to tackle resignation was by rendering a certain portion of the holdings rent-free.[119] Among numerous suggestions proffered by officials were proposals to remit the revenue on the ancestral tracts at least, with a view to encouraging the *ryots* to settle down by rendering their holding economically viable. Moderate rates of assessment were also suggested as an incentive to prevent the *ryots* from migrating elsewhere. The official missive was to prevent the latter at all costs, given Assam's reputation as a sparsely populated and consequently labour-deficit region. The colonial state was especially concerned because during the Burmese incursions, cultivation had already suffered immensely and was in imminent need of improvement. Many people, including men of rank and peasants, had reportedly fled elsewhere during the previous regime, some of whom did not return even after the province had passed into the hands of the British. This seemed to aggravate the problems of a land too sparsely populated to generate sufficient revenues in the first place.

The *ryots'* distress was compounded by the levy of uniform rates of assessment irrespective of the quality of the soil. Under the previous regime, land tax was not a simple tax on the land but was divided into several categories of claims depending on the nature and quality of the soil under cultivation as *rupit, faringhati* and *baotulla*.[120] Again, in areas annually inundated by the river, where cultivation was disturbed, taxes were levied on the ploughs and not upon the lands. Compared to this system, the colonial land revenue rates and taxes for the greater part of the nineteenth century were fairly uniform irrespective of the quality of the soil and the manner of cultivation – a point that was raised occasionally by officers of the new regime only to be shelved by the chief commissioner on the grounds that simplicity resulting from uniformity was imminent in administering the newly acquired territory.

A major source of discontentment among the peasants was the policy of regular tax enhancement irrespective of the inability of the peasants to pay the enhanced rates. Anandaram Dhekial Phukan mentioned this in his petition to Mills and urged the government to take necessary steps to improve cultivation, which was sadly lacking.[121] Peasant protests became an endemic feature of politics at the turn of the century as land revenue demand by the state almost quadrupled between 1865–66 and 1897–98.[122] The last-mentioned series of rebellions were triggered by serious anomalies in land classification, which sought to rectify the issue of flat rates of revenue with the aim of rectifying the revenue losses to the state. The Settlement Rules of 1893–94 announced enhanced rates of land revenue on the basis of a re-classification of land into first, second, third and possibly fourth grade on the basis of the sole criteria of demand for land on the ground that this indicated the value of land. These revised settlement rules on the basis of which rate enhancements were suggested caused immense dissatisfaction among the cultivators as also among the superior land holders.[123] They suffered from serious shortcomings. When the cadastral survey was made on the basis of which the re-classification was made, district officers were instructed to make arrangements to visit every village and find out the productiveness of the land concerned 'by general observation and local enquiry from the people' apart from the facility of bringing the produce of the land to the nearest market.[124] It is, however, indicative of the superficial nature of such enquiry that these officers were informed that they should not 'place much reliance on crop experiments which were liable to mislead, or to make any attempts to differentiate soils or to ascertain the profits derived from each field or by each cultivator'.[125] They were also asked not to consider the question of rent from sub-tenants, 'the practice of subletting in Assam Proper being rare'.[126] These standardized formats of enquiry did not take into account individual cases or local variations and was therefore not successful in generating a truthful picture of the condition of the peasants. Arupjyoti Saikia's study of Durrang and Kamrup, however, shows that the question of tenancy was indeed a major issue in some districts in Assam Proper. Saikia regards the inability to extract extra rent from tenants as one of the major factors that irked the landlords in the period leading up to the series of protests popularly referred to as the *Patharughatar Ran*.[127] Again land regulation rules assumed that all the lands belonging to a village necessarily fell within the same sub-class although there were considerable differences in the quality of land within the same village. Consequently, the burden of the same rate was bound to be different on occupiers of different categories of land. Interestingly, although people were asked to prefer any objections they had against either the classification or the rates, such objections were usually dismissed as invalid or inconsequential, 'the District Officers being generally opposed to making minute differentiations in this respect, and preferring the simplicity of placing all the lands in one village under one class'.[128] Thus, all the lands of a village were placed under the same sub-class for drawing up rates of assessment. Such an exercise was naturally cost-effective and did not involve more than a 'small temporary increase to the establishments of the District and Subdivisional Officers and to the office establishment of the director at headquarters'.[129]

The new settlement rules thus revised rates on the basis of a cursory survey that did not take into account some fundamental localized factors before drawing up the rates. This aspect of the revised rules drew the attention of the government of India later and was mentioned in a report submitted to the chief commissioner of Assam. Curiously enough, the ground for objection was not that these uniform rates affected the interests of those peasants who were overassessed but that 'Government interests were sacrificed for the benefit of the settlement-holder for the lands of each description could not be assessed at a higher rate than the worst lands of that description could bear'.[130] Accordingly, the chief commissioner of Assam was directed to take corrective measures. A letter to the chief commissioner observed disapprovingly:

> The Government of India understand that you agree with them in thinking that no effort should be spared during the currency of this settlement to place the land revenue assessments in Assam on a more satisfactory basis than this assessment laces them. It is not fair to the state, nor to the cultivator, that matters should remain on the present footing, which can only be regarded as provisional. The efforts of the administration should now be directed to the ascertainment of the qualities of each of the three great divisions of land – *basti, rupit* and *faringhati;* . . . next the area of each quality in each village should be determined; and finally, revenue rates should, by enquiry, observation and experiment, be fixed as fairly payable by each quality of soil. The present classification of villages can hardly be regarded otherwise than as a temporary expedient, and should make way for a true classification of soils and allotment of soil class rates, which offer the only firm basis for a proper assessment for land revenue.[131]

A typical feature of the countryside during British rule was the uneconomical size of the peasant's holding. The peasant was not offered land on concessional rates nor was he allowed to acquire wasteland on concessional rates as was conceded to European planters. In his report, Mills categorically dismissed the idea on the ground that the Assamese *ryot* was incapable of the task of managing additional land. Some fixed notions of primitiveness and incapacity mediated British attitude towards the indigenous peasants. What exacerbated the latter's inhibitions was, however, the lure of European capital investment in the cultivation of the newly discovered tea plants. Waste land was reserved for the European planters who received huge land grants for the purpose free of revenues or at nominal rates. Such concessions were denied to the Assamese peasants. Official indifference towards the growth of Assamese peasant economy was sought to be disguised under the rhetoric of indolence and lethargy of the Assamese peasant. It was claimed that the Assamese peasant preferred the security of tenancy to the volatility of bringing unmanned tracts under the plough. It is true that all waste land did not constitute rice land and therefore, could be brought under the plough with considerable human efforts. Hence, these tracts were not the most coveted ones. Yet, with a little encouragement from the government the peasant may have been induced to bring these tracts under cultivation. Instead of exerting itself in this direction, the British cited the lethargy of the Assamese peasant as a ground for encouraging immigration of peasants from neighbouring East Bengal in the twentieth century. In this manner, rhetoric obscured the reality of colonial indifference towards the indigenous peasant who was denied a favourable treatment unlike the cash rich European planter. This was counter-productive in the long run as only a small portion of land granted for plantation was actually brought under cultivation. Incidentally Scott had been open to the idea of granting waste land on lease on favourable terms to natives interested in bringing more land under cultivation.[132] Scott's purpose was to broaden the tax base by extending cultivation and to improve and modernize agriculture and thereby crop yield by pumping capital into agriculture. In 1827 he drew up a detailed proposal for granting waste lands to anyone who would engage to bring waste land under cultivation.[133] He died before he could translate his scheme into practice, and his successors preferred to grant land to European planters exclusively. The reason for this must be sought in the plantation-centric orientation of the economy. According to Amalendu Guha, the European planters would have been averse to the creation of a native landholding class.[134] The proposal was, therefore, decisively shot down by Mills in his report. The latter wrote,

> The Sudder Board have proposed to establish the subjoined rules
> for granting waste lands. In a country like Assam, where there is

a superabundance of land and a deficiency of labour, I strongly deprecate the granting of waste lands to natives of the province, except under peculiar circumstances: they have no capital, and their only resources is to seduce the Ryots to settle in these grants, so that as much or even more becomes waste in one place than is reclaimed in the other.[135]

One of the less talked-about effect of Ryotwari, but one that can hardly be ignored, was that the latter afforded the state the opportunity of washing its hands off the tenants who, consequently, received no protection from the state. This compounded the situation of this class whose numbers went on swelling on account of the abolition of slavery and the de-recognition of many former *paiks* for their inability to produce adequate evidence of their *paikan* status. Amalendu Guha states that no tenants enjoyed any kind of legal rights of occupancy and transfer over the lands they tilled.[136] The Assam Tenancy Act affording some protection to tenants was passed only in 1935 and came into force from 1937. Till then tenants in Assam Proper remained mere tenants-at-will.[137]

The excessive land revenue demand of the state coupled with the plantation-oriented economy discouraged the emergence of differentiation within the peasantry by denying both the bigger landlords and the small holders any incentive and, therefore, motivation for capitalistic investment. Assam failed to throw up a substantial class of rich peasants unlike most other regions in British India. The level of agricultural production remained poor in the absence of modernization whether by the land holders or by the state. That agricultural growth remained poor is best illustrated by the fact that despite the abundance of rice land in the region, Assam could not produce enough rice to meet its requirements. Rice became an important item of export in the colonial economy of British Assam.[138] The import of rice became the most visible symbol of the emasculation of the peasantry in the rural economy established by the colonial state. Throughout its existence, the colonial state did not pay any attention to the improvement of cultivation. The low level of surplus accumulated by the peasant compounded the burdens of tax enhancements and further drove the latter into the clutches of the money-lenders comprising Marwari merchants and retailers. That agriculture had ceased to be profitable may be surmised from the fact that most substantial land holders and peasants shifted to middle-class professions and services in the course of the nineteenth century.[139] The situation was serious enough to have drawn the attention of Sir Henry Cotton, the liberal chief commissioner of Assam, prompting him to mention it in his note to the government of India in 1898.[140] Peasant dissatisfaction with the colonial land revenue policies culminated eventually in a massive revolt in the 1890s against the government. Amalendu Guha rightly points out that the official land revenue policy in Assam led to the proletarianization of the Assamese peasantry.[141] In his work on the impact of Ryotwari on the Assamese peasants, Guha states that the prime motive behind the excessive revenue hikes was to flush out the *ryots* into the labour-starved plantation sector.[142] The failure of its policy to induce the local peasants to work on the plantations eventually induced the planters to outsource labour from outside the province in the long run.

VI

The benign state

Curiously enough, although the early British establishment did not hesitate to tamper with existing conventions and customs in the matter of demarcation of land rights derived from secular pre-colonial grants, it appeared eager to placate the religious aristocracy. The latter was allowed to enjoy their pre-colonial holdings, albeit with minor modifications. This section examines the colonial economic policies with regard to the rent-free land held by temples and Vaishnava *sattras* in Assam.

One of the benefits of colonial rule consisted of the restoration of law and order after the ravages of the previous decade in the hands of the dreaded Burmese, locally referred to as the *Man*. The withdrawal of the latter allowed fugitives – nobles, temple functionaries and common people – to return to their homes.[143] Right from the beginning, the administration of David Scott had been quite generous towards temples and provided occasional patronage to the latter in the form of financial assistance. Scott is said to have provided funds for the purchase of furniture and utensils at the local shrine of Kamakhya in Guwahati in addition to sanctioning an annual grant of Rs 1,100 for rituals.[144] It has been argued that the colonial state's approach towards shrines and places of worship, in general, was far less friendly than that of the erstwhile regime, which had actively patronized such institutions. Arjun Appadurai has argued that the delicate relationship between state, sect and temple was fundamentally altered under the colonial state.[145] Temples were not essential to the authoritative basis of British rule, and the exchange of gifts and honours between king and deity, characterizing the pre-colonial regime, largely ceased to exist under them. Temples in Assam were no exception to this general trend. Nevertheless, there are grounds for believing that British policies in Assam towards temples and other religious institutions were far from hostile – a factor that enabled the latter to revive and resume their ritual functions in the long run. It is our contention that in the case of Assam, certain strategic calculations on the part of the colonial state made for a different policy approach towards these institutions, which in turn ensured the material prosperity of the latter under the new regime.

That British rule would eventually benefit religious institutions was far from apparent when David Scott called for a re-examination of the fiscal benefits that temples and religious establishments had customarily enjoyed under the *Tunkhungia* regime.[146] The latter had granted huge expanses of un-assessed or rent-free land endowments to temples and religious personalities in the form of *debottar, brahmottar* and *dharmottar* tenures.[147] The latter were known in the revenue records as *lakhiraj* or un-assessed tenures, as opposed to *khiraj* or fully assessed tenures. The British were quite familiar with such grants, having encountered them in other parts of the country. Such transfers of revenue were termed as 'alienations' in British official parlance, in view of their inability to bring economic benefits to the state treasury. Everywhere in the country, such alienations were sought to be suitably managed with a view to bringing them back within the fold of the government's revenue administration.[148]

After an initial period of vacillation, David Scott imposed a tax on all *lakhiraj* or rent-free religious land grants, equivalent to one-third the rent then paid by lands not exempted. In the case of temples, where the land had been granted to the deity, the *Doloi* or temple servant involved with the daily management of temple affairs in many temples under the previous regime was identified as the custodian of temple property in all temples across Assam, and made accountable for the payment of the rent. Scott justified the measure on the grounds that a similar tax had been levied by the previous regime, in the last two or three years preceding the full occupation of Assam by the Burmese.[149]

In 1834, when Francis Jenkins was the commissioner of Assam, the grantees of rent-free tenures objected to pay the tax imposed by Scott on the grounds that the latter had intended it to be a temporary measure. Jenkins thereupon proposed that the government should confirm the holdings of all those claimants who could produce some sort of evidence in support of their claim that they had occupied their land rent-free under the previous government.[150] The proposal was turned down and a proclamation was issued on 25 August 1834, categorically stating that the new regime would have nothing to do with the pre-colonial entitlements, and was free to revoke them as and when it chose. The proclamation was carefully worded, leaving nothing to imagination:

> The British Government cannot be required to acknowledge as a right, claims to tenures which the claimants did not possess at the

time of the conquest of the country from the Burmese, neither could special exceptions granted by the Burmese, or their predecessors, be admitted as establishing claims which the conquerors were bound to acknowledge.[151]

This was followed by a directive that Captain Bogle, one of the officers of the Assam division, should be employed for making a full enquiry 'into all claims to rent-free land, on the part of the Rajahs, or as *dewuttur* and *dharmutter*, or any other plea, throughout the District of Assam' with the rejoinder that Bogle was to be empowered, subject to Jenkins's orders and control, to assess at full rates all the lands held in excess of what was held and possessed on bona fide grants before the British conquest.[152] It was decided that pending the *lakhiraj* enquiry, Scott's moderate rates were to be levied as before, from all land claimed as *lakhiraj* (i.e. as *debottar, bramottar, dharmottar* or on whatever plea) until brought under assessment at full rates, or until orders to the contrary were received from government.[153] Interestingly, despite careful attempts to rule out all ambiguities on the issue of the state's right to tax these lands, the proclamation could not disguise the dilemma of the new regime and its concerns over pushing its claims too far. This was evident from the decision to subject the matter to an inquiry commission rather than dismissing the entitlements outright. The state could neither dismiss arbitrarily nor sanction the totality of these alienations permitted by the previous regime.[154]

Scott himself was uncertain about the judiciousness of taxing the religious holdings. He cited precedence in order to gain legitimacy for his decision to impose tax on tracts hitherto considered inviolable. Known for patronizing native customs and practices, Scott was, at the same time, an astute administrator, who could not afford to relinquish the opportunity to reclaim these vast un-assessed tracts for the state. Bogle estimated the loss to the treasury on account of such tenures to be about Rs 150,000 annually.[155] Jenkins stated in one of his letters that 'Mr. Scott was apparently also induced to tax all the lands claiming exemption from the very great extent of the alienation attempted to be established, and from supposing that a very large portion of the estates would never be able to prove their claims, the validity of which he was then unable to investigate'.[156] The first agent was well aware that the land concerned constituted tracts of the best variety. Religious grants were usually made in *roopit* (*salee dhan*) lands or lands of the first quality, and if such was not available, a proportionate quantity of other kinds of land was usually given, consisting of twice the quantity of wet and three times the quantity of dry lands.[157]

The government of Bengal lost no time in acting on Scott's proposals. Orders were dispatched even before the contents of Scott's correspondence had been properly examined, and despite the fact that Scott's measures had evoked protests from appropriate quarters. The Court of Directors likewise did not see anything wrong with the proposed taxation and pointed out that the taxes were too moderate to cause any grievance to any one, especially since the people had already reconciled themselves to the loss of their privileges during the prolonged Burmese occupation of Assam. The dispatch from the Court of Directors reiterated the unquestionable right of the state to impose taxes:

> As the parties came to repossession by means of our conquest, of rights which were extinguished by the Burmese invasion, there can be no well grounded cause of complaints against the imposition of a moderate assessment.[158]

Despite such unambiguous statements of intentions, however, policy decisions during this period were anything but harsh, as the state made no attempts to modify Scott's mild rates. Examination of the colonial state's management of pre-colonial revenue entitlements reveals a larger tension in the economic relations of early British domination, between the urge to maximize the upward flow of revenue and the urge to maximize stability and order. This contradiction between the 'extractive' and the 'subsidizing' functions of British rule can be seen best in the conflict over *mirasi* (hereditary superior holdings in western India that usually carried with them the obligation to collect revenues) rights during the nineteenth century.[159] Laurence Preston and Nicholas Dirks, who have written on the subject of colonial administration of *inam* or religious grants, argue that despite initial dithering, the British government by and large added the *inam* holdings to the revenue records of the state.[160] The trajectory of such holdings in Assam, however, significantly differed in this respect, as we propose to argue in the following sections.

In 1832, Major Francis Jenkins was appointed as the Agent to the Governor General in the Northeastern Provinces. The former took an unusual step with regard to the matter of revenue-free land grants even before the report of the enquiry committee on *lakhiraj* tenures was out. Without bothering to consult his colleagues or superiors, Jenkins made a broad distinction between *debottar* lands, that is lands appropriated to temples, and other categories of religious land grants such as *brahmottar* and *dharmottar*. All 'bona fide' *debottar* grants, that is those grants that were 'authenticated' by means of deeds known locally as *sunnuds or phallis*, were confirmed revenue free, while in the case of 'valid' *brahmottar* and *dharmottar* grants, he confirmed the grantee in possession, subject to the payment of Scott's favourable rates, pending the investigation of the whole *lakhiraj* question. Henceforth, the erstwhile *lakhiraj* lands, which were assessed at half rates, came to be known as *nisf-khiraj*, and the category of tenures, which underwent full assessment, came to be known as the *khiraj* land. In all these cases, the claimants were required to authenticate their claims by means of deeds or *phallis* as the latter were locally called. The *lakhiraj* investigations went on till about 1860. Curiously, no report based on the inquiry was ever submitted to the government so that the holders of *brahmottar* and *dharmottar* lands continued to pay the half rates levied by Jenkins.[161] In 1879, the government of India recognized these estates as heritable and transferable, and subsequently they came to be regarded at par with land holders under the decennial settlement.

VII

Violating traditions

In defending his moderate treatment of temple and *sattra* holdings, Jenkins argued stoutly that it was necessary for the colonial state, as the rulers of the land, to fulfil the aspirations of the subject peoples by protecting and preserving the latter's customary rights.[162] To all appearances, Jenkins's defence was affective both in letter and in spirit, but the sheer hollowness of his claims is best illustrated by his persistence in demanding that the claims to entitlements be authenticated by means of *sunnuds* or *phallis* despite his realization that the latter were imprecise and inadequate as instruments of authentication. Jenkins continued to insist that all genuine claimants possessed and could produce *phallis*. In his note to Mills, Jenkins pointed out that 'in all the principal cases, especially of the larger temples, all the *lakhiraj* grants are supported by sunnuds or copper plates, phullees, and in greater part of the remaining cases, when phullees were not produced, there are sunnuds on thick strong paper, mohuzurs, scaled with the seals of the Rajahs or of the Bur Phokuns of lower Assam'.[163] In reality, neither the availability nor the reliability of the *phalli* could be taken for granted. Jenkins himself was forced to concede on numerous occasions that the *phalli* was not always a reliable source of information concerning land entitlements. The practical problems arising from an exclusive reliance on the *phalli* was voiced by Captain Brodie, the collector of Nowgong, in no uncertain terms:

In alluding to these it would have been satisfactory to have had sunnuds to refer to, but the fact is, that though there are about

100 claims to such lands registered, there are in this district very few men who have any written documents to produce in support of what they may lay claim to.[164]

Brodie admitted that during the Burmese rule, and through the confusion, which then existed, some individuals might have lost their title deeds. And yet, his colonial subjectivities did not allow him to believe that this could be a general phenomenon for 'people naturally look to the security of such proofs of their rights nearly as much as they would to the safety of their lives'.[165] He, therefore, concluded that a considerable number of claims were without any real foundation. On all such occasions, unless alternative evidences could be produced, Jenkins concurred with the decision of his officers in annulling the claims.

During this period the government received numerous appeals from claimants whose claims either had not been considered or had been only partly admitted on the basis of the *phalli*. Many such cases were settled by Jenkins in what came to be known as his *Faisalas*. In one such appeal, the descendants of the original Parbatiya Gossain, a Brahmin from Nadia, placed in charge of the Kamakhya temple by *swargadeo* Rudra Singha, claimed that a portion of their land had been resumed.[166] On enquiring why the claims had not been mentioned in the *phalli*, the respondent pointed out that the grantee had been customarily allowed entitlements in these *mouzahs* (revenue units).[167] Thereupon, an *Ameen* (one of the numerous revenue personnel involved with land survey activities) was sent to make a survey of the areas mentioned in the deposition. However, the claim could be settled only on the basis of the testimonies of local witnesses. Adjustments were made accordingly in the revenue statements.

Jenkins did not hesitate to take strong decisions when the occasion demanded, even if this impinged on pre-colonial customs and traditions that he had stoutly defended not so long ago. The finest illustration of this point comes from the manner in which he rode roughshod over the provisions of the *Perah Kaguz*, in the best interests of the administration. It has been already pointed out that these were measurement registers of the previous government and contained records of the extent and nature of the *lakhiraj* grants made by the Assam kings to their spiritual advisors/Gossains, Brahmins and other holy men as also to individuals for any particular services to the state. The drive to create compact holdings, discussed earlier in the previous section, shows how the process could be eminently intrusive and dissatisfactory. The authentication drive resulted in the resumption of at least a portion of the land held by temples and other categories of religious donees. This undoubtedly generated some tensions among a people used to notions of the sanctity of their entitlements. Such disturbances were, however, momentary and short-lived because the government ultimately conceded most of the temple-related entitlements and imposed only a nominal rate on the rest. The amount of land resumed by the state was also rather meagre compared to that which was confirmed with the donees. In his report to the government, Captain Bogle expressed his unhappiness at the huge extent of land declared *lakhiraj* or rent-free by Jenkins.[168] Even Mills was struck at the large quantity of land which had been confirmed at half rates and rent-free.[169]

Jenkins had indeed taken a rather lenient view at the time of assessment of hitherto un-assessed land. The former insisted that certain categories of land within the donated territory be exempted altogether from assessment in deference to the customs of the previous regime. He justified his decision on the grounds that the latter had not been included for assessment in the *Perah Kaguz* register of general survey. This included the jungle land and homesteads (*bari bustee*), since these were considered their hereditary property and hence not regarded as *pyke* land.[170] In doing this he had to overrule the opposition of Captain Bogle, who refused to admit such claims. What was more, Jenkins conceded more land to the claimants than they had actually pleaded for in their claims. When asked to explain his conduct, he pointed out to the great consternation of Mills that the claimants had often only sued for the amount of cultivated land in the Perah Kaguz, or in their phullees, whereas they had all along been in possession of the whole land as defined in the grant.[171] Jenkins's interpretation of the *Perah Kaguz* proved favourable for the claimants although it earned him the ire of his colleagues and superiors.

While it is nobody's contention that the confirmation of claims to entitlements increased the levels of cultivation in the *devottar tracts* declared *lakhiraj*, thereby improving the material prospects of the temples, the aforementioned measures definitely did not allow the conditions of temples to deteriorate because the means for the sustenance of these temples had been by and large preserved. It is true that during this period the right of temples to the services of the temple *pykes* against the latter's wish was also abrogated by the British on the grounds that the latter practice imposed a servile labour on the *pykes*.[172] While this decision may have created some consternation in the initial stages, it did not create too great a stir since by confirming the said land with the temples, the British actually placed the *pykes* at an acutely disadvantageous position vis-à-vis the temples. Under the circumstances, many of these *pykes* are likely to have entered into some sort of mutually beneficial negotiations with the temples, which suited both parties.

VIII

Imperial calculations

Why did the state adopt such a lenient policy towards temple-related land-holdings? The question merits consideration especially in the light of Francis Jenkins's decision to settle land in Assam with the *paiks* rather than with the pre-colonial Ahom elite. It has been pointed out earlier that Jenkins thought that security of tenures would induce the Assamese *ryot* to take up land for cultivation. The decision to authenticate the *devottar* and *brahmottar* grants (as *lakhiraj* and *nisf-khiraj*, respectively) with the existing donees, that is temples and priestly holders, instead of resuming them for redistribution among the *ryots*, thus, appears anachronistic, given the conscious decision to introduce a Ryotwari settlement in Assam. Jenkins's decision certainly caused great bewilderment among his colleagues most of who were in agreement about the sorry state of cultivation in these rent-free tenures. In his report on the province of Assam, A.J.M. Mills, who visited Assam in 1853 to enquire into the condition of administration in the province, condemned the *lakhirajdars* as 'the worst cultivators and rent-payers in the District' with a tendency to appropriate the revenues of the endowments to private uses. Mills was of the opinion that the holders of these tenures did nothing towards bringing under cultivation the large tracts of jungle land assigned to them.[173] The priestly class was held in suspicion by other members of the colonial bureaucracy as well. In this connection, Captain Butler wrote:

> The very great consideration shown to the priests by allowing them such an extent of country on half Khiraj rates, would from any other class of men have called forth the utmost gratitude, but the reverse is the case with these grasping priests; they may truly be said to be the only disaffected subjects of Government in the plains of Assam. They had lost almost everything under the Burmese reign, and on the British conquest have acquired grants they had lost all title or claim to. They may be considered the greatest impediment we may have to contend with in enlightening the rising generation. Possessed of great power over the minds of the people, bigoted, ignorant and avaricious, they did not in the smallest degree, through the means at their disposal, aid in the education of the people.[174]

Captain Butler's statement provides valuable insights into the imperatives of colonial policy towards temple and *sattra* land. It appears that the restoration of the pre-colonial religious entitlements was a strategic choice, meant to win over an influential section of the society to the cause of the empire. This was necessary for the state had already deviated significantly from the pre-colonial regime of privileges and reverence by refusing active patronage to these religious institutions. The colonial state had further stoked resentment among the pre-colonial elite by abolishing slavery and forced labour, which had formed the basis of the landed estates held by the latter. It is possible that the state did not want to risk further alienation of this section by completely denuding the influential temple and *sattra* leaders of their means of suste-nance, especially since the authentication drive undertaken by the state had already brought a sizeable part of these tracts under state control. Already there were indications that a section of the population comprising the dispos-sessed elite was highly dissatisfied with the colonial state on account of the arbitrary rejection of older entitlements and privileges. Maniram Dewan's petition to Mills, outlining a list of grievances, was an indication of the grow-ing disenchantment among this section with British rule.[175] In her work on Assam, Jayeeta Sharma describes how the state's initial reluctance to give much leverage to the Vaishnavite *mahantas* and *goswamis* later gave way to a conscious effort to keep them in good humour, though of course under complete subjection.[176] Colonial ambivalence towards this class bespoke its strategic calculations of the influence that this class continued to wield on the common people. For obvious reasons the state did not want to jeopardize its political stability by giving unnecessary provocation.

That the state meant to conciliate the religious elite is evident from the fact that many more concessions followed in the immediate post-mutiny years, notwithstanding the consequent loss to the imperial treasury. One notes a greater reluctance to trade the safety and security of the empire for increased revenues from the second half of the nineteenth century. State policy during this period sought precedents for its measures in pre-colonial conventions and usages. The debates accompanying an incident of defalca-tion by the *Doloi* of the Hajo Madhav temple in 1900 foreground this new shift in colonial policy decisions.

In 1900 when Narayan Bhattachajee, the *Doloi* of the Hajo Madhav temple, filed his security, it was found to be less than the amount due from him. Prior to this, the government of Assam had given a detailed account of the practice to be followed with regard to the general and temple *nisf-khiraj* holdings as well as the land held in excess of temple *lakhiraj* lands. The report stated:

> In the case of grants made for charitable or religious uses it is customary to take security from the temporary incumbent of the

office of manager of the trust for the due payment of the government demand. If the manager is unable to give security, the lands are placed in charge of the mauzadar. . . . The Chief Commissioner would continue this system of requiring security for the payment of revenue, and, in default of security, he would place the holding in charge of the mauzadar of the village in which it is situated.[177]

Accordingly, in 1876, the government ordered that lands found in the actual possession of an alienee in excess of the amount should be subjected to full assessment, if the excess was above 10 per cent, or else continued on the same terms as the rest of the holding. Narayan Doloi was, therefore, asked to furnish additional security, which he failed to do for some time. Meanwhile he was not stopped from collecting the revenue from the *ryots*. Having realized about Rs 5,000 from the *ryots*, Narayan Doloi tendered his resignation to the deputy commissioner and the *Bardeuries* who had elected him to the office of the *Doloi* without handing over the amount collected.[178]

Although certain anomalies in administrative practice were noticed on enquiry, the commissioner of Assam decided not to press charges. In fact, when the officiating commissioner of the Assam Valley Districts came up with a proposal to recover the arrears by attachment of the rent due to the temple by its *ryots* over and above the half that was payable as government revenue, the commissioner rejected the proposal after it was pleaded by the new incumbent to the office of the *Doloi* and the *Bardeuris* that this would leave them with virtually no funds with which to carry on the daily rituals at the shrine.[179] Instead, the chief commissioner chose to remit all outstanding arrears, indicating the state's reluctance to push its claims too hard. It was mentioned, however, that the concession must be treated as an exception rather than a rule.[180]

The issue of defalcation continued to haunt the officers as no attempt was made at legislation to ensure liability for rent payment in case of temple *nisf-khiraj* land. P.R.T. Gurdon, the deputy commissioner of Kamrup, wrote repeatedly, urging the government to adopt suitable legislation to prevent defalcation. Yet the commissioner of the Assam Valley Districts chose to play safe with regard to the matter. The former pointed out that Major Gurdon was quite right in in his reading of the law and that the legal status of temple *khiraj* lands was exactly the same as that of other *khiraj* lands, and that there was no legal bar to the sale of such lands for arrears of revenue. At the same time, he added that it was desirable that the means of realizing the revenue be found other than through sale of the land, since such a remedy was bound to 'ruin the temples, in which so many innocent persons, not responsible for non-payment of the revenue, are interested'.[181] When the issue surfaced again in 1903, the commissioner declared that temple *nisf-khiraj* lands could not be sold for arrears of revenue. Chief Commissioner J.B. Fuller clarified that the government was well within its rights as per the Land and Revenue Regulation to sell any defaulting estate which is transferable, that is barring those estates the proprietary rights over which are vested, not in an individual but in an institution such as a temple. He, however, felt that this would be too drastic a penalty in the case of temple lands.[182] His suggestion, instead, was that the government use this section as a threat to warn the temple management that in case of default the government would make use of the concerned provision. In addition, in order to facilitate the payment of security by the *Doloi*, the chief commissioner suggested that the state's demands should be limited to 25 per cent of the amount of the revenue. His justification for being lenient in the matter best reflects the ambivalence of the new regime as it sought hard to reconcile its urge to maximize the upward flow of revenue with the not-so-inconsequential concern for maintaining stability through a policy of patronage towards the influential sections of the indigenous population. The commissioner's letter best brings out this ambivalence, which dictated the official line of action towards religious holdings, which, in turn, benefitted temples in the long run:

> I sympathise with the desire of those who wish to prevent the malverisation of the revenue which the state has assigned. . . . I regret that in this province as elsewhere in India, endowments intended for religious purposes should be mismanaged or misappropriated with impunity. But the policy of the state being as it is, I could not sanction the interference of the executive officers of the government.[183]

Needless to say that the state's vacillations on the issue and its ultimate failure to enforce compliance were a source of relief to the concerned temple functionaries and enabled temple activities to continue uninterrupted.

The benevolence demonstrated by the state towards the religious grants enabled the *sattras* to survive and prosper while also ensuring the survival of temples. Although the new revenue regime did not live up to its claims of upholding and even improving the pre-colonial model of surplus appropriation, and was by no means friendly towards the *paik* turned *ryot*, it did not entirely destroy the socio-economic eminence of the middle-ranking section of pre-colonial society. While the upper class of aristocracy lost its preeminence and was forced to surrender its privileges, the class of middle-ranking service providers of the previous order was not wiped out. Either through their associations with the *sattras*, or through their access to literacy or their clever management of landholdings, they managed to stay afloat. Some even succeeded in augmenting their incomes through government jobs in the new bureaucracy. It was this section that constituted the nucleus of the colonial middle class.[184]

Notes

1 Sir Alexander Mackenzie, *The North-East Frontier of India*, 1884, Reprint, New Delhi: Mittal, 1995, p. 1.
2 Advertisement, dated Thursday, 20 May 1784, in *Calcutta Gazette, Selections from Calcutta Gazettes of the Years 1784, 1785, 1786, 1787 and 1788*, Calcutta, 1804, pp. 3–4.
3 Gunnel Cederlof, *Founding an Empire on India's North-Eastern Frontiers 1790–1840 Climate, Commerce, Polity*, New Delhi: Oxford University Press, 2014.
4 See Sanghamitra Misra, *Becoming a Borderland: The Politics of Space and Identity in Colonial Northeastern India*, New Delhi: Routledge, 2011.
5 See S.K. Bhuyan, *Anglo-Assamese Relations 1771–1826*, Guwahati: DHAS, 1949, for a detailed study of the Anglo-Burmese war leading to the annexation of the Ahom kingdom.
6 See Indrani Chatterjee, *Forgotten Friends Monks, Marriages and Memories of Northeast India*, New Delhi: Oxford University Press, 2013, for a discussion of the interesting ways in which nomenclatures and assessments of the so-called tribes were arrived at; see also Ajay Skaria, *Hybrid Histories: Forests, Frontiers and Wildness in Western India*, New Delhi: Oxford University Press, 1999.
7 See in this connection Bodhisattva Kar, 'Heads in the Naga Hills', in Partha Chatterjee, Tapati Guha-Thakurta and Bodhisattva Kar (eds), *New Cultural Histories of India*, New Delhi: Oxford University Press, 2014.
8 John Eliot, 'Observations on the Inhabitants of the Garrow Hills Made during a Public Deputation in the Years 1788 and 1789', in *Dissertations and Miscellaneous Pieces Relating to the History and Antiquities, The Arts, Sciences and Literature of Asia*, Vol. 3, A catalogue of Books Belonging to the Charleston Library, South Carolina, Published by A.E. Miller, 1826, pp. 11–45.
9 Ibid., pp. 11–30.
10 See in this connection D.V. Zou, 'Raiding the Dreaded Past Representations of Headhunting and Human Sacrifice in North-East India', *Contributions to Indian Sociology*, Vol. 39, No. 1, 2005, pp. 75–105, and Kar, *New Cultural Histories of India*. See Indrani Chatterjee for an insight into the systematic colonial displacement of women-centric practices in the Northeast.
11 Ibid., p. 27.
12 Lieutenant R. Wilcox, 'Memoir of a Survey of Assam and the Neighbouring Countries, Executed in 1825-6-7-8', *Asiatic Researches*, Vol. 17, 1832, p. 332.

13 Ibid., p. 334.
14 Captain Bedford, *Journal of a Voyage up the Brahmaputra*, 1826, appended to Wilson's *History of the Burmese War*, cited by Wilcox, *Asiatic Researches*, p. 337.
15 H.L. Cutter, 'Extracts from a Letter', dated 25 November 1837, *Baptist Missionary Magazine*, 1838, Vol. 18, November, p. 277.
16 Ibid.
17 See in this connection Ajay Skaria, 'Shades of Wildness: Tribes, Castes and Gender in Western India', *Journal of Asian Studies*, Vol. 56, No. 3, 1997, pp. 726–745, and Chatterjee, *Forgotten Friends Monks*.
18 Major John Butler, *A Sketch of Assam: With Some Account of the Hill Tribes*, London: Smith, Elder and Co., 1847, p. 34.
19 Mackenzie, *The North-East Frontier of India*, pp. 255–256.
20 Cederlof, *Founding an Empire on India's North-Eastern Frontiers*, p. 72.
21 See H.K. Barpujari, *Assam in the Days of the Company*, Guwahati: Spectrum, 1990.
22 See Sanjib Baruah, *India against Itself: Assam and the Politics of Nationality*, New Delhi: Oxford University Press, 1999, for a detailed exposition of the impact of separating the hills from the plains.
23 Cederlof, *Founding an Empire on India's North-Eastern Frontiers*, p. 10.
24 Ibid.
25 Sir Mackenzie, *The North-East Frontier of Bengal*, p. 7.
26 Ibid., p. 8.
27 Mackenzie, *The North-East Frontier of Bengal*.
28 Appendix to Captain R. Boileu Pemberton's *Report on the Eastern Frontier of British India*, Calcutta: Baptist Mission Press, 1835.
29 Captain John Bryan Neufville, 'On the Geography and Population of Assam, 1823', *Asiatic Researches*, Vol. 16, 1828; 'Shades of Wildness: Tribes, Castes and Gender in Western India', *Journal of Asian Studies*, Vol. 56, No. 3, 1997, pp. 726–745.
30 Neufville, *Asiatic Researches*, Vol. 17, 1832, p. 321.
31 Chatterjee, *Forgotten Friends Monks*.
32 See H.K. Barpujari, *Problem of the Hill Tribes of the North-East Frontier 1822–42*, Vol. 1, Guwahati: Lawyer's Book Stall, 1970; see also Baruah, *India against Itself*.
33 See Baruah, *India against Itself*.
34 Sir Walter Hamilton, *The East India Gazetteer*, London: Parbury, Allen and Co., 1828.
35 Mackenzie, *The North-East Frontier of Bengal*, p. 5.
36 Cited in N.K. Barooah, *David Scott in North-East India 1802–1831: A Study in British Paternalism*, New Delhi: Munshiram Manoharlal, 1969, p. 87.
37 Ibid.
38 Barpujari, *Assam in the Days of the Company 1826–1858*, pp. 16–17. There was a common feeling that the Manipuris possessed superior martial spirit than the Assamese. This has been emphatically noted by Sir Boileu Pemberton in his 'Report on the Eastern Frontier of India'. Pemberton observes, 'From this sketch of the history of muneepoor, and the vicissitudes through which it passed, the determined character of the people and

their rooted aversion to the yoke of the Burmahs are clearly shewn. . . . Their country is to be regarded principally as an advanced military position for the defence of the eastern frontier, and its utility must of course entirely depend upon its natural resources, and the efficiency of its military force' (p. 48).

39 Ibid.
40 Courtesy, N.N. Acharya, *Historical Documents on Assam and Neighbouring States*, New Delhi: Omsons, 1983, pp. 67–68.
41 See Bhuyan, *Anglo-Assamese Relations 1771–1826*, for negotiations leading to the annexation of Assam.
42 See Barpujari, *Assam in the Days of the Company*, for a detailed summary of the last days of the Ahom monarchy.
43 *Tour Diary of Captain Francis Jenkins, 1838*, Assam State Archive (henceforth ASA), Dispur.
44 Ibid.
45 Letter from Francis Jenkins, dated 21 June 1834, in *Letters Issued to the Government*, Vol. 10, 1834–35, ASA.
46 Captain Francis Jenkins, *Tour Diary of Upper Assam*, 1838, ASA.
47 Mrinalini Sinha, *The 'Manly Englishman' and The 'Effeminate Bengali' in the Late Nineteenth Century*, Manchester: Manchester University Press, 1995.
48 Jenkins, *Tour Diary of Upper Assam*.
49 See Barpujari, *Assam in the Days of the Company*.
50 Ibid. See in this connection Arupjyoti Saikia, 'Coal in Colonial Assam: The Dynamics of Exploration, Trade and Environmental Consequences', in K. Lahiri Dutta (ed.), *The Coal Nation: Histories, Cultures and Ecologies of Coal in India*, London: Ashgate, 2014.
51 See Barpujari, *Assam in the Days of the Company*.
52 For a discussion of the nature of the permanent settlement, see Tapan Raychoudhury's recollection of land management by *zamindars* in the eastern Bengal district of Bakarganj in the 1930s and 1940s in 'Permanent Settlement in Operation: Bakargang District, East Bengal', in Robert Eric Frykenburg (ed.), *Land Control and Social Structure in Indian History*, Wisconsin: University of Wisconsin Press, 1969.
53 See Eric Stokes, *The English Utilitarians in India*, London: Clarendon Press, 1969, and Ranajit Guha, *A Rule of Property for Bengal: An Essay on the Idea of the Permanent Settlement*, New Delhi: Orient Longman, 1982, for the intellectual origins of the British land revenue settlements; see also Frykenburg, ed., *Land Control and Social Structure in Indian History*.
54 For a discussion of the revenue settlement of the British in Assam, see Amalendu Guha, 'Assamese Agrarian Society in the Late Nineteenth Century: Roots, Structures and Trends', *IESHR*, Vol. xvii, No. 1, 1980, pp. 35–94.
55 See Barooah, *David Scott in North-East India*, p. 99; see Jayeeta Sharma, *Empire's Garden Assam and the Making of India*, Ranikhet: Permanent Black, 2011, for a discussion of British relations with the Vaishnava *sattras* in Assam. For a history of the *sattras*, see S.N. Sarma, *The Neo-Vasinavite Movement and the Satra Institution of Assam*, Guwahati: Guwahati

University, 1966; see also Dambarudhar Nath, *Satra Society and Culture Pitambardevs Goswami and History of Garamur Satra*, Guwahati: DVS Publishers, 2012.

56 Ibid., pp. 97–98.

57 Barooah, *David Scott in North-East India*, p. 98.

58 Ibid., p. 95.

59 See Nirode K. Barooah, 'David Scott and the Question of Slavery in Assam: A Case Study in British Paternalism', *The Indian Economic & Social History Review*, Vol. 6, No. 2, 1969, pp. 179–196.

60 Ibid.

61 See A.J. Moffat Mills, *Report on the Province of Assam*, 1853, Reprint 1984, Guwahati: Publication Board Assam.

62 Ibid., p. 5.

63 See Jayeeta Sharma, ' "Lazy" Natives, Coolie Labour, and the Assam Tea Industry', *Modern Asian Studies*, Vol. 43, Part 6, November 2009, pp. 1287–1324.

64 See Sanjib Baruah, *Durable Disorder: Understanding the Politics of North East India*, New Delhi: Oxford University Press, 2005.

65 *Assam Commissioner's Papers 1834–53*, File no. 681, ASA.

66 Guha, 'Assamese Agrarian Society in the Late Nineteenth Century', 1980, p. 58; also see Chatterjee, *Forgotten Friends Monks*.

67 Ibid.

68 Ibid.

69 See Bhuyan, *Anglo-Assamese Relations*.

70 See Guha, 'Assamese Agrarian Society in the Late Nineteenth Century'.

71 Mills, *Report on the Province of Assam*, p. 506.

72 Ibid.

73 Ibid.

74 See Barpujari, *Assam in the Days of the Company*.

75 Mills, 'Letter from Lieut. Colonel F. Jenkins', Appendix B, No. 275 of 1853.

76 *Translation of a Petition from Moneeram Borwah Dewan*, Appendix; K.B. Mills, *Report on the Province of Assam*.

77 Priyam Goswami, *Assam in the Nineteenth Century: Industrialization and Colonial Penetration*, Guwahati: Spectrum, 1999.

78 Introduction, *Assam Land Revenue Manual, 1886*, Dispur: Assam Secretariat Library (ASL).

79 Arupjyoti Saikia, 'Landlords, Tenants and Agrarian Relations: Revisiting a Peasant Uprising in Colonial Assam', *Studies in History*, Vol. 26, No. 2, 2010, p. 175.

80 'Notes by D. Scott (On Welsh's report on Assam)', courtesy, N.N. Acharya, *Historical Documents on Assam and Neighbouring States*.

81 Mills, *Report on the Province of Assam*, p. 3.

82 Ibid., p. 6.

83 Mills, 'Letter from Lieut. Colonel F. Jenkins', p. 60.

84 For the chief features of the *Khelwari* system of land tenure, see Amalendu Guha, 'Land Rights and Social Classes in Medieval Assam', *IESHR*, Vol. III, No. 3, 1966.

85 Ibid., p. 229.

86 Mills, *Report on the Province of Assam*, p. 7.
87 *Translation of a Petition from Moneeram Borwah Dewan*, Appendix; K.B.,
     Mills *Report on the Province of Assam*.
88 Guha, 'Land Rights and Social Classes in Medieval Assam', p. 232.
89 Ibid., p. 223.
90 See Guha, 'Assamese Agrarian Society in the Late Nineteenth Century';
     cited also in Baruah, *Durable Disorder*, p. 89.
91 Baruah, *Durable Disorder*, p. 89.
92 Ibid., p. 90.
93 Revenue Proceedings, 4–28 July 1835, Progs. 67, Vol. 911, WBSA.
94 Revenue Proceedings, 12 May 1834, Vol. 896, no. 15. WBSA.
95 Ibid.
96 *Assam Land Revenue Manual, 1886*.
97 See Guha, 'Assamese Agrarian Society in the Late Nineteenth Century'.
98 See Arupjyoti Saikia, 'The Moneylenders and Indebtedness: Understand-
     ing the Peasant Economy of colonial Assam, 1900–1950', *Indian Histori-
     cal Review*, Vol. 37, No. 1, 2010, pp. 63–88.
99 Guha, 'Assamese Agrarian Society in the Late Nineteenth Century'.
100 *Assam Land Revenue Manual, 1886*.
101 Ibid.
102 Ibid.
103 Ibid.
104 See Baruah *Durable Disorder*.
105 Ibid.
106 Ibid., *Assam Land Revenue Manual, 1886*.
107 Baruah, *Durable Disorder*.
108 *Assam Land Revenue Manual, 1886*.
109 Ibid., p. xlix.
110 Ibid.
111 Ibid., p. l.
112 Ibid., p. li.
113 Mills, 'Letter form Lieut. Colonel F. Jenkins'.
114 Ibid., p. 6.
115 Guha, 'Assamese Agrarian Society in the Late Nineteenth Century'.
116 Ibid.
117 Saikia, 'The Moneylenders and Indebtedness'; see also Guha, 'Assamese
     Agrarian Society in the Late Nineteenth Century'.
118 See Baruah, *Durable Disorder*.
119 See Mills, *Report on the Province of Assam*, 1854.
120 *Assam Land Revenue Manual, 1886*.
121 Mills, *Report on the Province of Assam*.
122 Guha, 'Assamese Agrarian Society in the Late Nineteenth Century', p. 51.
123 Saikia, 'Landlords, Tenants and Agrarian Relations', p. 175. See also
     Manorama Sharma, *Social and Economic Change in Assam: Middle Class
     Hegemony*, New Delhi: Ajanta, 1990.
124 See *Assam Land Revenue Manual, 1886*, p. li.
125 Ibid.
126 Ibid.
127 Saikia, 'Landlords, Tenants and Agrarian Relations'.

128 *Assam Land Revenue Manual, 1886*, p. liii.
129 Ibid.
130 Ibid., p. liv.
131 Cited in *Assam Land Revenue Manual, 1886*, p. liv.
132 See Barooah, 'David Scott and the Question of Slavery in Assam', pp. 102–103.
133 Ibid., p. 102.
134 Guha, 'Assamese Agrarian Society in the Late Nineteenth Century', p. 90.
135 Mills, *Report on the Province of Assam*, p. 16.
136 Guha, 'Assamese Agrarian Society in the Late Nineteenth Century', p. 80.
137 Ibid.
138 Ibid.
139 Ibid., p. 62. In this connection, Guha further observes, 'The surplus accruing to the rural rich only sufficed to maintain their higher than average standard of living. If there was no danger of their falling below their present condition of rural respectability, because of high fertility of the soil, there was no prospect of their ever rising above it either', p. 88.
140 Guha, 'Assamese Agrarian Society in the Late Nineteenth Century', pp. 88–89.
141 Ibid., p. 85.
142 Ibid.
143 See H.K. Barpujari, 'Management and Control of Religious Endowments in Assam', *Journal of the University of Gauhati*, Vol. XV, No. 1, 1964, pp. 35–44; and Gajendra Adhikary, *A History of the Temples of Kamrup and Their Management*, Guwahati: Chandra Prakash, 2001.
144 Barpujari, 'Management and Control of Religious Endowments in Assam', pp. 35–44.
145 Arjun Appadurai, *Worship and Conflict under Colonial Rule: A South Indian Case*, Cambridge: Cambridge University Press, 1981.
146 This was one of the four royal lineages among the Ahom rulers.
147 See Adhikary, *A History of the Temples of Kamrup*, for a discussion of the religious endowments of the pre-colonial regime in Assam.
148 See Laurence W. Preston, *The Devs of Cincvad: A Lineage and the State in Maharashtra*, Cambridge: Cambridge University Press, 1989, for a discussion of the colonial state's engagement with the *inam grants*; see also Nicholas B. Dirks, *The Hollow Crown: Ethnohistory of an Indian Kingdom*, Cambridge: South Asian Studies, 2007 (I thank Prachi Deshpande for drawing my attention to these books).
149 This tax, imposed during the later years of the Ahom rule, as an emergency measure by *swargadeo* Chandrakant Singha, was known as *Kharikatania*; see Adhikary, *A History of the Temples of Kamrup*, and Barpujari, 'Management and Control of Religious Endowments in Assam'.
150 See Madhumita Sengupta, 'Of Alienations: State, Temples and the Elite in Nineteenth and Early Twentieth-Century Assam', in *Occasional Paper*, CSSSC, No. 186, July 2013.
151 *Assam Land Revenue Manual, 1886*; this has also been cited by Adhikary, *A History of the Temples of Kamrup*.
152 *Assam Land Revenue Manual, 1886*.
153 Ibid.

154 See Dirks, *The Hollow Crown*, 1967, and Preston, *The Devs of Cincvad*, for the inconsistencies inherent in the colonial state's policy towards *inam* or rent-free religious land grants.
155 Revenue Proceedings, July1834, no. 6. West Bengal State Archive (henceforth WBSA).
156 Letter from Captain F. Jenkins, Assam Commissioner, dated 19 June 1834 to C. Macsween, Secretary to Government in the Revenue Department, Fort William, in *Revenue Proceedings*, 4–25 August 1834, Vol. 899, Progs. 20, WBSA.
157 Ibid.
158 See *Assam Land Revenue Manual, 1886*.
159 Appadurai, *Worship and Conflict under Colonial Rule*, p. 141.
160 See Preston, *The Devs of Cincvad*, and Dirks, *The Hollow Crown*.
161 See *Assam Land Revenue Manual 1886*; see also Adhikary, *A History of the Temples of Kamrup*.
162 *Revenue Proceedings*, 4–25 August 1834, Vol. 899, Progs. No. 20, WBSA.
163 Mills, *Report on the Province of Assam*.
164 Ibid., p. 25.
165 Ibid.
166 'Decree of Gen. Jenkins in Connection with Brahmottar Land of Prabatiya Gossains in Kamrup', 19 September 1846, no. 782, *Bengal Government Papers*, S.L. no. 1–3, 1848, ASA.
167 Ibid.
168 Mills, *Report on the Province of Assam*, p. 25.
169 Ibid., p. 24.
170 Assam Commissioner's Papers, 1834–53, File no. 681, ASA.
171 Mills, *Report on the Province of Assam*, p. 24.
172 Ibid., p. 26.
173 Ibid., p. 25.
174 Ibid., p. 25.
175 Ibid.
176 See Sharma, *Empire's Garden Assam and the Making of India*.
177 *Revenue A*, June 1904, nos. 17–37, ASA.
178 The *Bardeuris* were acknowledged as the highest class of temple servitors by the colonial state. See Adhikary, *A History of the Temples of Kamrup*.
179 *Revenue A*, January 1904, ASA.
180 Ibid.
181 Ibid.
182 Ibid.
183 Ibid.
184 See Sharma, *Social and Economic Change in Assam*, and Rajen Saikia, *Social and Economic History of Assam (1853–1921)*, New Delhi: Manohar, 2001.

2

LANGUAGES OF IDENTITY

In 1836, a letter was written by Indian Civil Service (ICS) officer Trevelyan, a close associate of Major Francis Jenkins, Agent to the Governor General in the Northeast, to the Calcutta Baptist missionaries. The following is an excerpt from the letter. Trevelyan observed:

> From this point (Sudiya) an impression may be made upon Burmah, from an exactly opposite quarter from that at which it has been heretofore entered by the missionary. The communication is open with Yunnan, the westernmost province of China, and it is the intention of the Indian government to send a mission there by this route, next cold season, for the purpose of inquiry about the culture of the tea plant. On the other side, Bhutan, and Thibet, and more countries and people than we have any accurate knowledge of at present, are open to the messengers of the Gospel; and, lastly, the Shun language, which is near akin to the Burmese and Siamese, and belongs to the Chinese family, furnishes a ready means of intercourse with perhaps a greater number of people than any other language in the world, except Chinese itself.[1]

The letter was meant to convince and hold out an invitation to the Baptist missionaries to set up a base at Sadiya in the easternmost region of what was then British Assam. Trevelyan was basically conveying what was in reality a scheme conceived by Francis Jenkins. The letter offers a crucial window into the priorities that the colonial state in Assam had set out for itself, as much as it offers valuable insights into the role and place of language in the official scheme of things in the region. Language was to be invested with nothing more than a functional role in the official scheme of affairs. The letter not only outlined the languages that would henceforth be chosen for patronage but it also presaged the centrality of the communicative aspect of language in the official framework of understanding with regard to vernaculars in Assam. This was clear enough also in Jenkins's subsequent letter to the missionaries where he set out the advantages that the former could hope to derive from their interactions with the Shyans or the Shans of Sadiya. Jenkins pointed out that given the fact that the Shan language was commonly spoken across a wide swath of territory, and the fact that sizeable sections of the population in Assam also hailed from the Shan stock and spoke one or the other of the Shan languages, it would ultimately be advantageous to the missionaries to cultivate the Shan languages. Jenkins's letter clearly foretold that henceforth the official policy would be to promote only those languages that held a potential for furthering commercial intercourse in the region as also those that had a wider following. His letter to the Baptist Society was carefully crafted, highlighting the special features of Sadiya – the site that he had himself proposed for the mission. Jenkins pointed out that the region was inhabited by the Singphos and the Khamtis whose dialects differed very little from those of the Siamese and the Burmese, while the characters in use were essentially the same. He added that there being constant communication between these peoples and the Burmese, the latter language was familiar in the region.[2] This meant that familiarity with the language of the Shans would enable the missionaries to expand their base towards Burma. He also added that people of the Shan stock could be found in most parts of Assam, implying that the mission's labours invested in Sadiya would be fruitful for the future of evangelical activities in the entire region of British Assam. With his characteristic enthusiasm, Jenkins noted:

> The Shans, too, with whom the Mission at Sudiya would be brought in contact, are a much finer and more intelligent people than the Burmese, and ten times as numerous. Their kindred races extend throughout the country whence arise all the mighty rivers from the Burhampooter to Kianguan (the river of Nankin); they occupy entirely the two frontier provinces of Ava-I-lookoom and Moong-.koom; they occupy all the east bank of the Irrawaddy; they stretch down the Salwen to Tenasserim. Laos, and Siam, and Cochin China are their proper countries; they compose half the population of Yunnan, a great proportion of that of Salwen, and stretch up into that district that has always baffled the Chinese, between Thibet, Tartary and Lechuen; whilst Assam is chiefly populated by the overflowings of this great people. The Cacharese are Shans; and the governing race of Upper Assam for many centuries, – the Ahoms – are a tribe from the highest eastern sources

of the Irrawaddy, and until very lately they kept up a communication with their parent stock. Here is an ample field. It is indeed boundless; for it extends over all the north and west of China, (for such is the extent of communication that we command from Sudiya,) and it embraces some of the most fertile and most temperate countries on the face of the earth.[3]

What Jenkins had outlined was a comprehensive plan meant to win over the missionaries with the lure of evangelical opportunities and to secure his own pet scheme of taming and disciplining the unruly hill dwellers through proselytization and evangelical activities. By the time Jenkins came to power in 1834, the discovery of the tea plant had begun to excite hopes of a flourishing plantation economy stretching to beyond the boundaries of British Assam towards the far east. Jenkins's invitation to the Calcutta chapter of the Baptist Missionary Society consequently was underwritten by specific strategic considerations. The Baptists were after all known for their unorthodox approach and keen interest in and successful conduct of evangelical enterprises in colonial settlements elsewhere, and were presumably therefore considered as pacific and 'safe' from the point of view of the 'natives' of the hill regions of Assam known for their unpredictable temperaments.[4] It was also no mere coincidence that Jenkins chose the people inhabiting the tracts east of Sadiya for evangelical intervention. He was keenly conscious of the fact that the region enjoyed a close proximity with Burma and western China, countries with which the East India Company was desirous of opening a commercial exchange. Jenkins was also aware that one arm of the Baptist association, the American Baptists, had already opened a chapter in Burma under the auspices of Rev. Adoniram Judson and was contemplating a further extension into China. In 1835, Mr Kincaid of the Burma Mission had made an attempt to reach Sadiya through Bhamo, Mogoung and the Hukong Valley, but he could not proceed beyond Mogoung on account of difficulties faced in procuring men and provisions.[5] The Agent to the Governor General had done his homework well and was ready to give shape to his schemes of bringing the hills under effective control. He was, therefore, more than generous in his pledges of support to the proposed mission and wrote:

> No attention of mine should of course be wanting to make the place comfortable to any missionaries, and I will be willing to contribute my mite to their establishment. You may mention, that I will subscribe 1,000 rupees, if a family is settled as a Mission at

Sudiya, and whenever they have had a press at work for six months I will be happy to double that sum, if I remain in charge of the Province.[6]

Jenkins's efforts to render the mission at Sadiya attractive to the prospective visitors must be seen in the light of the state's attempts to make the indomitable hill tracts more accessible to the British. In one of his journal entries, Brown observed that Captain Jenkins had written to him 'recommending the establishment of a station at Gowahati by our board with a particular view to the Garos – a numerous people in a savage state, residing on the hills south of Gowahati, and under the English government'.[7] This is a clear indication of how missionary activities were meant to be deployed in the service of the state, especially for taming the 'savage'. Given the key role of missionary activities in his scheme of things, Jenkins was careful to ensure the latter's success. He donated sums of money at regular intervals for the sustenance of the mission. The former also offered to grant some amount of waste land to the missionaries free of rent for 15 or 20 years so that the latter could set up a Christian colony. Needless to say such a plan received a warm response from Brown who communicated the same to the board with the hope that it would receive the board's approval since such a colony could 'be a radiating point whence a religious influence might be extensively spread'.[8]

Apart from the strategic and administrative implications of the letters written by Jenkins to the missionaries, the latter had immense significance for their insights into the state's policies vis-à-vis the vernaculars. These letters foregrounded the preponderantly commercial vantage point from which henceforth the state would visualize the vernaculars spoken in the region. Perhaps this was how Jenkins arrived at the decision to declare Bengali as the official vernacular of Assam in 1836. It is not possible for us to recount the precise manner in which the decision was taken in the initial stages, and allegations that the British were persuaded by their Bengali *babus* have thankfully been laid to rest. We have, however, Jenkins's statements which indicate that it was enough for him that Bengali was understood by the people of Assam. Once when confronted by mounting criticisms against the British government's policy of declaring Bengali as the official vernacular of Assam, Jenkins retorted:

To show more forcibly the manner or degree in which the Assamese were prepared for the adoption of the Bengali language . . . I will add a few words to exhibit the former connection of Assam with Bengal and Hindoostan, to prove that the Assamese were not so ignorant of the languages of their neighbours as the Missionaries would have Government to understand they were.

. . . long before the Ahom Rajahs were converted to Hindooism or Brahminism, the temples were established throughout Lower Assam, having large establishments of priests who read and taught the Hindoo sacred books in Sanscrit; and immediately after their conversion, the Rajahs brought in Kanóuge and Santipore Brahmins, for whom they instituted immense establishments, and invested with so much rank and power, that gradually the greater part of the authority of Government fell into their hands.[9]

To Jenkins it seemed a perfectly legitimate decision to institute Bengali, given not only the wide familiarity of modern standardized Bengali in Assam but also the close similarity between the dialects of Assam and those spoken in Bengal – an argument that he would advance eventually at the height of the language controversy. Later letters and reports indicate that it was rather convenient to have Bengali as the official vernacular since the latter afforded easy access to a pool of administrative personnel from Bengal as much as it allowed the state to make use of school books written in Bengali, thereby saving money in the process. Bengali was also viable for commercial purposes, as it enabled communication in a language already familiar to the group of Bengal-based European planters who were on the verge of investing in Assam. This was precisely the advantages of having Bengali that the inspector of schools, William Robinson, would also articulate in his defence of Bengali. It is easy to surmise that Robinson, a contemporary of Jenkins and an important functionary of the education department, would have been echoing the official line of reasoning. Yet it was Robinson himself who in 1839 had deemed it fit to produce a grammar of the Assamese language, and it would be legitimate to conclude that had he not spotted some distinctiveness in the local speech forms, he would not have taken the trouble of coming out with a separate grammar for what he called the Assamese language. However, Robinson's grammar did not contain any overt reference to the identity of Assamese, and the sole allusion of this order appeared in discussing the alphabet, consisting of the brief remark that for the most part it resembled the characters used in Bengali. When in 1841 Robinson published a detailed account of the province titled *A Descriptive Account of Assam*, he was prepared to engage with the subject of the identity of Assamese with greater eloquence. Interestingly, in this account, Robinson declared the two languages to be grammatically different. The similarities between the local speech and the Bengali language were, however, not lost on him. Hence, he expressed his surprise that the 'present dialect of the

Assamese' does not contain more traces of the language of the ruling class of Ahoms and observed that with the exception of a very few words of Ta i origin, Assamese 'seems to have been derived from the Sungskrit, and in most cases possesses a close affinity to the Bengali'.[10] Robinson clarified that the two languages were phonemically distinct – the Assamese language being 'distinguished by a slight difference in pronunciation', the most important of these being 'the substitution of s in Assamese for the Bengali ch, and a guttural h for the Bengali s and sh', adding that the form of three or four letters had also undergone a slight variation.[11] Robinson's account of Assamese, however, contained many contradictory remarks, such as his pronouncement that the grammatical features of Assamese and Bengali were 'considerably unlike' although there seemed to him to be scarcely any difference in their syntactical structures. It is telling that it was this single syntactical resemblance which Robinson was to foreground subsequently as the principal reason why Assamese and Bengali should be treated as cognates.

It is telling also that right after pronouncing Assamese and Bengali to be grammatically disparate, Robinson distanced himself from his earlier stance. At the height of the controversy over the identity of Assamese, in a letter written on 7 February 1859, Robinson, who was spearheading the state's opposition to Assamese, observed:

> Permit me further to observe that since the date when the Reverend Mr. Bronson and the other Missionaries of the Assam Mission agitated the question regarding the vernacular of Assam, I have had better opportunities than I then possessed of making a comparison between the dialect of Assam and the common colloquial dialect as spoken by the people in the adjacent districts of Bengal; and the result is, that I am more than ever convinced that the Assamese is nothing but a dialect of Bengali, and bears a very strong affinity to the dialects spoken in Dinagepore, Rangpore and Sylhet.[12]

It is curious to see how shifts in administrative positions could induce shifts on the issue of linguistic autonomy, the reason being that language for the British administration in Assam was a mere adjunct of its administrative concerns and strategic considerations. An early insight into this aspect of the colonial state's language policy in Assam may be gleaned from the introductory remarks in Robinson's grammar compiled in 1839, where he set out his reasons for producing the grammar. Robinson observed philosophically:

> Yet there are circumstances which seem to render the Assamese language in some measure worthy of notice. It is the language

usually spoken throughout that interesting country known as Assam, and by a population exceeding seven hundred thousand. . . . The country itself is now fast rising in importance. The extraordinary fertility of its soil – its varied productions, among which the tea plant ranks as the most important, – its extensive and hitherto unexplored mineral treasures, all tend greatly to augment its value and to render it a highly valuable acquisition to the British government. . . . An acquaintance therefore with the language of the country must be acknowledged to be important, especially to those who may enter it on mercantile speculations, for besides affording an intelligible medium of negotiation with the people, it will likewise furnish facilities for friendly intercourse with them whereby extensive information may be gleaned respecting the commercial advantages which the country affords.[13]

To Robinson, as much as to Jenkins and others in the colonial bureaucratic establishment, the decision to extend official patronage to a language was highly inflected by the commercial prospects of the language concerned rather than by the latter's sheer presence.[14] Jenkins's repeated letters to the missionaries during this period bespoke his impatience for the realization of his dreams. He was rather impatient that the missionaries should start their work immediately. So he proposed that men conversant with the Shan languages should be put in charge of the Sadiya mission since delay might happen in beginning the work if new members having to learn these languages were entrusted with the task of the mission. He therefore proposed that the mission society write for appropriate men for manning the mission at Sadiya to Rev. Adoniram Judson, the missionary who headed the Burma chapter of the mission. His letter to the mission contained the following words of advice:

> I know of no person to whom I would more willingly apply, to select a missionary, than Dr. Judson. The connection of the Sadiya dialects and tribes with the Burmese language and country, makes it obviously most important to get a gentleman from the Rangoon mission; otherwise we should be losing a year of precious time, whilst the individual was acquiring a competent knowledge of the Shan languages, which a Burmese scholar will master without difficulty.[15]

So far we have seen how the state's language policy in the region, from the very outset, was underpinned by its strategic and commercial considerations. This aspect of the colonial state's language policy in Assam will be taken up for further illustration in the chapter. It is important to note, however, that the debate on Assamese was to evolve eventually into a full-fledged ideological battle within the bureaucratic circle, with members of the bureaucracy venturing to offer contrary views on the issue of the identity of Assamese and the desirability of having the latter as the official vernacular of the province. Historiography's assessment of the colonial government in the war over language in Assam has been less than fair to the officials of the colonial state who chose to defend Bengali instead of Assamese. An assessment of the latter's role has taken the form of the latter's depiction either as innocent victims of manipulation by Bengali clerks desirous of retaining Bengali or as imperial strategists concerned with encashing the economic and administrative advantages of a single language. None so far has bothered to give them credit for participating in a shared battle of the ideologies. This chapter also foregrounds how the missionary discourse on Assamese was ultimately imbricated in larger ideological concerns other than the purely linguistic.

I

The uses of language

A British Baptist missionary, Robinson began his career as the headmaster of the Guwahati Seminary in 1839 and went on to become inspector of government schools in Assam. In 1854, at the height of the campaign for replacing Bengali with Assamese as the official language of the province, Robinson, as inspector of government schools, came forward to defend the move to accord institutional status to Bengali. In 'Some Remarks in Defence of the Use of Bengali', Robinson pointed out that the visual differences between the two languages would not have existed had Nathan Brown, the chief exponent of autonomy for Assamese in the missionary camp, not followed a phonemic method of spelling for the print version promoted by the Baptist Missionary Press at Sibsagar. Robinson argued that this version was profoundly inspired by the rules of orthography most common to the latter's part of the country, that is Upper Assam, and that there was in reality a far greater 'variety in the modes of pronunciation' in the region. That these were insufficient grounds for conceding autonomy to a language was, by then, to Robinson a matter of faith or so it will seem to anyone listening to his defence of Bengali. He cited the English case wherein similar differences had existed between the English language and its provincial dialects, which differed from the former in terms of orthography, grammatical forms and vocabulary. He concluded that similar differences between Assamese and Bengali could therefore not be conceded as sufficient grounds for ruling out the possibility of essential unity of the two languages.[16] That Robinson was not consistent in his grounds for advocating Bengali becomes clear when we read the following remark, which came close on the heels of the previous explanation. Robinson observed in a manner that was nothing, if not purely calculating:

> It will be better for the interests of the people, that we avail ourselves of the books that have been prepared, and may yet be published for the thirty millions of Bengal, in preference to creating a distinct literature for a comparatively small section of the people, merely for the sake of perpetuating what is at best but a dialectical difference.[17]

It is clear from the foregoing observation that it was considered far more advantageous to retain Bengali as the official standard, given the fact that public expenditure incurred on printing books in Assamese could be avoided thereby.

Robinson was not the only one to speculate about the likely advantages to the state from Bengali as the official vernacular. At the height of the language controversy, the state sought the opinion of its district officers on the issue of desirability and judiciousness of substituting Assamese for Bengali. However, even after these reports were received and studied, the government of Assam did not deem it expedient to revoke its earlier decision. A letter written at the eleventh hour by A. Eden, secretary to the government of Bengal, expressed the preferences of the lieutenant governor of Bengal for a status quo in no uncertain terms, notwithstanding the growing clamour for Assamese:

> I am directed to say that if the difference between Bengali and Assamese were so marked as Colonel Haughten supposed, the Lieutenant Governor would have been disposed to agree with him; but the information before his honour leads him to believe that the real difference between the two languages (if needed Assamese can be called a separate language) is confined to a very small number of vocables, and consists chiefly in inflexions and terminations. The character used, both for Bengali and Assamese is one and the same; and while Bengali has a considerable literature consisting both of original works and of translations, and more than one good Dictionary, there is no Assamese literature except a few bald translations of elementary books, nor anything deserving the

name of a Dictionary. The Lieutenant Governor has been assured by you that no practical inconvenience arises from the use of Bengali in the courts, as Bengali is thoroughly understood by all who are in the habit of attending there, and no one is prevented from writing and presenting a petition in Assamese if he chooses to do so. All the officers of the Commission are required to pass in the colloquial Assamese and the Amlah are nearly all natives of the province, so that no one speaking and understanding only Assamese can fail to make himself understood. Moreover, there is a considerable population in Assam (besides the hill tribes) who do not speak Assamese and barely understand it. To this people it is a matter of indifference whether the language of the courts be Bengalee or Assamese, and the latter has not even the advantage of being the universally spoken language of the province.[18]

Nowhere in this passage is there any overt attempt to contest the fact that the two languages – Bengali and Assamese – were not isomorphic in nature. Instead, there is a clear tendency to circumvent the issue of discrepancies by harping on the degree of intelligibility of the Bengali language to the people of Assam, the limited distribution of the print language proposed by the missionaries and the practical inconvenience arising from the lack of readable texts in Assamese. The state seemed to be unwilling to take on the responsibility of devising and organizing the necessary infrastructural apparatus for executing the change. Major J.C. Haughton, officiating commissioner of Assam, best exemplified the state's ambivalence on the issue. Despite his belief that there was no parity between Assamese and Bengali, he could not support the cause of Assamese unequivocally. Instead, he came up with an ingenious plan, which he felt would best serve the purposes of satisfying both local sentiments and the felt need to preserve Bengali. He therefore proposed the general use of Assamese as the medium of instruction in all village schools where that language was the vernacular, and its substitution for Bengali when used in the government offices.[19] Yet another statement from Haughton shows clearly that he did not anticipate any shortage of textbooks in Assamese, which was perhaps the biggest hurdle identified by some officials. The latter remarked, 'Elementary works in Assamese are already available and I am assured by persons warranted in giving such assurance, that the supply will fully keep place with the demand.'[20] Yet Haughton could not be persuaded to recommend the substitution of Assamese for Bengali at the official level, a fact that underscores the strategic advantages of Bengali to the administration.

II

A divided house

By the second half of the nineteenth century, the state was no longer able to evade the growing clamour of legitimacy with which the missionaries had invested the issue of the provincial vernacular. The demand to recognize the autonomy of Assamese and the latter's legitimate right to be recognized as the official vernacular had to be addressed on its own terms as this was now also the demand of the nascent provincial middle-class intelligentsia. This was precisely the point when men like Robinson chose to mount an ideological defence in support of Bengali. The debate becomes both interesting and complex from this point onwards as officials began to take contrary positions on the issue of autonomy of Assamese, making it difficult for the state to resolve the matter.[21] There were some who upheld the sanctity of standardization as a perfectly valid method of resolving disparities of speech practices much in the tradition of nineteenth-century language standardization in Europe. Some would go on to cite the immediate example of Bengali where standardization of the Bengali language in recent memory had superseded a fair amount of mutual unintelligibility of speech practices, especially in the districts of eastern Bengal to create a uniform Bengali print standard. For these officers the speech practices in Assam represented nothing but dialects of Bengali, having evolved out of a history of shared practices between the neighbouring territories. It was deemed sufficient that these speech practices were mutually intelligible with Bengali or shared an affinity with dialects of Bengali. The argument of intelligibility permitted much flexibility and would be similarly deployed by the missionaries to argue that the two languages were mutually unintelligible. Intelligibility could also sprout interesting interventions, with interested parties setting out to induce the same to prove a point. Again intelligibility as a criterion for arguing the identity of a language also allowed enough flexibility for foregrounding the differences between the written version and spoken varieties of a language. One official held the opinion that the confusion in settling the identity of the language had arisen from the fallacy of comparing the written language of one place with the colloquial of the other.[22] Col. Hopkinson, Agent to the Governor General and commissioner of Assam, also recounted how a certain Inspector Murray, who had initially regarded Assamese as a 'specifically different language', changed his opinion a year later after he had travelled in and mixed with the people of Mymensingh, Rajshahi and Cooch Behar. It seems that at the end of his sojourn, he could not 'fix a line where he could say, as dialects, that a

Bengalee dialect ended and an Assamese dialect began'.[23] The commissioner pointed out that there was not a single district in Bengal that did not have its dialectical peculiarities and that the Bengali spoken in Calcutta and its neighbourhood differed vastly from the dialects spoken in the districts of East Bengal. On a bemused note he added that if the peculiarities of the various East Bengali speech forms were held to constitute a distinct language, there would be in Bengal at least as many languages as there were districts.[24] Hopkinson pointed out that had the Baptist Mission in Assam derived from a parent branch in Calcutta instead of from one in Burma, one would never have heard of an Assamese language. Hopkinson's views were shared by some who pointed out that the Baptist missionaries were mooting for the autonomy of Assamese because they were ignorant of the multiple and largely congruous speech practices of the different districts of East Bengal, having come directly from America to Assam. A. Anley, district superintendent of police, felt that the language spoken by the people of Kamrup was 'nothing more than perverted Bengali', and explained that he had seen a judgement delivered by a Punchayut (a village council of elders and other esteemed residents) dated 46 years ago, before the British rule, and it was his opinion that if the latter was put in the hands of a Bengali scholar who was then asked to pronounce the 's' as 'h' and the 'ch' as 's', the person concerned would not have any difficulty in extracting its meaning correctly.[25]

Discrepancies in matters of speech in Assam were also often cited as grounds for denying the sheer impossibility of conceding a provincial standard. Thus, Henry Hokinson, the AGG, observed,

> Even in Assam, I may remark, the dialect of all the districts is not the same: for instance, in upper Assam – meaning by that Luckhimpore, Seebsaugor, and Nowgong – for the word 'they', we have 'sebilok'; in Lower Assam, or Kamroop and Durrung, 'tahun' or 'temra' . . . these instances might be multiplied ad infinitum.[26]

Hopkinson found the missionary demands to be perfectly preposterous and went as far as to question the latter's integrity in raking up the issue:

> If the language of Assam could be confounded with that of Bengal, then exclusive control over the most powerful of educational institutions was lost to them. Thus at Seebsaugor they conceived, and from Seebsaugor they promulgated, the Assamese dogma which was to extirpate the Bengalee heresy and which I now regard as really part of the creed of the Christian churchman in Assam.[27]

The commissioner had no patience whatsoever with the exponents of autonomy as, according to him, whatever differences there existed between the speech forms of Bengal and Assam were confined to the speech of Upper Assam. In his opinion the discrepancies were nothing but a greater vulgarization of Bengali proportional to an area's physical distance from the core region of Bengal. There were, however, many officials who felt strongly about the fundamental differences between Assamese and Bengali and insisted that Assamese should be installed in place of Bengali for the sake of justice and comprehensibility as the two languages were mutually unintelligible. Thus, both sides held completely contrary notions on the issue of the mutual intelligibility of the languages.

Among the officials who opposed Assamese were some who articulated cultural and racial considerations for defending their choice of Bengali. Many of the detractors of Assamese held that not all languages were capable of expressing sophisticated thoughts. Interestingly, there was much that was common between the discourses of these officials and the missionaries in this regard. The latter had held that Assamese was a copious language capable of developed and sophisticated literary expressions. All literary works produced in the region in the past were claimed as the literary heritage of Assamese to support this claim. On their part, many colonial officials also held that languages, unlike dialects, constituted a mode of informed literary expression. However, these officials did not consider the literary works purportedly written in Assamese as noteworthy. Curiously, their judgements were based not on actual examination of these works but on the poor opinion they held of the Assamese people, whom they regarded as a degraded and degenerate community, superstitious in beliefs and indolent in habits.[28] Such a people, in their opinion, could not produce works of merit. In the debates on the vernacular, one comes across arguments advanced by several officials that it was not expedient to accord official sanction to the local speech, not merely because it constituted a vulgarization of Bengali but also because of the desirability of retaining Bengali as the official language, on account of the prospects it held out for the superior cultural development of the people of the region. In this connection, R. Cornish, assistant commissioner, wrote,

> It (Assamese) may be a distinct offshoot from the Sanscrit, but it possesses no literature worthy of the name, and no standard of the written language. We may even concede that it is as fine a language as Bengali, but it has not yet passed through those stages which rendered a language a proper vehicle for conveying education, nor has it acquired that fixedness which is required of

an official language. It is at present only the tongue of a rude peasantry whose advance in civilization has been constantly checked by successive hordes of savage conquerors. . . . It is one thing to state that a language is spoken by a people, and another to prove that it should be made the official tongue. . . . It is right to insist on Assamese being the language of rudimentary education as it removes a barrier existing between the masses and learning but boys who aspire to the higher form of education can certainly afford the time necessary to master a cognate dialect, more refined and technical than their own, especially when a knowledge of it opens to them so large a field of literature and occupation. . . . I feel sure that Assam especially would suffer by it as it would tend to check the healthy currents of intercourse with Bengal, and make her administration more local and her people more prejudiced.[29]

Likewise, J.K. Graham, deputy commissioner of Durrang, argued that to reject Bengali would be 'to encourage the people to rely on a language having no literature of its own, and thus to keep them in a manner at a standstill, or it may almost be said to cause them to retrograde'.[30] This section of the bureaucracy argued from a purely racial perspective, attributing to Assamese the permanent disability to express informed ideas, which they felt could cause major practical inconveniences in the long run, implying, thereby, that the Assamese language would never succeed in inducting the requisite legal or technical vocabulary necessary for the future progress of the community.

Yet notwithstanding all this opposition, the government had to eventually bow to the growing pressure for declaring Assamese as the provincial vernacular. The General Department of Education of the government of Bengal met on 19 April 1873 to discuss the status of Assamese. After deliberating, among others, on the mass of opinion collected by the commissioner from the district and the subdivisional officers of Assam and from 'other gentlemen whom the Commissioner consulted', the committee adopted the resolution that Assamese should be the medium of instruction in all schools of Assam.[31]

III

Inducing uniformity

The state's decision to replace Bengali with Assamese did not resolve the problem of language for Assam as no normative solution to the issue could possibly do justice to what was a shared process of exchange that had historically evolved through proximate living and defied boundaries throughout its long and dynamic history of evolution. This was to be the bane of post-Enlightenment rationalism that threw its veil of obscurity over the lived history of speech. Having canonized Assamese, the colonial state set out with its newfound zeal, to obliterate all anomalies in speech practices and to bring the spoken forms closer to a uniform print standard which nonetheless did not conform to the print standard pioneered by the Baptist missionaries, the original advocates of Assamese and its principal ideologues. The state undertook to spell out, in unambiguous terms, the boundaries of Assamese in order to distinguish it from Bengali and to clear all ambiguities on this score. The following unequivocal declaration of the General Department of Education soon set the agenda for the future course of action:

> The people of Assam do not understand Bengali, and that the petitions written in name and the court proceedings are unintelligible to them, and the recent agitation proves clearly that the majority of the Assamese wish to have their own language for educational and court purposes.[32]

The state's concern that the boundaries between Assamese and Bengali be clearly distinguished inspired the General Department Notification in May 1885. The latter declared that the spelling of the names of the more important places in the province had been fixed by the chief commissioner of Assam and approved by the Governor General in Council, and that this should henceforth be strictly followed.[33] According to the approved rules, it was made mandatory to retain the local peculiarities of utterances of 'h' for 's' and 's' for 'ch' and 'chh' in partial acknowledgement of the style approved by the missionaries. The only deviant injunction was that the orthography of Assamese words should strictly follow the norms of the Sanskritic orthography instead of the phonemic orthography sanctioned by the Baptist missionaries.[34] These successive rulings were meant to accommodate both the state's cherished notions regarding fixed and impermeable linguistic boundaries and the Orientalist findings concerning the Sanskritic origins of the Indian languages, with the result that overlaps between Assamese and Bengali were simultaneously abrogated and reinforced. Thus, the chief commissioner soon mandated that words of common use among the local people, but suspected of Bengali 'origins', must be removed from the Assamese language. This resulted in a situation where Assamese was rendered entirely incomprehensible to a section of the people. Nothing possibly brings out the contrived nature of the entire exercise of 'standardization', as the examination of the primers submitted to a committee for selection and subsequent use in the schools. The latter had decided that one of the criteria for selection would be the fact that Assamese was essentially the language used throughout the books. In all, 58 competitors sent their books, out of whom the committee selected only 10. In this connection, the remarks of Major Clarke, deputy commissioner of Luckimpore, are worth noting. The latter writes,

> I have gone through all the 10 sets of books, and am quite disappointed to find that none of them is free from the defect for which the book received with Mr. Martin's letter No. 150, dated May 10th, 1873 had been rejected, viz., a large proportion of Bengali words.[35]

He added that Babu Hem Chandra's primer, *Adipath*, which was deemed the best of all the books, sent in, also contained, in a randomly selected extract, more than 40 pure Bengali words out of a total of 67 words in addition to several 'Bengali phrases and sentences'. Major Clarke's observation in this regard is quite telling:

> I must note that the advocates of Assamese will say that many of the words which I have marked as Bengali, are Sanskrit, and it is my conviction that no Assamese book can be written with a smaller proportion of Bengali words than Hem chandra has written. . . . In fact it is simply impossible to exclude Bengali words from so called Assamese books, and documents.[36]

He went on to recount the nature of the reaction to something written in the so-called pure Assamese. It seems that the inspector had asked examiners for the Vernacular Scholarship Standard to set their papers in both Bengali and Assamese, with the papers in the former to be used in the Cooch Bihar region while the ones in Assamese were to be used in Assam. The inspector was subsequently asked to send some of the papers printed in Bengali to the Assam centres of examination as it was anticipated that the papers printed in Assamese might not be intelligible to the candidates.[37] Not everyone was convinced that the decision to replace Bengali had been necessary or that it was justified. The irony of the entire situation caused Col. Hopkinson to remark with his characteristic sarcasm that 'it would be better to substitute (1) "Ahom", (2) "Ahomeea" or (3) "Ahomese" as the name of the language to be used in Judicial and Revenue Proceedings in the valley districts of Assam instead of "Assamese", for "Ahom" is the vernacular word, and

"Assamese" borrowed from the Bengalee for "Ahom", so that in employing the word "Assamese" we are discrediting and contradicting ourselves at the outset by using a Bengalee word to explain that we will not use Bengalee.'[38] After all, he added, one could no more do 'without Bengali than Shylock could get his pound of flesh without blood'.[39]

IV

A mission to fulfil

For the Baptist missionaries, the proposal from Jenkins to set up a base in Sadiya had held out a tempting promise of far-reaching evangelical consequences. Since the latter had always wished to expand towards China, the proposals were invariably greeted with enthusiasm. For a fairly long time their endeavours to expand their base of activities towards the far east had met with failure, primarily on account of the resistance of the kingdom of Ava. The members, therefore, took to the proposals immediately, hoping that through the proposed mission, they would be able in the near future to redeem their aspirations vis-à-vis China. Nathan Brown who was to take charge of the Sadiya mission was extremely hopeful that a step in the direction of Sadiya could open up avenues for a future transit to China. In his communications with the mission headquarters, he wrote:

> There is little doubt . . . that at the present time, Sudiya is the most feasible entrance, from the interior, to the empire of China. It is, in fact, precisely such a point of approach as the Board contemplated in their late resolutions. It is situated near the head waters of the Kiangku or Nankin river, which runs directly through the centre of China. The passage over to China from Ava may hereafter be practicable.[40]

Although on reaching Sadiya the missionaries were not exactly impressed by the low density of population and complained that the representations that had been made earlier had given a completely different picture of the place, they were hopeful about the new mission as this appeared to them to be a stepping stone to China. In a letter to the board, Cutter wrote:

> But there are around us many thousands of precious immortal souls, Asamese and Shyans, among whom we can labour unmolested; and a commencement might be made at once among several of the tribes around us. I certainly think this is one of

90

the most interesting missionary fields occupied by the Board, on many accounts, notwithstanding the population is so much scattered; and I hope, ere long, to see missionaries entering the *Celestial Empire*, and the dominions of his golden-footed majesty, from Sadiya.[41]

In the later part of the nineteenth century, Rev. P.H. Moore recounted that the principal aim of the mission had been not the Assamese but the vast masses of people beyond:

> But the importance of this province as a mission field is not confined to its own limits and to its present 5,000,000 of inhabitants. The fact of its location as a highway to Tibet and western China enhances its value from a missionary, as well as from a political and commercial point of view. Thus American Baptist Missionary Union occupied Assam in 1836 simply as a step towards entering China from the west. God turned us back, and has kept us here now fifty years. Was it because He saw that it was necessary that we first evangelize this valley and surrounding hills as a base of supply for more extended operations in the regions beyond, which are still an unknown quantity in all our Geographies, both physical and moral?[42]

Given the huge expectations generated by Jenkins's proposals, it was naturally disheartening for the missionaries when the mission at Sadiya failed to take off. It was at this point that the group of Baptist missionaries turned towards Assam. If for the state communicability had been the principal ground for choosing Bengali, the same ground was no less crucial for the missionaries eager to preach among the natives and attract the latter to the Christian doctrines. It was crucial, therefore, to their project to induce uniformity of speech, and in this respect their early experiences were rather disconcerting. Having convinced themselves a large section of the people residing in Sadiya spoke a uniform language called 'Assamese', they were soon dismayed to 'find not more than six or eight native Assamese who can read their own language in any character whatever, and but two who are able to write it'.[43] Although by his own admission, Brown had not yet 'obtained that perfect acquaintance with the language', that is Assamese, he concluded that the language of Carey's Bible translated and printed by the Serampore Press in 1820 was not authentic Assamese as it was 'not well understood by the common people', the reason inferred being that the tract contained 'so many Bengali terms'.[44] For the moment however, they avoided making any serious revisions as they did not know the language well themselves, and concentrated on learning Assamese from the people of Sadiya. Subsequently, when they undertook to revise Carey's Assamese Bible, they pointed out multiple errors in the work. Brown wrote in his journal, dated 1 May 1837:

> We find that Dr. Carey's translation . . . requires many alterations in order to be understood by the people around us. Dr. Carey never having resided in Assam, and being obliged to depend entirely upon a native interpreter, it would be surprising if the translation did not contain errors. The greatest fault is the introduction of many Bengali and Sanscrit words, totally unknown to the common people, and understood only by a few learned pandits. We make it our rule, however, to vary from Dr. Carey's translation only where it is absolutely necessary in order to make it intelligible to the natives. Still, the alterations required are so numerous as to make it almost a new translation, as you will judge from the fact, that in the Sermon on the Mount alone, we have been obliged to make no less than two hundred and thirty alterations.[45]

This passage provides us with the very first insight into what Brown construed as true Assamese. For Brown like many others of his age, lexical autonomy constituted one of the fundamental pillars of linguistic autonomy. Brown thus expected Assamese to contain 'few' words of Bengali or Sanskrit origin. Inducing uniformity in Assamese would not, however, solve all his problems, and he did not give up his hopes of preaching to the disparate populations of British Assam. Evangelical activities so far had shown no signs of progress, and it was imminent that the conversion rate be increased. It was imminent, therefore, that a common language of communication be conceived, if necessary, artificially to serve the purposes of preaching. The following letter addressed to Frederick James Halliday, lieutenant governor of Bengal, on 13 November 1854 by Miles Bronson, provides valuable insights into the existence of a twin motive behind having a uniform language:

> The Assamese language is the common medium of intercourse with the Mountain Tribes that surround this valley. The Bhutias, the Mishmis, the Miris, the Abors, the Khamptis, the Singphos, the Nagas – and various other Tribes compose a vast population, all of whom must be reached from this valley – and through the medium of the Assamese language. From their constant intercourse

with the Assamese some among them can speak the Assamese very well. Everywhere among them such interpreters may be found for a medium of communication. It is not probable that the languages of all these tribes can ever be reduced to system, and books and translation prepared for them to any great extent: but through the Assamese language as a common medium, much can be accomplished for them even at the present.[46]

As early as 1837 itself, Brown had come up with a unique scheme, which was contrary to all his stated theories of language structure but which would surely have resolved the problem of multiple languages that confronted the missionaries and seemed to handicap their objective of reaching out to the local people. In his journal in 1837, Brown wrote,

> Received today, through the kindness of Mr Trevelyan, a copy of an essay written by the Hon. John Pickering, on the uniform application of the English letters to the Indian languages of America – a plan no less advantageous to missionary operations here than to among the western Indians. In Saidiya I have not been able to find more than six or eight native Assamese who can read their own language in any character whatever, and but two who are able to write it. We are therefore obliged to give them an alphabet of some sort, and the only question is whether it shall be the expensive and difficult Bengali character, or the English. We have been induced to choose the latter, and more especially since, from present appearances, it seems nearly certain that the Bengali character will, in a few years be abandoned throughout India, and the English substituted in its place. In printing the Assamese, we shall follow Mr. Pickering's plan in every essential particular, and shall use the letters to express the same invariable sounds, whether in Asames, Khamti, Abor or Singpho, so that a scholar who has learned to read one, can read the whole.[47]

No scholarly engagement with language could possibly sustain such crude intrusions into natural languages, and the overt display of power that came with belonging to the ruling class is impossible to miss in the preceding statements. Ideology was thus clearly not sacrosanct and could be conveniently sacrificed for larger goals. Language for the missionaries was just a means to their ultimate mission of evangelism.[48] It is also telling that the tract was supplied to Brown by ICS Trevelyan, friend of the mission and Jenkins alike. When the board approved Brown's scheme of adopting the

Roman script, his joy knew no bounds. The former drew up an elaborate plan of overriding all internal inconsistencies in the Shyan language – an exercise that he was to use to good effect with regard to the Assamese group of languages. Brown exulted:

> We are glad to learn that the board approved of the application of the Roman characters to the Shyan language. In regard to any objections being offered to it by the natives, I do not think there is reason to apprehend anything of the kind. The Shyans are a scattered and subdued race; and having no central spot from where their laws and customs are regulated, as the Burmans have, they do not entertain those strong prejudices against all innovations which the Burmans manifest. The characters at present used by the Syans are entirely different from those used by their ancestors., the Ahoms, &c. They now use a sort of mongrel alphabet, chiefly borrowed from that of their Burman conquerors, but differing greatly in different sections of the country. We have not yet made any proposition to the Board for getting a fount of native SHyan characters cut, partly because the characters are so various in form that we could not yet tell what would in every case be the form most extensively known, and partly because there is no immediate opportunity for distributing Shyan tracts to any extent, there being at present no ready access to the main body of Shyans between here and Ava.[49]

It mattered little to Brown that the imposition of unity from above was not only highly intrusive but that it constituted a gross violation of the dynamism that informed speech formation and change in the world of the spoken languages. In blocking comprehension of this plurality and interchangeability of speech patterns, evangelical zeal as much as ideological leanings were equally liable.

Interestingly enough, the issue of uniformity of Assamese soon became a bone of contention between the members of the Baptist missionary fraternity themselves. The official reports of the mission reveal that there was a serious engagement within the mission with the issue of disparities in speech practices in Assam at this time. The Annual Report of the Mission to Assam in 1843 indicates that there was pressure to shift the mission station from Sibsagar to the Kamrup district, which was not only the capital of the province but also the headquarters of the commissioner of Assam with a sizeable population of 15,000 to 20,000 inhabitants. Once again, the influential camp led by Nathan Brown and others opposed the move to shift the headquarters of the mission from Sibsagar. The report claims that the principal objections to Guwahati arose on account of both the 'comparative sparseness of the Assamese population in its neighbourhood'[50] and the fact that 'the Assamese spoken in that vicinity is (was) a corruption of the pure Assamese, bearing nearly as close a resemblance to the Bengali as to the Ahom; and that such as it is, it is spoken by the lower classes, and is likely soon to be supplanted by the Bengali altogether'.[51] Although Brown and his supporters effectively thwarted the move to shift the mission base to Guwahati, the struggle was not easily won. One of the principal dissenters was Brother Danforth, who favoured the establishment of a separate mission in Guwahati that would cultivate a different linguistic medium in keeping with the differences between the speech forms in 'Assam Proper' or Upper Assam and Lower Assam. The latter had been investigating the *dhekeri* or the speech forms of Lower Assam for some time and was convinced of its distinctiveness from the usages practised in and around Sibsagar. Danforth wrote:

> I am inclined to think that the difference is so great between these two dialects that to preach the Gospel to the Dhekeri in the Assamese tongue will be fraught with constant embarrassment and perplexity. In my opinion to be a successful preacher, you must talk a language that can be comprehended by them without mental effort. I must therefore differ with you when you say that you think that this people can be reached through the Assamese language . . . the people of Gowahati talk Dhekeri or rather are Dhekeris.[52]

Danforth had spent almost seven years in Guwahati and was thus quite familiar with the linguistic situation of the most prosperous division of British Assam.[53] Significantly enough, although Brown did not agree with Danforth on the issue of speech discrepancies, he could not deny altogether the validity of *dhekeri*'s claim to distinctiveness from *Ujani* or the speech form of Upper Assam. Brown's ambivalence on the issue is evident from a letter written to Peck on 24 October 1854, where he says,

> I challenge any person to point out an equal extent of territory in any part of the world where there is a greater uniformity of pronunciation than in the Assamese, excluding, of course the Dhekeri of Kamrup – also the Kacharis and other hill tribes, to whom the language is not Vernacular and cannot therefore be expected to speak in its purity.[54]

In a passage indicative of great inner turmoil, Danforth stated,

> My investigation on this subject have been from the first trying and
> disheartening. The conclusions at which I have arrived have been
> most painful. They are the greatest trial I have ever met within
> my missionary work, but there is no use in believing that black is
> white because we desire to have it so. I would have this question
> otherwise, but . . . facts are facts and he is a fool who denies it.[55]

It is hard to miss the advantages of standard languages for communication purposes in a region too polyglot in terms of speech. The pressures of
evangelization on the Baptist Mission were expected to ease with the introduction of a standard language. Brown's letter to a person named Peck on
22 August 1850 expressed his misgivings about the activities of Danforth.
Brown confessed quite candidly:

> Bro Danforth has been for sometime making investigation in
> the Dhekeri language. . . . He had found so great a discrepancy
> between Assamese and Dhekeri that he is beginning to talk of
> designing a separate language for Kamrup. This would inevitably
> produce split in the mission and is what I have always been afraid
> would be the result of establishing a mission at Gowahati.[56]

That despite a huge amount of debate the issue was not sorted within the
mission society is clear from the words of Rev. P.H. Moor many years later:

> 'There is no distinct Assamese nationality.' Under the heading
> 'Prevailing Languages' the Report on the Administration of the
> Province of Assam for 185–86 gives forty distinct languages and
> dialects, some of which are known to include other dialects not
> mentioned in the Report. This variety of language is a fair index
> of the mixed ethnic elements in the population of the plains of
> Assam.[57]

In the immensely fraught exercise of standardization of languages, numbers also played a key role in ensuring the inclusion of a speech form for the
purpose of standardization, as the following passage by Brown effectively
demonstrates:

> I have long been in doubt whether, in the present circumstances
> of the mission, and while there are so many inviting fields among

the Assamese, it is the duty of any brother to devote his life to the study of a language, and to the translation of the scriptures into it, which is spoken by a few thousand people. The Nagas, who speak the Namsang language, according to the nearest estimate brother Bronson can make, amount to no more than about 6300 and of these, a large portion can already speak the Assamese language with ease. Whether we ought make a separate language for so small a tribe seems to be a serious question.[58]

Thus, the missionary discourse on Assamese did not constitute a disinterested scholarly engagement with the vernacular. The linguistic agenda of the latter appears, on examination, to have been informed, even if partially, by an evangelist urge to advance their base in the region. The conclusion, therefore, becomes inevitable that although ideology constituted the overarching rubric for understanding the essentially intrusive process of standardization, as Bodhisattva Kar argues, the discursive exercises of the Baptist missionaries in Assam were much more complex than a simple and straightforward ordering of speech in consonance with familiar conventions of language structure and use, as Kar's analysis seems to suggest.

In short, the expediency of having a language that was intelligible to all and sundry was thus an imminent requirement for the mission, an aspect that allows us to make sense of the missionaries' future course of action that pushed Assamese to the forefront of a debate. Brown was convinced that Carey's Bible had not succeeded in making a mark because it contained words that were not familiar to the people. This was perhaps the germ of the idea that the language of the Assamese people, that is Assamese, was distinct from Bengali and possessed a distinct lexicon – an inevitable property to have for languages, by the philosophy of the age. Brown was nonetheless not fully convinced about the mutual unintelligibility of Bengali and Assamese and admitted on occasions that 'the two dialects are so similar that a person who understands one could in a very short time understand the other', since 'about two-thirds of the words in common among the Assamese are the same as in Bengali, with some variations in pronunciation' (29 October 1838).[59] Yet, in their initial public defence of the autonomy of Assamese, the missionaries pushed ahead with the issue of lexical autonomy of Assamese as the principal attribute that made Assamese different from Bengali. Assamese was pronounced to be unintelligible to the ordinary speakers of Bengali and vice versa because the former possessed a huge repertoire of words of a different stock altogether. To this aspect were added later attributes of 'beauty' and 'copiousness' – designed to establish unambiguously the status of Assamese as a language in its own right.

The issue of a distinct lexicon could not however be resolved in the long run, and examples of a shared lexicon began to be cited from time to time by the officials of the colonial state, making it difficult to sustain the argument. Very soon therefore, the missionary rhetoric on linguistic autonomy of Assamese shifted its focus from the lexical element to the grammatical structure of languages as the ultimate determinant of the identity of a language. It was asserted that the principal difference between two languages was determined by disparities in their respective grammatical structures. The points of distinction between Bengali and Assamese, according to the latest discourse, hinged on their disparate grammatical structures. The shifting position on the number of 'Bengali' words in Assamese as well as the recasting of lexicon as less intrinsic to the discourse of linguistic autonomy underscores an overwhelming urge to establish Assamese as an autonomous subject in the ongoing battle over identity. Subsequent correspondences from the mission headquarters engaged with the grammatical structure of the Assamese language. Miles Bronson would thus argue that Assamese was to Bengali what Latin and French were to an English school boy since the two languages differed in their inflections, modes, affixes, prefixes, spelling and pronunciation. Once again, the missionaries were backed by solid linguistic philosophy that allowed them to privilege inflexions in deciding the autonomy of a language. The study of linguistics in Europe was overwhelmingly informed by the structures of the classical European languages, namely Latin and Greek, both of which were highly inflecting languages.[60] What, however, the missionaries did in order to project inflectional asymmetries between Assamese and Bengali is a different story altogether and one that was by no means fair and above board.

V

Beleaguered identity

The rigorous engagement with grammar by the missionaries coincided with the decision to choose the speech forms of Upper Assam, known collectively as *Ujani*, as the basis for creating a print standard. The speech forms prevalent in Upper Assam had the advantage of royal approval, as Sibsagar, the seat of the erstwhile Ahom monarchy, was located in the region. Incidentally, the first tentative tract in Assamese had already been prepared by the missionaries as early as 1835 while at Sadiya on the basis of their interactions with the people of Sadiya who spoke a language that the missionaries had identified as Assamese although they dubbed it to be some sort of 'barbarous Bengali'. Presumably the new print Assamese contained traces of scripts that Brown and his colleagues had come across in the region. The real advantages of *Ujani*, however, arose from their distinctive inflexional structure, which was well suited to distance them from Bengali. Not only did these upper Assam variants of speech possess distinctive syntactical properties, but they were also at the same time lexically different from the speech forms of Kamrup or Lower Assam, which possessed greater affinities with some of the neighbouring dialects of Bengali. The choice of these speech forms was thus deigned to serve the purpose of a language that was at once familiar to the people, or so the missionaries thought, and discrete from Bengali.

That the exercise was inherently problematic became obvious very soon. It became clear that speech forms that went by the common denomination of *Ujani* did not command universal following all over Assam. It was soon apparent that there was a wide variation in speech practices pursued by different sections of the very people dubbed as Assamese. The missionary-sponsored print standard modelled on *Ujani* came under criticism from sections of Assam's emergent middle-class intelligentsia claiming to represent the interest of Lower Assam. The latter submitted a petition to the government on behalf of the local speech of Lower Assam, which they referred to as Kamrupi. The latter contended that the speech long spoken in Lower Assam possessed attributes not shared by the speech forms familiar in and around Sibsagar. The petitioners questioned what they regarded as a deliberate move to promote the dialect of *Ujani* Assam or Upper Assam as the standard vernacular at the cost of Kamrupi and drew attention to the conspicuous absence of Kamrupi words in the new print language. The petition was signed by 1,226 persons, consisting of a cross-section of Lower Assam's middle-class elite (pleaders, *mauzadars*, manduls, Gossains, etc.), and submitted to the lieutenant governor of Bengal. It called for an explanation to the designation of the dialect of Upper Assam as the print standard. The petitioners stated:

> The Upper Assam dialect we beg respectfully to submit is spoken only by a small portion of the population of Assam, viz., those who reside in the two districts of Dibrooghur and Sibsagur and is altogether unimportant and meagre, and its capabilities and chances to make itself the language of this entire Province are extremely limited, as its comparative poverty in respect to written and published works does conclusively shew. The languages in vogue in the rest of the Province, though presumptously stigmatized by the Upper Assam people as provincial (Dhekie), on the contrary does manifest a remarkable and marked superiority in

this respect over its rival, as the large majority of written works and all the most approved publications together with the sacred and religious writings of the people of Assam are found to have been composed in it, the conclusion evidently to be based on these reasons is that the claims and the prospects of the patois of Upper Assam to be made and adopted as the common language of the entire people of Assam are altogether unfounded and chimerical. . . . The Upper Assam patois, the claims of which to be made, the court language of the whole province have been advanced by certain agitators at Sibsagar is comprehended by the uneducated classes of Lower Assam with almost the same amount of difficulty as the Bengali. The people therefore instead of reaping advantages by the change will continue still under the old accustomed abuses such as being misunderstood by the Judge and of being cheated by the Amlah. . . . The presumption of the Upper Assam people to force their own patois to the acceptance to the people of whole Assam would bear an air of absurdity had their wishes not been seconded by the noise created by the Missionaries who, we are sorry to witness, have already made a sad havoc with our language by adopting an abused system of spelling by phonetic representation, and by publishing a highly objectionable dictionary and one or two flimsy grammatical primers.[61]

The petitioners concluded by requesting that the prayer of the Upper Assam people to introduce their dialect in the courts of the Province be rejected and

the Lower Assam languages which is enriched with literature, and which is spoken over the larger part of the country and by the majority of the people be allowed to be enforced in all the courts throughout Assam.[62]

Recent scholarship has also focussed on the fact that Kamrupi Prakrit or Kamrupi Apabhramsa differed vastly from the Sibsagariya group of dialects in terms of phonology, morphology and vocables and that the latter contains a large number of Perso-Arabic words presumably derived from the region's close association with Mughal India.[63] The antiquity of Kamrupia has also been confirmed, with scholars recognizing definite traces of this form of Prakrit in the pre-Ahom inscriptions of Kamrup, despite conscious attempts on the part of the authors to produce the documents in authentic Sanskrit. It has been pointed out that even after the twelfth century the Kamrupi Apabhramsa was continued to be used for composing popular songs and ballads, in Mantra puthis or religious incantations as well as in the popular aphorisms of Dak.[64] Linguist G.A. Grierson, extensively quoted by the supporters of the one language theory, actually also considered Kamrupi as sufficiently distinct to merit attention. He mentioned this fact in his magnum opus *Linguistic Survey of India*. Grierson observed:

> The standard dialect of Assamese is that form of speech which is prevalent in and about Sibsagar. Over the upper part of the Assam Valley the language is everywhere the same. As we go west, we find a distinct dialect, which I call Western Assamese, spoken by the people of Kamrup and Eastern Goalpara.[65]

It was pointed out at the time that disparities between *Ujani* and the *Namoni* speech forms were induced by the deliberate politico-cultural distancing of the two divisions by successive *swargadeos* and their functionaries. The Kamrupis and the Durrangis – inhabitants of Lower Assam, comprising the British districts of Kamrup and Durrang, were not ordinarily allowed to enter the Ahom capital.[66] It seems that this restriction was rigidly enforced in Guwahati, which was the headquarters of the viceroy, or the Barphukan, with no Kamrupi being allowed to spend the night inside Guwahati. The gates were closed at dusk by which time all Kamrupis were required to evacuate the place and halt somewhere outside the enclosures if they wanted to come to the town the next day. Grierson also noted the condescending attitude nurtured by the people of Upper Assam towards the people of Western Assam and their culture. Grierson wrote:

> The Assamese spoken in the districts of Kamrup and Goalpara, which are the most western on the northern side of the Brahmaputra valley, is not exactly the same as the standard language of Upper and Central Assam, being influenced by the Bengali spoken immediately to the west, in west Goalpara and the Bengal districts of Rangpur. This form of Assamese is sometimes called dhekeri or, which is, however, considered as a term of opprobrium, having been first used when the portion of Assam now known as Kamrup and Goalpara districts was conquered by the Ahoms. The Ahom Raja gave the name of Sarkar Dhekeri or Dhekuri to this tract. According to Rai Gunabhiram Barua's Buranji, this name was given to this portion of Assam by the Ahoms to denote that it had been conquered, and consequently 'the people hated the name'.[67]

VI

The laboratory of Assamese

In their efforts to draw the boundaries of the Assamese language, the missionaries did not merely select a suitable speech form for standardization. They also handpicked a suitable orthography or mode of spelling that would serve their purpose of enhancing the visual distance of the print standard from words spelled in Bengali. It was decided almost unilaterally that the appropriate orthography for the print language should be a phonemic one, that is determined by the sound of the words rather than their root. Once again, the suitable orthography was hand-picked by Brown, who overlooked other styles of orthographic enumeration that were being used at the time, even after admitting that there were quite a few in circulation. Bronson admitted in his introduction to his dictionary that out of multiple orthographic styles, he had chosen the one followed by Jaduram Deka Barua, a 'learned Assamese Pundit' whose orthography 'much better corresponds with the actual pronunciation of the people than any other system met with'.[68] In his *Grammatical Notices of the Assamese Language*, published by the Baptist Mission Press at Sibsagar in 1848, Nathan Brown also confessed that there were in use a wide variety of styles of orthography in Assam. He confessed quite candidly that 'although as a spoken language, the Assamese has been fixed in its present form for centuries, it appears never to have been written on any settled and uniform principles of orthography'.[69]

Brown's choice of a phonemic orthography for print Assamese did not take into consideration the large number of Sanskrit *tatsama* and *tadbhava* words in the vocabulary of the spoken forms that went generically by the name of *Bhaxa*. This is curious, for in his introduction to his grammar, Brown had informed the readers that the Assamese language owed the greater portion of its vocabulary to Sanskrit:

> The Bengali alone excepted, it probably contains a greater proportion of Sanskrit derivatives than any other Indian tongue . . . It is remarkable that the Ahoms, who overspread and conquered the country and who now constitute a large portion of the population, should have been able to produce no alteration in the language of the original inhabitants; scarcely a single term in present use being traceable to the ancient Ahom.[70]

Brown was thus completely aware of what he was doing. It was a common-enough linguistic practice to spell words derived from Sanskrit according to their original spelling in the parent language. By adhering to this practice, however, the missionaries ran the risk of narrowing down the difference between Assamese and Bengali since the latter too contained a large number of words that were either Sanskrit or derivatives of Sanskrit. This was because other provincial languages in use in India also shared this property having originated as Apabhramsa of Sanskrit. The convention of following a Sanskritic orthography while spelling such words thus makes for a great deal of similarity among languages in India in general. One can presume that in the emotionally charged environment of nineteenth-century Assam, it was not deemed expedient to permit a great deal of resemblance between Assamese and its arch rival – Bengali. A phonemic orthography was therefore deemed more appropriate than a semantic one. This explains Miles Bronson's smug remark that out of the 14,000 words collected, there would be many that 'no Bengali scholar will understand'. Incomprehensibility was the need of the hour and had to be ensured at all cost if autonomy was to be affirmed.

The actual process of standardization, however, involved multiple acts of selection. One of the most important sources of inspiration for the missionaries was provided by Western linguistic canons. The best illustration of this is afforded by the manner in which Brown determined the 'appropriate' number of letters to have in the Assamese alphabet. Having examined the dictionary compiled by Jadunath Deka Barua, Brown concluded that there were some letters that did not possess a corresponding sound – a property deemed integral to European ideas of linguistics. These letters were therefore deemed 'surplus' as they seemed to serve no purpose whatsoever, and to axe these letters seemed to be the most judicious step to take.[71] Their very presence was deemed accountable for introducing a great variety in the modes of spelling. It was desirable, therefore, that these letters be removed altogether from the alphabet so that every letter could have a corresponding sound. Brown observed:

> The perfection of a written language evidently consists in its corresponding as far as possible, with the language actually spoken. In order for this, the following rule is indispensable, viz. That every sound should have its own appropriate character; and that every letter should express a single invariable sound. There will then be neither more nor fewer letters than the vocal sounds . . . . The Sanskrit alphabet, a modification of which is used for writing Assamese, contains fifty letters, while the number of sounds in Assamese is only thirty-six. The use of an alphabet containing so many redundant letters, has naturally led to the great variety

of spelling which we now find in native writers; the same sound being expressed by two, and sometimes by three and four different letters; while, not unfrequently, the same letter has been employed to express different sounds.

Brown proceeded to give a graphic description of the manner in which the task of getting rid of the 'useless' letters was accomplished:

In commencing the printing of books in this language, the members of the Assam Mission considered it important to establish a correct and uniform system of orthography. Three modes of procedure suggested themselves, viz.

To spell all words derived from the Sanskrit, and others as far as practicable, in accordance with the orthography of that language;

To adopt as a standard the orthography of some native writer, or approved Assamese manuscript; or

To select from different works those forms which were most agreeable to general usage, and which best correspond to the actual pronunciation.

The first method, it was found, would, if strictly followed, produce such distortions of the language as to render it nearly unintelligible. To bring back the spoken language to a correspondence with the original orthography was an evident impossibility; it was therefore necessary to make the orthography correspond with the pronunciation. This had been partially done in the native writings; to select a standard, however, was difficult; manuscripts not only differing from each other, but possessing no consistency or uniformity within themselves. The work which made the nearest approach to a regular system, was a manuscript Bengali Dictionary, with Assamese definitions, prepared by Joduram Deka Borua, a learned Assamese Pundit. The orthography of this work was found to correspond much better with the actual pronunciation than any other that had been met with; the greater portion of the redundant letters were discarded; while the general forms of words agreed, for the most part, with those found in the Buronjis.[72]

Brown was exultant about the outcome of his endeavour:

The alphabet being thus far simplified, it was discovered that only two redundant letters still remained; G to express the united sound of r and i; and k, used to represent the sound of S j. To these therefore the knife was applied without hesitation, and the written character brought to as exact a correspondence with the pronunciation, as the nature of the language will admit; every radically different sound having one and only one distinct symbol as its representative. In accomplishing this desirable end, not a single new character has been introduced; so that the language, as now printed, is read at once, and with entire ease, by natives who had previously been acquainted only with their own manuscripts.[73]

Despite such outright and systematic meddling to remove local styles of writing and induce homogeneity to a domain that had not known the same, the missionaries did not deem it incongruous to dub the print standard the authentic and legitimate language of the Assamese people – one that had been culled straight 'from the lips of the people'.[74]

Notes

1 Extracts from the letter written by Captain F. Jenkins to Mr Trevelyan of the Civil Service, Calcutta, *Baptist Missionary Magazine*, Vol. 16, 1836, p. 19.

2 Ibid.

3 Ibid., p. 20.

4 See Milton Sangma, *History of American Baptist Mission in N.E. India*, New Delhi: Mittal, 1987, for a history of the Baptist societies and their early interactions with William Carey, the Serampore Baptist missionary.

5 See A.K. Gurney, *History of the Sibsagar Field*, in The Assam Mission of the American Baptist Missionary Union Minutes, Resolutions and Historical Papers of the Second Triennial Conference held in Guwahati, 21–30 December 1889, pp. 20–30.

6 Ibid., p. 21.

7 Rev. Nathan Brown, 'Extracts from the Letters of Mr Brown', *Baptist Missionary Magazine*, Vol. 15, 1835, p. 5.

8 Rev. Nathan Brown, 'Letter of Nathan Brown', *Baptist Missionary Magazine*, Vol. 17, 1837, p. 173.

9 From Colonel H. Hopkinson, Agent to the Governor General, North East Frontier and Commissioner of Assam, to The Officiating Secretary to the Government of Bengal, General Department, Education Branch, Letter no. 13, 19 February 1873, WBSA.

10 William Robinson, *A Descriptive Account of Assam*, Calcutta: Ostell and Lepage, 1841, p. 253.

11 Ibid.

12 From William Robinson, Inspector of Schools, North East Bengal and Assam, to the Director of Public Instruction, Letter no. 288, Government of Bengal, General (Education), February 1859, nos. 23–24.

13 William Robinson, *Introduction to the Grammar of the Assamese Language*, Calcutta: Serampore Press, 1839.

14 For a study of how the fortunes of a script could depend on official patronage, see Prachi Deshpande, 'Scripting the Cultural History of Language: Modi in the Colonial Archive', in Partha Chatterjee, Tapati Guha-Thakurta and Bodhisattva Kar (eds), *New Cultural Histories of India*, New Delhi: Oxford University Press, 2014; see also Richard Burghart, 'A Quarrel in the Language Family: Agency and Representations of Speech in Mithila', *Modern Asian Studies*, Vol. 27, No. 4, 1993, pp. 761–804, and Christopher King, *One Language, Two Scripts: The Hindi Movement in Nineteenth Century North India*, Bombay: Oxford University Press, 1994.

15 Ibid., p. 152.

16 H.K. Barpujari, *The American Missionaries and North-East India (1836–1900)*, Guwahati: Spectrum Publishers, 1986.

17 Ibid., pp. 130–131.

18 From the Secretary to the Government of Bengal to the CoA, Letter no. 258t, GoB, General (Misc.), no. 64, September 1865, WBSA.

19 In one of his official notes, he made the following remark that is highly reminiscent of the Baptist missionary rhetoric, 'To me it appears certain that a native villager would not in a court of justice understand one word of his case, if the proceedings were recorded in Bengalee; neither would a pure native of Bengal be able to understand the same if read out to him in Assamese, although an educated Bengali or Assamese might probably be able to make out the purport of the written proceedings if he had leisure to study them', From Major J.C. Haughton, Officiating Commissioner of Assam (CoA), to the Secretary to the Government of Bengal, Letter no. 83c, GoB, General (Misc.), November 1862, no. 63, WBSA.

20 From Major J.C. Haughton, Officiating Commissioner of Assam (CoA), to the Secretary to the Government of Bengal, Letter no. 83c, GoB, General (Misc.), November 1862, no. 63, WBSA.

21 See Madhumita Sengupta, 'War of Words: Language and Policies in Nineteenth-Century Assam', *Indian Historical Review*, Vol. 39, No. 2, 2012, pp. 293–315.

22 Assam Commissioner's File, No. 471, Letter no. 1824, January 1873, p. 37, ASA.

23 Ibid., Letter no. 115, April 1873, p. 61.

24 From Col. Hopkinson, Agent to the Governor General (AGG), North East Frontier and CoA to the Secretary, to the Government of Bengal, GoB, General (Education), February 1872, no. 7, WBSA.

25 Ibid., Letter no. 239, June 1872, p. 6.

26 Letter from Col. H. Hopkinson, AGG and CoA to the Secretary to the Government of Bengal, GoB, General (Education), January 1872, no. 7, WBSA.

27 Ibid., p. 60.

28 John M'Cosh, *Topography of Assam*, Calcutta: Bengal Military Orphan Press, 1837, and Robinson, *Grammar of the Assamese Language*, for a glimpse into the colonial characterization of the Assamese people.

29 Assam Commissioner's Office, File 471, letter dated November 1872, ASA.
30 Ibid., Letter no. 339, June 1872, p. 18.
31 See Nagen Saikia, *Background of Modern Assamese Literature*, New Delhi: Omsons, 1988, p. 201.
32 Ibid., p. 203.
33 Assam Commissioner's File (General), No. 161G, 1877, ASA.
34 Bodhisattva Kar, ' "Tongue Has No Bone": Fixing the Assamese Language, c. 1800–c. 1930', *Studies in History*, Vol. 24, No. 1, 2008, p. 48.
35 From Major W.S. Clarke, Deputy Commissioner, Luckimpore, to the Personal Assistant to the CoA, Assam Commissioner's File 471, letter no. 268C, ASA.
36 Ibid.; see in this connection Alok Rai, *Hindi Nationalism*, New Delhi: Orient Longman, 2000, and Vasudha Dalmia, 'The Locations of Hindi', *Economic and Political Weekly*, Vol. 38, No. 14, 5–11 April 2003, pp. 1377–1384. These authors argue that modern print Hindi came into existence in the course of the nineteenth century. But even in mid-nineteenth-century, it was still in flux and there was little awareness of its existence as the common spoken and written language of the Hindus alone. The awareness of its Hinduness was imposed from above initially by colonial intervention and subsequently by the Hindu elite themselves when they took up the cause of Hindu-Hindi. See also Francesca Orsini, *The Hindi Public Sphere Language and Literature in the Age of Nationalism 1920–1940*, New Delhi: Oxford University Press, 2009.
37 Ibid.
38 Ibid., Letter No. G-306/T, September 1873, p. 81.
39 Ibid.
40 Ibid., p. 21.
41 Nathan Brown, 'Extracts of a Letter from Mr. Cutter', *Baptist Missionary Magazine*, Vol. 18, 1838, p. 277.
42 Rev. P.H. Moore, 'General View of Assam', in *The Assam Mission of the American Baptist Missionary Union Minutes, Resolutions and Historical Papers of the Second Triennial Conference Held in Gauhati, December 21–30, 1889*, p. 18.
43 'Journal of Mr. Brown', *Baptist Missionary Magazine*, Vol. 18, 1838, p. 119.
44 'Extracts from the Letters of Mr Brown', *Baptist Missionary Magazine*, Vol. 15, 1835, p. 5.
45 Barpujari, *The American Missionaries*, p. 151.
46 Ibid., pp. 138–139.
47 'Journal of Mr Brown', *Baptist Missionary Magazine*, Vol. 17, 1837, p. 119.
48 In this connection, see Jayeeta Sharma, 'Missionaries and Print Culture in Nineteenth-Century Assam', in Robert Eric Frykenberg (ed.), *Christians and Missionaries in India Cross-Cultural Communication since 1500*, Grand Rapids, MI: William B. Eerdmans Publishing Co., 2003.
49 'Extracts from Letters of Mr Brown', *Baptist Missionary Magazine*, Vol. 15, 1835, p. 7.
50 Barpujari, *The American Missionaries*, p. 125.
51 Ibid., p. 126.
52 Ibid., pp. 127–128.

53 See Rev. E.W. Clark, 'Labours of Early Baptist Missionaries in Assam', in Triennial Reports – 1890–92 published in the *Baptist Missionary Magazine*, Vol. LXXI, July 1891, Vol. 7, p. 61.

54 Barpujari, *The American Missionaries*, p. 129.

55 Ibid., p. 128.

56 Ibid., p. 127.

57 Rev. P.H. Moore, 'General View of Assam', p. 5.

58 *Missionary Magazine*, 1842, Vol. 22, p. 62, cited in Victor Hugo Sword, *Baptists in Assam: A Century of Missionary Service, 1836–1936*, Chicago, IL: Conference Press, 1935, pp. 64–65.

59 Ibid.

60 See John Lyons, *Language and Linguistics: An Introduction*, Cambridge, UK: Cambridge University Press, 1981.

61 By the end of the nineteenth century a section of Lower Assam's inteligentsia consisting of the likes of Shyamal Choudhury, Amrita Bhusan Adhikary and Kaliram Medhi had begun to forcefully assert the distinctiveness and antiquity of the Kamrupi dialect. Amrita Bhusan Adhikary claimed that the print vernacular must correspond to the language of the Namghosa of Sankardeb written purportedly in Kamrupi. Not satisfied with this, he further claimed that all eminent religious leaders and poets of pre-British Assam like Sankardeva, Madhavdeva, Mahendra Kandali, Ananta Kandali and Ram Saraswati had actually composed their works in the Kamrupi language. In 1910 the Tejpur Bandhav Samiti brought out a periodical called the *Assam Bandhav* (1910–17) to voice the growing discontent with the nature of language standardization carried out by the Baptist missionaries. The *Assam Bandhav* engaged in a series of debates with the contributors of *Banhi*, another contemporary periodical that advocated the uniformity of the Assamese language. Writers associated with the former included men like Taranath Chakravarty (editor), Pratap Chandra Goswami, Kaliram Medhi and Ambikagiri Roy Choudhuri. To emphasize the richness of the Kamrupi vocabulary, Kaliram Medhi chose to use many Kamrupi words in his essays, like 'Bhem' and 'Somajor Kramabikax', published in the *Assam Bandhav*. Later Pandit Padmanath Bhattacharya suggested in his 'Kamrupi Sasanavali' that the archaic forms of Indrapala's copper plates of the eleventh century AD, particularly the Guakuchi grant, was none other than a form of the then practised Kamrupi Apabhramsa unconsciously inserted therein by the local engravers.

62 Ibid.

63 U. Goswami, *A Study on Kamrupi: A Dialect of Assamese*, Guwahati: DHAS, 1990.

64 Ibid.

65 George Grierson, *Linguistic Survey of India*, Vol. 1, part 1, 1903–1928, p. 394. Best known as the author of the 11-volume *Linguistic Survey of India*, George Grierson was a member of the Indian Civil Service and served in Bengal (including present-day Bihar, Assam and Orissa) in various administrative capacities for nearly 15 years.

66 S.K. Bhuyan, *Anglo-Assamese Relations*, Guwahati: Lawyer's Book Stall, 1974, p. 271.

67 Ibid.; Grierson, *Linguistic Survey of India*, p. 414.

68 Nathan Brown, Introduction, *Grammatical Notices of the Assamese Language*, Sibsagar: American Baptist Mission Press, 1848.
69 Ibid.
70 Ibid.
71 See Kar, 'Tongue Has No Bones', for a detailed discussion of the ideological implications of the process of standardization undertaken for creating the alphabet.
72 Ibid., pp. IX–X.
73 Ibid., p. X.
74 Miles Bronson, *A Dictionary in Assamese and English*, Sibsagar: American Baptist Mission Press, 1867.

3

THE BURDEN OF PROGRESS

If Christian missions were crucial to Jenkins's scheme of administration, so was education of the masses. It was perhaps the only means that could allow the colonial state to effectively transfer its message to the latter. This in turn would be possible only if such an education could be imparted in the vernacular languages. Hence, at a time when Governor General Sir William Bentinck and his cabinet colleagues had decided that government funds should be used for educating the natives through the medium of the English language, in Assam Jenkins and his colleagues chose to reach out to the people through the official vernacular, that is Bengali. Veena Naregal has drawn attention to the fact that a vernacular education need not necessarily have been innocuous or absolutely well intended, although it certainly held out promises of a more universalized education. She shows how 'translation' of English tracts into the vernaculars could be an effective means of inferiorizing the colonized.[1] Naregal argues that no matter how colonial education was garbed, it was bound to act as an instrument of colonial ideological domination.[2] Other scholars like Gauri Vishwanathan have illustrated how indoctrination was enabled through a suitably designed curriculum of English literature in English-medium institutions in colonial India.[3] In Assam, to all intents and purposes, the colonial state appeared to take an active interest in the project of enlightenment through the dissemination of education among the masses through the medium of the vernacular. What, however, such education concealed was the ulterior motive to impart nothing beyond a basic minimum education to the masses so that the latter's intellectual inhibitions, perceived to be too many for the good of imperialist designs, could be overcome. This chapter delineates the somewhat distinct trajectory of colonial educational policies in Assam in the nineteenth century – discrete in nature from that followed in Bengal and elsewhere. Characterized by an emphasis on school-level education and an exclusion of collegiate and higher studies till at least the turn of the nineteenth century as well by an overt preference for the vernacular medium for imparting instruction, the state's rhetoric of progress masked its economic agenda for the region. This section argues that the educational project of the state was perhaps uniquely designed to cater to the revenue needs of a labour-deficit economy although it is evident that there was also in place a reluctance to undertake a more proactive policy presumably for deeper ideological and financial reasons. Throughout the nineteenth century, the state argued against the setting up of a college and advised Assamese students to travel to Calcutta for receiving higher education. Great care was, however, taken to hide the actual reasons behind this denial. The administration sought to justify its palpable disregard for higher education with reference to the backwardness of the Assamese people, and the imminent need for exposing the latter to the intellectual environment of colonial Bengal. The patronizing tone of official rhetoric and its stated modernistic stance on the issue of education was meant to and did convince people for some time about the honest intentions of the colonial state, the outcome being to inhibit the growth of a genuine critique, except for a brief spell, of the educational policy from within the province's emergent middle-class intelligentsia. The state's rhetoric of progress proved deceptive and served to divert the attention of the provincial elite by keeping the latter preoccupied with a preponderantly culturalist agenda, which served to delay the emergence of a radical anti-colonial consciousness among the provincial literati.

I

The rhetoric of disability

The colonial state right from its inception appeared concerned about the need for promoting education among the natives. Despite his brief tenure, David Scott put across a scheme for setting up village-level schools.[4] Accordingly, in 1826, 11 schools were set up in places like Guwahati, Nilachal, Desh Durrang, Hajo, Nowgong and Bishwanath. The tone and tenor of the official education policy in Assam were, however, set when in 1834, Francis Jenkins assumed office as the officer in charge of the Assam Division of Bengal province. Like many other aspects of Assam administration, Jenkins also laid the foundation of the modern system of education in Assam. Any standard history of colonial educational policy in Assam tends to begin with the following statement of Jenkins:

> On completion of our revenue settlements few will want the secured means of comfortable subsistence and but few will possess more.

These few in their present uneducated state do not suffice to carry on the duties of our courts the offices in which are nearly all filled by natives of Sylhet and Rungpore so that the old families of Assam are still losing influence in their own native province from being debarred those situations which lead to poorer or decent mainte-nance. This state of things appears to me pregnant with evil and I know no other method by which it could be remedied than by the government taking some active measures to provide instruction for the Assamese.[5]

What remains relatively underplayed in this passage that is read as an illus-tration of Jenkins's paternalist rule is the sheer dismissive tone with which the officer concerned regarded the state of education in the province. Jen-kins was more explicit in a subsequent passage:

To leave this matter (education) to the people would be to commit a duty incumbent in my opinion upon us to those who are mostly incapable of judging themselves and who from universal poverty caused perhaps greatly by our mismanagement are unable from want of means and intelligence to accomplish any progress that would satisfy us. . . . To leave the natives alone would approach nearly to parental neglect of children.[6]

Shortly into his tenure, Jenkins had formed a poor opinion about the state of education in Assam. He would often remark that education had not progressed in the province, despite sufficient encouragement given by the erstwhile monarchs. In his words, 'No country could previously boast of more splendid endowments – one quarter nearly of the cultivated land having been bestowed by the Rajahs on Brahmins, Dewalies, Shhusters and other religious sects and foundations.'[7] Jenkins stated that his poor opinion about the state of education in the province had been formed after due consultations with other officers. Jenkins, therefore, issued an official statement where he expressed his utter lack of faith in the future of educa-tion in the province, unless urgent measures were initiated by the state to redeem the situation:

All the officers whose reports are now forwarded have agreed upon the very low state of education in this province and that it is hopeless to expect any present improvement except the Govern-ment will (be) pleased to allow of the appropriation of lands and money for the maintenance of the school masters.[8]

Official accounts actually abounded with references to the backward state of education in the region. Mathie, deputy commissioner of Kamrup, referred to the extreme backwardness of the people in reading, writing and arithmetic, adding that it was the backwardness of the Assamese that had led the government to employ Bengalis and other foreigners to various government posts. Matthie's letter written to Jenkins in 1839 did echo the apprehensions flagged by Jenkins about the future prospects of education in the province if the Assamese people were left to sort the affairs by themselves. Matthie observed, 'It is however, necessary for me to observe from my acquaintance with the Assamese, that it is absolutely requisite that some indeed constant encouragement and even fostering attention should be shown by the European local authorities' to the educational establishments of the Assamese if they were to flourish.[9] He added in a deeply sceptical note, 'Otherwise I fear when the novelty wears off if left to themselves unnoticed at least until a year or two hence they will not be resorted to as their benefits although universally acknowledged by the Assamese have not yet from their infancy been properly felt.'[10] The tone of Matthie's letter and of Jenkins's declaration were both equally ominous, as these seemed to suggest that there was something intrinsic about the province's backwardness. The statement contained a subtle hint that the Assamese were somehow unable to comprehend matters intellectual – that they were, to be more precise, 'incapable of judging themselves'.[11] This note was significant as it set the tone for future policies in the domain of education in the region.[12]

Contrary to Jenkins's assertions, education in Assam in the pre-colonial period was not in any way different from that which could be found elsewhere in the subcontinent. *Tols* and *Madrasas* as also the Vaishnavite *sattras* constituted the chief institutions where knowledge of arithmetic, astronomy and Sanskrit/Persian were imparted to young boys. Such *tols* and cultures of education survived into the colonial period and have been mentioned by many nineteenth-century authors in their autobiographies. The rhetoric of 'want' spun by Jenkins and his officers, however, paved the way for the beginning of modern education in the region. What followed was a spate of proposals from officials to set up village- and division-level schools in the province. In 1837, Lieutenant Matthie came up with a scheme to start some village-level schools in zilla Kamrup of which he was the collector.[13] Lieutenant. Vetch, officiating magistrate of Durrang, also sought sanctions to set up schools in Chatgury, Durrang and Charduar. Jenkins himself presented a comprehensive scheme for state-sponsored education throughout his jurisdiction. Accordingly, in the next few years, the state took the initiative to set up several schools in the Brahmaputra valley. Jenkins proposed that schools should be set up at Gowalparrah, Goalputtee, Durrang,

Nowgong and Bishenath, that is stations 'where there was an European officer, who would attend to its welfare'.[14] Interestingly, official endeavours of the government of Assam to promote school-level education, whatever its limitations, constituted a significant departure from the colonial apathy for universal education in the rest of the country. The official disdain for mass education was rather old and had led everywhere in the country to the promulgation of a policy better known as that of 'downward filtration'. Such an approach implied that the state would take direct responsibility for and establish only a few schools, where Western education through the medium of the English language would be imparted to a limited number of people who would thereby fulfil Macaulay's description of the ideal subject, being 'brown in colour and white in taste'. The idea was that only those sections, already possessing a literate tradition, should be imparted some basic knowledge of Western literature and histories – elements that would enable them to communicate with and serve the colonial state in various capacities. The principal focus of the educational policy of the British Indian government in the nineteenth century was on higher education.[15] In fact, till the 1840s, the government failed to take any active interest in school education, which remained the sole concern of the Christian missionaries and of the affluent sections among the Indians.[16] It was only in the early twentieth century when Curzon was the viceroy that steps were taken to promote lower-level education for the masses.[17] It may be noted that schemes for promoting primary education among the masses through schools in the regional languages at the village and district levels had been proposed elsewhere, in the west by officers like Elphinstone, Munro and Adam, only to be shelved by a government unwilling to confront the financial implications of the task.[18] It was temporarily implemented in Maharashtra as Naregal shows only to be discarded later in favour of a higher dependence on English as the medium of instruction. It may be noted in this connection that the pan-Indian policy to provide official assistance to a few institutions in English and to the goal of education for a few was in general inspired by the Wood's Despatch of 1854.[19]

Jenkins's original proposal for setting up village-level schools did not meet with approval as a scheme of village schools was found to be too expensive to undertake, but the state instead sanctioned a number of middle-level schools in the vernacular in contradistinction to its avowed policy of 'downward filtration' and English education. It is interesting that although apparently solicitous of providing educational opportunities to many, Jenkins did not seem too keen to provide higher education to all and sundry. In this respect, his ideas were far too elitist for he 'proposed to commence the great work of civilization by giving instruction to a few selected Assamese youths of rank in Calcutta'.[20] However, such was the level of prejudice against the local people that even such a limited offer roused apprehensions in official circles and the Report on the General Committee of Public Instruction in Bengal for 1838–39 apprehended that 'the dissipated habits they would probably acquire in a large capital, would most probably entirely defeat the object in view'.[21]

By 1856, government vernacular schools were set up at the headquarters of each of the five districts of Assam Proper. According to one report, in 1839 alone, there were 20 'Purgunnuh Native Schools' in addition to the Guwahati Government School in Kamrup, where 795 youths received education in the vernacular, that is Bengali.[22] The report states that Matthie's scheme had been sanctioned 'to extend the benefits of vernacular education to the Assamese residing at a distance from the Sudder Station Government seminaries'.[23] In the Brahmaputra valley, these were supplemented by schools in the villages, which had nearly 4,000 pupils. Further, one English and seven Anglo-vernacular schools were set up at Guwahati and Sylhet, respectively. Three Anglo-vernacular schools were set up in Cachar and one in Goalpara. Primary education was largely left to private initiatives although some primary schools were also set up or funded by the government.[24] A normal school for training teachers was also set up in the valley at state initiative. The state also at the same time extended its aid to many other vernacular schools belonging to the middle and higher levels. The educational statistics for the districts of Kamrup, Durrang and Nowgong during 1856–60 illustrate the extent of state initiatives in the setting up of schools. In Nowgong the number of government-vernacular schools was 12 in 1856–57, and 8 in 1860–66. The figures for Kamrup during this period were 26 and 13, respectively, while those for Durrang were 9 and 6, respectively.[25] Education statistics of the period between 1892–93 and 1896–97 indicate a rise of about 28.8 per cent in public institutions.[26] The educational efforts of the state were presumably substantial for they prompted Reverend Whiting, the secretary of the American Baptist Mission in Assam, to remark that 'the Government appeared so much engaged in the matter (education) as to do away with the necessity of the Mission doing anything of that kind'.[27] Interestingly enough, the increase in the number of primary schools under government management was far more impressive than the increase in secondary institutions. While in the latter category there was an increase of 25 schools, during the same period there was an increase of 570 in the number of primary schools for boys while the girls' primary schools showed an increase of 111.[28] In 1891–92 the numbers for government secondary schools, primary schools, special schools and private institutions were 112, 2,365, 25 and 298, respectively.[29] In the same year, the percentage of pupils at different stages of instruction such as high stage, middle stage, upper primary stage, lower primary stage (reading printed books) and lower primary stage (not reading printed books) were 1.3, 2.8, 4.5, 76.4 and 15, respectively.[30] Between 1891–92 and 1896–97, there was very little change in these figures.

There was also an interesting departure with regard to the medium of instruction. Unlike elsewhere in the country, where by the 1850s the state had begun to show a distinct preference for English education, in Assam, the medium of education in the government schools of the lower and middle order (i.e. middle secondary schools) was Bengali, and English was merely taught as a subject. In Durrang in 1856–57, there was no government English school or aided English school, whereas the numbers of government vernacular schools and aided vernacular schools were 9 and 11, respectively. The trend was similar for 1860–61. In Kamrup, there was no government English school or aided English school in 1856–57 although there were 26 government vernacular schools. The trends were similar for 1860–61. English was, however, preferred at a higher level and was the medium of instruction in the first four classes of the high schools. In 1896–97, in public institutions, nearly only 7.9 per cent of the pupils learnt English and 3.7 per cent learnt the classical languages, while an overwhelming 97.4 per cent learnt the vernacular, whether Bengali or Assamese. The corresponding figures in private institutions in the same year were very close, being 341 for English and 406 for the vernaculars, while an overwhelming 6,426 learnt the classical languages.[31]

II

Manufacturing logic and desiring control

A letter written by the deputy commissioner of Luckhimpore in 1862 to William Robinson, inspector of schools, remarked that a vernacular education was best suited to a province like Assam, which was in a 'backward state'.[32] There are numerous indications in the colonial archives, of a mindset that regarded the Assamese as not quite ready for receiving education in anything other than the mother tongue.[33] This comes through loud and clear from overt references to the intellectual abilities of the people as much as from the highly utilitarian agenda that officials envisaged for education in the province. Matthie's early proposal for setting up Mofussil schools had envisaged a rather limited objective for education in the province, that of enabling the youth to 'qualify(ing) themselves generally for conducting the duties of village fiscal officers, and the business which is now in

very many instances for want of efficient Assamese, performed by foreigners from Bengal and other parts of India'.[34] The aims envisaged were rather
utilitarian in nature and did not indicate any intellectual possibilities in
terms of outcome. Jenkins himself nurtured very strong views about the
mental state of the people of Assam, for he wrote:

> These Assamese are intelligent and are most ready to be led by us,
> their European rulers in everything that does not directly infringe
> upon their superstitions to which they are wedded with all the bigotry
> to be expected of a race in a state little removed above barbarism.[35]

As late as 1862, we find William Robinson, inspector of schools, trying to
justify the principle of utility with regard to education in the province. He
observed:

> The desire for instruction in English among Assamese lads arises
> therefore solely from the prospects it affords of obtaining the
> more lucrative appointments open to them under govt . . . among
> a people whom we seek to raise from the lowest depths of igno-
> rance to an appreciation of the blessings of intellectual enlighten-
> ment, the principle of utility must, I presume be allowed to have
> its due weight as a native power.[36]

The choice of the vernacular instead of English for imparting education
in schools made it difficult for the British to procure books which had to
be brought all the way from Calcutta, given the fact that Bengali was the
official vernacular of the province. The approved list of textbooks in both
English and Bengali used in all recognized schools in Assam province were
usually those that were prepared by the Text-Book Committee, Bengal,
Calcutta, and sanctioned for use in Bengal schools by the Director of Public Instruction, Bengal. However, in the case of Bengali books in particular,
the standing instruction was that 'no Bengali books that are not approved
of by the Calcutta Text-Book Committee are to be used in Assam Schools,
with the exception of some elementary books on land measurement in the
Surma valley'.[37] It would have been far easier perhaps to introduce books
that could be locally produced. We hear Lieutenant Matthie lamenting
about the difficulties faced in procuring good books from Calcutta. The
decision to stick to Bengali despite such practical encumbrances, not to
speak of the expenses of transporting books from Calcutta, speaks volumes
for the prejudices nurtured by the ruling class about the local population.
The prejudices of the officers were shared by other agents of colonialism.

The Baptist missionary, Rev. Danforth, who had demanded a scientific education for the people of Assam so that the latter could look beyond the purview of government service, the scope for which was in any case narrow, found it necessary to preface his demand with the caveat that the education should be in the vernacular for 'to an ignorant, stupid and bigoted people like the Assamese, abstract studies are often difficult and unattractive even when communicated in the most common language' and hence 'how much more so must it be when veiled in a foreign tongue'.[38]

Yet the state's preference for a vernacular education for the province's population did not merely stem from an essential scepticism about the intellectual abilities of the people. There are indications that there were larger motives at work, which inspired the state to invest in nothing more than a highly limited and utilitarian education that would aspire for nothing more than acquainting the people with basic arithmetic and reading and writing skills that would equip them for lower-level jobs in government offices and on the plantations. The enthusiasm for vernacular education was however not reciprocated by the people, if field reports from the districts are anything to go by. On the contrary, these mention the tremendous enthusiasm for education in general and English education in particular among the people. One letter written by the deputy commissioner of Lukhimpore observed, 'All classes in the District are most anxious for the establishment of an English school.'[39] Urging the government to set up an English school in Dibrugarh, the officer concerned drew attention to the fast-changing socio-economic conditions of the province which made this imminent:

Hitherto the study of the vernacular has been the sole aim of the schools in this district and so long as the country was in a backward state it was as much as it was necessary.

From a remote unknown place the District of Luckhimpore is fast becoming a most important Division and as civilization advances improvement as regards Education is imperative.

Apart from the growing commercial prosperity of the administration, new laws and the gradual introduction of English in the courts render it essential that the youths educated in the schools should have the means of attaining greater proficiency in ordinary studies and above all that they should have the opportunity of acquiring English, a knowledge of which will henceforth be absolutely necessary to fit them for public employ.[40]

Reports sent by district officers were backed by several petitions presented in the 1860s by various sections of the people urging the government to set up English-medium schools. The state responded instead by providing financial assistance to a large number of Anglo-vernacular schools, which therefore proliferated in number.

Yet another unique feature of the colonial state's education in the province was the close vigil exercised by the state over the education sector. In Assam all executive officers were expected to inspect all schools in their respective districts. This included deputy commissioners, assistant commissioners and sub-divisional officers, chairmen of local boards and members of such boards.[41] This was despite the fact that the Manual of Rules and Orders of the Education Department in Assam compiled for the guidance of the deputy and subinspectors did not 'differ very much in principle from the corresponding rules which obtained in Bengal'.[42] In Assam, despite this, the state made 'backwardness' its principal criteria for tightening official control over the school sector. Such a step was in stark contrast to the situation elsewhere in India, where such measures of centralization appeared much later during the early twentieth-century regime of Lord Curzon.[43] Unlike other provinces, Assam was forced to adopt a two-tier surveillance system composed of the inspector of schools and his deputies and the executive officers of the state. By 1840, the schools in Assam had been placed under the supervision of an inspector of schools, and William Robinson became the first incumbent of this office. The official line of argument was that it was absolutely imperative that a closer and more effective surveillance be exercised over the schools of Assam for their efficient functioning.[44] Jenkins was not particularly pleased with the kind of supervision currently exercised by the inspector and desired a more regular and closer regime of supervision. He was so keen on this that, in anticipation of the sanction of the Council of Education which was examining his proposal, he arbitrarily placed the immediate supervision of the schools of his division on their respective subdivisional collectors. Later on, in his report on the province of Assam, A.J. Mills, visiting judge of the Sadar Dewani Adalat, summed up the idea behind the measure, which he wholeheartedly endorsed:

> Although the Collectors have little leisure to attend to schools, they will be able to exercise a more efficient supervision over the Masters than is obtained under the present system. The distance of the stations, the time a voyage up the Brahmapootra occupies, the number and inaccessible situations of the village schools, render it impracticable for the Inspector, who resides at Gowhatty, to do anything more than cursorily examine the schools, once a year some, and once in two years others.[45]

These measures, however, did not find favours with William Robinson (Robinson, 1841), who had proposed a more decentralized system of supervision through the appointment in each school of native examiners and superintendents with whom the Inspector of Schools would maintain a regular correspondence.[46] In a letter written to the commissioner of Assam in 1862, William Robinson proposed that schools should no longer be placed under the collector since 'they have already a variety of occupation and the schools have never functioned well under their management'.[47] Jenkins summarily rejected Robinson's views. Mills backed Jenkins's resolution on the grounds that 'in such hands (native) there would be no supervision at all'.[48] If Jenkins had at least favoured the existing system of conducting examinations through the Inspector, but Mills turned out to be even more emphatic in his advocacy of a more direct regulatory mechanism and urged that even the examinations be left to the care of the collectors. He recommended the complete abolition of the post of the inspector, thus advocating a total subordination of education in Assam to the administration. The Resolution on the Education Report for 1894–95 reiterated the imminent need for such a close surveillance by the executive arm of the government. It observed, 'The Chief Commissioner must again insist on Deputy Commissioners and Sub-Divisional Officers taking a proper share in the work of inspecting schools'.[49] The policy to be followed by the government in this matter was further summed up to drive home the absolute judiciousness of adhering to the aforementioned mode of functioning:

> In short, the inspection of schools is considered a legitimate part of the administrative work of all Executive officers. In Assam the educational functions delegated to Local Boards include the administration of grants-in-aid and special grants to Middle and primary Schools under private management, and management of Government Lower Primary Schools, which they are authorized to open when funds are available and the school supplies a recognized want, and the award of lower primary scholarships. The Deputy Inspectors are held responsible seeing that the boards do not grant money for educational purposes otherwise than in accordance with the grant-in-aid rules, and that these rules are observed by the Boards in their relations with aided schools. The Boards are not authorized to open either Upper Primary or Secondary Schools under their own management, and, except in backward places, with the sanction of Government, their lower primary schools are all examined for rewards in the same way as aided schools.[50]

The issue of duplicating efforts and of entrusting the work of supervision of schools to executive officers overburdened with their existing administrative responsibilities was opposed tooth and nail by William Robinson but to no avail. The latter pointed out numerous instances to show how such a policy had in the past jeopardized the healthy functioning of many institutions, but all his entreaties fell on deaf ears, indicating how closely integrated such a system of surveillance was to the administrative concerns of the British in Assam.

III

Political economy of education

The education policy of the British in Assam clearly envisaged very limited goals. A report from this period indicates that the latter was designed with very specific aims, and intellectual attainments presumably did not figure as one of the objectives. In his comments on the annual report of the commissioners of Assam on education in the Assam division in 1870, the lieutenant governor of Bengal categorically spelt out that the need of the hour in the region was the promotion of primary education, not because this would ensure education for the masses but because this would eventually create a class of intelligent labour. The latter's views were summed up by his secretary:

> The Lieutenant Governor considers that the reports received from the several districts of Assam . . . bear strong testimony . . . to the fact that their (the people of Assam) chief want is primary education . . . other gentlemen seem to mistake the object of Government, which does not wish to create mohurirs but intelligent labourers, who know their right hand from their left, and who can read and keep simple accounts.[51]

The lieutenant governor's report offers a valuable window that allows us to place both the vernacular thrust of education in Assam and the enthusiasm for school-level education in the right perspective. In addition to equipping Assamese youths for lower-level jobs in government offices, education was meant to help address what was becoming a major cause for concern for the establishment – the shortage of labour in the province. It was perhaps no mere accident that the colonial educational policy in Assam coincided with the colonial state's attempts to tackle the issue of labour shortage that had proved to be the bane of both the agricultural and the plantation sectors. The Assam government's promotion of school-level education and its drive for vernacular education were both targeted to bring education to the masses by making education simpler for the latter to comprehend and assimilate. Mass education was consciously adopted in order to counter the apathy of the Assamese peasant for sustained labour. The idea was to expose the local peasantry to the bounties of hard work and especially to the benefits of long-term agrarian settlements. The decision of the local government to sponsor middle- and higher-level secondary education in Assam, in contradistinction to its all-India policy of supporting education for the few, makes sense in the light of the state's attempts to disseminate some 'useful' knowledge among the population at large, with the hope that this would ultimately produce changes in life styles and habits, inducing the latter to take up commercial labour services in the long run. A basic minimum education for the general people was deemed imperative in Assam in the hope that this would counter the general aversion to hard work by fostering aspirations for better living and higher returns. That such a notion was in circulation for some time becomes clear from a letter written by Rev. Danforth to Judge Mills in 1853, in which the former observed:

> Assam, though a rich and beautiful valley, is greatly in want of population, and its resources lie undeveloped. The Ryots are satisfied to cultivate merely enough for their own use, and what little trade there is, is carried on almost entirely by the Bengallees and Kayahs. The want of an enterprising and impulsive spirit is everywhere seen, and until this monotony is broken up by drawing the attention of the natives to the advantages of commerce, and the blessings which honest industry is certain to secure, little can be hoped from the Province. I think I speak advisedly when I say that the taxes are almost the only motive that now moves the great mass of the people to put forth a single effort beyond what is required for the actual necessities of life. To find an antidote to this death like inertia . . . the means for arousing the slumbering energies of a people who have the natural ability for . . . developing the resources of the country and adding materially to its revenue, is a question alike interesting to the statesman and philanthropist. . . . The self-interest of every native is a motive sufficiently strong, when the means of securing domestic comfort and wealth are laid open before him and shown to be within his reach, to awaken a spirit of enterprise and call forth his activity. That education can do much toward unfolding the bright prospects of affluence is perfectly evident both from history and the nature of the case.[52]

Given the close official patronage enjoyed by the Baptist missionaries, it may be legitimate to infer that Danforth, as a member of the Baptist Mission group, was privy to the prevailing climate of opinion concerning education in bureaucratic circles. The very purpose of education so far as these men were concerned was perhaps to inspire the Assamese people to exert themselves physically for a better living. The motive of revenue maximization was an objective that was appended to initiatives in this field right from the beginning, and lofty ideals usually associated with a noble venture such as education were automatically relegated to the background or simply dismissed. This may have been the overarching framework within which education was envisioned in colonial India by the state. Gauri Vishwanathan has effectively demonstrated that colonial education in India was rooted in a larger political economy of the state. Vishwanathan argues that the overweening importance of literary studies and English literature in the teaching of English in India was designed to familiarize and thereby promote Victorian values deemed desirable for statecraft among the subject population.[53] This paper contends that among a people deemed 'inert' and inhabiting a region perceived as potentially rich and resourceful, the educational agenda of the state could and did become far more pragmatic in nature. There was an urgency to create a class of intelligent labour possessing some useful skills and practical knowledge. There was, hence, no room in this schema for higher learning for one and all, which had the potential to create an enlightened community capable of questioning the given paradigm. The state's policy thus envisaged a simple education for the many, and the vernacular medium was chosen as the perfect means to spread the ideologies of imperial rule among the many.

Not only did the state not exert itself to create more institutions where English was the medium of instruction, but it also carefully distanced itself over the years from secondary education. Of course, this policy had nothing to do with Assam per se, and had been inspired by the general decision of the British government taken in the 1870s to replace its earlier policy of direct participation in the school sector with a system of grants-in aid to supplement native efforts in setting up and managing schools. However, in a region like Assam, where the people had very little capital to invest, a policy that could and did produce disastrous consequences. The ill consequences and futility of a policy of withdrawing from direct initiative in promoting education in a region like Assam, where a moneyed class was severely lacking, were pointed out by many officers, with little impact on decision making. In the Annual Report of the Education Department for 1872–73, the inspector of schools recommended that the grants-in-aid system be considerably relaxed in Assam to enable the aided middle schools of the district 'to keep their heads above water'.[54] There were also appeals from the province's fledgling literati to revoke Campbell's grants-in aid system as being eminently unsuited for Assam. In one such petition presented to the viceroy on 22 August 1874, the people made the following fervent appeal:

> (in Assam) education has never come to that stage of progress as to warrant the withdrawal of Government aid in any slight degree. In Bengal the zemindars and the other rich men can very well take care of their schools and colleges; but alas! Where are such rich men in Assam? The number of families who can send down their boys to Calcutta for the purpose of receiving high education is so small that since the establishment of the university up to the present date there are in all Assam only four graduates. . . . This will clearly show how far the people of Assam can support their schools and colleges. It is to be hoped that what zemindars and other rich people are doing in Bengal will be done by Government.[55]

The failure to heed these suggestions meant that in a short time the number of schools in actual existence became disproportionately inadequate in comparison to the actual need for schools. One indication of the fact that the number of schools was not proportionate to the demand is the fact that indigenous seminaries such as the *maktabs* and the *sattras* remained very much in demand till nearly the turn of the century. The withdrawal of state support for these institutions in due course, however, greatly diminished their performance, which seriously jeopardized the cause of education in the plains, especially since the missionaries had already withdrawn from the sector by the later part of the nineteenth century.[56]

IV

Reinforcing privileges

In 1870 the Governor General in Council took the decision that henceforth state support should be extended to mass education only instead of higher education. The decision was sought to be implemented in many places in an interesting manner by lowering government schools in district civil stations to the status of aided schools and high schools to the status of district schools. In Assam where already the state had favoured lower-level education so far, further attempts to withdraw from secondary education met with strong disapproval from the elite. A section of the province's emergent middle-class intelligentsia presented an interesting memorial to the secretary of state for India on 28 June 1870, appealing for a reconsideration of the decision on the grounds that the policy was opposed to the pre-colonial aristocratic ethos of the region. The petitioners argued:

Your memorialists beg most humbly to state a most recognized fact of political science, that education should be imparted by a government to the people subject to its rule according to the law of demand and supply, like a commodity in the commercial market, and that mass education as at present obtaining in the country is amply sufficient for its requirements, there being indigenous pathsalas with guru teachers in almost every village having a sufficient number of juvenile population to form a school. This question should also be viewed in connection with the circumstances that the country had from time immemorial, close upto the planting of the standard of Britain, under a despotism of a mild nature, assisted by a strong and powerful aristocracy, who enjoyed a sort of quasi-feudal tenures. In a country which has been long ruled under a kind of policy of the above description, the democratic influence of the mass education should not be introduced in its full force all of a sudden and the small rudiments of that institution in this country, so essential to the well-being of the whole of India, now being regenerated in Assam under the benevolent auspices of the Government after its fall by the demolition of the old system of education, which the experience of history proves can never succeed to take root in Indian soil for an indefinitely long period of time. Under these circumstances . . . dispensing with higher education, and the substituting in its place of purely mass education, will prove to be a policy than which nothing can be more mistaken . . . owing to trade and industry being only in an incipient stage, there is not wealth enough in the country to supply the sinews of higher education if Government adopts the suicidal policy of retiring from the field of higher education, in consequence of which the chief blessing of the British rule, that is, the cultivation of Western learning, shall altogether disappear from the province.[57]

This petition underscored the fundamental anomalies of a middle and higher middle school–centric education policy, launched with much fanfare. What such a policy had ended up achieving was to put in place a highly elitist apparatus of education that had denied access to high school education to the bulk of the province's population and to English education, English being taught only as a subject till the middle level. Whatever little achievements had been made in spreading high school education gradually became something of a luxury after the state withdrew from direct participation in the sector. The initiatives of the Christian missionary institutions, on the other hand, were a study in contrast for these had set out to offer an opportunity to all categories of natives to study in English. However, the number of missionary schools was far less in Assam compared to Bengal since the state had rendered the missionaries' efforts virtually redundant through their concerted efforts to promote many middle-level and some secondary-level schools. High school education in Assam thus became possible only to a select few and along with it an access to English education, thereby reinforcing the aristocratic bias of the society. The petitioners, therefore, saw no irony in demanding that state-sponsored education should cater only to those sections possessing the cultural resources to make use of such an education so that they could retain their historical edge over the less-privileged sections of their countrymen.

By the middle of the nineteenth century, the state had admitted on many occasions that the Assamese were not exactly in imminent need of parental care and supervision and that they were actually an intelligent lot. Notwithstanding this admission, official educational rhetoric cited mental backwardness as the ground for proclaiming the absolute futility of setting up institutions of higher learning in the region. Jenkins had been concerned right from the beginning about the children of the erstwhile aristocracy who he felt deserved to be given special training and nurtured by sending them out of the province for a more wholesome education. As early as 1834, Jenkins, in his report on the state of education in the districts, had suggested that the best means of improving the education in the province was to 'give instruction to a few *Assamese youths of Rank* in Calcutta' under the impression that 'the habits and the acquisitions they would bring back with them could not fail to be of the happiest consequences' even if the government had to defray a part or whole of the expenses of maintenance (emphasis mine).[58] Jenkins was in fact quite categorical about his expectations from a higher education that would cater only to the elite:

> When the Upper classes perceive there is no other road to distinction than through the attainment of superior information and the means of producing it for their children is put within their reach, they will not allow them to be surpassed by those of the inferior ranks.[59]

Not only this, in a letter written to the secretary to the government of India informing the latter of the fact that eight boys from Guwahati School had been

selected for the Medical College and the Secondary Medical School in Calcutta, Jenkins exulted over the upper-caste background of the selected students. He noted in a self-satisfied tone that he was 'happy to say . . . the lads
sent are all of Assamese extraction and most of high caste and good connection'.[60] Higher education thus, if Jenkins had his way, would be for the select
few only and that too for those with considerable social and cultural capital –
a view that was soon accorded official sanction in the policy framework of the
provincial administration. Needless to say, such a policy was clearly anachronistic in the late nineteenth-century pan-Indian context of zealous govern-
mental intervention in the domain of higher education when universities and
colleges were being set up in several places, albeit to project the image of a
modernizing state. Money could not have been the primary obstacle, for
Assam was by then a viable commercial economy. Elsewhere in the country,
the development of colleges was fairly rapid during the period between 1857
and 1882 owing to the liberal encouragement given by the government.[61]
Orissa, a part of Bengal province, was sanctioned its first government college,
the Ravenshaw College, by 1878. So far as Bengal was concerned, there were
14 colleges before 1857, 9 of them located in Calcutta.[62] Since, in the case of
Bengal, colleges set up through missionary and Indian efforts outnumbered
those set up through government initiative, it hardly mattered that the latter
were few in number. In Assam, on the other hand, the absence of state efforts
was sorely felt as private initiatives were totally lacking.

In Assam, the only school to offer post-entrance education was set up in
1835. Named as 'Guwahati School', it was affiliated to the University of
Calcutta. It was decided at the time of its establishment that the continua-
tion of this school in the future would be contingent on the performance of
its students.[63] The Guwahati School was initially conceived as an institution
that would provide instruction upto the matriculation standard. However,
as there was no provision for imparting college education to students who
had qualified in the entrance examination of the University of Calcutta,
the Guwahati School was promoted to the level of a collegiate school
at par with FA (first arts) institutions of the University of Calcutta in 1865.
Prior to that, a few scholarships not exceeding Rs 10 used to be given to
each candidate willing to travel to Calcutta for pursuing FA degree. In
1876, however, the government took the sudden decision to abolish the
college section of the school, citing poor performance of the latter as the
excuse. This despite the fact that the General Report on Public Instruction
in Assam for 1880–81 had stated that the school had scored a 'tolerably fair
success' in the 'three preceding years at both the Entrance and First Arts
Examination'.[64] What was more, the decision was not revised despite the
improvement in the performance of the students over the next few years.

The decision resulted in a situation where there was no school in the province that taught a standard beyond the entrance level. Students who passed the matriculation examination had to go to colleges in Calcutta for further studies. Incidentally, several educational officers were of the opinion that the reduction of the Guwahati lower-grade college to the status of a zilla school was highly prejudicial to higher education, that students who appeared at the entrance examination were the sons of people who could scarcely afford to send their children to study in a Bengal college and that the expense of living and going to Calcutta prevented many boys from continuing their studies to the entrance standard.[65] Several memorials from the inhabitants of the province were also presented to the chief commissioner, praying for the reopening of the lower-grade college at Guwahati. Interestingly enough, although the chief commissioner admitted that there was merit in the advice of his own officers of the Education Department, he argued that these were only partially true. The General Report on Public Instruction in Assam for 1878–79 stoutly defended the official line of argument:

> I think the question is whether Assam needs a High School, and whether the money that would be necessary to maintain such a school could not be more profitably expended in other ways. . . . (Afterall) if results are any criterion, it would seem that the zilla schools in the districts of the Brahmaputra Valley have done rather better since 1876. . . . The reduction of the Gauhati High School to the status of a zilla school has had little or no effect on the results of the Entrance Examination. Again, I believe the greater advantages enjoyed by students in Bengal colleges – the students acquiring more liberal views by seeing more of the world and mixing with educated people – is an advantage which more than compensates for the additional expense of living away from their families in Bengal. I also consider that the money that would be necessary to maintain college classes at Gauhati could be more advantageously spent, either in improving the efficiency of the present zilla schools or in founding a class of school intermediate between the Primary and Middle-class schools, together with corresponding scholarships.[66]

It is quite likely that the government believed that studying in Bengal was in the best interests of the local youth. Alternately, the state might have been concerned about the additional expenses that installing higher educational institutions in the province would entail, but was constrained from revealing its true intentions to the people and hence was resorting to a face-saving explanation. The government did, however, reassure the people that 'should the people evince the strength of their desire for higher education, by raising a fund towards the support of college classes at Guwahati, he (the Chief Commissioner) would contribute from provincial funds a sum equal to that raised by public subscription. He thinks that in this, as in other matters, it is better that the help of the Government should be given in aid of independent effort than that the whole burthen of providing what is asked for should be borne by public funds'.[67] Predictably, no such fund could be raised because even this amount was deemed prohibitive.

The government's decision to push through its policies despite reports from its own officers alleging adverse impact is self-explanatory and throws light on a policy that was not meant to be reversed. There was actually no dearth of negative remarks. In the education report for 1871–72, Col. H. Hopkinson, Agent to Governor General, Northeast Frontier, and commissioner of Assam, mentioned with reference to the Nowgong district that there is a decline in the number of schools and pupils compared with 1870–71. He attributed this to some unnoticed defects in the education system. The first defect, according to him, was the grants-in-aid system because, 'there are no really opulent classes of natives in Assam, as in the districts of Bengal, in a position to come forward "liberally" to promote the cause of education. Almost all the native community are of the average class who are generally most apathetic and very indifferent to their own interests, and it is quite a mistake to expect them to raise by subscription an amount equal to what they get from the government in the shape of a grant'.[68]

Over the course of the next few years, there was a steady increase in the number of students seeking higher education in Bengal. According to the General Report on Public Instruction for 1891–92, there were 63 Assam students studying in first-year classes of Bengal colleges; 78 in second-year classes, of whom 25 successfully passed FA examination; 28 in third-year classes; and 36 in fourth-year classes, of whom 8 passed BA examination. In 1892–93[69] the same figures were 66 students in the first year; 73 in the second year, of whom 28 passed FA examination; and 24 and 41 students in the third and fourth year, and of the latter 17 passed BA examination. In the next year, the numbers rose to 82, 74, 20 and 36 in the first-, second-, third- and fourth-year classes, respectively, and of these 31 and 19, respectively, passed BA and FA examinations.[70] The reports also indicate that by now the students opting to pursue their studies in Bengal were distributed over a wider number of colleges, indicating in turn the diffusion of information in Assam about collegiate education in Bengal, which underscores the growing urge for higher education in the province. Tables 3.1 and 3.2 culled from the general reports on public instruction in Assam for 1893–94 and 1894–95 provide a list of colleges in Bengal in which the senior scholars had selected to read:

Table 3.1 Students in Bengal colleges during 1893–94 and 1894–95

Colleges in Bengal	1893–94	1894–95
City College	1	1
Dacca College	1	–
Duff College	1	–
General Assembly's Institution	1	4
Hugli College	1	2
Jagannath College	1	–
Jubilee Bhagalpur College	1	–
Medical College	2	2
Metropolitan College	2	–
Presidency College	3	5
Ripon College	–	4
Sibpur Civil Engineering College	–	1
Total	14	19

Source: Table prepared by author.

Table 3.2 Students in Bengal colleges during 1899

Colleges in Bengal	Number of students
Bangabasi College, Calcutta	1
City College, Calcutta	2
Dacca College	3
Free Church Institution and Duff College	1
General Assembly's Institution, Calcutta	2
Metropolitan Institution, Calcutta	3
Presidency College	4
St. Xaviers College, Calcutta	1
Victoria College, Cooch Behar	1
Total	18

Source: Table prepared by author.

The General Report on Public Instruction in Assam for 1894–95 also informs us that in that year two of the late pupils of Guwahati High School, two of Government High School, Sylhet, and one of High School, Silchar, passed MA examination of Calcutta University, and another of the Sylhet Government School's ex-pupil passed MA from Agra Central Muir Arts College. To appease the sentiments of the people, the government reiterated its previous offer to render partial financial assistance to supplement private initiatives undertaken for the promotion of higher education in the province. The General Report of Public Instruction for 1880–81 observed:

> Should the people evince the strength of their desire for higher education, by raising a fund towards the support of college classes at Gauhati, he (the Chief Commissioner) would contribute from provincial funds a sum equal to that raised by public subscription.[71]

Predictably, no such fund could be raised because even this amount was deemed prohibitive by an elite emasculated both by the dispossession of land and the emancipation of slaves, and by the closure of alternative opportunities of employment in the secondary and tertiary sectors. Irrespective of dissenting voices, Chief Commissioner Keatinge decided to continue the existing policy, invoking every now and then the recommendations in the Wood's Despatch in favour of the privatization of educational efforts. The chief officer of the province also reminded the people that it was imperative that the natives leave the insulated environment of their home province for their intellectual growth. Statistics of the swelling tide of college enthusiasts from Assam to Bengal were met with self-laudatory remarks that the policy of aiding students desirous of receiving higher education had begun to bear fruit.[72] The Report on the Progress of Education in Assam during 1892–93 and 1896–97 observed on a smug note: 'It should be noticed that the Assam Administration affords considerable help to Assamese youths of intelligence who wish to obtain the benefits of higher education, although it does not at present provide a first grade or a professional college within the province'.[73]

During this entire period, the only college that was begun at private initiative in Assam was the Murarichand College in Sylhet. In June 1892 Babu Giris Chandra Ray, a *zamindar* of Sylhet, started a second-grade college in the town of Sylhet under the name 'Murarichand College'. This was a purely private initiative, and the college was affiliated to the University of Calcutta. Of the total expenditure of Rs 2,847 incurred in setting up this college, Rs 840 came from fees, the balance being paid by the proprietor. The state did not provide any support to this institution.

131

Perhaps none was sought. In the very next year after its establishment, the college sent 11 candidates up to the FA examination, indicating clearly what the students of the province could achieve given the right opportunities.[74]

By the turn of the nineteenth century, although the state's educational policy with regard to collegiate education in the province remained unchanged, the official veto against institutions of higher learning began to cite additional grounds for denying the province its first college. In 1899, Sir Henry Cotton, the chief commissioner of Assam, and the man responsible for setting up the first college in Assam two years later, came up with the following explanation to justify his decision not to open a college in the province immediately. He observed:

> I have given my careful consideration to the proposal to re-establish a Government college in Assam. But I do not think it would prosper now any more than thirty years ago . . . local jealousies would go towards minimising the utility of any local institution. The centre of Assamese influence is admittedly in the Sibsagar district, and I find it stated there that if a college were established at Gauhati or Dibrugarh, or even at Tezpur, it would be more convenient for parents to send their sons to Calcutta than to a local college. I find those similar objections are put forward to any proposal to establish a college at Sibsagar or Jorhat. There is no central place in Assam where a college could be established which would be recognised in the same manner as Dacca is acknowledged in Eastern Bengal, Cuttack in Orissa, and Patna in Bihar. I am not anxious to give any encouragement to the feeling of provincialism which I find to be unfortunately too rife in the Assam valley districts, and would rather impress upon the educated Assamese of the present generation that they cannot be independent of Bengal in their language or associations, or in the advancement of their prosperity. They are as dependent on Bengal as Welshmen are dependent on England. Such dependence is not inconsistent with a true national sentiment. But the province cannot prosper in isolation, and I attribute the slowness of its progress in large measure to the unwise fostering by the Assamese among themselves of a policy of national exclusiveness. The establishment of a local college would, I am afraid, give a new lease of life to the existing tendency, and my proposals for encouraging higher education lie therefore altogether in the direction of helping successful candidates to continue their studies, not in Assam itself, but in the metropolis of India.[75]

It is hard to believe that the state's dillydallying on the issue of the college was inspired by its indecision on the choice of site for setting up the college. It is certainly ironical that the region's marginality to the colonial metropolis, that is Bengal, in matters of education, should be reiterated by the very person hailed for his immense contributions to the progress of education in Assam. In fact, Cotton seems to have nurtured his reservations about setting up a college in Assam till the very end – a fact that he candidly confessed in a gathering of Assamese intellectuals.[76] He had, from the very beginning, categorically declined to re-establish a government college in Assam. Instead, he had proposed that a hostel be set up in Calcutta for Assamese students. It was also proposed that the number of Assamese scholarships would be raised from 17 to 25. A note to this effect was drawn up and circulated for feedback and invited comments and criticisms, which proved crucial in the end in turning the tide of opinion in favour of a college. It is telling, however, that although a first-grade college had been demanded, what was ultimately conceded was second-grade college, which would teach only up to FA standard although 'the preponderance of opinion' favoured a first-class college teaching up to BA standard and only a 'a very influential minority' favoured a second-class college.[77] Even if we admit that the allegations made in the chief commissioner's note are true, it is curious that the state chose to pay serious attention to inter-valley rivalry, while overlooking the more forceful plea for establishing a college in Guwahati. The state was certainly being selective in considering local interests and not entirely for the merit of the concerned line of argument.

Colonial education in Assam by involving the state in the setting up of a large number of vernacular-medium schools did hold out promises of a universal education although to be truly successful such a policy should have been carried to its logical conclusion. Again, by making higher education accessible only to people of substance in society, colonial education ensured that the emergent educated middle class would be almost entirely upper class. Colonial education in Assam, thus, reproduced social hierarchies at least in the initial years after its inception.

Notes

1 See Veena Naregal, *Language, Politics, Elites, and the Public Sphere Western India under Colonialism*, New Delhi: Permanent Black, 2001; Naregal has shown how colonial education denied universal access to education, inferiorized the vernaculars and hardened social hierarchies by introducing a bilingual education system. According to Naregal, by its very nature, colonial education was destined to merely indicate but not fulfil possibilities of a laicized education.

2 Krishna Kumar has highlighted how colonial education could find many alternative modes of control beyond the standard apparatuses studied by scholars. See Krishna Kumar, *Political Agenda of Education: A Study of Colonialist and Nationalist Ideas*, New Delhi: Sage, 2005.

3 See Gauri Vishwanathan, *Masks of Conquest Literary Study and British Rule in India*, New Delhi: Oxford University Press, 1989. Vishwanathan argues that colonial education served specific purposes of disseminating Victorian morality and discipline through its emphasis on the reading of English literature.

4 See Archana Chakravarty, *History of Education in Assam 1826–1919*, New Delhi: Mittal, 1989.

5 'Letter from F. Jenkins, dated 21 June 1834', Letters Issued to the Government, Vol. 1, 1834–35; also cited in Chakravarty, *History of Education in Assam 1826–1919*, p. 10.

6 Letters Issued to the Government, Vol. 10, 1834–35, ASA.

7 Ibid.

8 Ibid.

9 Letter Received from Misc. Quarters, Vol. 4, No. 15, 1839, June 11, 1839, ASA.

10 Ibid.

11 Letters Issued to the Government, Vol. 1, 1834–35, ASA.

12 See Madhumita Sengupta, 'Orienting Progress? Some Aspects of Education in Nineteenth-Century Assam', *Economic and Political Weekly*, Vol. XLVII, No. 29, July 21, 2012.

13 Lakshahira Das, *Development of Secondary Education in Assam*, New Delhi: Omsons, 1990.

14 Report on the General Committee of Public Instruction in Bengal, 1838–39.

15 See Aparna Basu, *The Growth of Education and Political Development in India 1898–1920*, New Delhi: Oxford University Press, 1974.

16 Poromesh Acharya, 'Education in Old Calcutta', in Sukanta Chaudhury (ed.), *Calcutta: The Living City*, Vol. 1, Calcutta: Oxford University Press, 1990, pp. 85–94.

17 See Basu, *The Growth of Education and Political Development in India 1898–1920*.

18 J.P. Naik and Syed Nurullah, *A Student's History of Education in India 1800–1973*, New Delhi: Macmillan, 1974.

19 This provision of the Wood's Despatch has been criticized by many, including Veena Naregal, for promoting an exclusivist thrust among a section of the population; see Naregal, *Language, Politics, Elites, and the Public Sphere Western India under Colonialism*.

20 Ibid.

21 Ibid.

22 Bengal Government Papers, File no. 397, s. no. 1, 1839.

23 Ibid.

24 B.C. Allen, C.G.H. Allen and H.F. Howard, *Gazetteer of Bengal and North-East India*, 1901, Reprint, New Delhi: Mittal, 1979.

25 See W.W. Hunter, *A Statistical Account of Assam*, London: Trubner & Co, London, 1879.

26 Report on the Progress of Education in Assam during 1892–93 to 1896–97, p. 2, ASA.
27 General Department, Education Branch, Progs. 23 February 1859, West Bengal State Archives, WBSA.
28 Report on the Progress of Education in Assam during 1892–93 to 1896–97, p. 2, ASA.
29 Ibid.
30 Ibid., p. 3.
31 Ibid., p. 5.
32 Assam Commissioner's Papers, File no. 495, 1862–64, ASA.
33 See in this connection Chakravarty, *History of Education in Assam 1826–1919.*
34 Bengal Government Papers, File no. 397, s. no. 1, 1839, ASA; see Chakravarty, *History of Education in Assam 1826–1919.*
35 Letters Issued to the Government, Vol. 10, 1834–35, ASA.
36 Assam Commissioner's Papers, File no. 507 AC, 1862, ASA.
37 Report on the Progress of Education in Assam during 1892–93 to 1896–97, p. 34, ASA.
38 Danforth, Mills, ibid, Letter dated 19 July 1853 from the Danforth to MIlls, Appendix IA, Report on the Province of Assam.
39 Assam Commissioner's Papers, File no. 495, 1862–64, ASA.
40 Ibid.
41 Report on the Progress of Education in Assam during the Years 1892–93 to 1896–97, ASA.
42 Ibid.
43 Aparna Basu argues that Curzon's viceroyalty marked a turning point in government education policy. He formally abandoned the doctrine that the state should not interfere in education. Instead, he was for a policy where the state could have the initiative and control a planned system from the centre.
44 See Mills's Report for details; Aparna Basu has shown that it was Lord Curzon who initiated a policy of stricter control over schools in the rest of the country. The policy of strict vigilance of schools in Assam, thus, predated the introduction of similar, though not identical, measures in the rest of the country.
45 Mills's Report, p. 29.
46 Assam Commissioner's Papers, File No. 495, 1862–64, ASA.
47 Ibid.
48 Mill's Report, p. 29.
49 Report on the Progress of Education in Assam during the Years 1892–93 to 1896–97, p. 9, ASA.
50 Ibid.
51 Note by the Lieutenant Governor, Government of Bengal, General Department Education Branch, A, September 1872, Progs. 48–52, WBSA.
52 Letter from A.H. Danforth to Mills, dated 19 July 1853, Appendix I-A, Mills, Report.
53 Vishwanathan, *Masks of Conquest Literary Study and British Rule in India.*
54 Hunter, *A Statistical Account of Assam,* p. 83.
55 Government of India, Home (Public) B, September 1874, no. 166–167, NAI.

56 See Hunter, *A Statistical Account of Assam*.
57 GoI, Home (Education), 31 December 1870, no. 35, NAI.
58 Letters Issued to the Government, Vol. 10, 1834–35, ASA.
59 Ibid.
60 Ibid.
61 Naik and Nurullah, *A Student's History of Education in India 1800–1973*, p. 185.
62 Poromesh Acharya, *Calcutta: The Living City*.
63 H.K. Barpujari, *A Short History of the Higher Education in Assam*, cited in Saikia, *Background of Modern Assamese Literature*, p. 100.
64 General Report on Public Instruction in Assam for 1880–81, Oriental and India Office Collection, British Library, London (henceforth OIOC BL).
65 General Report on Public Instruction in Assam for 1878–79, OIOC, BL.
66 Ibid.
67 General Report on Public Instruction in Assam for 1880–81, OIOC, BL.
68 GoB, General (Education) A, September 1872, no. 48–52, WBSA.
69 GRPI in Assam for 1892–93, OIOC, BL.
70 GRPI in Assam for 1893–94, OIOC, BL.
71 GRPI in Assam for 1880–81 (GRPI henceforth), OIOC, BL.
72 Ibid.
73 Ibid.
74 GRPI in Assam for 1893–94, OIOC, BL.
75 IOR/L/PJ/6/540/File 926/26 April 1900, OIOC, BL.
76 Speech Delivered by the Chief Commissioner at Gauhati on 3 November 1899, Home A, February 1900, nos. 90–100, ASA.
77 IOR/L/PJ/6/540/File 926/26 April 1900, OIOC, BL.

Part II

4

NEW SOLIDARITIES
Print, politics and protest

The new middle class

In 1832, a few years after the East India Company's forces had conquered Assam from the Burmese, the acting Agent to the Governor General in Northeast India wrote a letter to the chief secretary of the British government at Fort William, in which he described a local employee of the British government of Assam in the following terms:

> The individual in question stood high in the confidence of Mr Scott, and is a man of large property and extended information and possesses some literary celebrity – he has visited Bengal and Hindoostan and has paid particular attention to the British system of jurisprudence and forms of Government regarding which he entertains liberal opinions. He also possesses some knowledge of our arts and sciences.[1]

This letter provides valuable insights into the social composition of the first batch of people who entered into the services of the British government in Assam. Pick up any standard book on Assam and we are told that the number of local people in British employ remained miserably low in the early part of British rule in Assam.[2] The unfamiliarity of the local people with the Bengal system of revenue administration, of which Assam was a part, necessitated the employment of Bengali clerks who had greater familiarity with the system. Irrespective of the number however, these men from Assam were all rather accomplished and worthy of the responsibilities thrust on their shoulders. A letter written by Adam White to his superior in 1832 sets forth the grounds for selecting these early stalwarts to their respective posts. The letter referred to Haliram Dhekial Phukan, who had joined the Guwahati Collectorate as a *Sheristadar* in 1825:

> I think you might derive much information from him, he is certainly clever in revenue business and enters readily into the ideal of Europeans. I should think he might afford great assistance in settling Durrang under European control.[3]

One of the principal criteria for selecting local people was their implicit knowledge of the pre-colonial system of governance, especially of their understanding of the revenue system and land rights. For instance, Scott is said to have obtained the land records of the previous regime from the Majumdar/Majindar Baruas, employees of the erstwhile regime, and hence, he incorporated the latter into the new revenue administration.[4] Reminiscing about their recruitment, Jenkins once observed,

> The officers who had the preparing and keeping of the Lakhiraj records were mozemdar burrooahs and mozemdars, in whose families the appointments were hereditary. We had three or four of these officers at the commencement of the investigation, who were personally conversant with the grants made during the reigns of the three last Rajahs, and they knew from their fathers what grants had been made through the reigns of the three last Rajahs, or back to the date of the *perah keguz*. These officers have been of great use in identifying grants, for in almost all instances one or other of them could recognize the handwriting in genuine mohuzurs.[5]

The Majindar-Barua was like a confidential minister of the king under the erstwhile regime, and combined the functions of a private secretary and advisor on foreign relations. David Scott also, in addition, appointed native surveyors, both Bengali and Assamese, to survey land in Assam preparatory to his promulgation of a new tax regime.[6] Archibald Watson, the compiler of David Scott's memoir, notes that the revenue department of the new regime made considerable use of the services of indigenous people:

> In the Revenue Department very important changes were effected. . . . Throughout the 26 pergunnahs in Lower Assam, the ryuts were allowed to elect their own choudhries, or native collectors, by whom the revenue was collected and paid in to Government. When the day of election occurred, they gave in tickets,

specifying the name of the candidate for whom they voted, and the majority of votes determined the election.[7]

Watson further noted that the same policy was followed in organizing the new judiciary, Scott having laid great store by native knowledge and opinion:

> In trying cases of murder, Mr. Scott, or his assistant, was aided by a jury, or, rather, a body of assessors, who gave in a verdict of guilt, or innocence, but had nothing to say to the sentence. These assessors were, generally speaking, (Assamese) public officers of the Civil Courts; but respectable Natives, unconnected with the Government, were encouraged to apply for permission to sit on these trials as members of the punchayut court; and it was only their apathy, ignorance of the functions of jurymen, and disinclination to give up their time for that purpose, which compelled Mr. Scott to rely, principally, upon the services of paid assessors. . . . Scott entertained a high opinion of the intellectual capacity of the Natives. About a year before his death, he recommended, that a Native should be appointed as assistant to the European officer in civil charge of Lower Assam, with the full powers of a European mofussil magistrate, in criminal cases, viz. of passing a sentence of two years imprisonment. Since his demise, this appointment has taken place. Upon the same principle he entrusted the decision of civil suits to them almost entirely. Three Civil Courts were formed at Goahattie, composed entirely of natives, and it was only in cases of large amount that a special appeal existed to himself. Fully aware of the evil of concentrating all authority in the European functionary in charge of a district, he erected subordinate punchyut courts, in each populous pergunnah, to whom all petty civil suits were referred, with a right of appeal to the higher courts at Goahattie, whilst the minor breaches of peace were referred to the choudhries, or native collectors of districts.[8]

Clearly, men considered suitable for the proposed situations were sought out and retained for various positions in the early days of British rule in Assam.

Yet another factor that was common to the group of men entrusted with various administrative posts was their literacy or ability to read either or all of the commonly used written languages in which official documents were usually composed, such as Persian, Sanskrit and one or other of the local scripts. Men like Haliram, Jajnaram and Harakanta were well versed in Sanskrit, Persian and sometimes in both although they were not conversant with English like their successors in government office. Some of them, however, picked up a workable knowledge of English through interaction with their superiors. In general, an important factor that distinguished these men was the social background from which they hailed. Most of them seem to have hailed from a service gentry background.[9] Their forefathers and in some cases they themselves had held important positions with the erstwhile regime of the 'Ahom' *swargadeos*, as the pre-colonial rulers of Assam were referred to. These men – the Rajkhowas, Baruas and Phukans – usually comprised the second- and third-tier officers of the erstwhile regime. They comprised the high-caste gentry possessing both moderate land resources and a certain amount of literacy, which had allowed them to serve the previous regime. Literacy once again allowed them to take up government service in the immediate aftermath of the takeover of Assam. Their administrative acumen enabled them to emerge as key functionaries of the new regime, which stood to gain substantially from their knowledge and expertise of key aspects of the previous regime. Many of the middle-ranking officers of the erstwhile regime were thus employed by the British in the lower rungs of the government's revenue and judicial services as *Sheristadars and Sadar Amins*. They were prized for their extensive knowledge of the previous system of governance, especially the nature of land rights and revenue entitlements of the pre-colonial state. These men were sometimes entrusted with the task of revenue collectors. Many of these people became *mauzadars* when assessment areas were divided into *mauzas*.[10] Radhanath was himself the son of Amvarish or Naga Majumdar-Barua during the reign of Lakshmi Singha, 1769–80.[11] Amvarish is said to have been proficient in Persian, Hindi, Bhutanese and Burmese. Harakanta later joined British government services as a clerk and rose to become a *Sadar Amin* with the powers of a second-class magistrate. Anundoram Barooah, the first ICS from Assam, was born into the family of the Majinder Borooah of North Guwahati.[12] One of his ancestors, Manik Chandra, was a Barkakoti under the Ahom ruler Sukampha. A descendent of this family, Gargaram Borooah was the last Majinder Borooah of the Assam king. Gargaram Borooah became a *Sadar Amin* or *Munsif* under the British. Anundoram Borooah was his son. Both Haliram (1802–32) and his brother Joggoram (1805–38) were the sons of Parashuram Barua, who was an important functionary of the erstwhile regime. He was given charge of the border post of Hadira Chowki on the Assam–Bengal border and collected excise dues on goods coming into the domain of the *swargadeo* from Bengal. He was also assigned the responsibility for guarding the frontier outpost from enemies. After his father's death, at the tender age of 14, Haliram was assigned his father's job. Later, *swargadeo* Chandrakanta Singha conferred on him the title of 'Dhekial Phukan'. When the Burmese raided Assam, Haliram fled with his brother and other members of his family to neighbouring Rangpur in Bengal. Subsequently, after the British conquest of Assam, he returned and was absorbed into the new administration as a *Sheristadar* in the collectorate. Haliram rendered invaluable service to the British government in settling the land revenues of Nagaon and Durrang. Later, he was transferred to Guwahati and became an assistant magistrate with a handsome salary of Rs 230 per month. Dinanath Bezbaroa, the father of Lakshminath Bezbaroa, belonging to the family of the Bezbaroa, or medical practitioners under the erstwhile regime, became a *Munsif* in the British administration of Assam.[13] Dinanath was the son of Chandrakantasimha, who was the chief physician of the Ahom monarch. In 1818, Dinanath was made the Bezbaroa by the Ahom king Purander Singha and also given charge of the Civil Sheresta.[14] Padmanath Gohain Barua's father Ghinaram Gohain Barua was the second child of Taoruru Buragohain, one of the highest functionaries of the Ahom regime. He became a *mauzadar* under the new regime in North Lakhimpur.[15] A sizeable section of those who secured government jobs in colonial Assam also hailed from a Vaishnavite *sattra* background and were substantial men of the society.[16] Thus, it is clear from the earlier survey that the small group of men who became closely associated with the founding years of British rule in Assam was made up of eminent members of pre-colonial society. They certainly stood to gain from their new positions as it allowed them to supplement their family incomes. For instance, for many of the newly appointed local revenue collectors, *mauzadari* or collectorship proved to be a financially rewarding employment, enabling them to accumulate considerable wealth.[17] In his autobiography, Lakshminath Bezbaroa states how his father Dinanath Bezbaroa and other members of his family were able to expand their landholdings with the help of money earned from government services.[18] It must not be forgotten, however, that these men were chosen because of their elite backgrounds and accomplishments. Colonialism may have introduced them to new avenues of employment, but they were certainly not new to social privileges. If anything, the colonial state itself benefitted immensely from their insights and acumen. Scholars working on colonial Assam tend to overlook this point in their zeal to demonstrate the favourable ties between the emergent middle class and the British.[19] It is often iterated that British rule came as a blessing for this class, but the fact of the matter is that they were also instrumental in giving stability to British rule.

The objective of this chapter, however, is not to delve into the issue of the social origins of the Assamese middle class since there is precious little that we can hope to unravel after years of debate on the subject. It is more or less well known that the middle class in Assam came into its own as a result of the emasculation of the upper tier of the Ahom aristocracy through dispossession following the implementation of new settlement rules by the British that exposed the latter to a tax regime, which eventually crushed them under its pressure. The second- and third-tier officers are, on the other hand, understood to have fared better under the new dispensation and emerged more powerful socially on account of their access to government jobs and the new institutions of a colonial but nonetheless new age culture defined in terms of 'modernity' and epitomized by Western education and Western values and new norms of pedagogy. There is no denying that everywhere in the subcontinent, British rule opened up new avenues of social mobility for sizeable sections of the population and that this enabled the growth of strong ties of loyalty between the colonial elite and their British patrons. Although everywhere the middle class acquired their cultural capital through the machinations of the colonial state, it is well known how the former eventually turned the tables on the British. In Assam however, there is a lack of serious antagonism between the colonial state and the provincial middle class till the turn of the century despite possibilities of hostilities held out by the language issue. We contend that British rule had more disagreeable features than one cares to admit and that there is every reason why the elite should have felt let down after the initial years of euphoria following the termination of Burmese rule. That they did not confront the British head-on over a number of issues that challenged their sensibilities for the better part of the nineteenth century, except for a short but decent beginning early on, was because they were deluded by the official policy discourses as well as by the turn of events from the middle of the century. This is not to deny that there was no soft corner for British rule but to observe that the institutional advantages of British rule cannot by themselves explain why the elite soft-peddled on a number of issues that were distinctly impairing their interests. Clearly, there is a need to re-examine the rhetoric of English rule in Assam for a clue to the reticence demonstrated by the middle class in confronting the misdemeanours of British rule. Hopefully, such an approach will allow us to explain the cultural preoccupations of the Assamese middle class till the turn of the century, when a fair degree of antagonism had begun to inform middle-class politics in other parts of the country. Colonial education policies had carefully nurtured the predominantly upper caste and upper-class background of the literati to a far greater extent than in neighbouring Bengal. Thus, the handful of people who benefitted from higher education had every reason to be grateful to the state for its endeavours even if they were not in agreement with the precise logic of the rhetoric of progress. It made more sense under the circumstances to enrich the 'mother tongue' as a counter to racist aspersions rather than confront the state on the matter. This explains the preoccupation of our intellectuals with issues of language when to all intents and purposes the principal provocation had been laid to rest by the 1870s. This chapter discusses the evolving dynamics of colonial middle-class aspirations and politics in Assam from its initial relation of affect with Bengali to its growing disaffection towards Bengali and through all this, its constant attempts to re-constitute *Assamiya* at times as a purified and pure derivative of Sanskrit and at others as a self-consciously literary language that had little or nothing to do with Bengalis. Through this evolutionary history, the chapter seeks to tease out the high caste, 'Hindu' and nationalist preoccupations of the middle class that by the middle of the nineteenth century sought to use language as a medium for the realization of their cultural aspirations.

I

Before Assamese

In 1829, the Samachar Chandrika Press of Calcutta published the first part of a book called *Assam Buranji Arthat Assam Deshiya Itihas* in Bengali. The name of the author was mentioned as Haliram Dhekial Phukkan. The brief preface by the author carried his name and also mentioned his *mulk* or place of origin as 'Assam'. The book was favourably reviewed by one Tarachand Chakraborty in the *India Gazette*, and later the review was reproduced in another Bengali magazine called the *Asiatic Journal and Monthly Register*, Vol. II, New Series. The same review seems to have been published before in the *India Gazette*. The positive response of the Bengali press indicates that the author was proficient in Bengali apart from being a good narrator. Haliram's book was not only the first printed history of Assam but also the first historical work to be published in the Bengali language. The favourable reviews and occasional mention of news related to the life and activities of Haliram in the Bengali press indicate that the book was quite obviously well received in the literary circuit of the colonial metropolis where print had already emerged as the new age medium for voicing informed opinion by the new and self-consciously Bengali middle-class 'public'. In 1833, Haliram's second book called the *Kamrup Jatra Paddhati*, which was an account of the principal sites of Hindu pilgrimage in Assam, was published. This time the language of composition was Sanskrit. Haliram was a familiar figure in the literary public sphere of colonial Calcutta by virtue of being a regular contributor to local newspapers and magazines such as the

Samachar Darpan, *Samachar Chandrika* and *Bangadoot*. It is said that he actively promoted the dissemination of Bengali-language magazines and newspapers in Assam.

Haliram's brother Joggoram Dhekial Phukan is also said to have published translations of English poems in Bengali and regularly contributed features such as letters to the editor and commentaries on social issues in the literary magazines of Bengal.[20] His contemporary, Jaduram Deka Barua, was like him, an avid follower and occasional contributor to the Bengali literary sphere. It is common knowledge that Bengali newspapers and periodicals like the *Samachar Darpan* and the *Samachar Chandrika* had a fairly good circulation among the reading elite in Assam. The popularity and huge circulation of Bengali-language publications in Assam led the leading Bengali daily *Samachar Darpan* to observe in a short passage titled *Assam Deshe Gyan Vriddhi* (The Expansion of knowledge in Assam), published on 30 July 1831:

> The respectable people of Assam keep in touch with events and activities in Bengal through Bengali newspapers. The number of newspaper subscribers in Assam is more than the number of subscribers in any district of Bengal. While we do not receive any letters from people from half the districts of Bengal, hardly a week goes when one or the other of the newspapers in Bengal do not receive any letters from the people of Assam.[21]

While Haliram was taught Sanskrit and Bengali in his childhood, his brother Joggoram was taught, in addition, Persian, Arabic and English. Assam's earliest batch of middle-class intellectuals evinced a remarkable readiness to embrace Bengali as the language of official communication and education. *Dangariya* Dinanath Bezbaroa chose to teach some preliminary Sanskrit and Bengali to his son Lakshminath at home before enrolling him in one of the numerous Bengali-medium schools that had been set up at state initiative in Assam under the label *Adarsha Bangali Vidyalaya* (Model Bengali Schools).[22] In his autobiography *Mor Jibon Smaran*, Lakshminath Bezbaroa recalls how it was considered fashionable among the Assamese youth in those days to speak in Bengali and also sing Bengali songs.[23] The familiarity of the earlier generation of men was often the outcome of the fact that many had taken refuge in Goalpara and other adjacent places of North Bengal during the days of the Burmese invasion. Others living in the lower Assam region of Kamrup and Durrang already enjoyed a great deal of familiarity with the speech practices of adjacent districts of Bengal right from the time when Bengal was a Mughal *subah* (province). Interactions with Bengal were old and more or less regular and ranged from commercial and military exchanges and frequent administrative negotiations to occasional religious interactions, which increased in volume ever since the conversion of the kings of Assam to Brahmanical Hinduism. One such priest who came to Assam at the invitation of *swargadeo* Rudra Singha was given charge of the Kamakhya temple atop the Nilachal Hill in Guwahati. He is said to have initiated a large number of the aristocracy to the *Sakta* forms of worship. All these interactions made for a fair amount of acquaintance with a variety of so-called Bengali speech practices. Yet the language spoken by people in the greater part of the valley had their distinct styles of intonation and usages that did not necessarily cohere to the usages popular in Bengal. This explains the frequent use of the expression *orthat* (in other words/or) by the author immediately after introducing a colloquial word or expression that he was certain his Bengali readers would not understand but which he himself could not help using perhaps in order to render the information more 'authentic' and to give a sense of the local peculiarities of speech.[24] Maniram Dewan's *Buranji Vivek Ratna*, on the other hand, was completely unapologetic in its choice of words and phrases, and his text is replete with phrases and idioms from the local lingo, most of which would not be familiar even to speakers of the so-called dialects of Bengal, let alone to speakers communicating in the refined and standardized Bengali language.[25] It is clear that what John Peter Wade in 1800 referred to as the *Bhaxa* may have had phonemic semblances with speech forms identified as proto-Bengali, but that most or many variants of the former practised in different parts of Assam did possess certain typical properties, which were rooted in the local syllogisms of Assam Proper and therefore beyond the comprehension of the people of Calcutta or other districts located away from Assam.[26] Despite this clearly discernible distinctiveness of local style/styles of expression, however, which had to be translated to a Bengali-reading public, there was in Assam no opposition to the government's decision to declare Bengali as the official vernacular of Assam. This chapter also therefore strives to understand the reasons for this profound silence of the literati.

Recent scholarship on the subject of language, outside Assam, offers a clue to the puzzle by throwing light on pre-colonial language use in the subcontinent. In her work on the making of a Telugu linguistic identity in the nineteenth century, Lisa Mitchell has argued that it was common for people in the past to use different languages for different purposes.[27] For instance, people might compose an official letter in Persian, record a land transaction in a language familiar to the local administration and perform religious rituals in Sanskrit, all at the same time.[28] In her detailed engagement with pre-colonial regimes of language use, Mitchell shows how by the twentieth century 'such context and task-specific language use was increasingly converted into different registers of the same language'.[29] Other scholars have highlighted the presence under pre-colonial regimes, of groups of scribes who routinely handled administrative correspondence and record keeping, and were, therefore, capable of communicating in multiple linguistic idioms.[30] The presence in Assam of such a multilingual scribal culture can be presumed from the diverse character of the *swargadeo*'s subjects, which necessitated communication in a variety of spoken and written languages.[31] Our study of the lives and practices of these scribes have been constrained, however, by a lack of records, and all that we have are some stray references which nonetheless convey a sense of the predominantly multilingual courtly culture that existed under Ahom rule. This was expected given the culturally diverse populations constituting the *swargadeo*'s subjects. The Ahom court maintained a class of officials whose task was to translate the king's message to neighbouring chiefs and rulers. These officials, called *katakis*, again communicated to the *swargadeo* the views and perceptions of the neighbouring rulers.[32] There is none better to illustrate this point than Amvarish or Naga Majumdar-Barua, the ancestor of Harakanta *Sadar Amin*, and a minister under *swargadeo* Lakshminath Singha (1769–80). His case illustrates the fact that multilinguality was a desired and highly cherished quality at the Ahom court. Amvarish is said to have been proficient in a large number of standard languages such as Persian, Hindi, Bhutanese and Burmese.[33] A high functionary at the court of the monarch, Amvarish is said to have served as the king's counsel on foreign relations. Diplomatic exchanges with regions outside the immediate domains of the Ahom monarch tended to increase with the beginnings of hostility with the Mughals. The presence of the Mughals along the borders of the *swargadeo*'s domain implied that occasional diplomatic exchanges with the latter could hardly be avoided. This entailed a certain degree of familiarity with Persian, and the presence at the court of officials capable of communicating in Persian was invariably cherished. Quite a few letters written in chaste Persian and addressed to Mughal officials have come to light. Learning Persian must have been quite in fashion for the aspiring young man of society for we hear that on his return from Calcutta Anandaram Dhekial Phukan appointed a *Munshi* (a functionary acting as an interpreter) to teach him Persian. This was long after the British government had done away with Persian for official work in 1835. Dhekial Phukan's desire to learn Persian thus underscores the social prestige associated with knowledge of Persian in elite society in Assam. Yet another language that was cultivated primarily for scriptural purposes was Sanskrit. Its predominantly religious function is indicated by Haliram Dhekial Phukan's decision to write his account of the holy shrines of Kamrup in the Sanskrit language. The latter's choice of *Bangla* to write his historical chronicle with an eye to expanding the latter's circulation and of Sanskrit for fulfilling a religious mission best illustrates the vastly different universe of language use in the pre-colonial world, many practices of which spilled over into early colonial society. The European notion of an all-purpose single language with very rigid boundaries of circulation was mapped onto a pre-colonial universe that was remarkably polyglot and flexible in matters of learning and using languages in various context-specific ways.[34] It is not surprising, therefore, that the early colonial elite did not react to the official choice of Bengali for Assam. Language was yet to emerge as a cultural marker of one's identity.

Admittedly, therefore, in keeping with the multilingual ethos of pre-colonial Assam, the language of literary compositions produced within the *swargadeo*'s domain was wonderfully diverse in their contents as much as these were remarkably hybrid in terms of the choice of languages. The corpus included historical chronicles locally referred to as *Buranjis* and poetical works dealing mostly with Vaishnavite themes. Verses were mostly composed in the pan-Indian *Brajabuli* tradition although they usually also contained a generous smattering of various colloquial and Sanskrit expressions. The stock of words was equally hybrid, making it difficult to map the language onto any structured linguistic schema. So far as the *Buranjis* were concerned, some were written in *Bailoong* or the old Tai-Ahom language of the Ahom rulers, while others were written in some sort of a mixed language abounding in all kinds of colloquialisms. In her study of the Tai-Ahom identity in the colonial period, Yasmin Saikia has also observed that the *Buranjis* were characterized by a great deal of variety in styles of orthographic enumeration.[35]

That the *Buranjis* were both inwardly hybrid and outwardly heterogeneous with regard to styles and usages is evident from the dilemma faced by those seeking to edit this genre of literature years later. Editing was deemed indispensable in order to render these works fit for consumption by a public used to a more standardized Assamese language, shorn of the hybridity characterizing the language of the *Buranji* literature. When the Department of Historical and Antiquarian Studies (DHAS), set up by the British government for preserving the antiquities and traditional literature of pre-colonial Assam, took up the project of printing some of these *Buranjis*, it was deemed imperative to undertake extensive editorial work to bring these local historical chronicles in sync with the established canons of language structure and use and render them comprehensible to the readers of the modern Assamese language. Sometime back, select chronicles from this genre had been subject to editorial interventions by the Baptist missionaries prior to their publication at the Baptist Missionary Press at Sibsagar. One such chronicle was the *Purani Assam Buranji* published in the popular missionary monthly, *Orunodoi*, some years after the magazine was launched. This chronicle was later included by Suryya Kumar Bhuyan in his compendium, the *Kamrupar Buranji*, published by the DHAS. In his introduction to the work, Surya Kumar Bhuyan, the first director of the DHAS and the man responsible for large-scale transcription and publication of *Buranjis* and other pre-colonial texts, observed:

> The manuscript . . . was collected between 1840–50 by Rev. Nathan Brown who was then in charge of the Mission at Sibsagar. There are directions here and there in the manuscript for preparing the press-copy for publication in the journal; and the manuscript also bears traces of the handiwork of Rev. Nidhi Levi Farwell.[36]

Clearly, the missionaries had to undertake quite rigorous editing to remove perceived 'anomalies' and discrepancies in style and substance in order to induce internal consistency and uniformity of the text. Bhuyan himself could not avoid the same kind of interventions to bring the other texts that he had used for compiling the *Kamrupar Buranji*, in line with consistent grammatical and phraseological usage deemed mandatory for a language to be taken seriously and on its own terms. His impatience with discrepant sentence constructions and spellings is palpable. He remarked:

> While the structure of the sentences is primarily Assamese the vocabulary is hybrid in places. Here and there the author or authors have emulated a conscious literary style by retaining words in their original Sanskrit forms rather than their Assamese variants and by using forms which were in vogue only in the poetic diction of the period.[37]

The preface to the *Kamrupar Buranji* presents other opportunities to study the hiatus between the pre-colonial and colonial understandings of language. There are occasional frustrations at the fact that the diplomatic letters exchanged between the representatives of the Ahoms and the Mughals 'represented a curious medley of Persian, Hindi and Assamese'.[38] For readers of a standardized Assamese, many of the words used would have been utterly incomprehensible without the careful editing that went into the publication of these pre-colonial texts. It is telling to hear the later-day editor of Kashinath Tamuli Phukan's *Assam Buranji*, first published by the

Baptist Missionary Press in 1844, observe that although the textual matter and the original spellings had been left undisturbed, an attempt was made to 'make the words and expressions uniform as far as possible'.[39]

The hybrid language of the *Buranjis* reflected the reality of a pre-colonial world devoid of rigid boundaries in the domain of spoken languages that allowed people to borrow freely from a wide variety of sources to enrich their stock of words and styles of expression.[40] Languages spoken at home and in ordinary conversation lacked written grammars till the Christian missionaries took up the task of compiling grammars of the *Bhaxa* or the ordinary lingo that they deemed to be not a little 'confused' and certainly 'mixed' in character. These spoken varieties were not bound by normative structures and could be remarkably fluid. People used varied syntactical styles, borrowing words and expressions indiscriminately, from a wide variety of sources and mixing them according to their convenience and taste to create communicative patterns that no modern-day structured language could legitimately claim as their very own. The spoken languages were consequently ill-defined and remarkably unbounded. The best illustration of the practice of drawing from a 'shared vocabulary' is provided by the *Buranji Vivek Ratna* of Maniram Dutt. Bodhisattva Kar correctly observes that Maniram's text resembles a 'disjunctive, even incoherent, patchwork of speeches' in its sheer refusal to abide by any uniform syntactical structure. Instead, the text 'shuttles between Sanskrit and a wide range of bhasha conventions'.[41] Maniram's text reflected the immense volatility and porosity of speech that was remarkably unfettered by the strict linguistic conventions of written grammars.

Nathan Brown, Baptist missionary and principal architect of language standardization in Assam, was bemused by the fact that literary production from the region and in the language which he identified to be strictly 'Assamese' constituted a medley of styles and conventions. He therefore sought to classify all pre-colonial Assamese texts into various categories depending on the degree of 'purity' of the language used. His observation at the end of this exercise is telling:

> The only Assamese books which can be regarded as a standard of good prose writing are the Buronjis, or histories, which have been written during the last two or three hundred years. Besides these there are but few prose works in existence. Translations of several mathematical and other Sanskrit works are to be found; but the language is less pure than that of the Buronjis. Most of the sacred writings of the Assamese are in poetry; which differs so widely from the spoken language, that the student who wishes to acquire

a correct style, should confine himself, at the commencement of his studies, entirely to prose.[42]

Clearly, Brown's 'pure' Assamese was one of the many variants used by authors of prose works, while the language of poetry did not correspond at all to any language spoken. Presumably, the provincial literati were accustomed to choosing their preferred idioms from diverse sources to suit the tastes of their patrons who may not have been a homogenous lot.[43] Scholars now talk about four broad groups of scripts practised in the region. These are the Gargaiya, Bamunia, Lakhari and Kaithali.[44] Presumably, there were many more scribal practices, some of which were subsumed under broader labels.

II

Travesties of bounding speech

Sudipta Kaviraj has argued that the rise of a distinct regional language in the subcontinent was often the outcome of some development linked to colonialism. He claims that in a pre-colonial world, the absence of enumeration made for 'fuzzy' identities, because people were not clear about boundaries/limits, that is the point where one's community ended and another began. This allowed a number of dialects to exist in neighbourly difference. Referring to pre-colonial Bengal, he points out that the prestige associated with languages like Sanskrit, Arabic and Persian did not allow the vernaculars to develop a strong normative form. It was easy to speak multiple languages because the core vocabulary consisted of Sanskrit, Apabhramsa and *desaja* words. It was impossible to draw a linguistic map because the 'frontiers where one language ended and another began were bound to be hazy'.[45] This meant that the dialect spoken in northwestern Bengal would be indistinguishable from neighbouring Maithili, whereas in the south, the language of Medinipur would be insignificantly different from that of Orissa. But the introduction of Western education prompted the elite to gradually drop the courtly Arabic/Persian or the priestly Sanskrit as languages of high culture, and to try and create a high-culture Bengali 'via the structural, sometimes even syntactic, imitation of English'.[46] Gradually, through the historical selection of the privileged dialect of some area, and by its promotion through the newly instituted print technology, this elite gave rise to a new norm language.

By contrast, European philology of the eighteenth century was strictly normative and highly deterministic. European nationalistic ideologies had already configured the notion of collective identities characterized by a single enduring 'mother tongue', which in turn was constituted by unique patterns of organization, possessing a wide variety of secondary 'dialects' which were deemed corrupt versions of the 'authentic' standard. These dialects were dubbed as deviations or anomalies introduced into the original language by the ill-informed and the ignorant.[47] Each language was also expected to possess a corresponding script internally uniform and cohesive. Those that did not possess these properties did not qualify to be treated as independent languages in their own rights and were relegated to the category of dialects of the one or other of the fixed and written standards.[48] The study of modern linguistics takes a radically different view of the nature and growth of languages. It is believed now that language variation is usually far more gradual and more or less continuous, over a wide area. Thus, speakers from two widely dispersed regions might be unable to comprehend each other's language, but there might be no point between any two adjacent dialects at which inter-comprehensibility breaks down.[49]

Interestingly enough, the interpenetration of speech patterns in geographically contiguous territories in India did not escape the notice of colonial officials or linguists like George Grierson, who carried out the mammoth task of surveying Indian languages. The following extract from a contemporary report on the hill tribes of Assam by the chief commissioner of Assam, Henry Hopkinson, will illustrate this point. Hopkinson once observed:

> The Khamptis and Singphos live apparently on most amicable terms. The Khamptis, owing to their written language, which is, for purposes of education and religion, adopted by the Singphos who possess no written character, may perhaps be held the superior of the two tribes – the Singphos have no priesthood, and using the religion of the Khamptis, Khampti priests occupy their temples and preside over all religious ceremonies as well as educate the lads of the villages who desire to learn.[50]

The element of a shared vocabulary in the languages spoken by people living in close geographical proximity did not escape the notice of Hopkinson. What he did with the information is, however, a different story altogether. Language was clearly not the only practice that was shared, and it serves to bring out the sheer absurdity of naturalizing political boundaries. Eminent linguist G.A. Grierson, author of the celebrated multi-volume *Linguistic Survey of India*, and the man behind the drawing up of scores of linguistic boundaries in colonial India, could not help noting the structural correspondence between speech forms practised in geographically contiguous territories in the north-eastern part of India. The latter observed:

> In Manipur and in isolated villages in Sylhet and Cachar where there are settlements of Manipuris, the Mayangs speak a mongrel form of Assamese, called by the name of the tribe. There are said to be about a thousand of these people in Manipur, while the number in Sylhet and Cachar is estimated at 22,500. Round the base of the Garo Hills, a kind of 'pigeon' Assamese, locally known as 'Jharwa' is used by the ruder tribes as a language of commerce. It is described as a mixture of Bengali, Garo, and Assamese, and is hardly worthy of being called a dialect of any language.[51]

Dr Grierson noted that the said language 'possesses the characteristics of both the languages (Assamese and Bengali) but at the same time differs widely from both'.[52] Thus, there was no dearth of information available to the early colonial architects of the social and cultural world of the colonized. These information certainly did not deter these men from imposing their own world view of language standards onto a culture where identities, if these existed at all, were at best fuzzy and indeterminate, simply because this was a world where vocabularies and styles of communication were not tied to geographical parameters. In her work on the Tai-Ahom identity in Assam, Yasmin Saikia argues that the linguistic community called 'Assamese' was a British invention since no traces of such a community can be found in any pre-colonial historical chronicle.[53] Arguing that society prior to the coming of the British was remarkably fluid with the king or *swargadeo* as the only legitimate centre of community identity, Saikia writes:

> In the buranjis of Assam we find a variety of images but no definite description of groups. Fluidity and elasticity are the two themes that are emphasized . . . the buranji upholds the fluid identity of a crossroads society that discouraged separation between communities. . . . Exclusive, demarcated identities were perceived as counterpolitic. Arguably, the people knew identity, but fixity was not the ethos. Thus, the boundaries between 'us' and the 'them' remained flexible. . . . The institution of the swargadeo served to realize a polity and gave some coherence to its fluid culture.[54]

The absence of any attempt at cultural demarcation in the *Buranjis* was in sync with the composite character of the subject population that, as Yasmin

Saikia states, 'had to be represented, if at all, as a composite community living within the *swargadeo*'s domain'.[55] Not only was the term 'Assamese' not mentioned by any of the authors of *Buranjis*, but none of them even made an attempt to classify local population into different categories on the basis of cultural attributes. By contrast, British accounts of the nineteenth century began to make a strict demarcation such as the one between the people of the hills and those of the plains, referring to the latter as 'Assamese' and describing them often as a group of taxable, revenue-paying peasants inhabiting the plain regions of Assam. Saikia points out that 'the blending of the various people into the Assamese produced a term with no clearly defined community or history'.[56] In her words, the British produced a name without a people.[57]

The clubbing of the population of the plains glossed over the mixed cultural backgrounds of the latter. Contrary to British colonial attempts to represent the plains peasantry as a homogenous lot, the latter were, in fact, fairly heterogeneous in social composition. It seems that all frontier tribes in Assam except the Akas had some members residing in the plains living as *ryots* and cultivating the land after the manner of the Assamese.[58] This implies that these groups would have retained some lingering links with their respective modes of cultural expression. This variety elided the colonial ethnographers. They went ahead and represented these plains people as the Assamese.[59] However, the British did not do anything beyond naming the community. Having created a community for the sake of governability, as Saikia claims, the British left the community undefined. The community so created remained bereft of a tangible identity till the missionaries endowed it with a cultural substance in the form of the Assamese language. The nineteenth century in Assam was the age of Assamese, when the missionaries engaged with the task of creating a uniform language out of a polyglossic speech and scribal culture practised by the motley groups inhabiting Assam's plain region. The Assamese language was, truly speaking, a construct, as Kar argues, like many similar nineteenth-century constructs, including *Bangla* or print Bengali. Like *Bangla*, in its next phase, Assamese was projected backwards as the ancient legacy of the Assamese community being the dominant peoples of the plain regions of British Assam. Assamese was represented as the original language of the people of Assam wrongfully upstaged by Bengali as the provincial vernacular. Through the efforts of the American Baptist Mission, supplemented soon by the able support of the emergent middle class, the Assamese language became entrenched for good as a cultural marker of an Assamese nationality. Assamese became henceforth the triumphant symbol of an Assamese identity that like the language itself was represented emphatically as primordial or eternal and for the moment beleaguered. By the turn of the century, Assamese nationalist self-fashioning had undergone considerable transformations. No longer satisfied with a limited number of cultural artefacts, the elite now felt impelled to generate a larger stock of cultural markers that could add substance to the notion of being an Assamese. Being Assamese henceforth would imply conforming to this large body of cultural imageries.

III

Contending identities

The battle over Assamese was far from over for the principal protagonists even after autonomy ceased to be an official issue. By the turn of the century Assamese became the site for yet another round of contestations. The intellectually fraught philological enterprise of the missionaries became even more contentious when sections of the province's middle class raised serious objections about the ideological premises of the new print language. This was after the missionary vernacular had been defended as the only legitimate Assamese by early stalwarts from among the nascent middle-class intelligentsia, like Anandaram Dhekial Phukan, the son of Haliram Dhekial Phukan. Even before the missionaries had tasted success with regard to their print vernacular, a serious debate unfolded over the issue of the 'correct' mode and style of spelling Assamese words. This task was taken up in earnest by self-proclaimed demagogues of Assamese such as Hemchandra Baruva, who claimed that the missionary orthography was all wrong as it was undermining the Sanskritic origins of Assamese.[60] In his *Axomiya Bhaxar Byakaran* (1859), Hemchandra Baruva therefore called for an orthography that would stick to Sanskrit norms while spelling *tatsama* and *tadbhava* words derived from Sanskrit. A new grammar written by Hemchandra Barua chose to give more prominence to the etymological origins of a word rather than to the sound and pronunciation of the latter in the matter of deciding the orthography.[61] Baruva also included a detailed discussion of other norms of language organization highlighted in Sanskrit grammars but deliberately left out as 'unnecessary', some norms of grammatical structure that missionaries had deemed significant in the formation of a language, such as those of *sandhi* and *samasa* or rules governing compounds. Curiously however, despite his admiration for Sanskrit norms, Baruva displayed remarkable eclecticism in adopting and inducting in his list of grammatical rules those traits of language structure that he deemed desirable and saw no harm in borrowing the same, if necessary, from a wide range of source languages with the objective of embellishing Assamese and giving the latter a modern look. Assessing his own work with the obvious satisfaction of a devotee who had done all he could in the services of his deity, Baruva observed:

> Sanskrit being the parent language of the Assamese literature, while solicitous to make the Grammar coincident with the Grammar of the Sanskrit; I have not overlooked such instances from the English and Bengalee, as could properly be introduced in to the grammar of the Assamese language; it can therefore be expected, that the Grammar will not contribute to the learning of the Assamese language only but it will conduce to that of the Sanskrit, Bengalee and English.[62]

Baruva's efforts to draw attention to the shortcomings of the missionary orthography resonated with the Orientalist fascination of men of the age of Hastings and Jones for the Sanskrit language which they perceived to be the parent of most known vernaculars of the country. Baruva's efforts received official endorsement when in 1873, the state announced the reversal of the earlier decision to recognize Bengali along with the promulgation that henceforth a Sanskritic style of orthography should be strictly observed in spelling those Assamese words which were derived from Sanskrit.[63] Baruva, incidentally, was not alone in his strong attachment to the Sanskrit language. Among the province's upper caste and upper-class intelligentsia, classicism or the revival of Sanskrit texts was becoming a popular trend as evinced by the large number of Sanskrit texts that were being translated into Assamese by the early years of the twentieth century.[64] Anundaram Borooah, the first Assamese ICS and a keen scholar of Sanskrit, made a valiant effort to revive Sanskrit studies by choosing to write a treatise titled *Bhavabhuti and His Place in Sanskrit Literature*. Here he went on to announce emphatically:

> To me Sanskrit is dearer than any other language. Its music has charms which no words can express. Its capability of representing every form of human thought in most appropriate language is probably not rivalled, certainly not surpassed by any other language.[65]

Classicism accompanied by attempts to purify Assamese and bring it close to the 'parent' stock, that is Sanskrit, thus went hand in hand and signified the onset of a conservative trend in language politics. It was this strong upper-caste bias that limited the scope for such low-caste enthusiasts of

Assamese like Nidhi Levi Farwell in the later years of assertive Assamese cultural nationalism. A regular contributor to the *Orunodoi*, Nidhi, a low-caste convert to Christianity and a close associate of Brown, had steadfastly refused to give up the phonemic orthography proposed by his mentor, Brown. The increasing cultural appeal of a sanitized *Assamiya* by the turn of the century left this early enthusiast behind.

Unlike Nidhi, for most of the provincial elite, after the official recognition to Assamese had been won, the choice in matters of orthographic style was not an easy one or as clear cut. Hence, in the coming years, Assamese continued to enliven cultural debates and inspiring myriad imaginings, none of which, however, pertained directly to the purely linguistic aspects of the language.[66] With the threat of Bengali still looming large in their minds, not all Assamese men of letters could agree with Baruva's theory of a Sanskritized and sanitized Assamese if only for the simple reason that holding on to Sanskritic norms could in the long run jeopardize the position of Assamese in Assam by reducing its disparities with Bengali. There were those who considered it judicious to minimize the language's proximity to Bengali by supporting a distinctive style of orthography and a near exclusive lexicon. In the process, the literati were split down the middle, with no clear consensus emerging on the issue for a fairly long time on what constituted the correct orthographic standard for Assamese. Some chose to take a middling position that would both establish the Sanskritic identity of the Assamese language and yet mark out the latter's audio-visual distance from Bengali. How contentious the issue had become can be seen from an incident that took place in 1873 when a committee was set up by the government to select primers for instruction at the secondary level. On that occasion, the latter received a letter from an organization that called itself the *Assam Literary Society*. The latter called upon the committee members to conform to certain rules proposed by the latter 'for the correct way of spelling and pronouncing Assamese words'.[67] The user was asked, among others, to pronounce 's' as 'ha', when not compounded with a consonant, and as 'ch' when compounded; to pronounce 'ch' as the Bengali way of pronouncing 's' while 'chcha' was to be pronounced a little harder than the way it was pronounced in Bengal. Again the reader was informed that in uncorrupted words of Sanskrit origin, 's' was to remain the same, while in words corrupted from the Sanskrit they should have the sound of 'ch'. Moreover, in words signifying the names of persons and places, 'ch' was to be substituted for 's'. It is not difficult to recognize in these prescriptions an attempt to strike a fine balance between an overwhelmingly Sanskritic style of spelling and one that would preserve the distinctive styles of pronunciation practised by the people. However, the issue of the correct orthographical standard continued to be debated in the pages of literary periodicals like the *Jonaki*, till the turn of the century, by which time a consensus emerged regarding the need to strike a balance between the classical and the local. Ultimately, what these exercises underscored was that the act of standardization was immensely fraught based as it was on the privileging of one single strand or trait as authentic when there were myriad other usages that could lay claim to authenticity with equal vigour and legitimacy.

That the issue of the origins of Assamese was more than a purely linguistic engagement for the nineteenth-century intellectuals became clear as the debate on orthography proceeded. Baruva who had been keen to establish the links between Sanskrit and Assamese exhibited a gross intolerance of 'non-Aryan' influences on Assamese despite the fact that speech forms identified as Assamese had co-existed all through their existence, with languages that were surely not 'Aryan' by any stretch of the imagination. This was a matter of pride to Baruva for he could then proudly observe as he did soon afterward that Assamese had successfully withstood the ravages of time to maintain its essentially Sanskritic character. Baruva wrote:

> The state of Assam was in the past dominated by the Baro Bhuyans and the Kacharis. Later the Ahoms came from the Northeastern hills and conquered the land. Although the Ahom language should have mixed with the already existing Assamese language, this did not happen possibly because the Ahoms were few in number and the Ahom language was the language of an uncivilised people (we all know that the thought process of the uncivilised being limited, it is difficult to express the sentiments of a civilised people through such a language; we do not know how far the Ahoms became civilized after coming to Assam). Hence the Ahoms learnt Assamese and the Ahom language fell into disuse.[68]

Such exclusivist outlooks were quite standard and were echoed by contemporaries like Hemchandra Goswami, who claimed in his *Axomiya Bhaxa* that although the word *Axomiya* had been derived from the word *Axam* which in turn was derived from *Aham*, the Assamese language had nothing to do with the language of the Ahoms who had migrated from a region beyond the geographical boundaries of Assam.[69] Through the debates for and against Assamese, the latter became entrenched as the predominant language of a group of people who were persuaded to imagine themselves as inhabiting a common cultural space from time immemorial.[70]

IV

Orunodoi, Jonaki *and the making of a linguistic identity*

In his eponymous work on the nationalist imagination, Benedict Anderson argues that it is print that plays a key role in the birth of nationalism by bringing together disparate people on a common platform and by providing them with a common theme on which to articulate their views.[71] Sumit Sarkar is perhaps right when he says that it is print more than education that enabled national communities in the subcontinent. The proliferation of a print culture in Assam from the middle of the nineteenth century certainly played a pivotal role in the growth of a small public, which became the principal medium for the dissemination of a literary nationalism centred round Assamese. Print was introduced in Assam in 1838 when the Baptist missionaries set up a printing press at Sibsagar. Initially, this was used to publish some Christian tracts, which were followed up by the publication of chronicles of a historical nature like Kashinath Tamuli Phukan's *Assam Buranji* and sundry other works. More sustained publications began with the launching of a vernacular newspaper-cum-magazine in 1846 called the *Orunodoi*. The latter immediately caught the fancy of the rapidly expanding literati, which had so far subscribed to Bengali-language newspapers and periodicals like the *Samachar Darpan* and the *Samachar Chandrika*. *Orunodoi* continued to circulate till 1883 when it was finally disbanded. Initially *Orunodoi* was published in two sections, magazine and newspaper, but from 1855 the newspaper section was discontinued and the magazine alone was published.[72] *Orunodoi* was the first newspaper from Assam to report on events concerning Assam along with various other news items and miscellaneous matters. *Orunodoi*'s principal contribution was to forge a literary public that could relate to each other through their reading of similar tracts and could also occasionally, through the medium of the *Orunodoi*, articulate informed views on issues of common interest to the emergent intelligentsia. *Orunodoi* enabled this public by publishing letters and tracts from local contributors on a variety of subjects ranging from history to social criticisms.

The subject matter of the *Orunodoi* was indeed eclectic. The first issue effectively summed up the focus of the new magazine. The title of the first issue read:

The Orunodoi, A monthly paper devoted to Religion, Science and General Intelligence, is printed and published at the Sibsagor Mission Press by O.T. Cutter, for the American Baptist Mission in Assam.

In the coming years *Orunodoi* carried a wide range of articles on themes as varied as news items, literary criticisms, scientific discoveries, geographical information, historical news and critical essays on issues such as language and social reforms. *Onek deshor samvad* or 'News from different countries' constituted a regular feature of the *Orunodoi*.[73] The magazine also contained didactic tracts from the Bible and sermons on Christianity as well as articles extolling the virtues of Christianity, but these themes were never allowed to dominate the pages of the *Orunodoi*. There were occasional articles on the Assamese language, the style and mode of spelling Assamese words and so on, but language also did not become the foci of attention of the *Orunodoi*. The magazine evoked a refreshing spirit of healthy inclusiveness by giving due importance to articles and tracts that highlighted the cultural and ethnic diversity of Assam. There were descriptions of the numerous ethnic groups inhabiting Assam, such as the Singphos, Miris, Akas and Daflas. A pioneer in the procurement and publication of old historical chronicles or *Buranjis*, as they were called in Assam, the *Orunodoi* never sought to thrust a homogenous past on the cultural sensibilities of its readers. Articles of history in the *Orunodoi* were therefore quite eclectic in terms of both their sources and contents. If the *Chutiya Buranji* described the activities of the *Chutiyas* – a small group inhabiting Assam's plain tracts, the *Durrung Rajvamshavali*, on the other hand, dwelt on the exploits of the Durrang kings of Lower Assam. The *Puroni Asomor Buranji* published in the pages of the *Orunodoi* was the only chronicle that dealt directly with the legacy of the Ahom rulers. Although the Baptists sounded the death knell for pre-colonial Assam's composite spirit by forefronting a single language, their literary venture, the *Orunodoi*, belied such a gesture by evoking the inclusive spirit of a cross-cultural society.

Orunodoi did not envisage the dominant voice of Assamese in Assam. Yet the magazine was crucial to the emergence of a critical public in the nineteenth century. Towards the later stages, it became a site for launching a cultural agenda through the enunciation of new expressions of behaviour that were said to behove a true Assamese.[74]

The biggest contribution of the *Orunodoi* was that it blazed the trail for yet another and more effective venture – the *Jonaki*, which became the most decisive medium for giving shape to the project of an Assamese Assam. The latter was the outcome of the efforts of Assamese students based in Calcutta. Securing the region firmly to a single language was the latter's pet project. Even after the grant of official status to Assamese in 1873, there was still scope for a multilingual culture in Assam. However, by the turn of the century, such a possibility was permanently snuffed out. With single-minded determination, the younger generation of Assamese intellectuals championed the case of an Assamese Assam, thereby extinguishing all possibilities of a multilingual province. In the 1880s some students from Assam residing in Calcutta, agitated by the dismal state of Assamese, agreed to pool together their meagre resources for launching journals and literary periodicals for promoting literary production in Assamese. The vernacular literary periodical *Jonaki* was pioneered by the latter, but there were two other literary periodicals that made their appearance at this time – *Assam Bandhu* and *Mou*. These gained immediate popularity and attained satisfactory circulation among the small but steadily expanding reading public in Assam. Later in 1888, expatriate Assamese students in Calcutta had launched a literary society called the *Axomiya Bhaxa Unnati Sadhini Sabha* or the Society for the Promotion of the Assamese Language. The principal aim of the society was to secure the literary credentials of Assamese by creating a reasonably big repertoire of literary works in the Assamese language. They also resolved to preserve older works from destruction by cataloguing and re-printing the latter as far as possible. The last, they felt, would place Assamese in the league of ancient languages, while increased literary production in Assamese would serve to establish the latter as a literary language par excellence.

The new vernacular periodicals were predominantly literary in nature unlike the infinitely more eclectic *Orunodoi*. The former drew on such modern literary genres such as poetry, novels, short stories, dramas and satires with occasional essays to break the monotony of contents. A significant shift achieved by the *Jonaki* was the publication of biographies of older writers in Assamese instead of biographies of eminent men from different fields as the *Orunodoi* had done. There was now more emphasis on historical chronicles and essays that dealt with the past in order to forge historical awareness among the readers. These periodicals thus achieved a critical shift in the nature of literary production at the turn of the century. The diversity of themes that had been a characteristic feature of the *Orunodoi* was replaced by a narrower focus on topics dealing with the Assamese language and literature. Such a possibility had been anticipated by the founder-editor of the *Jonaki*, Chandrakumar Agarwalla, in his prefatory note titled *Atmakatha* or 'Self-sketch'. Here the aims and objectives of *Jonaki* were clearly spelt out. The editor stated that *Jonaki* would concentrate solely on literature, science and society, taking special care to uplift the Assamese language from oblivion. *Jonaki* resolved not to concern itself with political affairs. Its chief focus was to promote Assamese among the people of Assam. Their principal mode of operation was to increase the number of literary production in Assamese and to establish the antiquity of the Assamese language. *Jonaki* made it very clear at the outset that it would follow a three-fold approach for the promotion of Assamese with the aim of (a) securing the exclusive claims of Assamese to the cultural sensibilities of the people of Assam, (b) according Assamese with an ancient lineage and (c) enriching Assamese with an expansive literary oeuvre.

In recent years many works have focussed on the myriad emotions that language came to inspire in people claiming to speak these languages. Scholars have examined the linguistic and literary practices through which intellectuals have ensured the construction of mother tongues anchoring a community's identity in terms of a single language and usually also a single history. In her highly acclaimed work *Passions of the Tongue*, Sumathi Ramaswami has shown how Tamil excited much passion and devotion in the late nineteenth century.[75] Likewise, Lisa Mitchell's detailed analysis of the emergence of a Telugu identity in the nineteenth century underscored the significance of literary and pedagogic interventions to the successful transition of Telugu from just a language among other languages to the status of the principal language or mother tongue for all Telugu-speaking people.[76] Mitchell shows how by the end of the nineteenth-century Telugu became a 'new personified object of adoration, pride, and devotion, as a subject of study, pedagogy and attention in its own right, and as a marker of identity'.[77] Mitchell dwells on the various literary practices through which Telugu's exclusive claims to the emotional and cultural sensibilities of the people of Andhra were secured, enabling Telugu to appear in a new personified and gendered incarnation to be affectionately addressed as 'Telugu Talli' or 'Mother Telugu'. The ascription of cultural values to language, these authors show, was not an automatic process but one that was shot through with various ideological and politico-cultural motives. The present work accepts the former as a valid framework for studying the trajectory of Assamese in the nineteenth century. For the new generation of Assamese intellectuals, the battle for Assamese was not easily won despite the substitution of Bengali by Assamese in 1873. The claims of Assamese to exclusive usage for literary and other purposes had to be secured beyond doubt. The crucial agenda for these young men thus consisted in the projection of Assamese as a language of literature both in the past and in the present. This involved the accomplishment of the twin tasks of gathering of evidences to boost the claims of Assamese to literary usage in the past and a simultaneous drive to make Assamese the sole language of literary compositions in the present.

A significant step in the direction was taken perhaps when these young enthusiasts chose the appropriate medium for showcasing the literary merits of Assamese. Unlike the Baptist missionaries, they did not opt to publish works in Assamese independently. Instead, they chose to produce literary periodicals – already an extremely popular form of literary production in Bengal. This choice of vehicle for communicating their ideas proved crucial to the success of their cultural agenda as this increased enormously the circulation of Assamese. Conventional print mediums would have been far more expensive and sporadic and therefore prohibitive at this early stage of proliferation of Assamese. Although it was the missionaries who had pioneered this form of literary production, it was the elite who used it with a zeal not seen before. Periodicals provided a single window to a wide range of compositions and genres and were therefore more tractable for the still fledgling reading community with scant means for purchase of expensive books on a regular basis. To the demagogues of Assamese, on the other hand, the periodical form of production afforded a single window to the literary range and scope of Assamese by allowing the juxtaposition of varied literary genres at the same time. Further, it allowed a constant circulation of Assamese in public memory by enabling regular production. Periodicals were also the products of collective effort and hence easier to sustain in the long run both from the financial and creative points of view. They allowed the nascent literati to practise economy in the size of their compositions which was crucial at a time when literary production in Assamese was still struggling to find its feet. Such intermittent production also permitted the community of writers the necessary time to compose longer works over a longer period of time; as such, works could now be serialized over successive issues. All this was definitely good for a fledgling community of writers struggling to disseminate a vernacular literary culture with as yet meagre creative and financial resources. The choice of literary periodicals as the chief vehicle of communication for Assamese served several important purposes at the same time.

Jonaki made biographies a regular feature of its issues. It published a series of biographies of literary personages. Tracts such as Bishnuprasad Agarwala's *Sankardev*, Dinanath Bezbaroa's *Sankardev Aru Ananta Kandali* and Sonaram Chowdhury's *Kavibar Ram Saraswati* belong to this category. Biographies of the same people were published by different authors at different times. In her work on the making of the Telugu identity, Lisa Mitchell identifies two important practices that were critical to the cultural metamorphosis of Telugu from just one language among several languages to the mother tongue of a group of people. Mitchell identifies the compilation of biographies of poets and the production of full-fledged biographies of the Telugu language as critical shifts in literary compositions during this period that played a crucial role in the evolution of Telugu.[78] Mitchell argues that the predominance of biographies of poets rather than the literary compositions of the latter as a creative oeuvre in Telugu literary compositions served to establish language as the sole yardstick of a common cultural tradition between poets and authors from diverse backgrounds and practising diverse literary genres. Language became the only common point of communication between these individuals who could now claim to be members of a common group by virtue of their use of a similar language. Biographies thus anticipated shared communities of the language. The second significant pedagogical intervention, according to Mitchell, was making language its own subject through the production of numerous biographies of the language itself describing distinct stages of its development from genesis to maturity. *Jonaki*'s emphasis on biographies of poets and authors served not only to push back the antiquity of Assamese and therefore increase its acceptability as a medium of literary composition but also to tie composer and reader together in a common bond of cultural affinity. *Jonaki* thus accomplished what even the missionaries did not manage to achieve. *Jonaki* also introduced book reviews as one of its occasional features, which further served to create an abiding interest in compositions in Assamese by enabling the reader to know about works that they had not managed to read in the original. Through various means *Jonaki* ensured that Assamese was never very far from the minds of the reading public that came to constitute the core of the new community and its chief members for some time to come. Through their ardent advocacy of Assamese, these early pioneers made language and nation synonymous, and service to language was upheld as service to the community/nation. Homogeneity and exclusivity became the hall marks of the new community. Although by Assamese these men referred to the whole of British Assam, they did not note the paradox of thrusting Assamese on the province's disparate speech groups. People were called upon to write in Assamese – an act that the first editor of the *Jonaki*, Chandrakumar Agarwalla, equated with service to the motherland. In his *Atmakatha* or Autobiography, the latter reiterated that promoting the language was equivalent to serving the motherland and must be passionately pursued.

V

Crafting an identity for Assamese

In one of his essays, Sudipta Kaviraj claimed that the 'constructedness' of the Bengali linguistic region is clear from attempts of Bengali high culture of modern times to give itself a long genealogy despite the fact that it is only in the period after the eighteenth century that some identifiable historical ancestor of the modern literary Bengali can be found.[79] Producing histories of the language was perhaps the most crucial aspect of literary nationalism and constituted the formative moment in the production of the mother tongue. This task was begun early and in earnest by Anandaram Dhekial Phukan, the son of Haliram Dhekial Phukan. In the middle of 1853, A.J. Moffat Mills, judge of the Sudder Dewany and Nizamat Adalat, Calcutta, was deputed to make a report on the province of Assam. Anandaram Dhekial Phukan, who was then a sub-assistant in Nowgong, submitted a detailed note titled *Observations on the Administration of the Province of Assam* to Mills on 4 July, in addition to making some oral submissions. Declaring Bengali to be a 'foreign tongue', Phukan argued strongly for 'the substitution, in the schools, of the Vernacular language in lieu of Bengalee (and) the publication of a series of popular works on the different branches of Native and European knowledge in the Assamese language'.[80] Asserting that Assamese alone should be the language of the courts, Phukan lamented the fact that although under the provisions of Act XXIX of 1837, the vernacular language of a district was directed to be used in the courts, a foreign language, namely Bengali, had been introduced into the courts of Assam. He pointed out that it was only to the officers and other persons connected with the courts that Bengali was intelligible, while the mass of the population and even private gentlemen possessed no knowledge of the language.[81] Claiming Assamese to be a distinct language that was the vernacular of the people, including the majority of the judges, Phukan argued,

> Bengalee bears no close resemblance to the Assamese than it does to the Uria language, and if the courts of Orissa be allowed the privilege of using the language of the country, we are unable to understand why the same benefit should have been withheld to the Assamese.[82]

Mills was sufficiently impressed by these arguments, as also by those of the Baptist missionaries who had made similar submissions, and in his report recommended that the Assamese language be restored in Assam.

In 1855, at the height of the agitation to establish the distinctiveness of Assamese, Anandaram Dhekial Phukan, who was by then a Sadar Amin, wrote *A Few Remarks on the Assamese Language and on Vernacular Education in Assam* under the signature of 'A Native'. One hundred copies of this were printed at the American Baptist Mission press at Sibsagar by A.H. Danforth and sent to the government of Bengal and distributed among leading persons in Assam. Being a public servant, Phukan perhaps did not consider it expedient to subscribe his name to the book as it contradicted the current government policy. Making out a strong case for Assamese as the 'vernacular language of the country', and as a language distinct from Bengali, Phukan wrote:

> The Measures that have been recently adopted by Government for the promotion of education in British India, have given rise to various discussions in this country, as to what is the most appropriate medium for educating the people of Assam. Some, from their imperfect acquaintance with the Assamese language, have contended, that the Bengali, the medium of instruction in Bengal, ought also to be adopted in Assam. . . . we allude to our right to use our native language, both in the education of the people and in the dispensation of justice.[83]

Phukan's plea was given wide publicity as the voice of the native for his legitimate rights and made a major impact on his contemporaries.

Phukan was also the first among the native intellectuals in seeking to provide a distinct genealogy to the Assamese language. Significantly enough, comparison with the literary claims of the Bengali intellectuals on behalf of the Bengali language was an indispensable part of Phukan's defence of the literary heritage of Assamese. Challenging the official statements that the Assamese language lacked a distinct literature of its own, he wrote:

> The Bengali can scarcely be said to have existed as a written language until the beginning of the present century, when the Missionaries of Serampore first moulded it into a form; Rajah Ram Mohun Roy wrote his Bengali Grammar; and other Native gentlemen, educated and trained up in the sciences and literature of Europe, reared up, during the last few years, a distinct literature, by the publication chiefly of translations from English works on different branches of learning. The Bengali translation of the Sanskrit Mahabharat by Kassi Dass, and that of the Ramayan by Kirti Bas, executed about a century and a half ago, may be said to be the only works of any importance in Bengali, that existed before the present Bengali literature sprung out from the efforts of Missionaries and educated natives. Now, we beg to affirm that the literature of Assam was in the year 1800 A.D. more extensive and varied than that of Bengal. The Mahabharat and Ramayan were translated into the Assamese language by Ramsaraswati and Sri Honkor nearly 400 years ago, long before Kirti Bas or Kassi Dass published their Bengali translations.[84]

As proof of his claims, Phukan provided an entire catalogue of Assamese books in the categories: (a) Hindu religious works, (b) history, (c) medicine, (d) drama, (e) arithmetic, (f) geography, (g) dictionary, (h) law and (i) schoolboy readers. He also drew attention to the latest Assamese works published by the Serampore Mission and the American Baptist Mission in Assam. He added that many books lay scattered and had not reached him and that a huge number of manuscripts were lost or destroyed during the Burmese wars and the Moamariya insurrections. He ends by asserting that the list provided wholly refutes the notion that the Assamese have no distinct literature of their own.

The impression made by Phukan's testimony was presumably strong for it led Edward A. Gait to specially mention it in his Report on the Progress of Historical Research in Assam in 1914. Gait cited Phukan's book as 'a well-written indication of the claim of Assamese to rank as a separate language'.[85] Local perception of Dhekial Phukan's contribution to the cause of Assamese is reflected in the words of Maheswar Neog, 'We believe that Phukan, without using the verbiage or methods of the linguist, has been able for the first time to have established the individuality of Assamese and its distinction from Bengali.'[86] Incidentally, Phukan's attempt to provide a suitable ancestry to the Assamese language had its precedent in missionary discourse. Danforth had noted in one of his letters,

> Shri Hungkor struck for the masses. He came down to the level of the people and translated from the Sanskrit these portions of the Hindu sacred books, and presented them to the people in their own favourite dialect.[87]

Through his writings, Phukan gave final shape to the narrative of Assamese as a literary language of sufficient antiquity.

The next stage of the task was accomplished by *Jonaki*. It not only effectively pursued the aim of crafting a substantial literary oeuvre in Assamese but also established a satisfactorily old genealogical history for Assamese. Essays on the history and development of Assamese became a regular feature of the periodical, with writers like Hemchandra Goswami and Lakshminath Bezbaroa contributing a series of articles on the subject. In his essays titled *Asamiya Bhasa*, Hemchandra Goswami traced the history of growth and development of Assamese language and literature. A familiar trope adopted by these authors, whether Goswami or Bezbaroa, was to remain evasive on the subject of the genesis of the Assamese language. Both chose to remain non-committal on this issue, deliberately creating the impression of an origin too remote and old to identify effectively. In one of his articles, Hemchandra Goswami remarked that the Assamese language must have been in existence long before the thirteenth century when the Ahoms were supposed to have arrived, because the Chinese pilgrim Hiuen Tsang was aware of the language and its distinctiveness from neighbouring Bengali and Oriya in the beginning of the Christian era. Goswami added that rather than being a corrupt form of Bengali, the Assamese language was in reality an evolved form of the language of the Aryan settlers of Kamrup, and hence, the origins of this language must be traced to the coming of the Aryans to this region.[88] Likewise, Lakshminath Bezbaroa, editor of the *Jonaki* from its third or fourth year, remarked in the seventh to eighth issue of the *Jonaki* that although not too many texts written in Assamese prior to the time of Sankardeva were available, there was not the slightest doubt that the Assamese language predated the latter. After all, the latter could not possibly have started from scratch. Bezbaroa was careful to negotiate the quantitative gaps in literary production through his rhetoric that evoked common sense to push the case of a suitable ancestry for Assamese. In his words,

> There had to be a language/dialect, however crude, for him (Sankardeva) to express his thoughts in it. The language must have had an ancestry of 1200 years for it to reach the stage in which the saint found it.[89]

One difficulty encountered by the devotees of Assamese in claiming older works for Assamese was frequent aspersions that the language of these works was not really Assamese. It was pointed out that Assamese contained numerous 'non-Assamese' words and usages. Thus, the strong presence of Maithili in the works of Sankardeva was frequently called to question. This was addressed by attributing the Maithili element in the latter's work to a self-conscious attempt by the poet-author to enlarge the readership of his works. Sankardeva's works were classified into two categories, namely drama and kirtan. The former was acknowledged to contain Maithili and other linguistic influences, while the latter was claimed to have been written in pure Assamese. The discrepancy was dismissed as an attempt on the part of the author-reformer, to endear his works to the general public, which had supposedly little respect for the local vernacular.[90] Another article published in the *Assam Bandhu* admitted that the language of Sankardeva's works constituted a mixture of Braj and Maithili with a smattering of Oriya, but hastened to add that this did not imply that these were not Axomiya texts (*Axomiya puthi*) since such overlaps were common in languages with a shared Sanskritic background.[91] Orientalist philological notions of the genetic relation between the principal vernaculars of north and eastern India, deriving from their common Sanskritic parentage, were conveniently appropriated and deployed to explain away incongruous and seemingly irreconcilable anomalies so that the antiquity of Assamese as a literary language could not be called to question.

Not satisfied with crafting a genealogy for Assamese, intellectuals of the nineteenth century also sought to foster impressions of a homogenous past that was sufficiently glamorous and strongly Aryan. Articles such as Anandachandra Agarwala's *Bamuni Konwar* and *Asamat Arya Basati* and Ratneswar Mahanta's *Jaymati Kunwari aru Langi Gadapani* belonged to this category. *Jonaki's* engagement with history was, however, very different from that of the *Orunodoi*, which had made a random selection of older narratives emanating from diverse sources and articulating diverse pasts. *Jonaki* was less eclectic, choosing to confine itself to Puranic or Ahomera narratives. Its privileging of Puranic accounts, discussed in more detail in Chapter 5, foretold an urge for homogeneity and anticipated a trend which became stronger subsequently. This was to discard heterogeneity in Assam's diverse historical and cultural traditions and impose on the latter a strictly tailored uniformity that conformed closely to the Puranic model of an Aryan past.

The *Assam Bandhu*, which began its publication prior to the *Jonaki*, in 1886, was equally devoted to the twin tasks of crafting a suitable ancestry for Assamese and in expanding the repertoire of works in the language. Not a self-proclaimed community exponent like the *Jonaki*, the *Assam Bandhu*'s publications of drama, poetry and fiction were, nonetheless, regularly interrupted with compositions evocative of a glorious past for the language and the region.[92] Its emphasis on the historical genre sought to project the age-old links and cultural affinities between the people of Assam and the inhabitants of Aryan India. The periodical sought to place Assam on the historical map of ancient India, thereby fulfilling the growing cultural aspirations of the provincial elite for recognition as a key participant in India's much-vaunted Puranic traditions. Historical writings predominated in the pages of the *Assam Bandhu*. Among these mention may be made of *Agor Din Etiyar Din* (The Past and the Present), *Purani Guwahati Nagar* (The Ancient Guwahati City), *Pouranik aru Tantrik Kamrup* (Kamrup of the Puranas and the Tantras), *Amar Manuh* (Our People) and *Bongali* (Bengalis).

The need to consolidate the position of Assamese meant not only that Assamese had to be provided with a genealogy but also that its status be secured at par with Bengali. Anandaram Dhekial Phukan was again the pioneer among the Assamese intellectuals in continuing the tradition set by the missionaries in this regard. He set the trend whereby the Bengali language became permanently etched as the competitive 'other', to be watched and outsmarted in terms of literary output. Apart from the passage from *A Few Remarks* that has already been quoted here is yet another allusion that will serve to illustrate the point:

> We are . . . informed that the want of zeal and promptitude in Assamese youths, led to the abandonment of every idea of giving the Assamese a sound English education. But we cannot forbear expressing our belief, that if no progress is made by all the pupils of an institution, defect in the system, and not in the scholars, must, in a great measure, be presumed. . . . That the Assamese are at least equal, if not superior, to the Bengalis in their mental capabilities will be conceded; and that thirst for European knowledge has now become almost universal in the country, may be proved from the deep anxiety which some Assamese parents have now begun to evince by sending their children to the Bengal colleges for education . . . and had not the climate of Bengal been most unfriendly to Assamese constitutions, numbers of our youth would, long ere this, have resorted to the Colleges of Bengal.
>
> (Translation mine)[93]

Significant in this passage is the clear transition from a sense of common language and its perceived heritage to a clear avowal of pride in the intellectual worth and abilities of the collective and simultaneously in an affirmation of collective interests. Henceforth, in the true sense, the Assamese collective could be said to have arrived.

The battle to assert the equality/superiority of the Assamese collective vis-à-vis that of the Bengalis was led in its subsequent stages by Lakshminath Bezbaroa. A few passages from his prolific writings will serve to illustrate this point. In one such work, he writes,

> It is not as if we envy the Bengalis but we desire that similar benefits should be extended to us and that the Bengalis instead of criticising us should help us to progress likewise.
>
> (Translation mine)[94]

In a more frontal attack on the Bengalis, he wrote,

> How developed is the Bengali language that these Bengali gentlemen dare criticise the Assamese language? Having brought out a

few state newspapers and having written a few Battala novels with plots stolen from English novels they have lost their senses. . . . People citing the antiquity of the Bengali must not forget that only recently Rammohun had taught the Bengalis prose reading. These Bengali babus had also tried to appropriate the Oriya language but failed. In Assam, however, they are still trying.

(Translation mine)[95]

The constant comparison with the Bengali language and with the Bengali 'community' thus became an indispensable part of the social and institutional history of Assamese.

The upshot of literary nationalism

The intensity of the Assamese elite's engagement with language and literature post-1874 had an intensely elitist bias as it did not allow them to consider more pressing socio-economic aspects of colonial rule. It is difficult to avoid the conclusion that the intensity of the vernacular project drew sustenance from the anxieties intrinsic to a distant education that was enforced on the Assamese youth by virtue of the reluctance of the administration in Assam to promote higher education. An enforced stay away from home in the impersonal environment of mess houses and in the alienating environment of a big city as well as forced migration lent a militant thrust to the nationalistic imagination of these young Assamese expatriates. It is typical, however, of the situation in Assam that despite the culpability of the colonial state in creating the conditions for forced migration, there was hardly any genuine animosity towards the colonial state till a fairly long time. It is crucial also that it was this small group of Assamese students who went to Calcutta for higher education and took to writing in due course, choosing to articulate in Assamese their emotions and aspirations for a distinguished mother tongue. With few exceptions, these men were associated with the vernacular literary periodicals for long periods of time. Travel for these men had not always been an easy matter and involved time, money and physical discomforts. Not everyone could afford to travel in style like Anandaram Dhekial Phukan, who is said to have travelled with a cook and an attendant for 25 days by boat to reach Calcutta. After a preliminary education at home, he was admitted to the English School at Guwahati in 1837, and after he had reached the top form in this school, he was advised by Commissioner Jenkins and Captain James Matthie to travel to Calcutta for completing his education.[96] Here he got himself admitted to the junior division of the Hindu College. Much has been said about the plight of Assamese students studying in Calcutta and their less-than-happy encounters with a confident Bengali literary culture. A fresh look at the subject would not be out of place in order to understand how the colonial metropolis reacted on the impressionable minds of these young migrants. The social impact of their metropolitan sojourn and the pressures of excelling in higher education in an alien environment were far from happy for many of the early stalwarts of Assamese. Once in Calcutta the Assamese students put up at various mess houses in the city and enrolled themselves in one of the numerous colleges of the city. The alienating effects of city life combined with the distance from friends and family made for extreme loneliness. Laksminath Bezbaroa effectively describes his feelings of loss at this stage in his autobiography *Mor Jibon Sworon*. Others like Padmanath Gohain Barua did not seem so unnerved by the experience and eventually came to cherish the cultural vibrancy of nineteenth-century Calcutta, if his account of his student days in Calcutta is anything to go by. Overall, however, the yearning for home in a distant city merged with new cultural sensitivities and the latter's complex negotiations with a confident and self-conscious Bengali literary culture inspired in these young men a desire for an Assamese Assam that could become an ideal 'homeland' for an Assamese-speaking community. The impersonal tenor of life in a big city for people who did not possess a permanent home within the precincts of the city usually could and did evoke all kinds of responses among a migrant population. In *Writing Social History*, Sumit Sarkar examines the alienating effect of the big city on Bengali men who came to Calcutta to work in the numerous government and private offices in the city. Sarkar highlights the fact that despite their prolonged sojourn in the various mess houses of the city, Calcutta could never carve out a place for itself in the literary imaginaire of the Bengali *bhadralok* (educated middle class) of the nineteenth century. The immigrants to the city continued to refer to their mess houses as *basha*, reserving the more familial and endearing expression *bari* for their ancestral homes in the village. If the colonial city produced nothing but alienation in its Bengali residents, it was only natural that it should seem less habitable to the Assamese students who had been forced to leave their province for no fault on their part. Moreover, an education away from home could and often did introduce all kinds of uncertainties in the lives of these young migrants. In 1844 when Anandaram Dhekial Phukan had been promoted to the senior division of the Hindu College, news of troubles in the family property reached him and he had to discontinue his studies and go back to Guwahati. His formal education consequently remained incomplete. He was not the only one who failed to complete education in Calcutta. The list included others like Chandrakumar Agarwalla,

Padmanath Gohain Barua and Lakshminath Bezbaroa. Of these, Chandra-kumar Agarwalla had everything going for him. The wealthy son of Harivi-las Agarwalla whose family had a business centre at 10, Armenian Street, Burrabazar, he was already staying in his own house and looking after the family business when he joined FA class of the Presidency College. Yet he failed to obtain a BA degree in the end. Lakshminath Bezbaroa's dreams of practising law were shattered when the University of Calcutta raised the percentage of pass marks in the Bachelor's examination, inducing the latter to file a litigation suite against the university authorities. Clearly, the experi-ence of education in Calcutta did not prove to be especially happy for many, and the dreams of receiving a higher degree at the end continued to elude many a young aspirant from Assam. It is not impossible and certainly worth considering that the social impact of an alienating education in the colonial metropolis had much to do with the virulent cultural nationalism of the turn of the century when Assamese had already become entrenched as the pro-vincial vernacular. The perceived insult to the mother tongue highlighted in all standard works on Assamese and derived originally from the story of Lakshminath Bezbaroa's reception in the Tagore household of his wife, Prajnasundaridevi, was an eminently personal experience, but this served to aggravate the sense of loss. Subsequent assaults on Assamese in the pages of Bengali literary periodicals like the *Prabasi* made matters worse.

VI

Middle class and the state

The intense preoccupation with language from the latter part of the nineteenth century and the possible belief in the good intents of the colo-nial state did not allow the middle class to address maladies of colonial rule. While the first part of the nineteenth century had witnessed some heightened engagements on the issue of the inadequacies of the new educational policy, the same impulse was conspicuous by its absence in the later part of the nineteenth century. There was a clear dearth of independent petitions and memorials unlike in the previous period. Nor did issues of education find any representation in the two leading ver-nacular periodicals of the time despite the fact that both had resolved to promote the material well-being of the 'mother land'. The colonial edu-cation policy that had driven the exponents of Assamese from home did not find any resonance in the literary enterprises of the expatriate Assa-mese students in Calcutta.[97] An examination of the contents of the first two – *Assam Bandhu* and the *Jonaki* – reveals an overwhelming concern with the need to forge a literary culture centred round the Assamese language. Neither the *Assam Bandhu* nor the *Jonaki* carried a single article on education during the period under review. Although thematically the lists of contents of the *Assam Bandhu* were quite diverse, there was a preponderance of compositions that deliberated on the 'history' of the region/community and on practices described as the community's very own. The silence of the *Assam Bandhu* was not in consonance with the broad theme outlined by its founding editor, Gunabhiram Barua. In his very first editorial, he had asserted that the journal would not indulge in administrative discussions, communal references and criticisms of others (*Poroninda*). Instead, the journal promised to contribute towards a wholesome development of the Assamese people by presenting 'useful' topics that would serve to broaden the community's outlook and ensure its progress.[98] The *Assam Bandhu*, however, belied this vision by leaving out such a significant matter as the limitations of colonial modernity from its very pages. A small sample survey of the contributions to the *Jonaki*, which was, perhaps, the most popular periodical of its time, reveals that from its inception in 1888–1900, the magazine did not publish a single article that talked about the need for improving the province's educational infrastructure.

The only journal that refused to be drawn into this literary battle was the *Mou*, edited by Bolinarayan Bora. *Mou* survived only for a year. It is said that the intense hostility of the Calcutta group of Assamese intellectuals expedited its demise. This periodical was unique in its call for an end to the anti-Bengali spirit (*BongaliBiddekh*) that animated the vernacular literary sphere. Its editor Bolinarayan Bora had caustically remarked in one of his articles, 'Bor pet kati Ra karilei DeshHitoishita?' (Does love for the community consist in merely inserting a line through Ba to make it Ra?)[99] *Mou* was, however, the only periodical in the nineteenth century to raise the demand for reversal of the state's policies for higher education. The periodical carried a series of articles denouncing the poor state of education in the province and urged the immediate need for promoting English education. In one of its articles published in January 1887, called *Uchcha Hikhkha*' (Higher Education), the author demanded an increase in the salaries of the school teachers to attract the best minds to education. The article merits attention for its vehement opposition to the government's education policy – a position not usual in the rhetoric of the regional elite in the nineteenth century.[100] It criticized the inadequacy of financial aid to education and commented sarcastically on the futility of spending huge sums of money to sustain the post of Inspector of Schools.[101] In its brief span of a year, *Mou* carried as many as three articles criticizing the state's educational policy. It placed a plethora of demands before the state, ranging from the increase in the number of schools in every district and the improvement in the quality of instruction to the promotion of English education in Assam. It called upon the government to raise the salary of the teachers to attract the best minds to education and exhorted the people of Assam to exert pressure on the government for reforms in the educational sector. Notwithstanding these timely critiques, *Mou*'s attempts to be forthright on the issue of anti-Bengali sentiments earned it the ire of its contemporaries and ushered in its ruin. *Mou* served to fill the vacuum created by the vernacular literary sphere's failure to assume a genuinely anti-colonial stance on an issue that could have become significant to the identitarian discourse of the middle class.

Not only did the middle class not react against the lack of opportunities for higher education closer home, but they also remained more or less silent on the excesses of the land revenue demands although this did not escape their notice. In his petition to Mills in 1853, Maniram Dewan had repeatedly referred to the 'unjust taxation' policy of the new regime. Maniram's criticism is, however, admissible given his personal grudge against the British, given the fact that he was one of those whose personal fortunes had suffered reverses under British rule. The same cannot be said of Anandaram Dhekial Phukan, who was not only a government employee but also one otherwise happy with the new regime and clearly one of the beneficiaries. Even such a loyal supporter of the British as Anandaram did not, however, fail to point out in the same petition about 'the defects in its (British) revenue and judicial administration as well as the improvements which it is now in the power of Government to effect' or to observe that 'the principle on which the public assessment is now regulated are far from being much favorable to the advancement of cultivation and the general improvement of the country'. Anandaram was scathing in his indictment of the misdemeanours of the collectors, over-assessment of the *ryot*'s land, imposition of illegal cesses and the difficult, protracted and expensive methods of judicial redressal instituted by the British that was utterly incomprehensible to the *ryots* and far too difficult for them to access. His appraisal was quite critical and unbiased. It is possible that Anandaram was voicing the feelings of men of his creed, who felt equally strongly about the nature and impact of new norms of settlements in Assam. Yet the petitions of Anandaram and Maniram are the only ones that we come across in our search for responses to British rule in Assam in the first, second and third quarters of the nineteenth century. There were of course incidents of royalist conspiracies which were crushed summarily.

However, one draws a blank when it comes to mapping the responses of the middle class, which though nascent was nonetheless existent, to what was obviously not a very happy state of affairs so far as the agrarian and revenue situations of Assam were concerned.

Notes

1 Foreign Political Records, 19 March 1832, No. 81, pp. 1–9 (NAI), cited in Amalendu Guha, 'Impact of Bengal Renaissance on Assam', *IESHR*, Vol. IX, No. 3, September 1972, p. 290.

2 See Rajen Saikia, *Social and Economic History of Assam 1853–1921*, New Delhi: Manohar, 2000; Sajal Nag, *Roots of Ethnic Conflict Nationality Question in North-East India*, New Delhi: Manohar, 1990, and A.K. Baruah, *Social Tensions in Assam Middle Class Politics*, Guwahati: Purbanchal Prakash, 1991.

3 Letter from White to the Agent to the Governor General, dated Jorhat 28 May 1832, Foreign Political Records, 23 July 1832, NAI, cited in Guha, 'Impact of Bengal Renaissance on Assam'.

4 Manorama Sharma, *Social and Economic Change in Assam Middle Class Hegemony*, New Delhi: Ajanta Publications, 1990.

5 Letter from Jenkins to Mills, Mills's Report, pp. 86–87.

6 Archibald Watson, *Memoir of the Late David Scot*, Calcutta: Baptist Missionary Press, 1832, p. 27.

7 Ibid., pp. 20–22.

8 Ibid., pp. 20–21.

9 For the debate on the social composition of the Assamese middle class in Assam, see Sharma, *Social and Economic Change in Assam Middle Class Hegemony*, and Saikia, *Social and Economic History of Assam 1853–1921*.

10 Ibid., p. 118.

11 Preface to Assam Buranji by Harakant Barua *Sadar Amin*, Guwahati: DHAS, 1962.

12 Surya Kumar Bhuyan, *Anandaram Barwa Jivan Charit*, Guwahati: Lawyer's Book Stall, 1955, p. 39.

13 Lakshminath Bezbaroa, *Mor Jivon Sworon*, Guwahati: Lawyer's Book Stall, 1999.

14 Maheswar Neog, 'An Outline of Lakshminath Bezbaroa's Life', in Maheswar Neog (ed.), *Lakshminath Bezbaroa, the Sahityarathi of Assam*, Guwahati: Gauhati University, 1972.

15 Padmanath Gohain Barua, *Mor Somvarani*, Guwahati: Assam Prakashan Parishad, 1971.

16 Sharma, *Social and Economic Change in Assam*.

17 Ibid., pp. 118–120.

18 Bezbaroa, *Mor Jivon Sworon*.

19 See in this connection, Hiren Gohain, *Assam: A Burning Question*, Guwahati: Spectrum Publications, 1985.

20 Samachar Darpan, 30 July 1831, cited in the Preface to the Assam Buranji.

21 Haliram Dhekial Phukan, *Assam Buranji*, Calcutta: Samachar Chandrika Press, 1829, Preface; also cited in Guha, 'Impact of Bengal Renaissance on Assam'.

22 Bezbaroa, *Mor Jivon Sworon*.

23 Ibid.

24 Preface to the Assam Buranji; also see Bodhisattva Kar, ' "Tongue Has No Bone": Fixing the Assamese Language, c. 1800–c. 1930', *Studies in History*, Vol. 24, No. 1, n.s. 2008, p. 27.

25 Ibid.

26 John Peter Wade, *History of Assam*, 1800.

27 Lisa Mitchell, *Language, Emotion, Politics in South India: The Making of a Mother Tongue*, Ranikhet: Permanent Black, 2009, p. 159.

28 Ibid.

29 Ibid.

30 See Velcheru Narayana Rao, 'Print and Prose Pandits, Karanams, and the East India Company in the Making of Modern Telugu', in Stuart Blackburn and Vasudha Dalmia (eds), *India's Literary History Essays in the Nineteenth Century*, New Delhi: Permanent Black, 2004.

31 See Kar, 'Tongue Has No Bone', p. 30.

32 Ibid.

33 Preface to Assam Buranji by Harakant Barua Sadar Amin, Guwahati: DHAS, 1962; cited in Kar, 'Tongue Has No Bone'.

34 See Kar, 'Tongue Has No Bone'.

35 Yasmin Saikia, *Assam and India Fragmented Memories, Cultural Identity and the Tai-Ahom Identity*, Ranikhet: Permanent Black, 2005, p. 120.

36 Suryya Kumar Bhuyan, *Preface to Kamrupar Buranji*, Guwahati: DHAS, 1958.

37 Ibid.

38 Ibid.

39 Kashinath Tamuli Phukan, *Preface to Assam Buranji*, 1844,Reprint, Calcutta: Majumdar Press, 1906 (further reprinted by DHAS, 1967).

40 See Kar, 'Tongue Has No Bones'.

41 Ibid., pp. 32–33.

42 Ibid.

43 See Nathan Brown, *Grammatical Notices of the Assamese Language*, Sibsagar, Assam: American Baptist Mission Press, 1848.

44 See Saikia, *Assam and India Fragmented Memories*, p. 6.

45 Ibid., p. 24.

46 Ibid.

47 See John Lyons, *Language and Linguistics: An Introduction*, Cambridge, UK: Cambridge University Press, 1981.

48 See Burghart, 'A Quarrel in the Language Family: Agency and Representations of Speech in Mithila'.

49 Lyons, *Language and Linguistics*; see King, *One Language, Two Scripts*, and Burghart, 'A Quarrel in the Language Family: Agency and Representations of Speech in Mithila'.

50 Letters Issued to the Government, 1872, Vol. 47, ASA.

51 G.A. Grierson, *Linguistic Survey of India, Vol. V, Indo-Aryan Family, Eastern Group, Part I; Specimens of the Bengali and Assamese Languages*,

Calcutta: Office of the Superintendent of Government Printing, India, 1903–1928, 1903, p. 394.

52 Ibid., p. 15.

53 Saikia, *Assam and India Fragmented Memories.*

54 Ibid., pp. 122–123.

55 Ibid., p. 125; Saikia convincingly argues that the nearest equivalent to the term 'Assam' may be found in the medieval chronicles of the Mughal period, none of which, however, contain any reference to the expression 'Assamese'. The *Baharistan-i-Ghaybi* of Alauddin Isfahani, alias Mirza Nathan, a Mughal general in the reign of Jahangir, uses the term 'Acham' to refer to the subjects of the *swargadeo.* The *Fathiyah-I-Ibriyah* of Shihabuddin Talish, a late seventeenth-century chronicle, refers to the people as the subjects of the 'Acham Raja' or the 'Achamers'. The first European account of the people is by Glanius, a Dutch mercenary who accompanied Mir Jumla to Assam. He refers to the local people as the 'people of Assam'.

56 Ibid., p. 59.

57 See Yasmin Saikia's doctoral dissertation titled *A Name without a People: Searching to be Tai-Ahom in Modern India*, University of Wisconsin–Madison, 1999.

58 'Report on the Aka Hills Expedition, 1883' by Captain H. St. P. Maxwell, Political Officer, Aka Field Force, ASL.

59 See Saikia, *Assam and India Fragmented Memories.*

60 In this connection, see Francesca Orsini, 'What Did They Mean by "Public"? Language, Literature and the Politics of Nationalism', *Economic and Political Weekly*, Vol. 34, No. 7, 13–19 February 1999, pp. 409–416. Orsini shows how during the late eighteenth and the early nineteenth centuries, the Hindi literati tried to lay down general principles and norms for Sanskritized Hindi, which alone was to be Indian Hindi.

61 See Kar, *Tongue Has No Bones*, for a detailed discussion of the contests over the orthography of the print Assamese.

62 Hemchandra Sharma Barua, Introduction, *Axomiya Bhaxar Byakaran* (Assamese Grammar), Gauhati, 1859.

63 Kar, *Tongue Has No Bones*, p. 48.

64 Catalogue of Assamese Books 1906–1953, Oriental and India Office Collections, British Library, London.

65 Anundoram Borooah, *Bhavabhuti and His Place in Sanskrit Literature*, 1877, Reprint, Guwahati: Publication Board Assam, 1971, p. 54.

66 See Madhumita Sengupta, 'War of Words: Language and Policies in Nineteenth-Century Assam', *Indian Historical Review*, Vol. 39, No. 2, 2012, pp. 293–315.

67 Assam Commissioner's File, No. 471, Letter no. 1412, ASA; see in this connection Orsini, 'What Did They Mean by "Public"?'. Orsini shows how *tadbhava* words (words of Sanskrit origin but phonetically modified through the ages) were systematically replaced by Sanskrit loanwords and 'foreign' (i.e. Perso-Arabic) words were avoided as much as possible. Thus, although in the nineteenth century Hindi was flaunted as the language of mass education (and the antithesis of English), the Hindi actually used in textbooks was the polite 'high' language of literary journals, p. 414.

68 Introduction, *Axomiya Bhaxar Byakaran*, Guwahati, 1859.

69 Hemchandra Goswami, 'Axomiya Bhaxa', *Jonaki*, Vol. 3, No. 5, 1890.

70 See Anindita Ghosh, *Power in Print Popular Publishing and the Politics of Language and Culture in a Colonial Society, c. 1778–1905*, New Delhi: Oxford University Press, 2006.

71 Benedict Anderson, *Imagined Communities: Reflections on the Origin and Spread of Nationalism*, London: Verso, 1963.

72 See Nagen Saikia, *Background of Modern Assamese Literature*, New Delhi: Omsons, 1988, p. 169.

73 See Jayeeta Sharma, 'Missionaries and Print Culture in Nineteenth-Century Assam: The Orunodoi Periodical of the American Baptist Mission', in Eric Frykenberg (ed.), *Christian Missionaries in India Cross-Cultural Communication since 1500*, Michigan and Cambridge, UK: Eerdmans, 2003; see also Tilottama Misra, 'Social Criticism in Nineteenth Century Assamese Writing: The Orunodoi', *Economic and Political Weekly*, Vol. 20, No. 37, 14 September 1985, pp. 1558–1566.

74 See Jayeeta Sharma, *Empire's Garden Assam and the Making of India*, Ranikhet: Permanent Black, 2011.

75 Sumathi Ramaswami, *Passions of the Tongue: Language Devotion in Tamil India, 1891–1970* (Studies on the History of Society and Culture, 1997), New Delhi: Munshiram Manoharlal, 1998.

76 Mitchell, *Language, Emotion and Politics in South India*.

77 Ibid., p. 69. Other works have highlighted the role of print in hardening linguistic boundaries. Christopher King has shown how during the later part of the nineteenth century, the Hindi press and a number of voluntary associations provided the necessary organization whereby the supporters of Hindi could transmit their aims to the literate public. The rapid expansion of publishing and journalism, later in the century, strengthened the existing differentiation between Hindi and Urdu and ruled out any assimilation between the two. The rural masses were left almost entirely untouched by the Hindi–Urdu controversy. See King, *One Language, Two Scripts*.

78 Mitchell, *Language, Emotion and Politics in South India*, p. 73.

79 Sudipta Kaviraj, 'The Imaginary Institution of India', in Partha Chatterjee and David Arnold (eds), *Subaltern Studies*, Vol. VII, New Delhi: Oxford University Press, 1993. In his words, 'But this culture requires a high ancestry; and consequently this highly confident literary culture gives itself an interestingly idiosyncratic and opportunistic genealogy. It is interesting to see it move in the tangled antiquities of a few contiguous and fluctuating regions to do its shopping for its historical past. For such purpose it happily appropriates Buddhist dohas from Nepal and the splendid poetry of Vidyapati as the undoubted ancestry of modern Bengali literature. We should not therefore be misled by the impressively ancient ancestry that regions and their languages press upon us. Often, the process by which the region comes into being is not much more ancient than the ones which make the Indian nation appear some years later, and sometimes the contributing processes are the same', p. 25.

80 Maheswar Neog, *Anandaram Dhekial Phukan: Plea for Assam and Assamese (with the Complete Text of Observations on the Administration of*

the Assam and a Few Remarks on the Assamese Language and on Vernacular Education in Assam), Jorhat: Asam Sahitya Sabha, 1977, p. 79.

81 Ibid., p. 118.
82 Ibid., p. 119.
83 Ibid., pp. 123–124.
84 Ibid., p. 161.
85 Ibid., p. 26.
86 Ibid., p. 26.
87 H.K. Barpujari, 'American Missionaries and North-East India/1836–1900 A.D.: A Documentary Study', 1986, p. 142.
88 *Axomiya Bhaxa*, composition read out by Hemchandra Goswami at the second annual meeting of the Axomiya Bhaxa Unnati Sadhini Sabha, *Jonaki.*
89 *Jonaki*, Pancham Bhag, 7th–8th Issue, 1816–1817 Saka.
90 Goswami, 'Axomiya Bhaxa'.
91 Hemchandra Goswami, 'Sankardeva Rachana – Sita Soyombor Natak', *Assam Bandhu*, Vol. 1, 1885, p. 109.
92 Francesca Orsini shows how in the nineteenth century, Mahavir Prasad Dvivedi's literary periodical *Sarasvati* sought to set a standard for prose writing by encouraging the production of works on biography, history and science instead of poetry and romance. Dvivedi perceived his role as editor-critic to create a certain Hindi-reading public in accordance with his notions of community service. See also Anindita Ghosh, An Uncertain 'Coming of the Book': Early Print Cultures in Colonial India, Book History, Vol. 6, 2003, pp. 23–55, for a study of how the popular Battala print culture in nineteenth-century Bengal resisted attempts by high print to set normative standards of literary production. See also Anindita Ghosh, 'Revisiting the "Bengal Renaissance": Literary Bengali and Low-Life Print in Colonial Calcutta', *Economic and Political Weekly*, Vol. 37, No. 42, 19–25 October 2002, pp. 4329–4338. Here Ghosh remarks, 'For long Bengal has been looked upon by historians as the harbinger of modernity in the subcontinent. Fortified with western education, Bengali intellectuals are supposed to have effected a western style "Renaissance" in contemporary thought and the liberal arts. These studies have focused exclusively on a dominant print-culture shaped by the educated elite, and have tended to assume a linear causal link between western education, control over print technology, and dissemination of occidental knowledge. The Bengali language itself is thought to have evolved into a modern vernacular, capable of communicating the most rational and sublime ideas. However, what this perspective overlooks is that print in 19th century Bengal was not used and engineered by dominant power groups alone. Given its cheapness and accessibility, the printed book enjoyed a wide circulation. Dominant ideas on literary taste and styles, also did not go unchallenged. It is important to bring back these reader groups into focus. Focussing on more commercial forms of print literature is a useful counterweight to historiography deriving from only "high" writings, that perpetuate images of an undifferentiated, enlightened, western educated Bengali middle class', p. 4329. Also

see Vasudha Dalmia, 'The Locations of Hindi', *Economic and Political Weekly*, Vol. 38, No. 14, 5–11 April 2003, pp. 1377–1384.

93 Neog, *Anandaram Dhekial Phukan*, pp. 170–171.

94 Ibid.

95 *Jonaki*, 6th Bhag–3rd Issue, *Bezbarua Granthabali*.

96 See Neog, *Anandaram Dhekial Phukan*.

97 See Madhumita Sengupta, 'Orienting Progress? Some Aspects of Education in 19th Century Assam'.

98 Gunabhiram Barua, 'Editor's Note', *Assam Bandhu*, First Issue.

99 'Axomiya aru Bongali', *Mou*, No. 2, January 1887 (translation mine).

100 'Ingrazi Hikhkha', December 1887, and 'Uchcha Hikhkha', March 1887, *Mou*, Guwahati: Prakashan Parishad, 1980.

101 Ibid.

5

INTIMATE HISTORIES
OF ASSAMESE

The nationalist trajectory of Assamese was by no means inevitable. This chapter explores telltale notions of an alternative community in the cultural imagination of the early intellectuals of colonial Assam, to put forward the assumption that the 'Assamese' community imagined around a common language was neither the first nor the only community imaginary to emerge from the region. Alternative ideas of groupness envisioned around alternate modes of solidarity had been conceptualized and proposed earlier although the latter failed to fire the imagination of the provincial intelligentsia. This chapter shows how in the long run these liberal and inclusive notions of nationality were superseded by more exclusivist subjectivities that held up language as the only legitimate marker of group identity for the so-called Assamese people.

I

A new solidarity: Haliram and his 'history'

Haliram Dhekial Phukan's *Assam Deshar Itihas yani Buranji*, written and compiled in 1829, was fairly novel in many ways. Apart from being the first purely indigenous attempt at publication from the region, the work is also now acknowledged to have been the first-ever history to be compiled in the Bengali language. For students of history, the value of the text, however, stems not from the contents of the work but from the inimitable style of narrative that had the authorial voice addressing the reader every now and then. The language and style of the narrative barely concealed an earnest and clear-cut agenda that was far more complex than the one that the author himself had ordained at the beginning of the text – that of

183

revealing Assam to the rest of the subcontinent's peoples. The agenda itself was stated quite unambiguously in the introduction:

> The availability of the printing press in Calcutta has made it possible for learned men to publish books of various kinds including accounts of different countries. However no book pertaining to Assam has so far been published. Many people are aware vaguely that there is a place called Assam Kamarupa, but no one knows where this country is or what this country is like. Hence it is important to write about Assam. This is crucial since after the occupation of Assam by the British many people are visiting this place. Owing to their ignorance about Assam they are finding it difficult to perform governmental activities. Hence for the benefit of all concerned, this work describing the history of Assam has been produced. This work has been divided into four parts and it is hoped that it will benefit many people.
>
> (Translation mine)[1]

Haliram's work possessed other interesting properties that set it apart from similar works written during this period. The author tried to push sell his compilation by offering to distribute copies free of cost to anyone interested in reading it. Another crucial aspect of his work was that it was not a sponsored or commissioned project like many other works that were being produced at the time. By his own admission, the author wrote the chronicle solely to fulfil his immediate and very personal urge to write a history of his *mulk* or land.[2]

Haliram's work was a curious amalgam of the modern and the conventional. It was 'modern' in as much as it belonged primarily to a genre of territorial history or historical narrative of a place/region and the people living therein. Although not yet familiar in British Assam, such a genre had already become a familiar mode of expression in the vernacular literary sphere of neighbouring Bengal with which Haliram had gained some acquaintance. It was certainly distinct from the older and more familiar genre of dynastic histories or family chronicles that had been quite the rage in the pre-colonial period almost under all previous regimes.[3] Another novel feature of Haliram's text was its attempt to provide a comprehensive account of all aspects of life – political, religious, economic, social and geographical – in pre-British Assam – an attribute that is not to be found in works of an earlier period. The author stated in the preface that he had divided his work into four parts. The first part contained an account of the kings of pre-British Assam; the second described the mode of governance, especially the administration of justice in Assam; the third contained geographical details of the region, including information about the hills and rivers of Assam; and the fourth enumerated the products of the region, castes, number of people and the mode of worship followed by the people. The scope of the work was far wider than any that had been contemplated so far.

At the time of the publication of the work, Haliram Dhekial Phukan was employed as a *Sheristadar* at the Guwahati Collectorate of the British administration. Soon afterwards, in 1832 he would be promoted to the post of assistant magistrate at Guwahati. A man seemingly well versed in Sanskrit and Bengali, Haliram was a frequent visitor to the colonial metropolis, Calcutta, and is known to have had access to the new class of social and intellectual elite in that city. He was certainly a regular contributor to contemporary Bengali newspapers like the *Samachar Darpan*. Widely popular and well known in the elite social circles of nineteenth-century Calcutta, Haliram's visits to the city were reported now and then in newspapers and other contemporary satirical works such as the famed *Alaler Ghorer Dulal* by Tekchand Thakur, a.k.a. Pyarichand Mitra.[4] A widely travelled man, he is said to have visited numerous places of Hindu pilgrimage such as Gaya, Kashi or modern Benaras and Prayaga, which was no mean feat in those days when transportation facilities were still rather basic. Although not exposed to Western education, Haliram was well informed and quite familiar with many of the emerging socio-cultural trends set in motion by the establishment of British rule. It is perhaps wise not to read too much into Haliram's choice of language, that is Bengali for his work, since young men in Assam in those days were fairly familiar with the language. The decision to write in Bengali was perhaps inspired by the author's desire to give maximum publicity to his work on Assam to a wider readership from outside the region. In fact, his choice of language was totally in keeping with his fervent desire to represent his *mulk*.

There seems no apparent reason to label Haliram's account as a 'nationalist' history as some seek to do.[5] The text was by no means self-consciously political, nor was it one where *des* (country) and people are synonymous with *rajatva* (realm) or statehood/sovereignty.[6] There is no such trace of the political in Haliram's narrative except a conscious desire to tell the story of the pre-colonial rulers in as much detail as possible. His narrative also does not betray any emotive attachment with the pre-colonial ruling class, nor does it articulate any apathy towards the colonial establishment. Yet Haliram's account makes a fairly strong attempt to present the people of Assam as a shared community of sorts although he is quite candid about the fact that a huge cultural gulf distinguished different sections of the people from each other. Haliram was certainly clear that his own beliefs and practices at least were at variance from those of certain sections of the people of the region that he claimed to be his 'home' or *mulk*. Hence, although the departures from the older genre of history writing in Haliram's work are fairly distinct, the work does not quite fit in with the common understanding of the overtly nationalistic. This chapter, however, goes beyond the conventional definition of the nationalistic to argue that Haliram's use of cultural parameters carried distinctly nationalist overtones. The first such trait is the treatment of land and people as synonymous in the text. Haliram uses the acronym *des* as coterminous with the people, which may be regarded as the first step in the 'imagining' of a shared community. In his chronicle, the people for the first time became the objects of historiographical enquiry. The other interesting feature of this work lay in its now-stated, now-understated objective of elevating Assam to a position of eminence within the subcontinent. Haliram clearly articulated his desire to see Assam emerge as a major destination for tourism and economic activities for people from outside the province. Haliram's enthusiasm for promoting Assam was almost equivalent to that of a publicist promoting his product – in this case the author's *mulk* – the expression that he uses to describe his relationship with the land. A fact to be noted is that Haliram's *mulk* was not just his place of birth but the larger spatial context within which were integrated both his place of birth and the place where he happened to reside in connection with his work. His *des* was, in fact, the larger territorial space of British Assam – a point that must be noted as an interesting departure from the earlier meaning of the term where *des* was coterminous with one's village and its immediate environs. This is not to deny that Haliram's emotive sentiments were a far cry from those that would soon grip the imagination of a later generation of Assamese middle-class intellectuals. What, however, makes the text intriguing to study for the historian is its uniqueness in the socio-cultural milieu of early nineteenth-century Assam. None before Haliram had ever written or spoken in quite the same manner.

Haliram's target readership was quite decidedly 'Hindu', for his book was steeped in a preponderantly Hindu imagery. He strongly denounced and dismissed as 'rumours' stories that circulated of the practice of sorcery and witchcraft purportedly pursued by women in Assam.[7] Instead, he devoted fairly lengthy passages for the delineation of Assam's close links and seemingly irrefutable cultural ties with a pan-Indian epic-Puranic tradition symbolized among others by an adherence to Brahmanical forms of worship. Convinced that Kamrup, an administrative division in British Assam with its headquarters in Guwahati, was none other than the famed Kamarupa of the Puranic literature, Haliram began his narrative with a description of the activities of kings associated in the Puranic literature with Kamarupa. In Haliram's account these Puranic characters came alive as real-life heroes, who through their deeds of valour had embellished Assam's past. Characters such as Mahiranga Danav and Narakasura were thus elevated to the level of historical characters quite unequivocally with no attempts to validate the latter's historicity. These were treated at par with irrefutably historical characters such as the Ahom princes. Entire passages described the glorious deeds of 'local' hero Mahiranga Danav, son of Brahma, one of the three principal deities of the Hindu pantheon. Narakasura, another local hero, was none other than the son of the great god Vishnu. There was not a little hint of pride in citing how Bhagadatta of the same family had fought off the Pandavas and had displayed enormous valour in the Mahabharata war. In this way, everything to do with the mythic Kamarupa was subsumed into the 'history' of British Assam in a rather uncritical manner, indicating the author's clear-cut ideological preferences for a certain kind of past. It did not bother Haliram that many of these textual references demonstrated polyvalent possibilities and fulfilled a highly allegorical function much in the same way that expressions like 'Kamarupa' could signify simultaneously a place name, the female body or female sexuality.[8] Haliram did not question these fantastic stories about his seemingly 'historical' characters, nor did he find it queer that he was treating characters like Narakasura and Mahiranga Danava as also Vishnu and Brahma at par with the Ahoms for whose existence there were unflinching evidences. That Haliram chose not to be constrained by the quest for historical validation bespoke his strong culturalist agenda. He gave the impression of being consumed by an overwhelming concern for securing Assam's position as a torch bearer of the Indic civilization. The paradoxical nature of Haliram's enterprise will be illustrated further in the subsequent section.

The task that Haliram seems to have set for himself – that of establishing Assam's Hindu credentials – could not be accomplished without representing Assam as an ideal space for Hindu ritualistic worship or Brahmanical forms of devotion. The latter's practice in the region had to be accorded an indeterminate antiquity. Haliram seemed to fulfil this requirement by recounting the names of Hindu shrines located in Assam with an eye to indicating their ubiquity in the region. One particular shrine that he chose to glorify in order to establish his larger point about the sanctity of British Assam was that of Kamakhya, located atop the Nilachal Hill in north Guwahati. This particular shrine, interestingly enough, had remained more or less hidden from the common people as the Ahoms had chosen to preserve it as a purely royal enclave, to which the general masses were not allowed any access whatsoever.[9] Haliram's work went to great lengths to prove that this shrine enjoyed the primacy of place among worshippers of *Sakti* or the female creative energy in Hindu pantheistic beliefs. Haliram's source of reference for claiming the primacy of Kamakhya was the Puranic literature, which seemed to epitomize for Haliram, the ultimate stage in the evolution of the creative genius and intellectual traditions of the ancient Aryans. On the basis of these textual traditions, Haliram represented the deity and her shrine as the principal object of veneration among Hindus all over.[10] Haliram carefully deployed stories from the Puranas to enhance the credibility of the shrine and render the latter attractive to a Hindu-reading public. 'Kamarupa Kamakhya', he reminded his reader, was one of those few shrines in the country where bodily remains of Sati, the divine consort of Shiva, had fallen after the former had been dismembered by the god Vishnu. Kamakhya was, however, singular as she bore the female organ of Sati.[11] Haliram's sources of information for a claim so profound belonged once again to the larger body of Puranic texts. The *Yogini Tantra* and the *Kalika Purana*, which Haliram cited for authority, were full of fantastic stories and mythical tales that could daunt the staunchest believer. What, however, is curious about our author is not that he accepted the Puranic renditions as genuine, which perhaps many of his contemporaries did, but that he rejected many other Puranic references and similar circulations as utterly baseless. It is this paradoxical nature of the author's choice of source matter for his work that makes it possible for us to treat his statements pertaining to prehistoric Assam as eminently discursive.

II

A nationalist agenda

Partha Chatterjee has argued that the intermingling of the modern and the pre-modern was a common characteristic of intellectual thought in colonized societies and an outcome of the ambivalent relationship that the colonial intelligentsia shared with the rulers.[12] The modern and the pre-modern were destined to remain intertwined in various domains of thought and practice in colonized societies so long as the bourgeois modern trends and practices introduced by colonialism retained their glamour and attraction for the colonized. Scholars like Sumit Sarkar have time and again warned against the use of binaries to assess practices and perceptions in colonized society as these binaries of the traditional and the modern are not capable of capturing the ambiguities of colonial thought and action. Such patterns of thought have therefore been explained through the prism of a third category called the 'colonial modern', which had the capacity to accommodate the dichotomous and the ambivalent.[13] As a category of embedded thoughts and practices, the category called colonial modern allows ample scope to understand and explain Haliram's numerous departures from a self-consciously modern position or subjectivity. Seen at from this perspective, Haliram had considerable reasons for deploying myths to serve his purpose. The principal discursive component of the *Assam Buranji* consisted of its stated objective of rendering Assam attractive to prospective visitors. The point to note here is how and in what ways Haliram made copious use of myths to illustrate the central thesis of his text. It becomes clear to readers before long that Haliram was not one who would uncritically accept myths in other contexts. By way of illustration, we may refer to Haliram's disdainful rejection of Ahom-origin myths that stated that the brothers Khunlung and Khunlai, regarded as the ancestors of the Ahoms and grandsons of Indra, had descended straight from heaven by means of a golden ladder.[14] He expressed his profound amusement and annoyance at these 'stories' and denounced the latter in no uncertain terms. This is what he had to say about these origin accounts that attributed a divine origin to the founders of Ahom dynastic rule in Assam:

> People of Ahom origin say that Khunllung and Khunlai, sons of Indra's son king Swarganarayan had descended from heaven through a golden ladder. Hence they are called swargadev. I cannot help elaborate on this trend. Despite being incarnations of god, both Sri Ramchandra and Basudev SriKrishna were born as ordinary human beings. Hence it is incredible that ordinary kings can descend from heaven in their mortal frames. However, these people refuse to see reason no matter how much we may attempt to explain to them. They refuse to treat as authentic works that do not contain references to these tales of Ahom origin. Hence I have inserted them in my account. I hope intelligent readers will know how to treat such materials.
>
> (Translation mine)[15]

Haliram's stated apathy towards myths as source materials for constructing effective 'histories' did not however deter him from using similar-origin myths to establish the credentials of Kamarupa's Hindu forebearers. This deliberate ploy is noteworthy as it throws into focus the functional aspect of his narrative. By choosing to ignore some stories as baseless, Haliram demonstrated that he was aware of the new historiographical knowledge that insisted on secular interpretations and temporal frames, but would use it selectively with regard to various other enterprises depending on the latter's suitability for serving his agenda. It leaves one in no doubt that Haliram was deliberately forsaking his modernistic subjectivities for a discursive end – that of establishing Assam's integrity to *Aryavarta*.

What were the larger implications of these traits? What did these occasional throwing away of one's usual reservations about myths and fables drawn really signify? To understand this, we need to examine the book further for certain other explicit and not-so-explicit trends. The book presented a highly favourable picture of social relations and societal practices in Assam. Haliram observes that societal norms followed in Assam were far more liberal and egalitarian than those practised in other provinces. He stated that in Assam even Brahmins could be penalized for their misdeeds, while a miscreant from some lower caste could hope for redemption if he was genuinely repentant for his sins.[16] Irrespective of his target readership from Bengal, or perhaps precisely because of the latter, he did not hesitate to condemn the Bengalis for their negligence of many evil practices such as early marriage, pointing out zealously that the people of Assam chose to get their daughters married only after the latter had come of age.[17] Haliram observed with obvious pride that women in Assam could and did seek separation from their partners in case of breach of trust in conjugal relations and could afford to refuse to readmit a partner till the latter had won back her trust. Earned.[18] The pleasure in the author's observation is almost palpable when he mentions these practices which, he knew for sure, was not to be found in Bengali society or for that matter among the people of neighbouring regions.

This chapter argues that the aforementioned traits in Haliram's text represented telltale signs of an inchoate nationalism. Haliram clearly felt that Assam like Bengal also possessed a shared community that shared a geocultural space notwithstanding the sheer heterogeneity of practices and beliefs. His arduous attempts to conjure a common history for the place represented an ardent desire to delineate this unity. By reacting to allegations of sorcery and witchcraft, he demonstrated his loyalty to what he believed was a common cultural heritage, which he felt must be defended against attempts at defamation. His *mulk* was no longer the small village where he had spent his childhood or the locality where he resided on account of his job. It was much bigger than that. He was comfortable with the idea that there would be matters which he would not be able to share with co-members of his community with whose beliefs and practices he did not always agree. Yet here were people with whom he could certainly share something tangible – whether in terms of a past, or of a common set of practices that he felt his people had forgotten and which he regarded as his sacred duty to remind them about. By choosing to tell the story of this community, Haliram became the first-ever exponent of a community identity in Assam. This community that Haliram posited was at once territorial and historico-cultural but by no means linguistic. Language was not indispensable to Haliram's cultural sensitivities, nor did it exist anywhere in his mental horizon. Haliram's notions of community would soon be out of sync with those that would come to animate the politics of a later generation of provincial intellectuals led by his son Anandaram. Haliram did not perceive language as anything more than a means of communication, and he was clearly not aggrieved when Bengali became the provincial vernacular.

In an engaging study of nationalist history writing in nineteenth-century Bengal, Partha Chatterjee identified the chief attributes of a 'Puranic history'.[19] He defined such a history as one where 'myth, history and the contemporary – all become part of the same chronological order; one is not distinguished from another; the passage from one to another, consequently is entirely unproblematic'.[20] The second feature of such histories, according to Chatterjee, is that here dynasties are founded by the grace of the divine power and kingdoms are retained only as long as the ruler is true to dharma. Chatterjee critiqued these histories as pre-nationalist and pre-political, characterized as these were by the absence of rationalist causal explanation and historical characters. By contrast, histories written in the latter half of the nineteenth century were more consciously political/modern, characterized as these were by historical periodization and identification of country (*des*) with realm (*rajatva*).[21] We would like to contend, however, that in the case of histories written in nineteenth-century Assam, it is impossible to make such a clear-cut distinction between early-colonial Puranic histories that were non-nationalist and a later genre of rationalist and nationalist histories that were uncontaminated by 'Puranic' elements. Halirama's text was both Puranic and political/modern at the same time. It possessed obvious discursive features that distinguished it from standard Puranic histories of an earlier period from the region. This paper contends that his deployment of myths to legitimize genealogy was a conscious and political choice to situate Assam within a chosen body of traditions. Ranajit Guha has argued that in Bengal by the second half of the nineteenth century there was an urgency to create 'an Indian historiography of India'.[22] Guha identifies this as an intensely political project for reclaiming power from the colonizers and traces it to Bankim Chandra Chattopadhyay's call to the subject peoples to write their own histories.[23] In *The Nation and Its Fragments Colonial and Postcolonial Histories*, Partha Chatterjee has argued that this project did not begin in the second half of the nineteenth century but much earlier when the principal features of a manner of recounting the past began to appear. Chatterjee traces the growth of nationalist historiography to these features of a commonly shared discursive formation.[24] According to Chatterjee, by the second half of the nineteenth century there were fairly elaborate instances of nationalist historiography that were portraying the political success of the British in India as a cynical pursuit of power.[25] Sumit Sarkar pushed the date for the emergence of nationalist history writing to an earlier period, tracing it to the writings of the members of the *Derozian Society for Acquisition of General Knowledge (1838–43)*.[26] Here we have argued that the nationalist process began in Assam much earlier when authors like Haliram accomplished an overtly political act by selecting what they wanted to include in their histories and how they wanted to represent their 'facts'. The manner of selection pursued in his text constitutes an overt act of assertion if only because he was not functioning in an intellectual vacuum. Some of his observations like the ones mentioned earlier in the paper indicate that he was aware, even if only vaguely, of some European conventions of history writing that he preferred to ignore for the time being. Haliram's history was something more than a conventional recounting of the past on the basis of Puranic citations. Here we have a history where the protagonists are sometimes gods and sometimes real men, while the temporal frame of the narrative oscillates between the secular/rationalist and the mythical/divine. Haliram's awareness of the need for secular explanations and for validation of his source materials and his skilful deployment of this methodology with regard to one category of sources and blunt refusal to do so with regard to another enables us to place his work within the larger genre of nationalist historiography.

III

Maniram Dewan and the idea of a composite nationality

It is perhaps befitting that a vision of composite nationality was to come from none other than the man dubbed as a rebel and executed by the Raj for his role in anti-colonial activities. Maniram Dutta Bor Bhandar Borwah, popularly known as Maniram Dewan, was perhaps the most controversial personality of nineteenth-century Assam. Ironically, the author of the *Buranji Vivek Ratna*, written sometime around 1858, has been berated by both the colonial state and fellow Assamese nationalists for pursuing a narrow self-interest.[27] Yet it was Maniram whose ideas of an inclusive community proved far ahead of his times.

Early in his career, Maniram had become an associate of the British East India Company's administration under David Scott, the agent to the governor general in the Northeast. In 1828, Maniram was appointed as a *Tehsildar* and a *Sheristadar* of Rangpur under Scott's deputy Captain John Bryan Neufville. Later, Maniram was made a Borbhandar (prime minister) by Purander Singha, the titular ruler of Assam during 1833–38. He continued to be an associate of Purander's son Kamaleswar Singha and grandson Kandarpeswar Singha. Maniram became a loyal confidante of Purander Singha and resigned from the posts of *Sheristadar* and *Tehsildar*, when the king was deposed by the British. By the 1850s Maniram had become hostile to the British and presented a petition to A.J. Moffat Mills, judge of the Sadar Dewani Adalat who was visiting Assam at the time, pointing out several shortcomings of the British administration in Assam.[28] He soon became involved in a series of seemingly seditious activities and was implicated for his role in instigating rebellion during the Revolt of 1857 and subsequently hanged to death.[29]

The *Buranji Vivek Ratna* was compiled in two volumes. Unfortunately, the first volume, which dealt with the political activities of the Ahom rulers, is lost to posterity. The second volume describes the social, cultural and economic facets of life under the Ahom rulers. A point to note about the work was that it was not written at the behest of any patron despite his close association with Kandarpeswar Singha, who was keen to restore his dynasty's rule in Assam. However, given the fact that Maniram himself had espoused the latter's cause on numerous occasions, one can surmise that the first part of Maniram's work describing the political history of Assam would have been an exposition of the achievements of the Ahoms. Although we cannot be absolutely certain, Nagen Saikia, the editor of the *Buranji Vivek Ratna*, seems to think, and correctly perhaps, that Maniram did not begin his work by listing the mythical and real kings and rulers of ancient Kamarupa.[30] Perhaps, this is a valid point, for Maniram clearly did not think much about the pre-Vaishnavite period, choosing to dub the pre-Ahom period in Assam as the *abhakatiya* period or the period of non-devotionality.[31] For him, civilized society was synonymous with the beginning of Ahom rule only because the same period coincided with the appearance of Vaishnavite devotion. The second volume of Maniram's work which is available to us is an exposition of the nature of social and cultural life in pre-colonial Assam.

It is to be noted that by the time Maniram submitted his petition to Mills in 1855, advocating the reinstatement of Ghunnokanth Singh Jubaraj to his ancestral throne, the idea of an Assamese community had already taken shape on account of the zealous drive taken by Anandaram Dhekial Phukan and the American Baptist missionaries. In his petition to Mills, Maniram also made it clear that the province of Assam belonged to the Assamese people whose economic interests had been grossly undermined by the employment policies of the British administration.[32] Yet the *Buranji Vivek Ratna* was remarkably unencumbered by the obligation to iterate notions of a singular identity for the province. The *Buranji Vivek Ratna* was written in a wonderfully hybrid language in keeping presumably with the varieties of local speech commonly used by people of his day.[33] The content of the book indicates a remarkably tolerant spirit despite the professed Vaishnavite leanings of the author. The work begins with a description of the festival of *Chongdeo* performed in the old 'Ahom' style by the *Deodhai* or *Bailoong* priests of the Ahoms. The author gave a detailed description of the different kinds of animals offered as sacrificial beasts to *Chongdeo*. The list included animals like pigs and bulls, which are completely inadmissible in ordinary Brahmanical sacrificial rituals.[34] The book proceeds to describe how in course of the sacrificial rites, the priests are possessed by the divine spirit that allows them to foretell the future. The entire passage is very matter of fact and bereft of any derisive attitude towards the practitioners of the *Bailoong* faith. Maniram is equally impassive in passages that described the advent of Brahmanical worship in Assam and the subsequent dissemination of the Vaishnavite faith in the region. It is obvious to the reader that the author's sympathies lay with the faith propagated by Srimanta Sankardev, and yet passages on *Sakta* worship and the *Bailoong* faith were rendered with utmost respect and utmost neutrality.

Maniram's *Buranji* is also remarkable in its dispassionate rendering of all cultural and social information pertaining to life during the pre-colonial period. Loyalty, if any, is demonstrated towards the Ahom courtly culture that is represented as one that promoted mutual tolerance of and respect for members of diverse faiths and practices. The text's repeated emphasis on the intermeshing of diverse strands of thought and practices under the Ahom regime betrays a conscious effort to represent Assam as the locus of a composite and transcendental cultural nationality which permitted differences. The text was certainly more political than Haliram's work in that its author certainly had definitive notions about the desirability in Assam of a government formed by popular participation and headed by a scion of the erstwhile royal family. His decision to focus on the diverse cultural matrix of the region was in a sense a conscious critique of the failure of the British to uphold the catholicity upheld by the pre-colonial rulers.

Maniram was clearly not ready to envisage a community that was anchored to a narrow cultural vision. Maniram's work was, truly speaking, evocative of a strong modernistic sensibility. Despite his strong ties with the royal house, the author did not use his work as a platform to talk about the glories of Ahom rule. Instead, he chose to talk about the societal, thereby making a significant departure from practices of literary representation followed by his contemporaries like Kasiram and Dutiram. By incorporating the social as a component of his history, Maniram, like Haliram before him, voted in favour of a whole new genre of history writing in Assam. His was not the narrow nationalism of the bigot but an all-inclusive nationalism in keeping with the multi-cultural ethos of the region.

IV

The transformation of history writing

Haliram's work may have been exceptional in espousing a specific kind of emotive attachment to land and faith, but this was not usual in Assam in the nineteenth century. What was far more common was an attachment to the ruling house and the practices of commissioning histories to recount the glories of the ruling dynasty – a practice that continued into the early years of colonial rule in Assam. History writing itself was a fairly common practice in Assam during the early part of the nineteenth century if we go by the number of works produced although authors of such works did not choose to publish them. These works were preserved as handwritten manuscripts to be published later at the initiative of the government. With the exception of the account left by Harakanta *Sadar Amin*, these written narratives were all commissioned by *swargadeo* Purander Singha, the last Ahom monarch who was allowed by the British to rule Upper Assam till 1838. The earliest work in the category of commissioned histories consisted of the *Assam Buranji Puthi* written by Kasinath Tamuli Phukan. The latter was first published in 1844 by the Sibsagar branch of the American Baptist Mission with the subtitle *Indravamshi Assam Maharaja Sakalar Biboron* or *A Descriptive Account of the Kings of the Indravamshi Dynasty*. All these works commissioned by the last Ahom monarch and his successor sought to evoke a certain type of memory – one that harked back to the immediate pre-colonial past with the narrative centred around the symbolic figure of the *swargadeo*. The purpose behind such representations would not be hard to guess. The monarch wanted to convey to the British the fallacy of the latter's decision to take over Assam from the erstwhile rulers and also to rouse latent pro-monarchical sentiments among the remnants of the pre-colonial aristocracy, many of whom were already smarting from their loss of privileges under British rule. As proof of this, one need only consider the numerous royalist conspiracies that took place during the tenure of Scott, compelling him to recommend a partial restoration of Ahom rule, a possible solution to the crisis, and to appease the dispossessed aristocracy.[35]

A work that departed in one crucial respect from the previous works, although by and large belonging to the older genre of dynastic accounts, was a work that was written towards the end of the nineteenth century by Harakanta Sharma Barua Chaudhury *Sadar Amin*, a functionary of the new regime and a man with roots in the pre-colonial past like Maniram.[36] Harakanta had received an education in the old style and joined British government service as *mohuri* or clerk in the Kamrup Collectorate. He served the colonial state in various capacities such as treasurer, *Peshkar*, *Sherastadar*, deputy collector, *Munsif* and finally rising to the position of a *Sadar Amin* with the powers of a second-class magistrate. Born in 1813, Harakanta retired from government service in 1877 and died at a ripe old age in 1900. Like his predecessors, Harakanta was as much a man of the past as of the present. In his editorial note to the *Assam Buranji* by Harakanta *Sadar Amin*, historian Surya Kumar Bhuyan states, 'Harakanta was, a spectator of the last phase of Ahom supremacy as well as the foundation and consolidation of British power in Assam. . . . He came in contact with men of the old regime as well as of the new, and was thus a most competent authority on the order which had passed away'.[37]

Harakanta's *Assam Buranji* begins in a conventional manner by describing the origin theory of the Ahoms. It then goes on to recount the history of the Ahom rulers from Khunlung and Khunlai till the termination of Ahom rule in 1826. What is interesting is a passage in the preface where the author observed that the *Assam Buranji* compiled by Kasinath Tamuli Phukan was incomplete in many respects and that he meant to rectify these shortcomings. In his words:

> Their compilation should have incorporated numerous important incidents and facts, which were unfortunately omitted, perhaps to avoid Prolixity. For this reason we have commenced writing this chronicle having based it on the earlier one . . . referred to. I have, with due discrimination and diligence collated informations from many other Buranjis and reports heard from the lips of reliable Ahom Phukans, Baruas and others.[38]

The passage quoted above is unique for its evocation of historiographical integrity that was not acknowledged as an intrinsic quality of history writing in those days. It is possible that the author was aware of some modern conventions of history writing such as the need to tap different kinds of sources, collation of data, and authentication of source materials and so on. Harakanta's work was modern also because he put together a rather a comprehensive picture of the past. This is evident from his furnishing of details such as those pertaining to the names of Ahom functionaries, the latter's obligations and other information pertaining to the actual functioning of the Ahom administration. In producing this work Harakanta was acting on his own impulse and one cannot help detect a scholarly enthusiasm for producing a complete and authentic account of the past as it were.

However, unlike Haliram, Harakanta did not propose an altogether novel model of cultural solidarity. On the contrary, his notions were still rather archaic and his account of Ahom dynastic rule indicated a great deal of preoccupation with the previous regime. It was as if the shadow of Ahom rule still loomed large over his mental horizon. While he clearly understood and acknowledged that the old days had passed for good, he was still to adopt and adapt to the ways of the new age in a way that would make the new sensibilities an integral part of his intellectual framework. The reason for this was perhaps that Harakanta did not have the kind of exposure that Haliram or even Maniram did. It is possible to argue that Harakanta's perceptions reflected those of most of the people of his age and time. This was a time when people were yet to come to terms with the new era with its attendant ideas and institutional practices which were so different from those of the previous regime. Harakanta did depart however in his induction of a female character into his list of cultural heroes of Assam. His famed inclusion of Queen Jaymoti was more modern than the male-centric histories that had been written so far. The inclusion of Rani Jaymoti constituted a crucial departure from standard modes of representing the past and merits attention. This step signified an unambiguous attempt to create cultural icons. Clearly his intervention was not meant to satisfy royalist egos but indicate tentative steps towards conceptualization of a shared community that was meant to draw sustenance from acts of glory by iconic members-whether dead or alive. The project seems to have been at a rather incipient stage and it is not possible to tell from the text at least in what way the author perceived its scope. The contours of a community are however unmistakably present in the author's mental landscape. What is important to note is that these emergent contours do not point by any means towards consciousness of a mutually shared language but are rather indicative of a very inclusive vision of community identity that drew sustenance from a shared memory of rule by an illustrious line of rulers.

By the turn of the century history writing in Assam had undergone a notable transformation. Histories written and produced from this period onwards were almost invariably language centric. Intellectuals vied with each other in their zest for producing histories of the Assamese language and by extension, histories of the Assamese community.[39] There was a palpable urge to accord a decent antiquity to Assamese, the use of which was now projected backwards. A large number of these works were published in the form of essays in vernacular literary periodicals. The concern with language and literary histories diminished the attraction for dynastic histories. Consequently, only a few dynastic histories were written and published during this period. The only author who continued to exhibit a sustained interest in dynastic histories was Gunabhiram Barooah. He continued to take a great deal of pleasure in exploring the history of the Ahoms till the turn of the century. In 1884, Barooah produced a detailed history of the Ahoms in his *Assam Buranji*. He followed this up by a series of essays on the Ahoms called *Agar Din Etiyar Din* (Time Then and Now) in the periodical he edited and produced, that is the *Assam Bandhu*. He also wrote a series of essays called *Alikhito Buranji* (Unwritten Chronicle) in the *Jonaki*, the leading vernacular literary periodical of the time.

While there were obvious resonances between the style and content of Barua's history and those that animated the work of Haliram, the former was distinctly more clearly nationalistic in character. Perhaps it would be true to say that Barua's manner of delineating the lives and activities of his protagonists seemed to carry forward the legacy of Harakanta Sharma Barua. For Gunabhiram Barua, history was the history of great men and women whose legacies could be cited as evidence of the greatness of the land. Hence, in a manner highly reminiscent of the colonial practice of relegating all acts of glory by the colonized to the past, Barua took satisfaction in the fact that the people of ancient Kamarupa had been far superior to the present inhabitants of the land in wisdom, might and wealth.[40] It is a different matter that such an explanation allowed Barua to make sense of the present state of bewilderness to which colonial subjection had pushed the people of Assam. Taking refuge in the past would increasingly become the only option available for the colonial elite. Barua, writing in the mid-nineteenth century, could not help feeling wistful:

> Kamarupa was a glorious land. It is popularly regarded as the land given to Bhagavati as her dowry. Its glories have been recounted in the Puranas. The very name of its capital, Pragjyotisapura, tends to reinforce such an impression . . . this country (desa) has always had an independent existence. It has never been subordinated to any other country. By the grace of god it is hoped that it will rise once again for the present administrative system is conducive to its revival.[41]

Like Haliram, he was keen to delineate the region's close cultural ties with the 'Aryan' heroes, especially since he felt overburdened by the realization that the region had a population that was predominantly non-Aryan. Barua was, thus, quick to point out that rulers from the region had maintained fairly close and regular contacts with their Aryan kinsmen from the north. By way of evidence, Barooah cited references to Duryodhana's marriage to Bhagadatta's sister, Bhanumati, Parasurama's journey to the Brahmakunda located to the east of the Kamarupa for washing off his sin and similar incidents. Like Haliram, Barooah considered such references as unimpeachable evidence of the continued geo-cultural significance of Kamarupa, meaning thereby ancient Assam, to *Aryavarta*. In the concluding section of the book, Barooah provides a list of artefacts that he described as being survivals from Kamarupa's Aryan past. In listing what he called the material remains of Kamarupa, Barooah, interestingly, no longer cited textual references. Instead, he chose to tap local historical memory and folklores to draw up an inventory of these 'objective' symbols of Assam's Aryan antecedents. The list of Puranic archaeological ruins of British Assam according to Barooah consisted of a stone house in the southern part of the modern-day Kamarup district, which local memory had ascribed to Chand Saudagor, the mythical character of the Puranic tale of Lakhkhinder and his wife Behula mentioned in the Padma Purana. Barooah referred, likewise, to other ruins in Tejpur, ascribing them to Bana of the famous Usha-Aniruddha account who had reportedly fought Krishna in order to prevent the latter's grandson from marrying his daughter, Usha. Folklores associating these sites with mythical events were deemed sufficient for fixing their communion with the Aryan heroes mentioned in the Puranic accounts. Barooah could thus rejoice that local memory had preserved intact the peculiar historical associations of these ruins when all other marks of identification had faded away.

Barooah's nationalistic subjectivities did not allow him to negotiate some of the sophisticated methods of historical enquiry that had been introduced in India by the Europeans and with which Barooah seemed to have had an early interaction. More than Haliram, Barooah exhibited a keen sense of the meaning and implications of historical enquiry that in the nineteenth century entailed the all-important practice of authentication of one's sources. By 1884, when Gunabhiram Barua wrote his *Assam Buranji*, such historiographical practices had already begun to be adopted by many of his contemporaries. Barua himself demonstrated his scepticism of the acceptability of Puranic tales as reliable source materials for producing authentic histories. This did not, however, deter him from accepting, albeit partially, many of the claims made by these texts without any attempt whatsoever to authenticate the reliability of the accounts contained therein. Barua's awareness of these practices prevents one from dismissing outright his work as fabulous history or his text as a pre-modern construct. Rather, he should be regarded as a colonial intellectual overburdened by the task of seeking a decent place for himself and the community to which he purportedly belonged within a respectable tradition. This overwhelming nationalistic urge played havoc with his objective self, preventing him from rejecting the old for the new as was the wont of many colonial intellectuals during this period. This often led him to throw away scholarly caution to the wind and make bold assumptions on the doubtful basis of homophonic words and phrases such as the one that he extended in his attempt to understand the origin of the name 'Assam'. Barooah wrote:

> This place is also called Acham, a word that can be traced etymo-logically to the Sanskrit word 'Achaman'. This name was given when it was seen that the people of this region performed Acha-man since they had been Aryanised.[42]

Barooah did not bother to cite his sources before making such a claim. The sheer confidence of his assertions was breathtaking in their nonchalant disregard for any kind of authentication.

It has been pointed out already that Gunabhiram Barooah represented the quintessential colonial intellectual trying to come to terms with varied modern ideas and institutional practices while at the same time trying to negotiate a deep-rooted fear of being pushed aside in the emergent nation. The prospect of marginalization was a nagging fear and served to hinder one's attempts at assimilation of a large number of new practices associated with the coming of modernity. These twin acts of negotiation were also at times conflicting such as when one was called upon to define one's community concerns as well as the latter's place amidst a motley group of mutually competing communities. Called upon to make a choice between his community identity and his academic integrity, Barua thus chose to privilege the community to the emerging discipline of critical history writing like so many other intellectuals of his time and age both within and outside Assam. Hence, while, on the one hand, he was informed enough to lament that India lacked a truly historical vision and literature devoid of mythical absurdities drawn from sundry epics and Puranas, he could not dismiss this genre of literature outright as fantastic and ahistorical. It was easier for him to dub the latter as 'semi-historical' literature, whose label allowed him to selectively make use of components therein for constructing a suitable genealogy for the Assamese community. He therefore argued passionately that it was quite possible to construct an appropriate historical account of India with the help of Puranic materials. The ambivalence of his position comes out in his caveat that the latter must be well supplemented by occasional references to other categories of textual sources. His remarks in this connection are suggestive of his angst:

> Historians are known to draw their information from citations in Puranic stories, temple inscriptions and sundry other sources. If it is possible to reconstruct the past on the basis of these materials, then can we not accept the Puranic accounts or the customs and practices prevalent in the country as historical source materials for drawing inferences about the past? It may not be correct to dismiss the Puranic accounts as utterly baseless and useless. The Puranas contain references to each and every state of India. Even if we cannot accept them entirely, we can still decode them to glean significant information about the contextuality and temporality of the narrated incident.
>
> (Translation mine)[43]

In the preceding passage, Barua seems to be laying down a distinct methodology for translating Puranic citations into authentic historical evidence. According to him, this entailed a careful weighing of such citations against the testimony of local traditions or a community's historical memory. This was precisely what he claimed to have done in his own account. He gave detailed illustrations of how this could be achieved. Barooah argued that the reference to the rebirth of Kamadeva, for example, could be interpreted to imply the suitability in the past of this place for meditation and quiet contemplation on account of the plenitude of hills and forests that served to isolate it from other regions. In fact, he came up with a full-fledged theory of the likely manner of Aryan penetration of the region. According to this, at the time of the discovery of the region by the Aryans, it was ruled by 'uncivilised and cruel races', some of whom later acknowledged the supremacy of the Aryan conquerors who raised one of them to the throne. Barooah unhesitatingly identified this king as Naraka of the Puranas.[44] Eager to accord a Hindu-Arya ancestry to his community, Barooah could hardly afford to ignore the Puranic literature, which was his last chance of securing Assam's ties with a tradition much sought after in colonial India. Often in his account of the Pala rulers, Barooah subjected his sources to a process of commonsensical interrogation of the kind that he claimed to have applied to his Puranic source materials. This was how it was carried out. Regarding the local belief that the last of the Pala kings was overthrown by the cowherd employee of Brahmin priest, Barooah summarily dismissed this as a fabrication on the grounds that this was an oft-cited incident in many other local traditions and, therefore, likely to have been borrowed to serve a certain purpose. But the story was not summarily dismissed as being devoid of all value as a historical source material and was interpreted to indicate the accession, at that time, of a complete stranger to the throne. Statements such as these lead on to suspect that the notion of historical evidences so integral to European historiographical practices of the eighteenth and nineteenth centuries had already begun to intrude upon the historical consciousness of local intellectuals. However, the profoundly ideological nature of the task of constructing a community history that these men had set for themselves stood in the way of the full implementation of these methodological innovations for the writing of more analytical histories.

Barooah, however, drifted from Haliram in one significant respect. Haliram was clearly not comfortable with the Ahom legacy and did not hesitate to declare them as a separate category of people who differed ostensibly from the rest of the plains peoples. Despite their conversion to Hinduism, Haliram did not deem them 'clean' enough to accept water from their hands. His engagement with Ahom history was also rather impersonal. Gunabhiram, on the other hand, did not display any overt signs of discomfort with the legacy of the erstwhile rulers of Assam. On the contrary, he appropriated the latter and sought to build it into his narrative as a symbol of the achievements of the Assamese people. He may have taken a keen interest in delineating the Aryan past of Assam, but he did not make any derogatory remarks about the Ahoms or their habits. In fact, he did not treat the latter as a separate category of people. His silence on this aspect conveyed a sense of cultural assimilation and integration rather than that of asymmetry and dissonance. His skilful and seamless blending of the Ahom and Aryan pasts conveyed a sense of cultural continuity in the history of the region that allowed him to underscore the ultimate triumph of the Hindu faith in Assam. Gunabhiram's narrative was thus predominantly a narrative of the Assamese people that bespoke of cultural continuity and integration. Barooah did not betray any impulsive appreciation of Ahom-era achievements. Barooah seamlessly integrated the Ahom past to convey the impression of a continuous history. His message to his readers was that Ahom-era institutions and influences constituted just one of many traditions through which the Assamese community had been moulded. Ahom rule was presented not as the history of a separate people after the manner of Haliram's history but as one of the many legacies of the Assamese community.

V

New spatial histories and the growing eminence of Guwahati

An emergent trend amidst the plethora of cultural histories that animated the historiographical landscape during this period was the compilation of spatial histories. A key text belonging to this genre was the *Ancient Geography of India* written in 1877 by Anundoram Borooah.[45] Borooah was a self-professed Indologist, who believed in the sanctity of Sanskrit texts as irrefutable evidences for studying ancient India's historical traditions. The first ICS from Assam, Borooah was also a scholar of Sanskrit as well as an ardent admirer of the language. He once wrote:

> To me, Sanskrit is dearer than any other language. Its music has charms which no words can express. Its capability of representing every form of human thought in most appropriate language is probably not rivalled, certainly not surpassed by any other language.[46]

Borooah was keenly interested in locating 'place names' mentioned in Sanskrit texts onto the map of modern India – a practice pioneered by European Indologists who believed that it was possible to reconstruct the geographical knowledge of the ancient Indians (read 'Aryans'). The region of British Assam had already secured a place within the sacred geographical space of *Aryavarta* through selective readings of Puranic references to Kamarupa and other places in its vicinity as place names located in modern-day Assam.[47] Bodhisattva Kar has shown how in the manner of textual Indologists before him, Borooah set out to rebuild the spatial history of modern Assam. Thus, he would cite references in older texts, such as the Mahabharata and local oral traditions, to claim that the 'important' kingdom of Kamarupa lay to the north-east of Pundra Desa and extended from the banks of the Karatoya to the extremities of Assam. Allusions to the army of the fabled Kamarupa king Bhagadatta as fighting on the side of the beleaguered Kaurava prince, Duryodhana, were interpreted literally to mean the historical significance of kings from ancient Assam to the larger history of India. He next tried to draw up the precise historical boundaries of 'Kamarupa' by unequivocally thrusting some of these names on to the map of modern Assam. Thus, if the Sabha Parva of the Mahabharata mentioned Bhagadatta as having fought with Arjuna for eight days with an army of Kiratas, Chinas and dwellers on the sea coast and the Udyoga Parva mentioned Arjuna as having assisted Suyodhana with an army of Kiratas and Chinas, for Barooah this would imply simply that the territories of Bhagadatta had extended up to the Himalayas in the north and the borders of China in the east. Barooah supplemented his argument with reference to allusions in the said text that Bhagadatta had presented Yudhistira with fine horses, jewelled ornaments and swords with hilts of ivory at the Raja-suya festival. This was the decisive evidence for the author since 'horses are not indigenous to Assam while a fine breed of ponies is to be found in Bhootan'.[48] This, for the author, was proof enough of the fact that Bhaga-datta's kingdom had stretched as far afield as modern Bhutan.

Borooah, however, could be quite eclectic in matters of sources of infor-mation for his account. A swift shift from textual sources to local memory as and when he deemed fit was considered permissible in his scheme of things. Switching from one to the other allowed him the ease with which he could then mould the contours of his history. Thus, while identifying the capital of the ancient kingdom of Kamarupa, Barooah did not hesitate to make up for the lack of supportive data in the texts by resorting to popu-lar stories. In this connection he observed:

> The ancient capital of Kamarupa was at Pragjyotisa or Pragjyo-tisapura on the Lauhitya, by which the Brahmaputra is generally known to the people of Upper Assam. Local tradition identifies it with modern Gauhati. . . . The hill of Asvakranta on the other side of the river is still pointed out as the place where the demon Naraka fell and the marks of his great opponent Krisna's horse's hoofs are still shewn to the credulous devotees who flock its tem-ple or bathe in the sacred waters of the river.[49]

Local memory could thus serve as a useful conduit for written evidence when the latter was unavailable as a referral. This method was highly convenient for constructing an account that served to satisfy the cultural pride of the emergent intelligentsia for a homeland within India's sacred Aryan space. Bodhisattva Kar observes that the most remarkable feature of Borooah's *Ancient Geography of India* was its unhesitating identifications especially since the doubts and reservations, which characterized a later generation of archaeologists, were erased out of existence in Borooah's text.[50] Gunabhiram Barooah did not lag behind in the matter of construc-tion of spatial histories that would re-create the 'past' of the valley. British Assam, for Barooah, was an amalgam of multiple kingdoms mentioned in the Puranas and other Hindu texts. Gunabhiram Barooah could not help acknowledging the recentness of the British boundaries of Assam, but he soon rationalized the difference in extent of present-day Assam and the much smaller dimensions of ancient Kamarupa through a theory of emasculation of the neighbouring kingdoms of Sonitpur, Hirimba and Kaundilya, and their subsequent annexation by Kamarupa leading to the formation of modern Assam. What mattered for the author was the fact that he could situate a large chunk of modern Assam that he tacitly referred to as the core territory on the Puranic map of ancient Kamarupa. In his words:

> The name Assam for the province is a modern term. This was not the name of the place in the past and the boundaries of the state were also not the same. This place has been mentioned in the Mahabharat, Kalika Purana, Bhagavat, Yogini Tantra and such other texts. If we look at texts such as the Purana, we shall see that today's Assam consists of Kamarup, Sonitpur, Hirimba, Manipur and Kaundilya of the past. Gauhati was known as Pragjyotishpur in the Puranas. This was the kingdom of Bhagadatta, the son of king Naraka. . . . Sonitpur is today's Tejpur. This was the capital of the famous Bana Raja of the dynasty of Bali Raja. . . . Kaundilya is today's Sadiya. This place was the kingdom of Rukmini's father Bhismak.
>
> (Translation mine)[51]

Subsequent authors like Sonaram Chaudhury were even bolder in their assertions of Assam's Aryan connections, giving free rein to their imagination.[52]

The search for specific pasts that informed history writing in nineteenth-century Assam did not emerge as a fully autonomous act of self-avowal. It was by no means an isolated exercise. This genre of history was preceded by, and drew its inspiration from, an earlier body of Indological scholarship spearheaded by Orientalist scholars since the time of Warren Hastings. The methodology followed in spatial histories of this sort was to identify Sanskrit texts wherein correspondences between historical and colonial 'regions' or spaces located on the map of British India could be sought. The hunt in texts for the limits of the geographical knowledge of the ancient Indians gave rise to feverish toponymic exercises, which saw Indologists picking up presumably place names from Sanskrit texts and trying to locate them on the map of modern India on the basis of something as flimsy as phonemic semblances.[53] From the later part of the nineteenth century, the choice of sites for and the pattern of order of archaeological excavations tended to be dictated by such toponymic exercises.[54] Haliram's endeavour to find older names for modern locations in British Assam, thus, drew its inspiration from the Orientalist quest for the geographical space inhabited by the Aryans.[55] Bodhisattva Kar has argued that the practice of toponymic identifications in colonial India was far from being an innocuous and innocent pursuit of knowledge.[56] Rather, it was a 'major site of ideological investment that worked to naturalize the space of British India', and, although the process was dialogic, 'the genre itself was framed within the cultural demand of colonialism upon the native to produce an unbroken and authentic historical tradition'.[57] Finding exact locations for place names in texts was immensely fraught, given the numerous ambivalent references that included, not infrequently, multiple site information for certain places making it impossible to affix it to a specific point on the map. Kar argues that the toponymic literature produced by Indologists served a valuable purpose for early intellectuals seeking to counter the stigma of inferiority be it with regard to the Europeans or people from other parts of the subcontinent, as was the case of intellectuals from Assam seeking to counter perceptions of a non-Aryan past for their province. The sanctity accorded to *Aryavarta* and the Brahmanical tradition in European scholarship made it worthwhile to locate one's own culture and traditions within this esteemed heritage. Kar argues that works by Indian authors were even more culpable of historical distortions. The Indian works tended to be more confident in their assertions to the utter disregard of all ambivalent and discrepant citations, thereby communicating a sense of uncontested spatial history.

The pride of place accorded by the Orientalist scholars to history and antiquity percolated down to colonial society. It made the search for a suitable and sufficiently old past a worthwhile intellectual exercise for all kinds of demagogues desiring a cultural capital for their respective creed. History writing emerged as a crucial tool in such a competitive environment for all kinds of politics over identities. Instead of being transformed into an impartial and impersonal exercise for the representation of facts, the study and communication of which had begun to concern European historiography by the end of the nineteenth century, history writing in India became for the colonized a weapon with which to strike at the very foundations of their subordinate status. Ranajit Guha has shown how an outstanding feature of the counter-hegemonic claims made by the Indian Nationalist Movement was the use it made of the Indian past.[58] Nationalist historiography, according to Guha, was nationalism's answer to the hegemonic pretensions of the Raj. In nineteenth-century Assam, history writing assumed a critical significance as the weapon of a beleaguered community anticipating threats from various quarters. In this sense, men like Haliram and Gunabhiram anticipated Bankim Chandra Chattopadhyay's call in 1880 for a truly Indian historiography.[59]

The urgency demonstrated by the literati in staking a claim to the Aryan legacy was perhaps not misdirected, given the serious apathy demonstrated in the colonial state's approach towards the excavation of material remains from the region and their preservation. The quest for historical artefacts in Assam began rather late. As late as 1894, the government of Assam woke up to the issue of historical enquiry into Assam's past. In 1894, Chief Commissioner Sir William Ward approved a suggestion made by Sir Edward Gait that enquiries should be made into the ancient history of the province. Thus, on 18 July 1894, Charles J. Lyall, the officiating commissioner, issued a note pointing out that 'the time had come for a sustained and systematic endeavor to arrest the process of destruction of such historical manuscripts as survived in the province' and that *buranjis* in the Assam valley districts and, similar materials for history in other parts of the province, might either be acquired or copies made for the translation of the Ahom *puthis*, many of which were believed to be of historical value.[60] The chief commissioner advised that 'the enquiry might profitably be extended to the libraries of the *Sattras* or religious establishments of the great Gosains of Upper Assam', adding that the most important work to be done immediately was 'to catalogue and rescue from oblivion the historical records of Assam'.[61] The delay in addressing the obvious treasure trove of historical literature from Assam, the presence of which was attested as early as 1800 by John Peter Wade, indicates an essential disdain for Assam's 'non-Hindu' and 'non-Turko-Mongol' past – the two dominant traditions worth addressing in British official perception of the subcontinent's history. One can only speculate whether Assam's failure to fit into any of these labels became its biggest handicap in the matter of attracting official attention. Thus, the Archaeological Survey of India set up in 1871 under the aegis of Sir Alexander Cunningham did not deem it worthwhile to conduct a survey in Assam till the early twentieth century. It may be noted that ruins of temples had been reported from the region from the 1840s by Major Hannay. Two such sightings are reported in Upper Assam in 1848 and in Kamrup in 1851. Despite this, surveys were not conducted in the region, presumably because of fear that such ruins would be too few to 'justify any extensive scheme of conservation work', as T. Bloch observed in the first Archaeological Survey Report on Assam in 1906–07.[62] It is rather telling that the report should begin with the following remark that 'of all the countries in India, to which the civilization of the Aryans gradually extended, Assam seems to have been one of the last'.[63] There was clearly a degree of indifference built into the official approach towards the region.

A direct fallout of textual Indology's fascination for toponymic exercises was to help entrench notions of a core space within British Assam.

Nationalist historiography's privileging of the geographical space of *Arya-varta* led to Western and Central Assam being perceived as the most sacred theatre wherein were performed the valiant deeds immortalized in the epics and the Puranas. The ultimate outcome of all these endeavours was to pitchfork Guwahati, the headquarters of the Western division of the British government of Assam and otherwise a nondescript place as per missionary descriptions of the early nineteenth century, into an eminently important place with significant historical linkages, in short, a place central to the so-called Assamese culture and civilization. Over the years this perception grew into a natural desire to see Guwahati becoming the centre of colonial Assam in the form of the administrative capital of the new regime. As long as Purander Singha was alive and ruling in Sibsagar, the latter continued to hold primacy of position for the pre-colonial elite. However, its decline was foretold when the centre of gravity shifted towards Guwahati, if only because of its proximity to Bengal. If the British dislodged Sibsagar physically from its position of eminence, the nineteenth-century intellectuals dislodged Sibsagar from the cultural map of Assam and the emotional sensibilities of the people. That Guwahati had become so significant culturally to the new elite, with their new-found affinities for a Hindu past, became apparent when in 1874 the government of Assam decided to shift the capital of Assam to Shillong. Apart from its salubrious weather, there were other reasons to render Shillong attractive to the government as a provincial capital. The chief commissioner felt that Shillong had greater advantages over Guwahati. The latter had earned an ill reputation as an unhealthy station owing to frequent flooding of the Brahmaputra at Bharalu and the creation of swamps, which became the breeding grounds for mosquitoes. The need for improving the sanitary condition of what was the chief station of the province had come up for discussion and corrective measures such as the construction of bunds had been suggested. The official correspondence in this regard iterated the advantages of Shillong quite unequivocally:

> Gowhatty is thirteen hours by post nearer to eight districts of the province than Shillong. But thirteen hours is no great difference of postal communication; while, of the districts to which Shillong is nearer than Gowhatty, one, Cachar, is perhaps the most important in the province. If Sylhet should ever be added to this province then Shillong will be thirteen hours nearer than Gowhatty to the larger part of the population under the chief Commissioner's control. . . . Gowhatty is the capital of lower Assam only. The capital of Upper Assam is Sibsagar, while with Sylhet and Cachar Gowhatty has little or no communication. It is merely a mofussil station, and has no

claim over other places in the province by population or trade. . . . On the other hand, in a province containing so large a European population as Assam, it is probable Shillong will become a large and important sanatorium to which the tea planters and others will resort during the hot season. . . . It is true that at present Shillong is difficult of access, but the difficulties are natural ones. A traveller from Upper Assam to Shillong is detained perhaps for a fortnight on the bank of the river waiting for the steamer; at Gowhatti he finds no dak bungalow; on the road to Shillong he finds no carts or other means of conveyance, nor proper rest-houses. All these difficulties are being removed. The road is only practicable for carts at present for ten miles from Gowhatty, but in a country where road-making is so simple and easy as in the Khasi Hills, the completion of the cart road need not be long delayed. It is no uncommon thing for officers to ride from Gowhatti to Shillong by the present road in one day. When the present difficulties have been removed, the Chief Commissioner believes that Shillong will be accessible from out-lying stations as any provincial capital in India, which does not lie on a line of rail. . . . Not only is there the difficulty of finding space to build on in Gowhatti, building is there more expensive than at Shillong. Building can be done both more cheaply and expeditiously at Shillong than at Gowhatty. To Gowhatty lime is brought by boat from beyond Suddya – a distance of 332 miles; – at Shillong both coal and lime are found within twenty miles. . . . Situated as it is at sixty miles distance from two distinct means of water communication with Calcutta and the coast, Shillong possesses, the chief Commissioner considers, a very important political advantage. It is accessible from two opposite directions by routes lying through valleys inhabited by people of different religions and different races. It is hard to understand circumstances under which it could be cut off from communications with the Ganges, Calcutta, and the coast. . . . Finally, I am to say that, other things being equal, the Chief Commissioner thinks that the climate is sufficient to recommend Shillong in preference to Gowhatty. He has shown that it enjoys several advantages besides that of climate.[64]

No matter what the advantages of Shillong were to the state, the decision did not find favour with the Assamese middle class. Several petitions were addressed to the government requesting a change of decision and strongly advocating the case of Guwahati as the place best suited to be the capital of Assam. It was the perceived cultural significance of Guwahati to the Assamese people that was iterated over and over again in some of these petitions. Thus, one such petition made a fervent appeal that the capital be removed to Guwahati.[65] The language of the petition dwelt less on the issue of the suitability of Guwahati from the point of view of administrative convenience and more on the fact that the shift from Guwahati to Shillong 'involves a very great injustice to Assam and the Assamese'.[66] It also, of course, pointed out that Guwahati had the advantage of being connected by the Brahmaputra which formed the highway of communication between Assam and the rest of the empire, while Shillong is situated remotely in the recesses of the hills. The point to note is, however, the emphasis that the capital be located within 'Assam Proper'. The petition read:

> Gauhati may be called the centre of the nine districts of Assam. The remaining two, viz, Cachar and Sylhet, cannot outweigh in importance the nine districts on this side. (Hence) A Commissioner with revenue and sessions powers can very well manage the affairs of those two districts, and the presence of the chief authority of the land in the hills does not appear to be at all necessary. The advantages of the largest town in Assam are denied to the Assamese, the Chief Commissioner of Assam being among the Khasiahs. If Gauhati is objected to on the score of climate, any other district town in the valley may be chosen, and we beg Your Excellency's kind interposition for fixing the Chief Commissioner's seat anywhere within Assam proper.[67]

David Ludden's work in recent years sheds light on the nature of spatial politics. It demonstrates how spatial discourses can be inflected by nationalist sensibilities, leading to attempts to naturalize territorial boundaries productive in the end of serious spatial inequities.[68] Beginning as a project to contest marginality, Assamese nationalism thus ended up in imbricating itself in a politics of domination that sought to silence voices other than their own. The choice of Guwahati over Sibsagar, the seat of the erstwhile royalty of Assam, was no doubt inflected by administrative changes instituted by the British, which elevated Kamrup and Guwahati in the spatial scheme of things. This aspect of Guwahati's spatial location dovetailed neatly with the cultural politics of the plains people, who constituted the chief members of the newly imagined Assamese community. It is a reflection ultimately of the contingency of spatial boundaries that Guwahati, located in the region, treated disdainfully under the Ahoms as *dhekeri* and constituting the margins of Ahom territories was pitchforked into a position of eminence within the newly constituted space of British Assam. The ministrations of the people, of course, served no purpose as the government went ahead and made Shillong the headquarters of the province in 1874. The new Viceroy, Lord Keatinge, in his report to the authorities in Calcutta noted the advantageous geographical location of Shillong between the Surma and the Brahmaputra valleys, the prospects of expanding trade and commerce, and the growing importance of the place to the burgeoning plantation industry, apart from its pleasant climate, among the factors that had influenced this decision.[69]

VI

New social and cultural histories

Before long came the realization that it was not enough to have a single attribute for claiming groupness. From the middle of the nineteenth century the task of fleshing out the community began in earnest by ascribing and prescribing a whole set of desirable properties and practices. This pedagogic exercise helped define the essence of Assameseness to its presumed members and was informed presumably by a quest for something tangible with which to define an Assamese identity. Like many other trends, in this sphere too it was Haliram who had showed the way. The exercise had begun in his attempts to attract prospective tourists, traders and merchants to Assam. In an effort to draw up a favourable picture of the society in Assam, Haliram described Assamese society as more liberal and egalitarian than those in other provinces. He pointed out that in Assam even Brahmins could be penalized for their misdeeds, while even a miscreant from some other lower caste could hope to be rehabilitated on repenting for his sin. He followed up this issue with a curious comparison with Bengalis, who were condemned as being less mindful of evil practices such as early marriage. The Assamese, on the other hand, got their daughters married only after the latter came of age.[70] Haliram pointed out that women in Assam were allowed to seek separation in case of breach of trust and till the husband had established his innocence.

Haliram's son Anandaram Dhekial Phukan continued his father's unfinished agenda. Although he did not produce conventional histories, he actively participated in the exercise of image building for the community by bringing into focus a cultural attribute that had gone relatively unnoticed. In his petition to Judge Mills in 1853, Anandaram celebrated what he described as a unique cultural quality of the people of Assam. Titled *A Few Remarks on the Assamese Language*, the document observed that 'a considerable collection of historical works of considerable authenticity, composed in original Assamese, and styled Buronjis, had, it appears existed since the thirteenth century of the Christian era'.[71] Anandaram explained:

> In no department of literature do the Assamese appear to have been more successful than in History. Remnants of historical work that treat of the times of Bhagadatt, a contemporary of Raja Judhisthir, are still in existence. The chain of historical events, however, since the last 600 years, have been carefully preserved, and their authenticity can be relied upon. It would be difficult to name all the historical works, or as they are styled by the Assamese, Buronjis. They are numerous and voluminous. According to the customs of the country, a knowledge of the Buranjis was an indispensable qualification in an Assamese gentleman; and every family of distinction, and specially the Government and the public officers, kept the most minute records of historical events, prepared by the learned pundits of the country. These histories were therefore very numerous and generally agreed with each other in their relation of events. A large number is still to be found in the possession of the ancient families.[72]

Trained in one of the most illustrious of colleges set up by the British in Calcutta, the colonial metropolis, Anandaram seems to have been fully aware of the usual criticism that the ancient Indians lacked a historical tradition in the true sense of the term. By positing the local culture of history writing, Anandaram seized on one of the most effective weapons with which to combat the threat of marginality that the people of Assam presumably faced. Anandaram's motives become clear when we consider the larger passage from which the preceding excerpt has been taken. This is in the nature of a comparison between the literary oeuvres of Bengali and Assamese. It is evident that Anandaram felt obliged to strengthen his claims to the superiority of the Assamese people by marshalling substantial 'evidence' for buttressing his claims. He would soon draw up a formidable and fairly long list of books purportedly written in Assamese on various subjects in order to strengthen his argument that Assamese had a justifiable claim to antiquity and proficiency.

Anandaram's elevation of *Buranjis* to the level of histories in the modern sense of the term glossed over the fact that these documents had served a variety of purposes in the pre-colonial cultural tradition of record keeping. Many of these were actually written to promote family or individual valour and, consequently, deliberately omitted or distorted incidents to suit their purposes. In her work on *Buranji* writing in Assam, Lila Gogoi acknowledges that private *Buranjis* were at times manipulated but hastens to add that this was not the case with those that were produced on state orders and preserved in the royal archive or *Gandhiya Bharal*.[73] These were 'impersonal and objective'. It is hard to see how this conclusion was arrived at as by the admission of the same author, most of these records were destroyed.[74] The personalized nature of the *Buranji* literature and disparities in style and statements were evened out in the nationalist imagination of Phukan eager to stake claims to an intellectual tradition on behalf of his community.

For quite some time after Anandaram's petition, the task of fleshing out the cultural components of Assameseness remained unattended as the *Orunodoi* exhibited no interest in the process. Quite a few local individuals were now contributing frequently to the periodical, and still in its entire course of existence, one comes across only a single article that offered to describe some social attributes peculiar to the Assamese. Titled 'Asamiya aru Bongali', this article praised the absence of rigidity in Assamese society, which purportedly allowed a man to pursue an occupation not traditionally practised by members of his caste group. The very same behaviour, he pointed out, would earn a person considerable opprobrium in Bengal and might lead even to social ostracism.[75] Society in Assam, as the author concluded with relief, was far more liberal than that in Bengal. Almost towards the end of its brief existence, the *Orunodoi* published a series of articles by a non-resident Assamese gentleman. Written under the pseudonym *Ejon Asamiya Lok*, in the form of letters addressed to the readers, and titled *Kalikatar pora oha Potro* (Letters from Calcutta), these articles evoked a cultural solidarity by exhorting the Assamese people to write in Assamese and indulge in scholarly pursuits while imbibing a strong moral character.[76]

Writings belonging to this genre increased in intensity with the launching of the *Assam Bandhu*, a periodical edited by Gunabhiram Barooah in the 1880s. He took the lead role in defining the chief components that constituted Assameseness. Through a number of essays called *Agar Din Etiyar Din*, Gunabhiram Barua drew attention to traditional Assamese forms of recreation such as singing of the Bihu songs, playing hide and seek, dancing to the tune of the drum and climbing trees.[77] The author also highlighted preferred and commonly consumed food items such as sour fish, rice, vegetables and various kinds of sweets such as coconut sweets, fried and puffed rice sweets made with jaggery and rice pancakes.[78] In his essays which were serialized in successive issues of the *Assam Bandhu*, Barooah referred to dresses ordinarily worn by women such as the *Mekhela Chadar* and the *Cholong*, and men's dresses comprising the *Churiya Cheleng* and the *japi*, the last being a hat to cover the head.[79] Barooah's essays formed the prelude to a series of articles that dwelt on similar themes. These included *Bongali, Amar Manuh, Bihu, Kirtan, Amalok, Assamiya Ru Bideshi Saaj and Assamar Bhasa Buranji*. These articles celebrated a whole range of Assamese cultural forms such as 'traditional' festivals like the *Bihu*, common forms of music such as the *kirtan* and common styles of dressing with special emphasis on the *Mekhela Chadar* for women. One author went to the extent of discouraging women from wearing sarees as this could dilute their distinctiveness from women of other parts of India, where saree was the common attire of the female sex. Women were, instead, exhorted to dress in the traditional Assamese style, as this was the attire that became them.[80] Likewise, men were asked to wear garments that could be called as 'innately Assamese'.[81] Essays such as these were often written on a wistful note and were full of longing for a time when the people of Assam had led a simpler and more unostentatious way of life.

These essays sought to accord a more tangible essence to something called an 'Axomiya'. The later part of the nineteenth century was thus a crucial turning point in the cultural history of the 'Assamese' when conscious efforts began to be made to mould the experiences of being an Assamese into the embodiment of a common set of social and cultural practices that could evoke a commonly shared historical memory. By the time the *Jonaki* began to publish a series of essays called *Asamar Unnati* (The Progress of Assam) at the turn of the century, by a host of authors including men like Kamalakanta Bhattacharya and Lambodar Bora, Assamese had already evolved into 'a language of belonging' with its expansive repertoire of cultural and social attributes.[82]

Notes

1 Haliram Dhekial Phukan, 'Preface', *Assam Deshar Itihas yani Buranji*, Calcutta: Samachar Chandrika Press, 1829.
2 Ibid.
3 See Raziuddin Aquil and Partha Chatterjee, eds, *Histories in the Vernacular*, New Delhi: Permanent Black, 2011, for a discussion of how the new methods of historiographical enquiry introduced by the Europeans were sought and adopted by the new literati of the colonial period; see also Partha Chatterjee, 'The Nation and Its Pasts', in *The Nation and Its Fragments, Colonial and Postcolonial Histories*, Princeton, NJ: Princeton University Press, 1993.
4 Cited by Suryya Kumar Bhuyan in his editorial note to Haliram Dhekial Phukan's *Assam Buranji*.
5 See 'Editorial note' by Lakshinath Tamuli Phukan in *Assam Buranji*, by Haliram Dhekial Phukan, Reprint, Assam Publication Board, 1958.

6 See Partha Chatterjee, 'Histories and Nations', in *The Nation and Its Fragments Colonial and Postcolonial Histories*, Princeton: Princeton University Press, 1963.

7 See Bodhisattva Kar, 'Incredible Stories in the Time of Credible Histories: Colonial Assam and the Translations of Vernacular Geographies', in Raziuddin Aquil and Partha Chatterjee (eds), *History in the Vernacular*, New Delhi: Permanent Black, 2008, for a historiographical study of myth-making in the context of colonial Assam, especially with regard to the production and circulation of the well-known myth of 'Kamakhya's sheep'.

8 See Bodhisattva Kar, 'What Is in a Name? The Politics of Spatial Imagination in Nineteenth-Century Assam', *CENISEAS Papers*, 2004.

9 Haliram Dhekial Phukan, *Assam Buranji*, p. 58; see also Gunabhiram Barua, *Jonaki*, Dwitiya bhag, Pancham Sankhya, 1822, p. 167. Read about an author's imaginary reconstruction of the Durga puja festival performed by the Ahom royal family in Rajanikanta Bardoloi's novel, *Rahdoi Ligiree*, Guwahati, 1949.

10 *Assam Buranji*, p. 83.

11 Haliram offered an interesting justification for the alleged primacy of the former with regard to the other Sakta shrines of the country. Citing the Puranic legend according to which Sati's genitalia fell on the Nilachal Hill when Vishnu dismembered her body to cool down Shiva's anger, Haliram writes that the shrine's eminence stemmed from the precise factor that 'the female organ being (is) the most desirable part of the female body' ('Striloker sarbangapekhkha joni sprihaniya bote'; translation mine), *Assam Buranji*, p. 81.

12 Aquil and Chatterjee, *Histories in the Vernacular*, p. 7.

13 Ibid.

14 Ibid., pp. 23–24.

15 Ibid.

16 Ibid., p. 85.

17 Ibid., p. 88.

18 Ibid.

19 See Chatterjee, *The Nation and Its Fragments*.

20 Ibid., p. 80.

21 Ibid., p. 96.

22 See Ranajit Guha, 'An Indian Historiography of India: A Nineteenth-Century Agenda and Its Implications', in *Dominance Without Hegemony: History and Power in Colonial India*, Cambridge, MA: Harvard University Press, 1997.

23 Ibid., p. 153.

24 See Chatterjee, *The Nation and Its Fragments*.

25 Ibid.

26 Sumit Sarkar, *Writing Social History*, New Delhi: Oxford University Press, 1997, p. 19.

27 For a full-length biography of Maniram Dewan, see Benudhar Sharma, *Maniram Dewan*, Guwahati: Assam Jyoti, 1950. See H.K. Barpujari, *Assam in the Days of the Company 1826–1858*, Guwahati: Spectrum, 1980, for a short but insightful study of the allegations against Maniram Dewan and the precise functioning of colonial justice with regard to rebels.

215

28 See Appendix to A.J. Moffat Mills, *Report on the Province of Assam*, 1854, Reprint, Guwahati: Publication Board, 1984.
29 See Barpujari, *Assam in the Days of the Company*, for a discussion of the chain of events leading to the execution of Maniram Dewan.
30 Maniram Dewan, Introduction, *Buranji Vivek Ratna*.
31 Ibid., p. 15.
32 See 'Translation of a Petition Presented in Person by Moneeram Dutt Borwah Dewan on Account of Ghunnokanth Sing Joobaraj and Others', pp. 605–617, Mills, *Report on the Province of Assam*.
33 See in this connection Bodhisattva Kar, '"Tongue Has No Bone": Fixing the Assamese Language, c. 1800–c. 1930', *Studies in History*, Vol. 24, No. 1, n.s. 2008, pp. 27–76.
34 Ibid., pp. 2–4.
35 See Nirode K. Barooah, *David Scott in North-East India 1802–1831: A Study in British Paternalism*, New Delhi: Munshiram Manoharlal, 1970 for an account of the nature of discontentment during the last years of David Scott's tenure.
36 See also Kumudchandra Bordoloi, ed., *Sadar Aminor Atmajiboni*, Guwahati: Lawyer's Book Stall, 1991.
37 S.K. Bhuyan, ed., *'Preface' to Assam Buranji* or *A History of Assam*, Reprint, Guwahati: DHAS, 1962, p. ii.
38 Dewan, *Buranji Vivek Ratna*.
39 History was everywhere in the colony acquiring a new pedagogical status, with a significant shift occurring at the level of history writing from the middle of the nineteenth century, identified by Partha Chatterjee. See Chatterjee, *The Nation and Its Fragments, Colonial and Postcolonial Histories*, Princeton, NJ: Princeton University Press, 1993; see also Guha, *Dominance without Hegemony*.
40 Gunabhiram Barua, *Assam Buranji*, p. 212.
41 Ibid., p. 213.
42 Ibid., p. 10.
43 Ibid., p. 20.
44 Ibid., p. 5.
45 Anundoram Borooah, *Ancient Geography of India*, 1877, Reprint, Guwahati: Publication Board, Assam, 1971.
46 Anundoram Borooah, *Bhavabhuti and His Place in Sanskrit Literature*, 1877, Reprint, Guwahati: Publication Board Assam, 1971.
47 See Kar, *Studies in History*, for a full description of toponymic exercises identifying ancient Kamarupa with modern Assam.
48 Borooah, *Bhavabhuti and His Place in Sanskrit Literature*, pp. 68–69.
49 Ibid.
50 See Bodhisattva Kar, 'What Is in a Name? Politics of Spatial Imagination in Colonial Assam', *CENISEAS Papers*, No. 5, 2005, p. 21.
51 Barua, *Jonaki*, p. 5.
52 For a detailed discussion of the article by this author published in the 1889 issue of the *Jonaki*, see Jayeeta Sharma, *Empire's Garden Assam and the Making of India*, Ranikhet: Permanent Black, 2011.
53 Kar, 'What Is in a Name?'.

54 See Upinder Singh, *The Discovery of India, Early Archaeologists and the Beginnings of Archaeology*, New Delhi: Permanent Black, 2004; see also Kar, *What Is in a Name?*

55 See, in this connection, Thomas R. Trautmann, *Aryans and British India*, New Delhi: Sage Publications, 1997.

56 Kar, *What Is in a Name?* p. 3.

57 Ibid.

58 Guha, *Dominance without Hegemony.*

59 See Chatterjee, *The Nation and Its Fragments.*

60 E.A. Gait, *Report on the Progress of Historical Research in Assam*, Shillong: Assam Secretariat Printing Office, 1897.

61 Ibid.

62 Major S.F Hannay, 'Notes on the Ancient Temples and Other Remains in the Vicinity of Suddyah, Upper Assam', *Journal of the Asiatic Society of Bengal*, Vol. 17, 1848, p. 18, and 'Brief Notice of the Sil Hako or Stone Bridge in Zillah Kamrup', *Journal of the Asiatic Society of Bengal*, Vol. 20, 1851.

63 T. Bloch, 'Conservation in Assam', *Archaeological Survey of India Annual Report, 1906–07*, pp. 17–28.

64 Letter from Secretary to the CoA to Secretary to the GoI, Letter no. 101, 2 May 1874, Shillong, Home (Public), May 1874, nos. 265–267, NAI.

65 Ibid.

66 Ibid.

67 Ibid.

68 David Ludden, 'Spatial Inequity and National Territory: Remapping 1905 in Bengal and Assam', *Modern Asian Studies*, Vol. 46, No. 03, May 2012, pp. 1–43.

69 Imdad Hussain, *From Residency to Raj Bhavan: A History of Shillong Government House*, New Delhi: Regency Publications, 2005.

70 See Haliram Dhekial Phukan, *Assam Buranji*, Calcutta: Samachar Chandrika Press, 1829.

71 Anandaram Dhekial Phukan, 'A Few Remarks on the Assamese Language', in Maheshwar Neog (ed.), *Anandaram Dhekial Phukan: Plea for Assam and Assamese*, Jorhat: Assam Sahitya Sabha, 1977, p. 161.

72 Ibid., pp. 163–164.

73 See Lila Gogoi, *The Buranjis Historical Literature of Assam*, New Delhi: Omsons, 1986, p. 173.

74 Ibid., p. 172.

75 Haliram Dhekial Phukan, 'Asamiya aru Bongali', *Orunodoi*, June 1847, p. 148.

76 'Kalikatar Pora Aha Patro'; see successive issues of the *Orunodoi.*

77 'Agar Din Etiya Din', *Assam Bandhu*, Part II, 1886.

78 Ibid., Part I, 1886.

79 Ibid., Part II, 1886.

80 Ratneswar Mahanta, 'Asamiya Aru Bideshi Saaj', *Assam Bandhu*, Part I, 1885.

81 Ibid.

82 Expression borrowed from book of the same name by Chitralekha Zutshi, *Languages of Belonging: Islam, Regional Identity, and the Making of Kashmir*, New York: Oxford University Press, 2004.

6

REPRESENTING TRADITIONS, RECASTING HISTORY[1]

The moves to purify Assamese and invest it with a Sanskritic ancestry, described in the previous chapters, coincided with attempts to assert the Hindu identity of the emergent community at least in the nineteenth century. In this chapter we explore certain patterns of cultural behaviour that indicate a growing attachment towards rituals and norms identified as Brahmanical Hindu. Indrani Chatterjee's study of the Northeast bears out the larger Vaishnavite cultural tradition of the trans-Himalayan region to which Assam belonged.[2] It was here that the fifteenth-century saint, Sankardeb, had preached the *Eksaran dharma*. Sankardeb, his direct disciple, Madhavdeb, and their numerous successors were responsible for forging strong Vaishnavite traditions, which were kept alive subsequently by the *sattras* or monastic establishments that proliferated under the Ahoms. However, the lived history of Vaishnavite practices and initiations in the region was far from being unilinear in pattern and permitted a mosaic of unorthodox practices and belief systems which invariably contributed to the proliferation of the faith. In many ways, the nineteenth century brought about a shift in the dynamism that characterized the practices of Vaishnavism in the region as also in the general pattern of devotional practices pursued by the people referred to as 'Assamese'. Lakshminath Bezbaroa's attempts to streamline the *sattras* represented one such attempt to induce order in the functioning of the latter institutions and to make them conform to a more puritanical mode of functioning.[3] More relevant for our purpose, however, is the fact that the nineteenth century marked critical shifts in devotional practices by creating a congenial environment for the proliferation of Brahmanical Hindu practices, especially those connected with temple worship, which had witnessed significant attrition in the preceding era under the impact of the Vaishnavite faith. We have seen that the colonial state's favourable handling of rent-free religious endowments enjoyed by temples rescued the latter from total oblivion into which they had been pushed by

the general indifference of the common people as well as by the depredations of the Burmese in the early years of the nineteenth century. This has
been discussed in Chapter 1. The establishment of political stability by the
British, as well as the colonial state's favourable handling of the rent-free
land held by temples, improved the material condition of the latter under
colonial rule. This chapter explores the growing affinity for temple worship
among a section of the emergent middle-class intelligentsia, and especially
the phenomenal ascendance of the shrine of Kamakhya located in the North
Kamrup division of Lower Assam. A local deity of pre-Ahom antecedents,
Kamakhya was one of many similar shrines dedicated to female divinities
in the region, such as the shrine of the *Kasai kheti Gossaini* in the Jaintia
hills. The antiquity of these shrines, as well as the actual nature of worship
pursued for these deities or of the identities of people who visited these
shrines, remain shrouded in mystery. These shrines were later subsumed
under an expanding Brahmanical Hindu belief system and came to be associated with *Sakti* worship or the veneration of the female power constitutive of one among many sectarian practices within the Hindu pantheistic
belief system. Patronized by the Ahom monarchs from the seventeenth
century, the shrine of Kamakhya remained nonetheless a predominantly
royal enclave till the coming of the British when David Scott supposedly
offered monetary assistance to sustain ritual activities in the shrine.

I

Vasihnavism in Assam: revisiting a pre-colonial tradition

In 1829, Haliram Dhekial Phukan, a native of the British province of
Assam, published a book called the *Assam Buranji*, or a historical chronicle
of Assam.[4] Written in Bengali for a wider readership, this book not only
tells us what a prominent member of the emergent middle-class intelligentsia thought but also offers valuable insights into the pre-colonial history
of devotional practices followed in the region. A substantial part of the text
is devoted to the author's lamentations about the declining state of Brahmanical Hinduism in Assam. He states regretfully that the Hindu faith had
fallen into disuse since nearly three-fourths of the population was under the
influence of the *sattras* or Vaishnavite institutions founded by the followers
of the fifteenth-century reformer saint, Sankardeb. In 1833 Dhekial Phukan published another book called the *Kamrupa Jattra Paddhati*, with the
avowed aim of reversing the strong apathy for the Brahmanical faith and
shrines dedicated to the Brahmanical deities among the local people. In a
letter addressed to the editor of the Calcutta-based Samachar Chandrika

Press which published the work, he stated that his objective in writing the book was to acquaint tourists and the general public with *Kamrupdesh* about which people outside Assam were by and large ignorant.[5]

Dhekial Phukan's anxieties underscored the steady erosion of Brahmanical Hinduism in the region since the sixteenth century under the onslaught of the neo-Vaishnavite movement preached by Sankardeb's followers. Early British accounts written soon after the acquisition of Assam observed that temples were not the foci of devotional worship for the majority of the people. The *Gazetteer of Bengal and North-East India*, compiled in early 1900, noted that Hindu temples were very few in number, especially in the Assam valley.[6] Instead, the work observed almost every village contained the *namghar* or prayer hall where people assembled for prayer and worship. The lack of patronage for temples is also corroborated by Chief Commissioner P.R.T. Gurdon, who stated in his report in 1902 that temples like the Madhav temple at Hajo and the Sukleshwar temple at Guwahati were 'in a state of rapid decay'.[7] Francis Jenkins, commissioner of Assam, was sufficiently swayed by the palpable disregard for Brahmanical Hindu institutions and practices in the region, to remark, 'Brahmins are not the Gooroos of the Assamese, nor are they in the least repute amongst them, except when it may be from occasionally holding respectable secular offices.'[8] Contemporary writers like Maniram Bor Bhandar Barua, the author of the *Buranji Vivek Ratna*, and Gunabhiram Borooah, the author of the *Assam Buranji*, have also referred to the preponderance of the Vaishnavite faith in nineteenth-century Assam.

There were quite a large number of Vaishnava sects, each controlled by their respective *sattras*. The latter was a monastic or semi-monastic organization led by the chief preceptor or the Gossain.[9] The *guru* or master offered *saran* or initiation and was held in reverence by the disciples who regarded him as second only to God. It was customary for an average Assamese to take the *saran* on attaining maturity. Travelling across Assam in 1851, the ethnographer E.T. Dalton noted the tremendous popularity of one such sect. Dalton observed:

> I know of none that for the general respectability and intelligence of the disciples, their number and their success in making proselytes, are more deserving of attention than the Mahapurushiyas or votaries of the Borpetah Shostro, a religious community widely spread throughout lower Assam, and extending into Cooch Behar and N.E. Rungpore.[10]

Dalton states that the Kamrup district itself possessed 195 *sattras* subordinate to that of Barpeta.[11] Dalton's early study of the Barpeta *sattra*, one of the most important and influential *sattras* of Assam, and one that enjoyed immense following in the Kamrupa division, provides us with the first detailed insights into the devotional life led by members of the *sattras*. The growing popularity of the neo-Vaishnavite sects would have forced Brahmanical Hinduism into total oblivion had it not been for liberal patronage to temples and priests by the erstwhile rulers in the form of periodical land grants and donations. The conversion to Hinduism, of the erstwhile rulers in the seventeenth century, allowed the Hindu shrines to withstand the general apathy and helped them survive alongside the *sattras*.[12]

The ascendancy of Vaishnavism was accompanied by newer forms of devotion such as incantations or *nama kirtana*. Unfortunately, we do not have any evidence to track precisely what earlier forms of worship the neo-Vaishnavite modes of devotion replaced, but it is possible, given the rather unorthodox functioning of the new faith, that older household deities and cults continued to be venerated.[13] One ethnographer who studied the rituals practised in the Dakhinpath *sattra*, in the first decade of the twentieth century, has remarked: 'The worship of Krishna was the essence of religion in all of them, but at Dakhinpath there was no objection to the worship of Durga and other Saktis as an accessory'.[14] The same author also noted the elaborate rituals observed by the *Gosains* and the *bhakats* in the *sattras* adding that in the Auniati *sattra* in particular the ceremonial 'came closer to the ordinary Hindu type'. It was this catholic spirit of Vashnavism in Assam that must have promoted a wide variety of modes and practices of devotion by those who came under the influence of the faith. In the villages a least, many local cults survived and continued to receive a great deal of attention. These included those of the serpent goddess *Manasa*, *Dharma* in the form of a bull and so on.[15] Given, however, that Sankardeb had preached a form of monotheism, there must have been a general increase in the veneration of Vaishnavite deities from the sixteenth century onwards. One may also infer with some degree of legitimacy that congregational chanting and the reading of the sacred texts, that is, the *Bhagavadgita* and the *Bhagavatapurana*, became far more ubiquitous as modes of devotion than practices of regular visits to shrines and the performance of sacrificial rituals. Chanting of *Harinaam* or the name of the Vaishnavite deity, *Narayana*, was done either individually or congregationally in *namghars*, which, therefore, became a ubiquitous feature of village life in Assam. The central object of veneration in the *sattras* and the *namghars* was the *Bhagavad Geeta* or the book recounting the conversation between Arjun and Krishna, characters in the epic *Mahabharata*. Both Dalton and Charles Eliot have left detailed accounts of the inner life of these Vaishnava monasteries. They mention that all kinds of prayer in these *sattras* was congregational in nature and consisted of the singing of spiritual songs accompanied by the clapping of hands and the striking of cymbals and other musical instruments and the reading of the *Bhagavat* in Sanskrit.

The publication of Haliram Dhekial Phukan's *Kamrupa Jattra Padhddhati*, in 1833, assumes a critical significance in the context of a society that did not consider Brahmanical Hindu rituals as fundamental to their existence.[16] The discursive value of this text is enhanced by the self-proclaimed agenda of the author to attract prospective 'Hindu' pilgrims to Assam. The text provided a list of Hindu shrines in Kamrup, taking care to highlight the religious significance of each and every shrine and the latter's suitability for hosting key religious ceremonies. By dwelling at length on the merit of individual shrines, and the possible outcome of worshipping at the latter, and by comparing such merits with those which one hoped to gain from similar shrines elsewhere, this work made a valiant and conscious effort to project the religious sanctity of Assam (*sthanamahatya*) to prospective Hindu pilgrims from other parts of the country.

Brahmanical Hinduism gained a stronghold in the region in the coming years although Haliram did not live to witness the transition. This chapter draws its assumptions in this regard from vernacular literary periodicals that reflected the self-perceptions of their middle-class patrons in the nineteenth century. The chapter contends that the new-age deliberations on 'Hinduism' and the significance attached to religion by the Orientalists in their assessments of Assamese society intertwined with complex nationalist aspirations to open up a space for Brahmanical forms of devotion in the nineteenth century. Another significant factor that went a long way in reviving temple worship was the colonial state's sympathetic handling of pre-colonial land entitlements enjoyed by temples. This came as relief to these institutions ruined by the depredations of the Burmese forces and the apathy of ordinary people.

II

Ethnographic delusions

Curiously enough, the immense following enjoyed by the Vaishnavite *sattras* in Assam failed to impress the early colonial authors and compilers of the numerous ethnographic reports on Assam produced in course of the nineteenth century. Without exception, these authors, be they travellers, ethnographers and officials by profession, displayed a remarkable lack of comprehension when it came to interpreting the practices of Vaishnavism in the region. It is impossible to say, in the absence of adequate records, how these assumptions were generated, but one can surmise that Orientalist scholarship was a key factor in inspiring notions of a 'Hindu past' for the subcontinent.[17] These early studies assumed almost seamlessly that Vaishnavism practised in Assam was but a mere sub-sect of Hinduism essentially similar to the parent religion in its beliefs and practices. It was a different matter that such conflation was in gross violation of the uniqueness and disparate religious experiences of Assam that set it apart from other regions of the so-called Indic heartland. It would have been far more politic to consider Vaishnavite practices in Assam as being closely integrated with one of the myriad forms in which Buddhism was practised in Tibet, Bhutan and other places in the trans-Himalayan region where Buddhism still survived. After all, places like Hajo and Tezpur in British Assam continued to receive Tibetan Buddhist pilgrims well into the British period. Vaishnavite practices in Assam also resonated with the larger and connected history of Vaishnavism in eastern India with a fairly familiar network of pilgrim sites which inspired the medieval reformer Sankardeb to undertake his pilgrimage preparatory to his preaching of the *Eksaran dharma* in Assam.[18] Instead, however, colonial historiography chose to place religious observances and practices in the valley in the broad category of Brahmanical Hindu. In 1800, John Peter Wade's *History of Assam* assumed unequivocally that the current religious establishment in Assam was derived from the conversion of the monarch and his subjects to the Hindu faith by the Brahmans of Santipoor, Nuddea and other Western districts.[19] It was almost as if this sweeping generalization had set the tone for later studies such as that of Francis Buchanan-Hamilton – the man who carried out the arduous task of surveying the Bengal districts during 1807–14. Hamilton noted that the reigning dynasty had fallen under the influence of Brahmanical rituals.[20] This is curious, for Hamilton had earlier in his report observed that very few among the Brahmins of Assam or Kamrup 'worship the Saktis or female destructive spirits' and 'that they are chiefly of the sect of Vishnu'.[21] He also noted that the instructors of the worshippers of Vishnu lived in 'Chhatras' and that they were very powerful, several of them having from 10,000 to 15,000 entirely devoted to their service.[22] It is clear, however, from the lack of substantive details or a well laid-out comparison, which the distinctiveness of worship in the region had failed to produce any serious impression on his intellect. When John M'Cosh chose to write his *Topography of Assam* in 1837, the matter had been almost resolved, and consequently, he dismissed the issue in a single sentence, which said 'the natives of Assam chiefly consisted of Hindoos'.[23] By contrast, *A Descriptive Account of Assam*, written in 1841 by William Robinson, was more discerning in its observations. Robinson echoed Buchanan-Hamilton's observation that the Brahmins of Assam were mostly devoted to the worship of Vishnu and that only a small portion were *Saktas*.[24] He also mentioned that most of the temples in Assam were lying in ruins. He further observed that the temple of Kamakhya drew only a few devotees during the day, whether on the occasion of festivals or otherwise. However, instead of choosing to follow his observations to their logical conclusion, Robinson preferred to conclude that the people of Assam had succumbed to the influence of the Brahmanical faith.

The second half of the nineteenth century was characterized by a preponderance of ethnographic surveys. Driven by an urge to carry out extensive fieldwork-based surveys, these studies, surprisingly, failed to exhibit any distinctiveness of approach. Without exception, these surveys echoed the impressions of the earlier genre of colonial historiographical literature. Consequently, there was no paradigm shift in their understanding of the religious pursuits of the people. Even the makers of the province's first census did not bother to make independent judgements despite their access to first-hand information collected through circulation of elaborately crafted questionnaires. The answer to this mystery lies in the failure of census officials to design more nuanced questionnaires that could tease out information pertaining to the disparate manner in which people practised their religions. The emphasis on broad labels under which people's practices were conveniently subsumed ignored the unique flavours of devotional life in a region that was culturally diverse. The census, by giving simple options such as 'Hindu', 'Muslim' and 'others' to the people, robbed them of their right to choose and enter the religious affiliations that approximated their individual styles of devotional worship. Even when their relatively simplistic methods of enquiry generated data that were clearly not in sync with their preconceptions of religion, these were not treated with the criticality that they deserved. Consequently, the assessment ended up becoming nothing more than a mere normative understanding of society instead of generating a nuanced and analytically rigorous framework of representation. The following passage will serve to bring out the anomalies of the census enumerations and their clichéd understandings of colonial society. The first census report of 1881 stated:

> Much interest attaches to the manner in which the Hindu propaganda is carried on in the Assam valley. The head proselytisers are the Goshains, who are mostly Brahmins from Nadiya and (professedly) from Kanauj. A few great houses in Kamrup follow the Tantrik form of religion and are allowed to marry, but all the Goshains of upper Assam are Vaishnava, and most of them are

celibate, living in shattras or monasteries, with the sacred shrine in the centre, and the cells of their chief followers, to the number sometimes of several hundred, disposed in order around it.[25]

What the surveyors found was non-trivial, but these peculiarities of religion, as it was practised by a sizeable section of the population in Assam, could not persuade the survey authorities to revisit the predominant understanding of the Hindu. The first census did not regard the aforementioned specificities of practices pursued in Assam as anything but Hindu. Nor did the makers of the first census bother to take into account the enormous following that these Vaishnava *sattras* obviously enjoyed in Assam although the data collected make it impossible to overlook this pattern. Referring to the overwhelming influence of these *sattras*, the census of 1881 observed:

Whatever their denomination, the Goshains wield a vast spiritual authority, have adherents in many parts of the country, with a headman in each village in which adherents are numerous, and send out from time to time emissaries to exhort the faithful, to reprove the lukewarm, to inflict punishments on offenders against moral laws, and to invite and attract converts. One Goshain has his special followers among the Mataks, another among the Domes, a third in one part of the country, a fourth in another. They have already absorbed all the Ahoms, the ancient ruling race in this valley, and they now swell the number of their converts mostly from among the aboriginal tribes of Kacharis, Lalungs, Miris, Mikirs and so on. Even some of Nagas of the Sibsagar frontier have of late been drawn within the attractions of one of the Goshains and acknowledge themselves his disciples.[26]

The observations made by the census report for 1881 did not lead to an interrogation of the standard representations of religious practices in Assam as Hindu. Nor did these provoke any discussion on the distinctive features of Hinduism as practised in Assam. Even when the disparities were noticed and commented upon, as in the second census report on Assam in 1891, they failed to inspire any critical response. The second census of 1891 casually mentioned that the phenomenon of conversion was a relatively unknown feature of Hinduism in Assam:

Although figures cannot be given to show the extent to which Hinduism has spread during the past ten years, it is well known that the work of proselytization is steadily going on. The time-honoured theory that a man cannot become a Hindu unless he is born a Hindu has long since been demolished.[27]

Somehow such observations failed to translate into a proper appreciation of the fact that religion in Assam did not quite conform to the established norms of Hinduism as understood by the British. Consequently, no alternative framework of representation for religion was ever proposed for Assam. The peculiar features of Vaishnavism in Assam were ultimately labelled as quotidian Hindu norms of worship that did not merit additional attention or an alternative framework of representation.

III

Inventing traditions

Orientalist scholarship was culpable of far greater violations than the mere oversight of Assam's distinctive Vaishnavite past. Religious ethnography in Assam designated the precise mode of Brahmanical worship practised in the region as *Sakta-Tantrik*. The latter had a special connotation in nineteenth-century Orientalist scholarship. Rituals observed by the practitioners of this faith were believed to be associated everywhere in the country with female spirits and the gratification of sexual pleasures through the practice of erotic cults. Assam's insertion into the latter tradition was determined by the chance discovery, in the late eighteenth century, of two texts containing references to a deity designated as Kamakhya, which was also, incidentally, the name of a local shrine venerated by the people of the province. Orientalist scholarship, which had already identified modern Kamarupa with British Assam, lost no opportunity in associating textual allusions to 'Kamarupa Kamakhya' with the shrine located atop the Nilachal Hill in Guwahati. The two were immediately and irrevocably clubbed and myths and rituals mentioned in these texts were unambiguously ascribed to Kamakhya and the mode of worship practised at this shrine. This literal translation of textual references glossed over the fact that the word, *Kamarupa* was used in these texts, with polyvalent meanings making it impossible to translate the expression into a place name.[28] Bodhisattva Kar has argued that this linear interpretation fulfilled a significant imperialist purpose. It legitimized the empire by making its territorial space isomorphic with the ancient *Aryavarta*.[29] In short, 'Kamarupa's' territorial location within the geo-body of the British province of Assam fulfilled an imperial need. It did not matter that the same had been resolved through questionable historiographical means.

The exercise of treating the two texts as the chief determinants of devotional practices in the region was equally suspect and outright ideological. One of these texts that referred to 'Kamarupa Kamakhya' was the *Kalika Purana*, which incidentally had come into prominence in Bengal sometime in the eighteenth century in connection with the celebration of the Durga Puja festival in Bengal which had begun to gain ascendancy in Bengal since this time.[30] The text became immensely popular on account of its detailed exposition of rituals associated with the annual worship of Durga. In 1799, a section of this text was translated by W.C. Blaquiere under the title 'Rudhiradhyaya' or 'Sanguinary Chapter' and published in the *Journal of the Asiatic Society of Bengal*. The published extract described the manner of propitiation of Goddess Kamakhya. The chapter contained a lengthy exposition of how and in what vessel blood offerings to the deity were to be made.[31] On the basis of its contents and style of narration, the text was immediately pronounced to be *Tantric*.[32] This classification was determined by the text's graphic descriptions of blood sacrifices and the sexual dalliances of the deities. The other text, the *Yogini Tantra*, written presumably in the sixteenth century, was similarly classified as a *Tantric* text on the pretexts after an analysis of its contents revealed a similarity in contents and manner of delineation of the same.

The classification of texts as *Tantric* had by the middle of the nineteenth century become a simple and straightforward affair. Orientalist scholars in India had identified an entire corpus of religious literature and rituals as embodiments of the so-called *Tantric* tradition believed to be practised by esoteric sects in different parts of the country. Such classification did not take into account the profound lack of uniformity, whether in terms of contents or styles of narration, among this motley group of works. Orientalist scholarship gave wide publicity to the highly erotic nature of rituals practised by the cult members for acquiring occult powers. A much-discussed theme that evoked simultaneously curiosity and disgust among British scholars, *Tantric* rituals came to signify the evil face of the Hindu faith. Ronald Inden has argued that such scholarship sought to construct India as the quintessential 'other' in comparison to the West.[33] Conceived as an essentially passionate, irrational, effeminate world, India was set in opposition to the progressive, rational, masculine and scientific world of modern Europe, and *Tantra* was quickly singled out as India's darkest and most irrational element in addition to being the most exotic feature of the exotic Orient.[34] Recent scholarship on the subject holds that Orientalist categorization and denigration of certain practices as *Tantric* constituted a conscious investment in the rationalization of British rule in India.[35] This chapter argues that the canonization of the *Kalika Purana* and the *Yogini Tantra* as texts of authority with regard to the shrine of Kamakhya in

Assam was an issue that was resolved without adequate physical verification of ritual practices actually performed at the shrine. In fact, the very choice of the 'Rudhiradhyaya' or the 'Sanguinary Chapter', for translation, out of sundry other chapters in the *Kalika Purana*, was also immensely fraught as it demonstrated a fascination for certain types of ritualistic formulae over others. Such an approach served to filter less-extravagant details out of cognition. It is telling that Rev. William Ward, the first missionary to mention the ritual worship of the Kamakhya in 1817, did not once refer to the bloody rites that were later pronounced to be indispensable for Kamakhya's worship. On the contrary, his work offered an innocuous representation of the rites associated with the deity. Ward wrote:

> This goddess is worshipped daily by persons of property before a
> pan of water or some other substitute; and also by many Shaktus
> on the 8th of the moon in both quarters. . . . A few persons receive
> the initiatory rites of this goddess, and worship her as their guard-
> ian deity.[36]

Ward's statement also left no room for doubt that the veneration of the deity was by no means a universal phenomenon.

The making of a stereotype with regard to the representation of the shrine actually began with Francis Buchanan-Hamilton. It is noteworthy that the latter did not visit Assam even once in course of his survey of the eastern districts of the British Indian territories. His account of Assam was based on hearsay. It goes without saying that his verdict on Kamakhya was entirely textual. Buchanan pronounced the *Yogini Tantra* as the 'highest authority concerning everything related to Kamrup'.[37] Notwithstanding his earlier observations regarding the marginality of the *Sakta* mode of worship in Assam, Hamilton pronounced that the *Tantras* contained the key to an understanding of the religious practices of the people of Assam.[38] The subsequent account of William Robinson accepted this classification unquestioningly when he declared that the shrine of Kamakhya was the principal seat for the practice of *Tantric* rites. Robinson even provided a detailed description of the rituals purportedly practised at the shrine. There was no mention of the source of his information. Invariably, his information was also drawn exclusively from the *Yogini Tantra*, and not from any ethnographic survey of rituals actually practised at the shrine. This, however, did not deter Robinson from making the following observation:

> Here the most abominable rites are practised, and the most licen-
> tious scenes exhibited, which it is hardly possible to suppose the

human mind, even when sunk to the very lowest depths of depravity, could be capable of devising.[39]

Robinson's assertions were far more sweeping than those of Buchanan. He claimed that the entire province had succumbed to the spell of the deity although Kamrup in Lower Assam was the 'grand source' of the *Tantric* system of magic. Robinson's account proved to be a turning point in the representational history of the shrine. Kamakhya was henceforth classified as a site for the practice of extreme *Tantric* rites demanding bloody sacrifices and sexual excesses of all kinds. Along with the shrine, the province itself acquired an identity that was belied by the heterogeneity of religious practices pursued by the region's diverse population. Even if one assumes that the so-called *Tantric* practices were performed by some sectarian groups, they were certainly not predominant. On the contrary, Dhekial Phukan makes it amply clear that the former constituted one out of many other genres of worship practised by the people. It is telling, however, that there is no attempt to define the precise nature of rituals constitutive of the *Tantric* in Assam by one who was clearly familiar with the temples in Kamrup. In fact, the urgency demonstrated by Phukan for standardization of devotional practices in the region bears testimony to the heterogeneity characterizing modes of worship in Assam. It is equally telling that travel accounts of the nineteenth century written by pilgrims visiting the shrine also failed to detect anything unusual in the mode of veneration practised at the shrine.[40]

IV

Contending pasts

Kamakhya's insertion into the *Sakta-Tantric* body of tradition and its representation as the principal place of worship in Assam were immensely fraught with the usual incongruities and elisions that characterized colonial studies of indigenous practices.[41] Contrary to Orientalist representations, the shrine of Kamakhya appears to have experienced shifting fortunes from time to time. According to the *Darrang Rajavamsavali*, or the court chronicle of the kings of Durrang in lower Assam, the temple was found in a dilapidated condition in 1565 CE by the Koch king Naranarayan and his brother Silarai, who constructed the present structure and rescued the shrine from total oblivion by assigning charge of daily rituals to a Brahmin priest, Kendu Kalai, brought from elsewhere for the purpose.[42] The state in which the temple was found by the Koch monarch indicates at best the volatile history of veneration of the deity associated with the shrine. In fact, the shrine does not appear to have been prominent before the eleventh century. The earliest inscriptional reference to the shrine cannot be found earlier than the eleventh century and is attributed to Indrapala although the references in the said inscription are sufficiently vague and contain no direct references to Kamakhya. In fact, the deity mentioned in the Gwaku-chi grant of Indrapala is *Mahagauri* and *Kamesvara* instead of Kamakhya.[43] Scholars think that the shrine was earlier dedicated to a non-Brahman female cult, which was later integrated within the Brahmanical Hindu pantheon. Irrespective of this, however, the shrine failed to command uninterrupted veneration, prompting active interventions from the *Tungkhungia* monarchs to overhaul the management of the shrine in the seventeenth century. It is common knowledge that *swargadeo* Rudra Singha handed over charge of the temple to Krishnaram Bhattacharya, a *Sakta* Brahmin who was brought for the purpose from Malipota in Nadia in Bengal. Designated Parbatiya Gossain, on account of his residence atop the Nilachal Hill, he was responsible for standardizing rules of worship in temples across the *swargadeo*'s domain. The *swargadeo* and many of his nobles were initiated by the Gossain into the new faith. Author-writer Rajanikanta Bardoloi mentions in his novel *Rahadoi Ligiree* that the *swargadeos* introduced the custom of performing Durga Puja at the shrine and the common people had little access to the rituals or to the temple precincts.[44] Thus, the process of assimilation with the Brahmanical order in Assam happened rather late and followed the usual pattern of appropriation of local cults and practices into the Brahmanical fold. Royal patronage of a certain order facilitated erasure of earlier properties and practices through enforced adoption of new patterns to suit the dominant ideology.[45] The identity of the shrine of Kamakhya, thus, experienced numerous shifts over the years to suit the demands and expectations of successive ruling clans, belying Orientalist attempts to ascribe a fixed and transcendental identity to it. In fact, local historical chronicles of Assam called *Buranjis* abound with references to royal intervention in favour of preferred modes of devotion. Silarai, the brother of the Koch king Naranarayan, is said to have brought two Bhattacharya Brahmins from Gaud in Bengal and settled them in the Koch kingdom.[46] The *Smriti Kaumudi* composed by one of them, Pitambar Siddhantabagish, laid down the ritual norms, which were henceforth followed during the Durga Puja festival in the Koch kingdom. Omission of royal intervention as one of the primary agents of change in the pre-colonial period constituted a serious elision in Orientalist representations of indigenous traditions. Fixity of norms was, truly speaking, a colonial innovation, unanticipated in the culture of pre-colonial societies. With regard to the

Kamakhya, notions of the shrine having been Hindu, much less *Tantric-Hindu*, were a foregone conclusion tailored to suit the tone and tenor of Indology's text-based scholarship, as Kar shows in his study of colonial geography's toponymic approach.[47]

Further, even if we concede that the shrine in whatever form was venerated long before the eleventh century, there is no specific archaeological evidence to indicate that the rituals observed at the shrine were esoteric in nature, far less that they were inclined towards the erotic. Unlike some other local shrines from where erotic sculptures have been discovered, Kamakhya has not produced any such specimen. Sculptures of female divinities found in the vicinity also do not indicate erotic possibilities. The discursive nature of Kamakhya's representational history under colonial rule is illustrated by shifts in Orientalist ethnography of the shrine from the turn of the century. This shift synchronized with a serious attempt to reclaim British Assam for 'Aryan' India, in what Kar regards as colonial attempts to legitimize British rule in the region.[48] Toponymic identifications of local sites with Puranic place names, thus, coincided with reiterations of the antiquity of Kamakhya and its sanctity within the Hindu pantheon. From the beginning of the twentieth century, the process was reinforced through archaeological initiatives that sought to discover and identify monuments in the region as remnants of the Aryan legacy. British Assam's integrity to the Indic heartland had to be established on multiple registers, and the insertion of local religious practices into the great Indian tradition constituted a related discursive exercise. Consequently, the constant foregrounding of the erotic in Kamakhya was replaced by an invoking of the sacred and the antique. *Kamrup and Gauhati* written by K.S. Macdonald, and published in 1902, typified this discursive shift. Macdonald was a missionary of the Free Church of Scotland and had been persuaded by an acquaintance to collect materials on the *Tantras* sometime in 1900.[49] He is said to have acquired translations of a large number of *Tantras* from his friends although he did not live to publish his research. The present work was the outcome of his research on the *Tantras*, which presumably led him to learn about Assam given the perceived associations between the two in Orientalist scholarship. Macdonald wrote:

> Assam is the most easterly acquisition of the early Aryan invaders of India. Kamrup contains places which were the scenes of numerous mythological occurrences as related in the Epics, the Puranas and Tantras. The popularity of the place with gods and men is indicated by the two proverbial sayings (1) that 'Elsewhere deities are scarce but in Kamrup they are found in every house' and (2) that 'men who go to kamrup never leave it' and by the statements that

Kali was born there; that there the most sacred or secret part of her body was deposited; that the Sakta religion originated there, that there salvation from sin and freedom from rebirths are easily got, and that the Tantra scriptures were written, – any one of which if true, would make Kamrup famous and popular with Hindus for all time.[50]

Macdonald paid scant attention to the erotic rituals that had been integral to the accounts of his predecessors. Statements that 'in the great Hindu Epics and in the Puranas and Tantras alike we find indications of the religious and political importance assigned to Kamrup', marked a definite transition from the negative appraisals of the previous century.[51] Evidences culled from the *Puranas* were furnished to project the shrine as a premier seat of Hindu worship since remote antiquity.

Macdonald's attempts to shift the focus away, albeit momentarily, from Kamakhya's rituals towards its antiquity and interiority to mainstream Hindu iconography and worship, seemed to echo the tone and tenor of colonial administrative practices mentioned in the earlier paragraph. The *Tantric* rituals were, therefore, relegated to Assam's prehistoric past and ascribed to the influence of indigenous forms of worship on the pure and pristine cultural practices of the immigrant Aryans. As Macdonald categorically stated, 'To the original aboriginal cult of its inhabitants we think Tantricism is indebted'.[52]

The relegation of unacceptable practices to the pre-Aryan period was an old Orientalist trope that enabled the British to explain admirable traits in India's history without jeopardizing their own claims to authority and superiority.[53] That Macdonald's colonial subjectivities remained firmly in place is evident from his regurgitation of the old stereotypes of earlier British ethnography concerning the sexual promiscuity and eroticized rituals encouraged by the devotees of Kamakhya although he choose, significantly enough, not to be judgemental about the veracity of such accounts.[54] His ambivalence was that of a colonial subject, although in seeking to rectify Assam's berated status as a cultural outcast, he confirmed his locus within a shifting trend of administrative thoughts and practices concerning Assam.

V

The nationalist turn

The Baptist missionary newspaper *Orunodoi* published a series of poems titled *Tirthar Vivaran* and *Tirthayatra* by the Assamese convert Nidhi Levi Farwell, at the turn of the century. Highly didactic in nature, these poems warned readers to be wary of the wiles of Brahmin priests who robbed credulous devotees by prescribing obscurantist and obnoxious rituals. They described with great derision some of the customs, rites and rituals practised in the temples of Kamakhya and Hajo. Coming as these essays did, several years after the launch of the Orunodoi, and the frequency with which they were published within a close span, as well as the intensity they displayed, invest these compositions with a discursive significance. The author, Nidhi Levi Farwell, was an eager contributor to the *Orunodoi* and wrote frequently on diverse themes ranging from general knowledge to the glories of the Christian faith although this was the first time he had launched a frontal assault on Brahmanical rituals. The reason behind this unusual criticism may have been a surge in pilgrim interest in the Hindu shrines at the turn of the century although we have no concrete data to prove this. Nidhi was bound to be concerned, given the fact that the Baptist Mission had miserably failed so far to produce any visible impact on the religious sensibilities of the local population of the Brahmaputra valley.[55] It was not long before they gave up their proselytizing activities in the Assam valley and chose to concentrate on the Garo and the Khasi hill districts.

With the establishment of rail links between Assam and Bengal in the 1880s, Assam began to attract pilgrim tourists from Bengal and other parts of the country.[56] Kamakhya soon emerged as the principal tourist destination, with people from neighbouring Bengal and other parts of India flocking to the shrine, presumably attracted by the latter's highly publicized *Tantric* associations. Associated with instant gratification of desires, *Tantric* rites were the subject of immense curiosity throughout the country at this time. Kamakhya's purported links with these forms of worship, as well as its famed association with fertility rites, catapulted the shrine into instant fame and attracted pilgrims in large numbers. Nidhi Levi Farwell was, however, less likely to be concerned about visitors from outside the province. Given the fact that the Baptist Mission still nurtured some hopes of proselytization in the valley, it is possible that Nidhi was especially concerned about local pilgrims who now frequented these shrines in larger numbers. Although it is impossible to quantify the number of local pilgrims visiting the Hindu shrines in the absence of recorded data, it is possible to gain some insights into shifts taking place at the level of devotional worship if the contents of the vernacular literary periodicals of this period are anything to go by. For instance, Gunabhiram Baruah, a prolific contributor to these periodicals, and a key member of the emergent intelligentsia, observed that the Durga Puja, which had been a strictly royal affair in the pre-colonial period, was now being observed with great pomp in the region. Baruah mentioned the phenomenon in the 'Saumar Bhraman', an essay published in the *Jonaki*, the leading literary periodical of the period, in 1890. Barua observed:

> In the past Durga puja was not popular among the common people of our country. . . . Raja Surath lost his kingdom after performing Durga puja along with Chandipath and animal sacrifice. Since then the worshipping of the Durga idol became confined to the king's family. Restrictions were placed on mass worship of the idol. The devi puja is also performed in some temples including the kamakhya. . . . The rest of the people used to attend the rituals and festivities carried out by the king. . . . But under the British no such restrictions exist. . . . Now the Sakta people here are also celebrating the Durga puja according to their ability.
>
> (Translation mine)[57]

What Barua witnessed was not an isolated event. The shift in devotional practices may also be gleaned from the considerable number of articles in these periodicals on themes drawn from the two Hindu epics, that is the Ramayana and the Mahabharata, and the Puranic literature. Quite a large number of books were produced dealing in subjects drawn from these texts.[58] The trend underscored a growing interest in Hindu mythological subjects that was not without its consequences on the modes of devotion. The shift did not go unnoticed in the census records. Barua mentions that Brahmanical practices had begun to infiltrate the *sattras*, which were highly influenced now by caste restrictions. The Census Report of 1881 observed: 'This revolt against Brahmin supremacy has almost spent its force, and some of the most important Kolitashattras are beginning to elect Brahmin Goshains'.[59]

The ascendancy of Brahmanical Hinduism in Assam, which these trends underscored, is best exemplified by the immense popularity that the shrine of Kamakhya came to acquire in the days ahead. The phenomenon was anticipated by the vernacular literary sphere which began to take an acute interest in the shrine from the turn of the century. Kamakhya became the focus of much-animated discussion in the literary public sphere, with debates ranging on issues concerning its ancestry and religious symbolism, especially its purported associations with *Tantric* rituals. The pattern was set by the province's leading literary periodical *Jonaki*, which published a series of articles on the shrine at about this time. Written by one Matiram Das, these articles unequivocally asserted the antiquity and religious significance of the shrine to the people of Assam. Das's language reflected the ardent admiration of a devotee and the nationalistic self-pride of an 'Assamese' intellectual:

> The Kamakhya temple . . . is the chief centre of Bhagavati Maha-maya which proclaims the eternal glory of the ancient Aryans. . . . Both in antiquity and beauty this temple has virtually no parallel in our country. This is the principal pilgrimage centre of the Hindus. . . . Nearly all Hindus from the rest of the country visit the shrine.[60]

In the course of the twentieth century, Kamakhya became the central focus of an enormous body of discursive literature that made the latter the site for launching a full-scale war on the Orientalist denigration of Assam in general and the shrine in particular, as one that encouraged objectionable and obscurantist religious rituals. Writers like Hemchandra Goswami, Bani Kanta Kakati, Birinchi Kumar Barua and Rajanikanta Bardoloi returned to the theme at various points of time in their careers.

A key feature of the middle-class discourse on Kamakhya during this period, which allows us to regard such rhetoric as highly nationalistic in their discursivity, was its strongly defensive tone. Kamakhya became enmeshed in the growing nationalist consciousness that cast its powerful spell on the provincial literati from about this time. We argue that Kamakhya's appropriation into the nationalist discourse as a symbol of community pride and solidarity was determined by the negative manner of depiction of the shrine in Orientalist scholarship that served to turn the tide of middle-class public opinion in favour of the shrine. Confronted with the negative publicity, some members of the elite chose to distance the region from questionable practices by situating the latter in the past, that is before the advent of Sankardeb's Vaishnavism. To the first category belonged scholars like Hemchandra Goswami. In an article on the Assamese language, the latter observed:

> Before Sankardeb the bond of language had become as lax as possible in Assam. Both the Brahmin and the Sudra had forgotten that religion constituted the key to human progress. With the decline of the Buddhist faith, instead of the lofty ideals of the Aryan religion, the lowly aspects of the latter became popular among the common people. Beliefs in spirits and other superstitions were preventing the people from focusing on Narayanas as the Ultimate Being and the source of all incarnations. Society had sunk to the lowest depths of corruption and depravity. It was at

this crucial juncture that Sankardeb was born to save mankind and religion from total obscurity and to reorganize the community.

(Translation mine)[61]

Yet another section of the elite proudly projected Kamakhya as a triumphant symbol of the province's achievements in the religious domain. The latter took obvious pleasure in pointing out that Assam was regarded as the premier centre of the *Sakta* form of worship by people from other regions. Writers like Haliram Dhekial Phukan and Gunabhiram Baruah belonged to this category. What, however, concerns the scholar is the complete transformation of Hemchandra Goswami's views on the so-called *Tantric* rituals before long. This ardent admirer of Assam's Vaishnavite legacy underwent a complete turnaround on the subject in a matter of few years. In a lecture delivered in 1920, as the chairman of the Axam Sahitya Sabha, he projected the *Tantras* as the proud legacy of the people of Assam:

> You all know that Kamarupa is the land of the Tantras. It is said that the Tantra Shastras were born in this land. The Tantras are the source of the Mantras. From the ancient times many civilized communities have admitted the effects of the Mantras on the human body and mind. . . . As a result of Western learning, a section of people used to cover their years at the very mention of the Tantras. . . . but people are now considering the Tantras respectfully. We hope that a time will come when the Assamese people will understand the true meaning of the Tantras and will be attracted towards these texts. Many of you have heard that with the help of the mantras men can influence ferocious beasts like snakes, tigers and bears. That these Mantras which originated in Kamarupa had once influenced the whole of India, is evident from the fact that even now the Mother Kamakhya of Kamarupa is referred to in connection with Mantras. People elsewhere even now refer to the people of this land as magicians. The name Assam may not be familiar to many, but few would not recognize 'Kamarupa Kamakhya'. . . . The Mantras are our old legacy.
>
> (Translation mine)[62]

The nationalist investment of Kamakhya as a much-venerated shrine of sufficient antiquity was part of the larger Assamese project of situating British Assam within the geographical and historical domain of Aryan India. Since the middle of the nineteenth century, the provincial intelligentsia had striven to establish British Assam's claim to the great Indian tradition culled from the *Itihasa-Purana* 'sources'.[63] The corresponding efforts were, therefore, two-fold. As Bodhisattva Kar has shown, on the one hand, the provincial elite sought a correspondence between Aryan place names and sites within British Assam.[64] Closely related to this were attempts to establish the historical antecedents of the people by drawing up lineage histories stretching back as far as the days of the Mahabharata. These histories were specially crafted to establish Assam's proximity to the geo-body of Hindu-India. The trends and patterns discussed in this chapter represent early indications that Brahmanical Hinduism was beginning to edge its way into the religious imagination of the Assamese middle class via their cultural project of securing a Hindu ancestry.

VI

Being Hindu being Assamese

From an obsession with Sanskritization of the language to a growing interest in Hindu iconography was perhaps a logical step, but what was ominous was the Assamese intellectual's determination to distance himself from Assam's diverse cultural ethos. With the progress of efforts to reinforce the boundaries of the community, assaults on the region's 'tribal' cultures gained in momentum. About this time the *Assam Bandhu* published an article titled *Garo Brittanto* by Ratneswar Mahanta, where the author severely denounced what he called the 'detestable' food habits of the Garo community, adding that the character and habits of these people led one to feel that they were none other than the demons mentioned in the Shastras.[65] In another article 'Bongali', Bengalis and hill tribes alike – such as the Khamptis, the Singphos, the Garos, the Bhot Abors – were designated as foreigners, equally uncivilized and unclean in their habits and practices.[66] Not satisfied with evoking cultural cohesion, some among the provincial intelligentsia also evoked a superior status for the community on the basis of the 'purity' of practices. These trends had been anticipated as early as 1859 by Haliram Dhekial Phukan, who remarked that although the Ahoms had been reformed after their conversion to Hinduism, it is still not possible to take water from their hands and that Brahmins who perform their crematory rites are regarded as lowly.[67] These tendencies were reinforced at the turn of the century by the growing fascination for Hinduism, which generated an exclusivist outlook and representations of the Assamese as caste Hindus and therefore racially untainted by contamination or intermixture with 'tribes' such as Garos or the Abors. There was simultaneously also an attempt to create a distance between the Assamese and the Ahoms as a separate people despite attempts to reclaim the Ahom martial legacy for Assam. The ruling class was demarcated as a separate Hinduized community that lacked an 'original' connection with Brahmanical Hinduism and hence was not quite Hindu. This narrowing of boundaries disrupted the broader understanding of Hindu that had allowed the absorption of many so-called non-Hindu peoples within the folds of an amorphous Hinduism that no one had cared to define. The *Buranji Vivek Ratna* written by Maniram Dewan recounted how becoming a Hindu had been a fairly common and easy practice associated with aspirations to upward social mobility – the phenomenon commonly described as Sanskritization.[68] Written sometime around 1855, the book by a prominent member of the Ahom traditional elite recounted an interesting feature of the Shiva temple purportedly established by Aurva Rishi at Devgaon, where the Kacharis ritually offered wine and meat to the deity, till they were instructed in a dream by the god himself to appoint a Brahmin priest for his worship. Dewan points out that even after the divine injunctions had been met with, the area adjoining the temple continued to remain predominantly non-Vedic, and for a long time, there was no trace of the Vedic rites and practices outside the temple on the southern banks of the Brahmaputra. The myriad ways in which one could be a Hindu in the days of the *swargadeo* now gave way to a strict definition of the faith in terms of a derived set of practices and entry into the group became impossible. This closure put an end to the assimilative process set forth by the Ahoms and divided hearts for good. The cultural agenda of the new middle-class elite set a dangerous precedent that opened the Pandora's box of politics with regard to group identities in the years to come.

A significant follow-up to the aforementioned trend was the tightening of caste rules. The neo-Vaishnavite movement started by Sankardev had a liberalizing influence on society although it did not succeed in eliminating caste altogether. The proselytizing drive of the later *sattras* had further generated conditions for intermixture of peoples – something that the Ahom rulers had also actively promoted.[69] A much-reported feature of pre-colonial society had been the alterity of castes as well as the absorption of tribal groups into the caste hierarchy. Sometime in 1640, the Ahom ruler is said to have issued an injunction identifying certain families only in Upper Assam as authentic Brahmin.[70] This indicates the fact that 'becoming a Brahmin' was permissible in Assam – a fact that was noted and perhaps caused some consternation among the orthodox sections who brought the matter to the king's notice.[71] Audrey Cantlie's anthropological survey of villages in Assam, as also the Census Reports of the nineteenth and twentieth centuries, indicates that the process of assimilation of tribes into caste society, as also social mobility within caste society did not come to

an end during the colonial period.[72] Cantlie noted that 'the majority of
Assamese castes are heterogeneous in origin and open to infiltration from
below' and that 'Assam still contains a large tribal population in process
of conversion'.[73] The process of initiation by a Vaishnavite Gossain often
enabled such assimilation by inducting norms of ritual purity among the
new entrants that usually set the latter apart from the rest of their kin who
had not taken *saran* from a *guru*.[74] The process of assimilation continued
after the coming of the British. Cantlie's own observations as late as 1948,
as also the census reports indicating 'increase' in the number of Hindus,
bear this out. Yet the process may not have been as smooth as it once was.
Cantlie herself notes that certain groups were no longer accepted for initiation by some Gossains.[75] It has to be remembered that Vaishnavism in
Assam did not really target social stratification along lines of caste but tried
instead to mitigate its influence.[76] While this implies that caste restrictions
survived within the *sattras* from an earlier period, one gets the impression that these were reinforced to some extent during the nineteenth and
early twentieth centuries both within and outside the *sattra* institutions.
Restrictions on commensality or inter-dining within the *sattra* indicate an
increasing concern with ritual purity.[77] Cantlie also refers to emphasis on
ritual purity by groups aspiring either to enter caste society or to move
higher up in the caste hierarchy. One way of attaining a purer status was
to abstain from eating meat and certain types of food or of refusing to
accept food from certain people unlike in the past.[78] Nath mentions the
disowning of the Ahoms by some *sattradhikars* immediately once it was
clear that the latter had lost their position of eminence.[79] Nath's study of
the *sattras* during the colonial period indicates public debates on the issue
of untouchability within the *sattra*, with many *sattradhikars* openly root-
ing for preserving the caste restrictions. It is possible that they were merely
reiterating what was an already-established tradition, but the conclusion
becomes inevitable, given evidences of caste alterity in pre-colonial Assam,
that caste rules were beginning to be enforced with renewed vigour from
roughly the nineteenth century.

An indication of what seems to have been a growing concern with ritual
status was the sudden engagement with 'appropriate' rules of marriage in
Assamese weddings. At least two prominent middle-class intellectuals from
the period – Hemchandra Barua and Gunabhiram Barua – engaged with
the subject of marriage in their works. Although none of these authors
were judgemental about any specific form of marriage practice, they identified those practices that were of 'non-Aryan' origin.[80] Successive issues of
the literary periodical *Jonaki* carried articles on marriage by authors like
Ratneswar Mahanta.[81] The male upper-caste concern about the need to

discipline women is underscored by articles like *Tirota* (Women), which urged women to devote themselves to the well-being of their husbands.[82] Essays like this reflected a concern about heterodox practices and the need to confront the latter by insisting on norms of ritual purity. These essays also reflect society's concern for the women becoming too radical to tackle.[83] Invariably, such an obsession with ritual status stemmed from a nationalist impulse, but they were also ultimately the result of colonial practices of enumeration that left little room for the fuzzy and the liminal. In 1902, in response to a directive from the Home Department, the chief commissioner of Assam appointed Major P.R.T. Gurdon as superintendent of ethnography in Assam.[84] The purpose was to 'prepare as far as possible a systematic account of the tribes and castes of this province, somewhat in the form adopted in the Tribes and Castes of Bengal'. The idea for such a project had originated in a suggestion by the census commissioner in 1882, when the data from the census operations of 1881 were being processed. Such a project was expected to benefit 'many branches of the administration in this country of an accurate and well-arranged record of the customs and the domestic and social relations of the various castes and tribes'.[85] Apart from the underlying notion of inflexibility that informed such an enterprise, the study was premised on crude essentialist principles. The resolution observed:

> The entire framework of native life in India is made up of groups of this kind, and the status and conduct of individuals are largely determined by the rules of the group to which they belong.[86]

The questionnaire that was circulated as part of this project revealed strong preconceived notions, making it impossible to give unconventional answers that did not fit the stereotype. The following selective list of questions will be sufficient for elucidating the point:

> Do the castes employ Brahmans for religious and ceremonial purposes? If so, are the brahmans received on terms of equality by other Brahmans? If they do not employ Brahmans what class of people serve them as priests?
>
> Are any ceremonies performed for the propitiation of (a) ancestors in general (b) childless ancestors (c) men who have died a violent death, and, if so, of what nature and at what seasons? Is the ceremony of sraddh performed or not?
>
> Is the caste, or any of its sub-divisions, named after any animal, plant, weapon or instrument? Do they show their reverence for

any such object either by special worship, abstaining from killing, eating, cutting, burning, using or naming it?

Fishermen, do they catch fish only or also crocodiles and tortoises?

Name any implement or mode of working which is characteristic of the caste, and note whether there is any form or detail of their main occupation by abstaining from which they believe themselves to be raised above others of the same craft.

Do they habitually prostitute their (1) unmarried, (2) married women?

Which of the following articles of food do the caste eat or abstain from eating: flesh, wine, monkeys, beef, pork, the flesh of cloven-footed or uncloven-footed animals, scaley or scaleless fish, crocodiles, snakes, lizards, jackals, rats, other vermin. . . . Is there any special article of food their abstaining from which tends in their opinion to raise them above some or other caste which does not abstain from it?[87]

It is hardly necessary to add that these questions were inspired by a rigidly sacerdotal understanding of the so-called Hindu castes. Answers to such questions could be merely monosyllabic, leaving no room for more elaborate deliberations. The myriad experiences of being a Hindu or a Vaishnavite in pre-colonial Assam could not be encompassed within the ambit of such a deterministic questionnaire. Thus, in Assam Maniram Dewan could claim to be a devout Vaishnavite and yet lament that regular rituals in the *Sakta* shrine of Kamakhya were beginning to be neglected after the coming of the British. In his description of the pre-devotional period (*Abhaktiya kal*), Dewan mentions how before the coming of Sankardeb, 'Hindu Brahmins' in Assam had debased themselves by not conforming to ritualistically sanctioned behaviour.

It is hard to believe that the rush to conform to rigid norms of a pan-Hindu identity did not affect the near monopoly of the *sattras* to the devotional loyalties of the people. Although a broader survey of the socio-cultural impact of colonialism on the *sattras* is outside the purview of this book, there are strong signs to suggest that the *sattras* were forced to adhere more closely to a narrower definition of Brahmanical Hinduism that came to the forefront during this period as a result of the intersections of print and the vernacular standard, which enabled a forum for debating issues and created a common pool of debatable matters. The growth in the conservative spirit within the *sattra* led to the foundation in the 1930s of an organization in Nowgong that called itself the *Sri Shankardev Sangha*.[88]

The organization's call to go back to the liberal spirit of the original faith preached by Sankardev indicates a dissatisfaction at some levels about the growing rift between the *sattras* and the simple and liberal faith preached by the saint-reformer. The call for reforming the *sattras* given out by Lakshminath Bezbaroa sometime later reflected the same concern.

Notes

1 Work for this chapter was facilitated by an internal grant from IITGN, Project No. IP/IITGN/HSS/MS/201415-14.

2 See Indrani Chatterjee, *Forgotten Friends Monks, Marriages and Memories of Northeast India*, New Delhi: Oxford University Press, 2013.

3 See Jayeeta Sharma, *Empire's Garden Assam and the Making of India*, Ranikhet: Permanent Black, 2011.

4 Haliram Dhekial Phukan, *Assam Buranji*, Calcutta: Samachar Chandrika Press, 1829.

5 Haliram Sharma Dhekial Phukan, *Kamrup Jattra Paddhati*, Calcutta: Samachar Chandrika Press, 1833, Reprint, Guwahati: Assam Prakashan Parishad.

6 B.C. Allen, ed., *Gazetteer of Bengal and North East India*, 1905, Reprint, New Delhi: Mittal, 1979.

7 Assam Sect. Progs, No. 76, January 1902, Assam State Archive (henceforth ASA), Dispur, Assam.

8 Francis Jenkins, *Diary and Notes of Captain F. Jenkins, Commissioner and Agent to the Governor General for Assam and the North Eastern Part of Rungpore, 1837–1841*, Calcutta: Baptist Mission Press, 1868.

9 D. Nath, *Satras in Colonial Assam: Their Response to the Emerging Socio-Political Issues*, Lecture-V, Guwahati: ICHR-NERC, 2007, p. 6; See also Sharma, *Empire's Garden Assam.*

10 Captain E.T. Dalton, 'Notes on the "Mahapurushiyas", a Sect of Vaishnavas in Assam', *Journal of the Asiatic Society*, Vol. XX, No. VI, 1851, pp. 455–469.

11 Ibid.

12 See S.N. Sarma, *The Neo-Vaishnavite Movement and Satra Institution on Assam*, Guwahati: Gauhati University, 1998, and Nath, *Satras in Colonial Assam*; see also Sharma, *Empire's Garden Assam.*

13 In a study of religious practices followed in British Assam, conducted in 1910, the author noted the differences in the practice of Vaishnavism in different sattras. Referring to the disparities between the *Bamunia sattras* and the *Mahapurushia sattras*, the author noted: 'The various communities exhibited slight differences in doctrine and practice, but insisted on the observance of caste and especially on the necessity of religious teachers being Brahmans, while they were tolerant of idolatry and even of the worship of non-Vaishnava deities. They also allowed the flesh of goats, pigeons, and ducks to be eaten. The adherents of Madhab Deb were distinguished by the name of Mahapurushias: they repudiated idolatry and the ascendancy of Brahmans, admitting, and even preferring, Sudras as religious guides.' Charles N.E. Eliot, 'Hinduism in Assam', *Journal of the Royal*

Asiatic Society of Great Britain and Ireland, Vol. 42, No. 4, October 1910, pp. 1155–1186, p. 1171. The Bengali periodical *Janmabhumi* in 1924–25 carried an article by Bijoy Bhushan Ghosh Chaudhury, who observed that the *Mahapurushia* followers of the Barpetasattra were accustomed to consuming various forms of meat, fish and eggs unlike the Vaishnavites in Bengal.

14 Eliot, 'Hinduism in Assam', p. 1179.
15 See Maheswar Neog, *Religions of the North-East*, New Delhi: Munshiram Manoharlal, 1984.
16 Ibid.
17 See Romila Thapar, 'Imagined Religious Communities? Ancient History and the Modern Search for a Hindu Identity', *Modern Asian Studies*, Vol. 23, No. 2, 1989, pp. 209–231, and Ronald Inden, 'Orientalist Constructions of India', *Modern Asian Studies*, Vol. 20, No. 3, 1986, pp. 401–446.
18 See Chatterjee, *Forgotten Friends Monks*.
19 John Peter Wade, *An Account of Assam*, 1800, ed., Benudhar Sharma, Reprint, Guwahati: Assam Jyoti, 1927.
20 F. Hamilton, *An Account of Assam*, first compiled in 1807–14, Reprint, Guwahati: Department of Historical and Antiquarian Studies Assam, 1963.
21 Francis Hamilton, *An Account of Assam*, first compiled in 1807–1814, Reprint, Guwahati: Department Of Historical And Antiquarian Studies Assam, 1963.
22 Ibid.
23 John M'Cosh, *Topography of Assam*, 1837, Reprint, New Delhi: Logos Press.
24 Robinson, *A Descriptive Account of Assam*, Guwahati, 1841, Reprint, Delhi: Sanskaran Prakashak, 1975.
25 Report on the Census of Assam, 1881.
26 Ibid.
27 Report on the census of Assam, 1891.
28 See Bodhisattva Kar, 'What Is in a Name? The Politics of Spatial Imagination in Nineteenth-Century Assam'.
29 Ibid., p. 3.
30 Cited in Ralph W. Nicholas, 'A Review of Worship of the Goddess According to the Kalikapurana', by K.R. Van Kooij, *The Journal of Asian Studies*, Vol. 36, No. 1, November 1976, pp. 172–174. For a detailed study of Goddess Kamakhya, see Bani Kanta Kakati, *Mother Goddess Kamakhya*, Guwahati, 1948. For a study of the *Kalika Purana*, see K.R. Van Kooij, *Worship of the Goddess According to the Kalika Purana*, Leiden, 1972.
31 'The Rudhiradhyaya or Sanguinary Chapter', translated from the Calica Puran, by W.C. Blaquiere, Esq, *Asiatic Researches*, Vol. 5, 1799.
32 See in this connection, Hugh B. Urban, *Tantra, Sex, Secrecy, Politics and Power in the Study of Religion*, California: University of California Press, 2003, and *The Economics of Ecstasy: Tantra, Secrecy and Power in Colonial Bengal*, New York: Oxford University Press, 2001. For a general discussion of the construction of traditions, see Eric Hobsbawm and Terrence Ranger, eds, *The Invention of Tradition*. Cambridge: Cambridge University Press, 2012, and Romila Thapar, *Cultural Transaction and Early India*, New Delhi: Oxford University Press, 1987; For the construction of traditions in British India, see Bernard S. Cohn, *Colonialism and Its Forms of Knowledge:*

The British in India, Princeton: Princeton University Press, 1966, and Lata Mani, 'Contentious Traditions: The Debate on Sati in India', in Kumkum Sangari and Sudesh Vaid (eds), *Recasting Women Essays in Colonial History*, New Delhi: Rutgers University Press, 1989.

33 Ronald Inden, *Imagining India*, Oxford: Basil Blackwell, 1990.

34 Ibid.

35 See Jeffrey J. Kripal, ed., *Encountering Kali: In the Margins, at the Center, in the West*, California: University of California Press, 2003.

36 William Ward, *A View of the History, Literature and Religion of the Hindoos Including a Minute Description of Their Manners and Customs and Translations from Their Principal Works*, Vol. 1, London: W.H. Pearce, 1817, p. 141.

37 'History of Cooch Behar', being an extract of a passage from Dr Buchanan's *Account of Rangpur* (revised and communicated by Major F. Jenkins), 1838, *Journal of the Asiatic Society of Bengal* (ed.), James Princep, Vol. VII, Part I (January to June), p. 3.

38 Ibid., p. 11.

39 Robinson, *A Descriptive Account of Assam*, p. 258.

40 Anukulchandra Bhattacharya, *Kamakhya Bhraman*, Calcutta, 1899, and *Assam Pradesher Bishesh Biboron*, compiled by Gopalchandra Basu, Calcutta, 1877 (transcript found in the National Library, Kolkata).

41 See Bernard S. Cohn, *Colonialism and Its Forms of Knowledge*, and Nicholas B. Dirks, *The Hollow Crown: Ethnohistory of an Indian Kingdom*, Cambridge: Cambridge University Press, 1988.

42 Cited in Jae-Eun Shin, 'Yoni, Yoginis and Mahavidyas: Feminine Divinities from Early Medieval Kamarupa to Medieval Koch Behar', *Studies in History*, Vol. 26, No. 1, 2010, pp. 1–29.

43 See Birinchi Kumar Barua, *A Cultural History of Assam*, Guwahati: Lawyer's, 1951.

44 Rajanikanta Bardoloi, *Rahadoi Ligiree*.

45 See Jae-Eun Shin, 'Yoni, Yoginis and Mahavidyas: Feminine Divinities from Early Medieval Kamarupa to Medieval Koch Behar', p. 21; Shin argues that the local goddess cult at Nilachal in Guwahati was transformed over the years through association with different groups of multiple female divinities such as the Yoginis and the Mahavidyas. Shin argues that a local goddess cult was adopted and utilized in the process of regional state formation, p. 9.

46 Debendranath Bhattacharya, *Axamat Saktipuja*, Guwahati, 1977.

47 Kar, 'What Is in a Name? The Politics of Spatial Imagination in Assam', *CENISEAS Papers*, No. 5, Guwahati: Centre for North East India, South and Southeast Asian Studies, 2004.

48 Ibid.

49 See Ernest A. Payne, *The Saktas: An Introductory and Comparative Study*, London: Oxford University Press, 1933.

50 K.S. Macdonald, *Kamrup and Gauhati in Assam*, Calcutta: Traill and Co., 1902 (reprinted from the *Indian Evangelical Review*, April 1902), p. 1.

51 Ibid., p. 2.

52 Ibid., p. 8.

53 See in this connection, Thomas. R. Metcalf, *Ideologies of the Raj*, Cambridge: Cambridge University Press, 1998, and Francis G. Hutchins, *The*

Illusion of Permanence: British Imperialism in India, Princeton, NJ: Princeton University Press 1967.

54 Macdonald, *Kamrup and Gauhati in Assam*, pp. 11–12.

55 See Victor Hugo Sword, *Baptists in Assam: A Century of Missionary Service, 1836–1936*, Chicago, IL: Conference Press, 1935.

56 See Bodhisattva Kar, 'Incredible Stories in the Time of Credible Histories: Colonial Assam and the Translations of Vernacular Geographies', in Raziuddin Aquil and Partha Chatterjee (eds), *History in the Vernacular*, New Delhi: Permanent Black, 2008.

57 Gunabhiram Barua, 'Saumar Bhraman', *Jonaki*, Dwitiya Bhag, Pancham Sankhya, 1822, Saka (AD 1890), p. 167.

58 Catalogue of Assamese Books 1906–1953, Oriental and India Office Collections, British Library, London.

59 Report on the Census of India/Assam, 1881; see Jayeeta Sharma for a discussion of the Brahminization of the sattras.

60 Sri Matiram Das, 'Kamakhya Mandir', *Jonaki*, Notun Khanda, Pratham Bhag, Dwitiya Sankhya, 1823 Saka, AD 1901, pp. 894–895.

61 'Assamiya Bhasha', Lecture delivered at the Assam Sahitya Sabha, 1870, *Hemchandra Goswami Rachanavali*.

62 Ibid., 1920.

63 See in this connection Partha Chatterjee, *The Nation and Its Fragments*. See also Ulrike Stark, 'Hindi Publishing in the Heart of an Indo-Persian Cultural Metropolis', in Stuart Blackburn and Vasudha Dalmia (eds), *Indian's Literary History Essays on the Nineteenth-Century*, New Delhi: Permanent Black, 2004, for the creation of a Hindu Hindi or the creation of a Hindu literary tradition through publication of Sanskrit classics in Hindi translation by Lucknow's Newal Kishore Press in the nineteenth century; see also Vasudha Dalmia, *The Nationalization of Hindu Traditions Bharatendu Harischandra and Nineteenth-Century Banaras*, New Delhi: Oxford university Press, 1997, and Prachi Deshpande, *Creative Pasts Historical Memory and Identity in Western India 1700–1960*, Ranikhet: Permanent Black, 2007.

64 Kar, 'What Is in a Name?'.

65 Ratneswar Mahanta, 'Garo Brittanto', *Assam Bandhu*, Part 1, No. 2, 1885.

66 'Bongali', *Assam Bandhu*, Part 1, No. 3, 1885.

67 Phukan, *Assam Buranji*, 1859, p. 89.

68 See M.N. Srinivas, *Social Change in Modern India*, New Delhi: Orient Blackswan, 1995.

69 See Yasmin Saikia, *Assam and India Fragmented Memories, Cultural Identity and the Tai-Ahom Identity*, Ranikhet: Permanent Black, 2005.

70 Cited in Audrey Cantlie, *The Assamese: Religion, Caste, and Sect in an Indian Village*, London and Dublin: Curzon Press, 1984, p. 233.

71 Cantlie observed this phenomenon while examining social mobility among the Kaibarta community in Sibsagar, p. 249.

72 Audrey Cantlie, *The Assamese*, ibid.

73 Ibid., p. 249.

74 Ibid., p. 234.

75 Ibid., p. 269.

76 Ibid.; see also Nath, *Satras in Colonial Assam*.

77 See Nath, *Sattras in Colonial Assam.*
78 Cantlie, *The Assamese*, p. 249.
79 Nath, *Sattras in Colonial Assam*, pp. 18–19.
80 See Gunabhiram Barua, *Assam Buranji* and Hemchandra Baruva, *Notes on the Marriage Systems of the Peoples of Asam*, Guwahati: Anandaram Barua, 1908.
81 Ratneswar Mahanta, 'Tirota', *Jonaki*, 1889; Krishna Kumar Barua, 'Bibaha aru Samaj', *Jonaki*, Chaturtha Bhag, Tritiya Sankhya, 1891.
82 Purnakanta Sharma, 'Tirota', *Jonaki*, Dwitiya Bhag, Pancham Sankhya, 1890.
83 See Tanika Sarkar, *Hindu Wife, Hindu Nation: Community, Religion, and Cultural Nationalism*, Ranikhet: Permanent Black, 2013.
84 General Department Home A, April 1902, Nos. 4–12, NAI.
85 Abstract from the Proceedings of the Government of India in the Home Department (Public), dated Simla, 23 May 1901, enclosed in 'Ethnographic Survey in Assam', General Department, Home A, April 1902, NAI.
86 Ibid.
87 Ibid.; see Bernard Cohn, 'The Census, Social Structure and Objectification in South Asia', in *An Anthropologist among Historians*, New Delhi: Oxford University Press, 1998, and Nicholas Dirks, *Castes of Mind Colonialism and the Making of Modern India*, Permanent Black, 2003; see also Shekhar Bandopadhyay, *Caste, Protest and Identity in Colonial India: The Namasudras of Bengal, 1872–1947*, New Delhi: Oxford University Press, 2011.
88 Cantlie, *The Assamese.*

CONCLUSION

Assam's colonial history was full of stereotypes that produced an image of the land and its peoples as strangely inadequate in numerous ways. The common ground in the apparently unrelated domains of land revenue, language, education and religion consists of a series of discourses that stemmed from a calculated disdain and at times a sheer ignorance of meanings that had once informed modes of living in the region constituting British Assam. One of the chief objectives of this book is to push back the date of colonization of the region to beyond 1826 and to highlight the all-encompassing nature of colonial subjugation in Assam that made British Assam distinct from the rest of India's colonial subjects. The book argues that the nature and character of the movement for an Assamese identity that took centre stage from the nineteenth century onwards cannot be adequately understood as an isolated outcome of the colonial state's language policy, often the starting point of any standard history book on Assam. The saga of colonization in Assam was more potent in character than what may be usually seen elsewhere in the country. At stake were the region's liminal socio-cultural and economic practices nurtured by the pre-colonial rulers through a highly sophisticated mechanism of accommodation and adaptation. This book foregrounds the sure and steady erosion of this liminal politico-cultural zone in the nineteenth century under the impact of colonial rule. It contends that the pre-colonial culture of shared practices began to give way in the nineteenth century under the weight of singular frames of understandings and hegemonic norms and standards. Many of these frames were unconsciously adopted by the people, while some were stoutly resisted, but shifts in earlier modes and practices of living were irreversible. Admittedly, Assam was no exception to what was after all a pan-Indian phenomenon. What, however, aggravated the situation in the Northeast was its immense diversity as well as the delicate fabric of inter-community relations that could not withstand the assault

247

of hegemonic norms and standards and pushed the region, sooner rather than later, into the throes of an ethno-political crisis. Assam was treated as a margin in colonial policy framework right from the beginning. The aspect of uncontrolled immigration from neighbouring Eastern Bengal, which the British enabled and which undoubtedly constituted a major element in this process of colonization, was just one part of a far bigger process of denial of the ethos and spirit of the land and its peoples and involved a complex process of subsumption of beliefs and practices that if left alone had the potential to indicate a more viable and sustainable mode of life in culturally sensitive and diverse Northeast. In my opinion, standard claims that the British treated Assam as a 'land frontier' are highly inadequate in explaining how, when and why Assam became a 'frontier' in colonial official discourse and especially in narrating what being a frontier entailed and implied. This book contends that the expression 'becoming a frontier' is far more appropriate in indicating the comprehensive and complex process of emasculation that Assam experienced under colonial rule and which worked both discursively and materially to gloss over the claims of the region and its peoples by denying them certain fundamental entitlements that the rest of colonial India's subjects were found to be enjoying. This book examines the fundamental premises informing colonial policies in British Assam in the seemingly unrelated domains of land revenue, language and education in order to understand this phenomenon of marginalization. The book tries to foreground the exceptionalities intrinsic to Assam's colonial experience that made it distinct from the pan-Indian colonial experience. The choice of period is deliberate. The nineteenth century constituted the foundational moment in the region's colonial history when much of the policies and premises of colonial rule were shaped and put in place from which little variation took place in the subsequent years. Needless to say, these changes have been examined with reference to pre-colonial modes and practices to bring out the true import of colonial rule in Assam.

Although the study affirms the exceptional nature of Assam's colonial experience, as well as the nature of reactions triggered by colonial modes of governance, one also acknowledges the fact that there was much that was common between the colonial histories of Assam and the rest of India. Imperialist motives and financial concerns of the Raj governed most of its policies in the country. In Assam as elsewhere, again, the major innovation that sustained nationalist response was print. Print constituted the inevitable outcome of colonial rule and along with modern education came to signify the progressive face of colonialism. Adopted by the Western-educated colonial middle-class elite, print became the primary medium of protest against rule. Assam was no different in this matter although for some reasons, nationalism in Assam did not immediately assume anti-colonial proportions. Nationalism in Assam swiftly took a cultural turn immersing itself in literary debates and anti-Bengali rhetoric, without directly addressing the basic premises of the political economy of the colonial state. This book argues that this peculiar trajectory of Assamese middle-class nationalism set it apart from other regions where the nineteenth century proved to be the seedbed of anti-colonial consciousness and even resistance. The course of Assamese middle-class politics was dictated by the nature and substance of colonial policy decisions premised almost invariably on discourses of 'progress' that served to turn attention away from the true intent of the policy makers. Above all, official rhetoric and discourse served to present the state in a beneficent light. Although one concedes that the growth of community consciousness was by and large the outcome of the general spirit of community solidarity that followed in the wake of Western education, Western ideas and print culture in the subcontinent, it is hard to sustain the argument that the specific nature of community that the middle class in Assam evoked in the nineteenth century grew organically out of the ideas and thoughts introduced by Western education. The book warns against taking community consciousness in Assam for granted. It contends that the narrowing of the contours of cultural boundaries in Assam was the logical culmination of a series of policy decisions on the part of the state and more significantly of the stated and unstated prejudices intrinsic to these decisions stemming from the colonial understanding of local society. It was an outcome of repeated attempts to undermine local practices as 'backward', of aspersions on the competence of the people of Assam and especially of overt comparisons made with the Bengali-speaking people. Some of the assumptions underlying colonial policies primarily in the domain of education but also reflected from time to time in debates on language and religion were not without their effects on the self-perception of the emergent Western-educated middle class in Assam. Needless to say, such assumptions and prejudices produced a sense of unhealthy competition that resulted in converting the Bengali into the 'other'. The making of communities may well have been the outcome of Western ideas and print communication as well as of the overall spirit of community belonging that became the hallmark of sociability in the nineteenth century, but its militant spirit and narrow contours in an otherwise syncretic cultural zone need to be complicated for an effective understanding of the phenomenon.

The social composition, as also the mental world of the new middle class that became the principal agents of change in Assam, was forged, first and foremost, through new economic policies that ruthlessly decimated the existing means of sustenance from land and other pre-colonial entitlements but did not replace these with new modes of livelihood in industry, trade or administrative occupations. The systematic closure of avenues of employment killed hopes of economic mobility for young aspirants. Yet, curiously enough, the growing angst failed to find expression through any overt means of anti-colonial resistance such as could be seen in many places outside Assam. This book examines how responses generated as a consequence of the passing of the old order of society were almost invariably cultural in essence and directed not towards the colonial state but towards the Bengali other. It further examines the hegemonic aspirations of the middle-class agenda which increasingly denied the cross-cultural ethos of the region. An intense homogenization followed as hegemonic tendencies manifested themselves in many ways – whether in the form of calls for conformity to 'Hindu' religious practices or to notions of a common and uniform past. Religious boundaries were consequently redrawn and norms of social behaviour redefined in the interests of homogeneity to convey impressions of unitary patterns of behaviour that community identities demanded as their defining criteria. History emerged as a significant object of scrutiny and a crucial site for the affirmation of togetherness as claims of shared practices in time came to constitute the essence of public discourse. The writing of history gained momentum, and the meaning of history changed now to become fixed, immutable and authoritative even as the practice of history writing itself was acquiring new modes of authentication. Thus, both the meaning and the writing of history changed to accommodate the new-found sensibilities of the literary elite. The social horizons of the community were progressively narrowed to include other social and cultural practices such as food habits, dressing practices and aesthetics as eligibility criteria for gaining entry into the community. These, therefore, emerged as additional terrains where uniform standards should be imposed. As if this was not enough, these norms and standards were declared not only as ubiquitous, sacred and inviolable, but also as old. By projecting them backwards in time, these were made into 'traditions' that were further accorded sanctity in the pages of the new cultural histories of the Assamese community. The nineteenth century was a period when something called an Assamese identity was endowed with a tangible past, present and future, and this could happen only at the cost of denying a larger and older history of shared existence. The book thus provides a window to these complex cultural negotiations that became the hallmark of the nineteenth century.

The choice of the nineteenth century for exploring these trends has been guided by the feeling that this is a less-explored period and one that has borne the brunt of a stereotypical understanding so far as the history of Assam is concerned. The various shades in policy decisions, as also the numerous sensibilities that made up the imaginary world of middle-class Assamese nationalism, have been duly considered. If the book chooses not to proceed beyond the nineteenth century, it is because the subsequent period has already received more than its fair share of consideration from scholars across the social science disciplines. The questions of immigration, hardening of cultural boundaries among some of Assam's plain and hill populations, the communalization of politics and the subsequent course of Assamese language debates have all been studied by numerous scholars, and one feels that there is hardly anything left to add. On the contrary, the nineteenth century happened so far to be a much-neglected field of study although the lag is gradually being filled up with some eminently engaging work that seek to interrogate the received wisdom of conventional approaches. This book seeks to contribute to this emerging field of Northeast India studies by examining the many worlds of Assamese middle-class sensibilities and the role of colonialism in shaping them. The work seeks to focus on strategy debates to bring out precise influences and negotiations leading up to policy decisions. The idea has been to contextualize these policies by gaining an insight into the mindset of the executive. The focus on print culture has its limitations and leaves out of its trajectory the responses of the majority of illiterate peoples who were co-opted into the Assamese community. The absence in Assam of something like a field of popular literature that could provide insights into the mental world of at least a section of the lower middle class, if not the entire population, necessarily limits the scope of this work. At the same time, one has to admit that print matter had various modes of circulation and found its way through various means into the heart and minds of people who did not actually read them, thereby involving these sections in the high debates of the literate classes.

The findings of the book suggest that individual British response to issues of language and land revenue was not always predictable and cannot be mapped through standard interpretations of the colonizer as ever hostile and calculating. Individual official responses could and did vary widely, and in many cases, terms of the debate were decided by what was 'appropriate' and 'good' for the people rather than what was necessary in the interests of the state. This is not to suggest that ultimate official policy decisions were not premised on strategic calculations. Again, there was no automatic solidarity between the state and the missionaries. On the contrary, the aims of the state and those of the Christian missionaries were often mutually conflictual, as the language debate in Assam clearly demonstrates. Even within the missionary fraternity, ideas could be at variance although in the end the logic of dissemination of the faith predominated. In terms of social processes, one cannot help noting the overall parity in pattern in terms of the emergence of an educated and highly articulate middle class that took to print with a remarkable alacrity, the emergence of new modes of sociability, the growing emphasis on history to bolster community claims and so on. The rush to embrace the new education and history was quite pan-Indian in characteristics. What is outstanding is the elite's failure to draw up a more inclusive community in sync with the heterogeneous cultural ethos of the region's pre-colonial past. The nationalist schemes for progress or *unnati*, as outlined in successive articles of the *Jonaki*, were intellectually limited in that despite suggesting a plethora of measures for the realization of progress such as industrial development, dissemination of education, hard work, sincerity of efforts and promotion of the vernacular, they fell short of outlining a constructive critique of the colonial rhetoric of progress. Nor did the authors come up with any concrete plans for realizing these goals. One is not suggesting, however, that strong response to colonial denials was utterly absent but that it was highly limited and inadequate when judged from a pan-Indian perspective. The statement also needs to be qualified with regard to the response evinced by the sections below the middle classes who resisted colonial exploitation tooth and nail.

In reading the socio-economic and cultural experiences of colonial rule in Assam, one is reminded of Sumit Sarkar's caveat in *Modern Times* that one must guard against binaries of any type in assessing pre-colonial and colonial histories. Yet one cannot help noting Assam qualifies for such binaries of assessment when it comes to discussing principles of governance underlying pre-colonial and colonial modes of functioning. It is hard to miss the latter's unsuitability for the region's complex geo-cultural morphology. Again, the findings from Assam throw up a lot of elements that challenge long-cherished stereotypes which are only now beginning to be interrogated such as the one that print and modernity went hand in hand. The case of Assam validates Sarkar's observation that print and vernacularization need not always prove to be liberating and could instead cause greater harm by imposing and fixing 'authoritative single meanings'. Moreover, print was also not always liberating and could be used to articulate many orthodox beliefs even if we grant that at times this was done deliberately as a knee-jerk reaction to colonial denigration. This is evident in the new elite's attempts to propagate Hindu histories, beliefs and rituals through print, and their reticence in forefronting the much more familiar and liberal history of neo-Vaishnavism in Assam. There is no denying the fact that print did throw up 'new opportunities' for hitherto marginal sections like women by creating new modes of articulation. Overall, this meant new possibilities, which would produce far-reaching changes although their full potential was yet to be realized. The public sphere that print and vernacularization enabled in the nineteenth century was real but limited. However, its most significant outcome in nineteenth-century Assam was in fostering a community consciousness that was represented as old and enduring. The findings from Assam also throw light on the many faces of colonial rule. The case of Assam throws up evidences that constitute the very antitheses of the long-held notion that British-educational policies necessarily promoted English education. The study affirms that policies varied according to specific situations. However, the strongest contrary feature so far consists of the response of the new middle-class elite, who proved Sumit Sarkar's caveat that everything that happened in the nineteenth century did not point towards anti-colonial resistance.[1] While it is easier to identify a nascent and ever-growing anti-colonial consciousness, the same did not lead to timely resistance to colonial categories of rule. The Assamese peasantry on the other hand did not suffer from any such constraint and could, consequently, react to colonial exploitation with much more spontaneity and vigour.

Note

1 Sumit Sarkar, *Modern Times India 1880s-1950s Environment, Economy, Culture*, Ranikhet: Permanent Black, 2014.

GLOSSARY

Babu title attributed to the order of lower-level clerks who worked for the British Indian bureaucracy, most commonly used to refer to the Bengali clerical order, later used to denote all Bengalis.

Bailoong a class of priests also called the Deodhais, associated with the religious practices of the Ahoms.

Bandi/beti male and female slaves or service personnel employed in the household in pre-colonial Assam.

Bari garden.

Basti homestead.

Bhakat members of the Vaishnavite monastic order sworn to celibacy.

Bhaxa the spoken vernacular.

Brahmottar land granted free of rent to Brahmins.

Buranji local chronicles; the term is used currently to refer to works of a historical nature.

Chamua rent-free land enjoyed by the nobles of the Ahom rate as service tenures.

Dangariya a nobleman of high status working for the Ahom state.

Devottar land granted free of rent to temples and religious institutions.

Dewan term used to denote local business agents of the East India Company.

Jhum shifting or swidden cultivation.

Khiraj land that payed full revenue.

Lakhiraj land that paid no revenue to the state, usually land gifted to religious functionaries or temples.

Mauzadar revenue collector responsible for a mauza.

Mauzah unit of revenue assessment.

Namoni administrative division in British Assam signifying 'lower' and consisting of the districts of Kamrup, Barpeta and Durrang.

GLOSSARY

Nisf-khiraj land that paid half of the revenue liable on a piece of land, once again a concessional rate granted in consideration of some act of merit.

Paik a subject of the Ahom state liable to render service obligations.

Parbatiya pertaining to the hill; the epithet came to be associated with the Brahmin preceptors of the Ahom royal family on account of their residence on the Nilachal Hill in Guwahati.

Ryot peasant or cultivator, also referred to as the 'raiyat'.

Sadar Amin a native judge of the civil court in the British Indian judicial system.

Sanad usually a land charter or deed granted by the ruler.

Sattra Vaishnavite monasteries.

Sattradhikar head of a sattra, also referred to as the Gossain or Mahanta.

Swargadeo literally lord of the heaven, title assumed by the Ahom rulers.

Ujani administrative division in British Assam signifying 'upper' and consisting of the districts of Sibsagar, Lakhimpur and Dibrugarh.

BIBLIOGRAPHY

Primary Sources

Unpublished

I. Proceedings and Files

Oriental and India Office Collection, British Library, London

a. Assam Proceedings (Home) from 1874 to 1880.
b. Public and Judicial Department Records: Annual Files from 1836 onwards.

National Archives of India, New Delhi

c. Proceedings of the Government of India in the Home Department, Education Branch from 1854 to 1899.
d. Proceedings of the Government of India in the Home Department, Public Branch from 1836 to 1899.
e. Proceedings of the Government of India in the Home Department, Miscellaneous Branch.
f. Proceedings of the Government of India in the Home Department, Revenue Branch.
g. Proceedings of the Chief Commissioner of Assam from August 1887 to July 1888.

Assam State Archives, Dispur

h. Letters received from miscellaneous quarters.
i. Letters received from the government.

257

j.   Letters received from the Board of Revenue.
k.   Letters issued to the government.
l.   Assam Commissioner's Papers.
m. Assam Commissioner's Files.
n.   The Political History of Assam Collection.
o.   Bengal Government Papers.

West Bengal State Archives, Kolkata

p.   Proceedings of the Government of Bengal in the General Department, Miscellaneous Branch, from 1859.
q.   Proceedings of the Government of Bengal in the Political Department, Political Branch, from 1859.
r.   Proceedings of the Government of Bengal in the General Department, Education Branch, from 1859.
s.   Proceedings of the Revenue Department, select volumes from 1834, 1835.

II. *Private Papers and Manuscripts*

Oriental and India Office Collection, British Library, London

a.   Papers of Captain (later Major General) Francis Jenkins (1793–1866), including letters, book and private journals relating to surveys in Arakan and Assam, and a description of the Brahmaputra valley, 1831–38, IOR/Mss Eur/F257.
b.   Translation of an original History of Assam by John Peter Wade (1762–1802), 1797, IOR/Mss Eur/D103.
c.   Buchanan-Hamilton (Francis) Papers (extracts compiled c. 1824–29, from various papers and maps relating to Burma and Assam), IOR/Mss Eur/D106.
d.   Papers of and related to Sir Henry John Stedman Cotton (1845–1915), Chief Commissioner of Assam, 1896–1902, IOR/Mss Eur/D1202.

Department of Historical and Antiquarian Studies, Guwahati

e.   Maniram Dewan, *Buranji Vivek Ratna*, 1838 (transcript).

National Archives of India, New Delhi

f.   History of Freedom Movement Papers, Phase II, 1885–1919.

BIBLIOGRAPHY

III. *Newspapers and Periodicals*

The Orunodoi
Assam Bandhu
Mou
Jonaki
Baptist Missionary Magazines (select issues)
Journal of the Assam Research Society
Asiatic Researches/Journal of the Asiatic Society of Bengal, select issues
Probashi
Jonmobhumi

Published Sources

Gazetteers

Assam District Gazette
East India Gazetteer
Rangpur District Gazetteers/ Eastern Bengal and Assam
Imperial Gazetteer of India, vol. 1

Government Reports, Census Papers and Others

Annual Reports of the Archaeological Survey of India, 1902–10.
Archaeological Survey of India – Cunningham Reports, vols 1–23.
Assam Land Revenue Manuals.
Captain Jenkins's Tour Diary of Upper Assam, 1838.
Catalogue of Assamese Books, 1906–53 (checked the ones published in the first two decades of the twentieth century).
General Report on Public Instruction in Assam from 1874 to 1900.
Report of the General Committee of Public Instruction of Bengal, 1838–39.
Report on the Administration of Land Revenue in Assam.
Report on the Administration of the Province of Assam from 1876 onwards.
Report on the Census of India/Assam for 1881, 1891, 1901 and 1911.
Report on the Eastern Frontier of British India, Captain R.B. Pemberton, 1835.
Report on the Province of Assam, A.J.M. Mills, 1854 (reprinted), Publication Board Assam, 1984.
W.W. Hunter, *A Statistical Account of Assam*, London, 1879.

BIBLIOGRAPHY

Books and Articles

Account of the Burman Empire and Kingdom of Assam (compiled from the works and M.S. Documents of the following most eminent public functionaries, viz, Hamilton, Symes, Canning, Cox, Ley-Den, F. Buchanan, Morgan, Towers, Elmore, Wade, Turner, Sisson, Elliott & C. & C), Calcutta, 1939.

A.C. Hazarika, ed., *Bezbaroa Granthavali*, Guwahati: Assam Sahitya Sabha, 1988.

Adam White, *A Memoir of the Late David Scott* (compiled by S.K. Bhuyan), Gauhati: DHAS, 1988.

(Sir) Alexander Mackenzie, *The North-East Frontier of India*, 1884, Reprint, New Delhi: Mittal, 1995.

Anandaram Dhekial Phukan, *Asamiya Larar Mitra*, 1849, ed., Gunabhiram Barooah, Reprint, Goalpara, 1875.

Anundoram Borooah, *Ancient Geography of India*, 1877, Reprint, Guwahati: Publication Board, Assam, 1971.

———, *Bhavabhuti and His Place in Sanskrit Literature*, 1877, Reprint, Guwahati: Assam Publication Board, 1971.

Archibald Watson, *Memoir of the Late David Scot*, Calcutta: Baptist Missionary Press, 1832.

B.C. Allen, C.G.H. Allen and H.F. Howard, *Gazetteer of Bengal and North-East India*, 1901, Reprint, New Delhi: Mittal, 1979.

Charles N.E. Eliot, 'Hinduism in Assam', *Journal of the Royal Asiatic Society of Great Britain and Ireland*, Vol. 2, No. 44, October 1910, pp. 1155–1186.

Clements R. Markham, *A Memoir of the Indian Surveys*, 1871, Reprint, Cambridge: Cambridge University Press, 2015.

Dinesh Chandra Sen, *History of Bengali Language and Literature*, Calcutta: University of Calcutta, 1911.

E.A. Gait, *A History of Assam*, 1905, Reprint, Guwahati: LBS Publications, 1962.

———, *Report on the Progress of Historical Research in Assam*, Shillong: Assam Secretariat Printing Office, 1897.

Francis Hamilton, *An Account of Assam* (first compiled in 1807–14), Reprint, Guwahati: Department of Historical and Antiquarian Studies Assam, 1963.

(Captain) Francis Jenkins, *Diary and Notes*, Calcutta: Baptist Mission Press, 1868.

G.A. Grierson, ed., *Linguistic Survey of India, Vol. V, Indo-Aryan Family, Eastern Group, Part I; Specimens of the Bengali and Assamese Languages*, Calcutta: Office of the Superintendent of Government Printing, 1903.

Gunabhiram Barua, *Assam Buranji*, 1884, Reprint, Guwahati: Assam Prakasan Parishad, 1972.

Haliram Dhekial Phukan, *Assam Buranji*, Calcutta: Samachar Chandrika Press, 1829.

Haliram Sharma Dhekial Phukkan, *Kamrup Jattra Paddhati*, Calcutta: Samachar Chandrika Press, 1833.

Harakant Barua Sadar Amin, *Assam Buranji*, Guwahati: DHAS, 1962.

———, in Kumudchandra Bordoloi (ed.), *Sadar Aminor Atmajiboni*, Guwahati: Lawyer's Book Stall, 1991.

H.B.L. Cutter, *Phrases in English and Assamese*, revised by E.W. Clark, Sibsagar, Assam: A.K. Gurney Printer, 1877.

Hemchandra Barua, *Hema Kosha, or an Etymological Dictionary of the Assamese Language*, ed. P.R. Gurdon, Calcutta: Baptist Mission Press, 1900.

Hemchandra Goswami, ed., *Purani Assam Buranji*, 1922, Reprint, Guwahati: Assam Sahitya Sabha, 1977.

Hemchandra Goswami Racanavali, Guwahati: Assam Sahitya Sabha, 1972.

Hemchunder Shurma, *Axomiya Bhaxar Byakaran*, 1859.

Horace Hayman Wilson, *Narrative of the Burmese War, 1824–26*, Calcutta: Horace Hayman Wilson, Esq, 1827.

(Major) James Rennell, *Journals Written for the Governors of Bengal during His Surveys of the Ganges and Brahmaputra Rivers, 1764*, Calcutta: Asiatic Society, 1910.

J.D. Anderson, *A Short Vocabulary of the Aka Language*, Shillong: Assam Secretariat Printing Office, 1896.

John Butler, *A Sketch of Assam*, London: Smith, Elder and Co., 1847.

———, *Travels and Adventures in the Province of Assam during the Residence of Fourteen Years*, London: Smith, Elder and Co., 1855.

John M'Cosh, *Topography of Assam*, 1837, Reprint, New Delhi: Sanskaran Prakashak, 1975.

John Peter Wade, *An Account of Assam*, 1800, Reprint, Guwahati: Assam Jyoti, 1927.

Kaliram Medhi, *Assamese Grammar and the Origin of the Assamese Language*, 1936, Reprint, Guwahati: Publication Board of Assam, 1998.

Kasinath Tamuli Phukan, *Assam Buranji*, 1906, Reprint, Calcutta: Majumdar Press.

(Rev.) K.S. Macdonald, *Kamrup and Gauhati in Assam*, Calcutta: Traill and Co., 1902.

Lakshminath Bezbaroa, *Mor Jivon Sworon*, Guwahati: Lawyer's Book Stall, 1999.

Mary Mead Clark, *A Corner in India*, Philadelphia, PA: American Baptist Publication Society, 1907.

Michael Symes, *An Account of an Embassy to the Kingdom of Ava in the Year 1795*, London: W. Bulmer & Co., 1800.

Miles Bronson, *A Dictionary in Assamese and English*, first edition, Sibsagar, Assam: American Baptist Mission Press, 1867.

Monier Williams, *Hinduism*, London: Society for Promoting Christian Knowledge, 1906.

Montgomery Martin, *The History, Antiquities, Topography and Statistics of Eastern India*, Vol. V (Rangpur and Assam), 1838, Reprint, New Delhi: Cosmo Publications, 1976.

Nathan Brown, *Grammatical Notices of the Assamese Language*, Sibsagar, Assam: American Baptist Mission Press, 1848.

Padmanath Bhattacharya Vidyavinod, D. Sarma (eds), *Kamarupasasanavali*, Guwahati: Publication Board Gauhati, 1981.

Padmanath Gohain Barua, *Asamar Buranji*, 1899, Reprint, Guwahati, 1976.

———, *Jiboni Sangraha*, Tejpur, 1925.

———, *Mor Somvarani*, Guwahati: Assam Prakashan Parishad, Guwahati, 1971.

P.H. Moore, ed., *Twenty Years in Assam*, 1901, Reprint, New Delhi: Omsons, 1982.

Lieutenant R. Wilcox, 'Memoir of a Survey of Assam and the Neighbouring Countries, Executed in 1825–6–7–8', *Asiatic Researches*, Vol. 17, 1832.

Reginald Arthur Lorrain, *Grammar and Dictionary of the Lakher or Mara Language*, Guwahati: DHAS, 1951.

S.O. Bishop, *Sketches in Assam*, Calcutta: City Press, 1885.

S.R. Ward, *Glimpse of Assam*, edited and published by S.R. Ward, Calcutta, 1884.

Sir Walter Hamilton, *The East India Gazetteer*, London: Parbury, Allen and Co., 1828.

William Griffith, *Travels in Assam, Burma, Bhutan, Afghanistan and the Neighbouring Countries*, 1847, Reprint, New Delhi: Mittal, 1982.

William Robinson, *A Descriptive Account of Assam*, Guwahati: Government Seminary, 1841, Reprint, New Delhi: Sanskaran Prakashak, 1975.

———, *Grammar of the Assamese Language*, Calcutta: Serampore Press, 1839.

(Rev.) William Ward, *A View of the History, Literature and Religion of the Hindoos: Including a Minute Description of Their Manners and Customs, and Translations from Their Principal Works*, Vol. 1, London: W. H. Pearce, 1817.

William E. Ward, *Note on the Assam Land Revenue System*, Shillong: Secretariat Press, 1897.

Secondary Sources

Books and Articles

Ajay Skaria, *Hybrid Histories: Forests, Frontiers and Wildness in Western India*, New Delhi: Oxford University Press, 1999.

———, 'Shades of Wildness: Tribes, Castes and Gender in Western India', *Journal of Asian Studies*, Vol. 56, No. 3, 1997, pp. 726–745.

Alok Rai, *Hindi Nationalism*, New Delhi: Orient Longman, 2000.

Amalendu Guha, 'Assamese Agrarian Society in the Late Nineteenth Century: Roots, Structures and Trends', *IESHR*, Vol. XVII, No. 1, 1980, pp. 35–94.

———, 'Impact of Bengal Renaissance on Assam: 1825–1875', *IESHR*, Vol. IX, No. 3, September 1972, pp. 288–304.

———, 'Land Rights and Social Classes in Medieval Assam', *IESHR*, Vol. III, No. 3, 1966, pp. 217–239.

———, *Planter Raj to Swaraj: Freedom Struggle and Electoral Politics in Assam, 1826–1947*, New Delhi: ICSSR, 1977.

Ania Loomba, *Colonialism and Postcolonialism*, London & New York: Routledge, 1998.

Anima Dutta, *Assam Vaishnavism*, New Delhi: Mittal, 1989.

Anindita Ghosh, *Power in Print Popular Publishing and the Politics of Language and Culture in a Colonial Society 1778–1905*, New Delhi: Oxford University Press, 2006.

———, 'Revisiting the "Bengal Renaissance": Literary Bengali and Low-Life Print in Colonial Calcutta', *Economic and Political Weekly*, Vol. 37, No. 42, 19–25 October 2002, pp. 4329–4338.

Anjali Sarma, *Among the Luminaries in Assam*, New Delhi: Mittal, 1990.

Aparna Basu, *The Growth of Education and Political Development in India 1898–1920*, New Delhi: Oxford University Press, 1974.

Apurba Kumar Baruah, *Social Tensions in Assam Middle Class Politics*, Guwahati: Purbanchal Prakash, 1991.

Archana Chakravarty, *History of Education in Assam 1826–1919*, New Delhi: Mittal, 1989.

Arjun Appadurai, *Worship and Conflict under Colonial Rule: A South Indian Case*, Cambridge, UK: Cambridge University Press, 1981.

Arupjyoti Saikia, *A Century of Protests: Peasant Politics in Assam since 1900*, New Delhi: Routledge, 2013.

———, 'Coal in Colonial Assam: The Dynamics of Exploration, Trade and Environmental Consequences', in K. Lahiri Dutta (ed.), *The Coal Nation: Histories, Cultures and Ecologies of Coal in India*, London: Ashgate, 2014.

———, 'Landlords, Tenants and Agrarian Relations: Revisiting a Peasant Uprising in Colonial Assam', *Studies in History*, Vol. 26, No. 2, 2010, pp. 175–209.

———, 'The Moneylenders and Indebtedness: Understanding the Peasant Economy of Colonial Assam, 1900–1950', *Indian Historical Review*, Vol. 37, 2010, pp. 89–109.

Ashis Nandy, 'History's Forgotten Doubles', *History and Theory, Theme Issue 34: World Historians and Their Critics*, Vol. 34, No. 2, May 1995, pp. 44–66.

Atul Chandra Hazarika, ed., *Bezbaroa Granthavali*, Guwahati: Sahitya Prakash, 1988.

Audrey Cantlie, *The Assamese: Religion, Caste, and Sect in an Indian Village*, London & Dublin: Curzon Press, 1984.

Bani Kanta Kakati, *Assamese: Its Formation and Development*, Guwahati: Lawyer's Book Stall, 1941.

———, *Mother Goddess Kamakhya*, Guwahati: Lawyer's Book Stall, 1948.

———, *Purani Kamrupar Dharmar Dhara*, Pathsala: Bani Prokash Mondir, 1955.

Benedict Anderson, *Imagined Communities: Reflections on the Origin and Spread of Nationalism*, London: Verso, 1983.

———, *The Spectre of Comparisons: Nationalism Southeast Asia and the World*, London: Verso, 1998.

Benudhar Sharma, *Maniram Dewan*, Guwahati: Assam Jyoti, 1950.

Bernard S. Cohn, 'The Census, Social Structure and Objectification in South Asia', *Folk*, Vol. 26, 1984, pp. 25–50.

———, *Colonialism and Its Forms of Knowledge*, Princeton, NJ: Princeton University Press, 1996.

Birinchi Kumar Barua, *A Cultural History of Assam*, Guwahati: Lawyer's, 1951.

Bodhisattva Kar, 'The Assam Fever', *Wellcome History*, No. 23, June 2003, pp. 2–4.

———, 'Heads in the Naga Hills', in Partha Chatterjee, Tapati Guha-Thakurta and Bodhisattva Kar (eds), *New Cultural Histories of India*, New Delhi: Oxford University Press, 2014.

———, 'Incredible Stories in the Time of Credible Histories: Colonial Assam and the Translations of Vernacular Geographies', in Raziuddin Aquil and Partha Chatterjee (eds), *History in the Vernacular*, New Delhi: Permanent Black, 2008.

———, *The Politics of Spatial Imagination in Assam, CENISEAS Papers*, No. 5, Guwahati: Centre for North East India, South and Southeast Asian Studies, 2004.

———, ' "Tongue Has No Bone": Fixing the Assamese Language, c. 1800–c. 1930', *Studies in History*, Vol. 24, No. 1, 2008, pp. 27–76.

Carol A. Breckenridge and Peter van der Veer, *Orientalism and the Postcolonial Predicament*, Philadelphia: University of Pennsylvania Press, 1993.

Chitralekha Zutshi, *Languages of Belonging Islam, Regional Identity, and the Making of Kashmir*, London: Hurst and Company, 2004.

Christopher King, *One Language, Two Scripts: The Hindi Movement in Nineteenth Century North India*, New Delhi: Oxford University Press, 1994.

Clifford Geertz, ed., *Old Societies and New States*, Glencow: The Free Press of Glencoe, 1968.

Dambarudhar Nath, *Satra Society and Culture Pitambardevs Goswami and History of Garamur Satra*, Guwahati: DVS Publishers, 2012.

———, 'Satras in Colonial Assam: Their Response to the Emerging Socio-Political Issues', in *Lecture Series Publication*, Lecture-V, ICHR, Guwahati: North-East Regional Centre.

Daud Ali, ed., *Invoking the Past: The Uses of History in South Asia*, New Delhi: Oxford University Press, 2002.

David Ludden, *Peasant History in South India*, Princeton: Princeton University Press, 1985.

———, 'Spatial Inequity and National Territory: Remapping 1905 in Bengal and Assam', *Modern Asian Studies*, Vol. 46, 2011, pp. 483–525.

———, 'Where Is Assam? Using Geographical History to Locate Current Social Realities', in Sanjib Baruah (ed.), *CNISEAS Papers*, Guwahati: OKD Institute of Social Change, 2003, Paper No. 1.

D.D. Mali, *Revenue Administration in Assam*, New Delhi: Omsons, 1985.

Debendranath Bhattacharya, *Axamat Saktipuja*, Pathshala: Bani Prakash, 1977.

Dinabandhu Dehury, 'T.E. Ravenshaw and the Spread of Education in Orissa', *Orissa Review*, April 2005, pp. 40–46.

Dipesh Chakrabarty, 'Postcoloniality and the Artifice of History: Who Speaks for "Indian" Pasts?', *Representations*, No. 37, *Special Issue: Imperial Fantasies and Postcolonial Histories*, Winter, 1992, pp. 1–26.

——, *Provincializing Europe*, Princeton, NJ: Princeton University Press, 2007.

D.V. Zou, 'A Historical Study of the "Zo" Struggle', *EPW*, Vol. 14, 3 April 2010, pp. 56–63.

——, 'The Pasts of a Fringe Community: Ethno-History and Fluid Identity of the Zou in Manipur, Indian Historical Review', Vol. 36, No. 2, 2009, pp. 209–235.

——, 'Raiding the Dreaded Past Representations of Headhunting and Human Sacrifice in North-East India', *Contributions to Indian Sociology*, Vol. 39, No. 1, 2005, pp. 75–105.

Edward W. Said, *Orientalism*, New York: Vintage, 1979.

Eric Hobsbawm and Terrence Ranger, eds, *The Invention of Tradition*, Cambridge: Cambridge University Press, 1983.

Eric Stokes, *The English Utilitarians in India*, London: Clarendon Press, 1969.

Ernest A. Payne, *The Saktas: An Introductory and Comparative Study*, New York: Oxford University Press, 1933.

Francesca Orsini, *The Hindi Public Sphere (1920–1940): Language and Literature in the Age of Nationalism*, New Delhi: Oxford University Press 2009.

——, 'What Did They Mean by "Public"? Language, Literature and the Politics of Nationalism', *Economic and Political Weekly*, Vol. 34, No. 7, 13–19 February 1999, pp. 409–416.

Francis G. Hutchins, *The Illusion of Permanence: British Imperialism in India*, Princeton, NJ: Princeton University Press, 1967.

Francisco J. Gil-White, *The Study of Ethnicity Needs Better Categories*, 2006, available from http://www.psych.upenn.edu/~fjgil/.

Fredrik Barth, *Ethnic Groups and Boundaries: The Social Organization of Cultural Difference*, Illinois: Waveland Press, 1969.

Gajendra Adhikary, *A History of the Temples of Kamrup and Their Management*, Guwahati: Chandra Prakash, 2001.

Gauri Vishwanathan, *Masks of Conquest Literary Study of British Rule in India*, New Delhi: Oxford University Press, 1989.

G.C. Spivak, 'Can the Subaltern Speak?', in C. Nelson and L. Grossberg (eds), *Marxism and the Interpretation of Culture*, Basingstoke: Macmillan Education, 1988, pp. 271–313.

Gunnel Cederlof, *Founding an Empire on India's North-Eastern Frontiers 1790–1840 Climate, Commerce, Polity*, New Delhi: Oxford University Press, 2014.

——, '"Natural Boundaries": Negotiating Land Rights and Establishing Rule on the East India Company's North-Eastern Frontier 1790s–1820s', in

Crispin Bates and Alpa Shah (eds), *Savage Attack Tribal Insurgency in India*, New Delhi: Orient Blackswan, 2014.

Harinath Sarma Dalai, 'Asamat Sakti Sadhana aru Sakta Sahitya', in Hiren Gohain (ed.), *Assam: A Burning Question*, Guwahati: Spectrum Publications, 1985.

H.K. Barpujari, *The American Missionaries and North-East India (1836–1900)*, Guwahati: Spectrum Publications, 1986.

———, *Assam in the Days of the Company*, Guwahati: Spectrum, 1990.

———, 'Management and Control of Religious Endowments in Assam', *Journal of the University of Gauhati*, Vol. xv, No. 1, 1964.

———, *Problem of the Hill Tribes of the North-East Frontier 1822–42*, Vol. 1, Guwahati: Lawyer's Book Stall, 1970.

H.K. Bhabha, 'Of Mimicry and Man: The Ambivalence of Colonial Discourse', 28 October, Vol. 28, Discipleship: A Special Issue on Psychoanalysis, Spring, pp. 125–133.

Hugh B. Urban, *The Economics of Ecstasy: Tantra, Secrecy and Power in Colonial Bengal*, New York: Oxford University Press, 2001.

———, *Tantra, Sex, Secrecy, Politics and Power in the Study of Religion*, Berkeley, California: University of California Press, 2003.

Ichhimuddin Sarkar, *Aspects of Historical Geography of Pragjyotisa-Kamarupa*, Calcutta: Naya Prokash, 1992.

Imdad Hussain, *From Residency to Raj Bhavan: A History of Shillong Government House*, New Delhi: Regency Publication, 2005.

Indrani Chatterjee, *Forgotten Friends Monks, Marriages and Memories of Northeast India*, New Delhi: Oxford University Press, 2013.

Jae-Eun Shin, 'Yoni, Yoginis and Mahavidyas: Feminine Divinities from Early Medieval Kamarupa to Medieval Koch Behar', *Studies in History*, Vol. 26, No. 1, 2010, pp. 1–29.

James Scott, *The Art of Not Being Governed: An Anarchist History of Upland Southeast Asia*, New Haven, CT: Yale University Press, 2009.

Jayeeta Sharma, *Empire's Garden Assam and the Making of India*, Ranikhet: Permanent Black, 2011.

———, ' "Lazy" Natives, Coolie Labour, and the Assam Tea Industry', *Modern Asian Studies*, Vol. 43,No. 6, 2009, pp. 1287–1324.

———, 'Missionaries and Print Culture in Nineteenth-Century Assam', in Robert Eric Frykenberg (ed.), *Christians and Missionaries in India: Cross-Cultural Communication Since 1500*, Michigan: William B. Eerdmans Publishing Co., 2003.

Jeffrey J. Kripal, ed., *Encountering Kali: In the Margins, at the Center, in the West*, California: University of California Press, 2003.

Jogendranath Bhuyan, *Unniso Satikar Asom Samvad*, Dibrugarh, 1998.

John Edwards, *Language, Society and Identity*, Oxford: Oxford University Press, 1985.

John Lyons, *Language and Linguistics: An Introduction*, Cambridge, UK: Cambridge University Press, 1981.

Joy L.K. Pachuau, *Being Mizo Identity and Belonging in Northeast India*, New Delhi: Oxford University Press, 2014.

J.P. Naik and Syed Nurullah, 'A Student's History of Education in India 1800–1973', New Delhi: Pan Macmillan, 1976.

Kanak Lal Barua, *Anandaram Dhekial Phukanar Jivan Caritra*, 1880, Reprint, Guwahati, 1971.

———, *Early History of Kamarupa*, Guwahati: Lawyer's, 1966.

Krishna Kumar, *Political Agenda of Education: A Study of Colonialist and Nationalist Ideas*, New Delhi: Sage, 2005.

Kumkum Chatterjee, 'Communities, Kings and Chronicles: The Kulagranthas of Bengal', *Studies in History*, Vol. 21, No. 2, 2005, pp. 173–213.

Kumud Chandra Bordoloi, ed., *Sadar Aminar Atmajivani*, Guwahati: Lawyer's Book Stall, 1960.

Kunal Charabarty, 'Cult Religion: The Puranas and the Making of the Cultural Territory of Bengal', *Studies in History*, Vol. 16, No. 1, 2001, pp. 1–16.

Lakshahira Das, *Development of Secondary Education in Assam*, New Delhi: Omsons, 1990.

Lata Mani, 'Contentious Traditions: The Debate on Sati in India', in Kumkum Sangari and Sudesh Vaid (eds), *Recasting Women Essays in Colonial History*, New Brunswick, NJ: Rutgers University Press, 1990.

Laurence W. Preston, *The Devs of Cincvad: A Lineage and the State in Maharashtra*, Cambridge: Cambridge University Press, 1989.

Lila Gogoi, *The Buranjis Historical Literature of Assam*, New Delhi: Omsons, 1986.

Lisa Mitchell, *Language, Emotion, Politics in South India: The Making of a Mother Tongue*, Ranikhet: Permanent Black, 2009.

M. Kar, 'Assam's Language Question in Retrospect', *Journal of the Indian School of Social Sciences*, Vol. 4, No. 2, September 1975, pp. 21–35.

Madhumita Sengupta, 'Orienting Progress? Some Aspects of Education in Nineteenth-Century Assam', *Economic and Political Weekly*, Vol. XLVII, No. 29, 21 July 2012, pp. 53–60.

———, 'War of Words: Language and Policies in Nineteenth-Century Assam', *Indian Historical Review*, Vol. 39, No. 2, 2012, pp. 293–315.

Maheswar Neog, *Anandaram Dhekial Phukan: Plea for Assam and Assamese*, Jorhat: Asam Sahitya Sabha, 1977.

———, *Nidhi Levi Farwell*, New Delhi: Sahitya Academy, 1985.

———, 'An Outline of Lakshminath Bezbaroa's Life', in Maheswar Neog (ed.), *Lakshminath Bezbaroa, the Sahityarathi of Assam*, Guwahati: Gauhati University, 1972.

———, *Religions of the North-East*, New Delhi: Munshiram Manoharlal, 1984.

Manorama Sharma, *Social and Economic Change in Assam: Middle Class Hegemony*, New Delhi: Ajanta, 1990.

Manu Goswami, *Producing India*, New Delhi: Permanent Black, 2004.

Michiel Baud and Willem Van Schendel, 'Toward a Comparative History of Borderlands', *Journal of World History*, Vol. 8, No. 2, Fall 1997, pp. 211–242.

Milton Sangma, *History of American Baptist Mission in N.E. India*, New Delhi: Mittal, 1987.

Nagen Saikia, *Background of Modern Assamese Literature*, New Delhi: Omsons Publications, 1988.

Nagendranath Basu, *Social History of Kamarupa*, Calcutta: The Jain Siddhanta Prakashak Press, 1922.

Nayanjot Lahiri, *Marshalling the Past: Ancient India and Its Modern Histories*, Ranikhet: Permanent Black, 2012.

———, *Pre-Ahom Assam: Studies in the Inscriptions of Assam between the Fifth and the Thirteenth Centuries AD*, New Delhi: Munshiram Manoharlal, 1991.

Neeladri Bhattacharya, 'Pastoralists in a Colonial World', in David Arnold and Ramchandra Guha (eds), *Nature, Culture, Imperialism: Essays on the Environmental History of South Asia*, New Delhi: Oxford University Press, 1996, pp. 49–95.

———, 'Remaking Custom: The Discourse and Practice of Colonial Codification', in R. Champakalakshmi and S. Gopal (eds), *Tradition, Dissent and Ideology*, New Delhi: Oxford University Press, 1996.

Nicholas B. Dirks, *Castes of Mind Colonialism and the Making of Modern India*, Princeton, NJ: Princeton University Press, 2001.

———, *The Hollow Crown: Ethnohistory of an Indian Kingdom*, Cambridge: Cambridge University Press, 2007.

Nilmani Mukherjee, *The Ryotwari System in Madras 1792–1827*, Calcutta: Firma K.L.M., 1962.

Nirode K. Barooah, *David Scott in North-East India 1802–1831: A Study in British Paternalism*, New Delhi: Munshiram Manoharlal, 1969.

———, 'David Scott and the Question of Slavery in Assam: A Case Study in British Paternalism', *The Indian Economic & Social History Review*, Vol. 6, No. 2, 1969, pp. 179–196.

N.N. Acharya, *Assam and Neighbouring States Historical Documents*, New Delhi: Omsons, 1983.

Parikshit Hazarika, 'The Kamurpi Apabhramsa', *Journal of the Assam Research Society*, Vol. 18, 1968.

Partha Chatterjee, *Agrarian Relations and Politics in Bengal: Some Considerations on the Making of the Tenancy Act Amendment 1928*, Calcutta: Centre for Studies in Social Sciences, 1980.

———, 'Anderson's Utopia', *Diacritics*, Vol. 29, No. 4, Winter 1999, pp. 128–134.

———, 'Bengal: Rise and Growth of a Nationality', *Social Scientist, the National Question in India Special Number*, Vol. 4, No. 1, August 1975, pp. 67–82.

———, *The Nation and Its Fragments, Colonial and Postcolonial Histories*, Princeton, NJ: Princeton University Press, 1993.

———, *Nationalist Thought and the Colonial World: A Derivative Discourse*, London: Zed Books, 1986.

———, ed., *Texts of Power Emerging Disciplines in Colonial Bengal*, Minneapolis: University of Minnesota Press, 1994.

————, 'Transferring a Political Theory: Early Nationalist Thought in India', *Economic and Political Weekly*, Vol. 21, No. 3, 18 January 1986, pp. 120–128.

Partha Chatterjee and Anjan Ghosh (eds), *History and the Present*, New Delhi: Permanent Black, 2002.

Paul R. Brass, *Ethnicity and Nationalism Theory and Comparison*, New Delhi: Sage Publications, 1991.

————, *Language, Religion and Politics in North India*, Cambridge: Cambridge University Press, 1974.

Peter Robb, 'The Colonial State and the Construction of Indian Identity: An Example on the Northeast Frontier in the 1880s', *Modern Asian Studies*, Vol. 31, No. 2, pp. 245–283.

Pierre Nora, Representations, No. 26, Special Issue: Memory and Counter-Memory (Spring, 1989), pp. 7–24.

Poromesh Acharya, 'Education in Old Calcutta', in Sukanta Chaudhury (ed.), *Calcutta: The Living City*, Vol. 1, Calcutta: Oxford University Press, 1990, pp. 85–94.

Prachi Deshpande, *History in the Vernacular Historical Memory and Identity in Western India 1700–1960*, Ranikhet: Permanent Black, 2007.

————, 'Scripting the Cultural History of Language: Modi in the Colonial Archive', in Partha Chatterjee, Tapati Guha-Thakurta and Bodhisattva Kar (eds), *New Cultural Histories of India*, New Delhi: Oxford University Press, 2014.

Prasanjit Duara, *Rescuing History from the Nation: Questioning Narratives of Modern China*, Chicago: Chicago University Press, 1995.

Priyam Goswami, *Assam in the Nineteenth Century: Industrialization and Colonial Penetration*, Guwahati: Spectrum, 1999.

Rajanikanta Bardoloi, *Rahdoi Ligiree*, Originally published in 1930; Reprint, Guwahati: Sahitya Prakasa, 1949.

Rajat Kanta Ray and Ratnalekha Ray, 'The Dynamics of Continuum in Rural Bengal under the British Imperium', *Indian Economic and Social History Review*, Vol. 10, No. 2, 1973, pp. 103–128.

Rajen Saikia, *Social and Economic History of Assam, 1853–1921*, New Delhi: Manohar, 2001.

Ramesh Chandra Kalita, *Assam in the Eighteenth Century*, New Delhi: Omsons, 1992.

Ranajit Dev Goswami, *Banikanta Kakati Aru Axamar Bouddhik Xomajor Iti-hax*, Academic Committee, Maligaon: L.C. Bharali College, 1995.

Ranajit Guha, *An Indian Historiography for India in Dominance without Hege-mony History and Power in Colonial India*, Cambridge: Harvard University Press, 1997.

————, *A Rule of Property for Bengal: An Essay on the Idea of the Permanent Settlement*, New Delhi: Orient Longman, 1982.

————, *The Small Voice of History*, Ranikhet: Permanent Black, 2009.

Ratnalekha Ray, *Change in Bengal Agrarian Society, 1765–1850*, New Delhi: Manohar, 1979.

Raziuddin Aquil and Partha Chatterjee, eds, *History in the Vernacular*, New Delhi: Permanent Black, 2011.

Richard Burghart, 'A Quarrel in the Language Family: Agency and Representations of Speech in Mithila', *Modern Asian Studies*, Vol. 27, No. 4, 1993, pp. 761–804.

Robert Eric Frykenburg, ed., *Christians and Missionaries in India Cross-Cultural Communication Since 1500*, Michigan and Cambridge: Eerdmans, 2003.

———, *Land Control and Social Structure in Indian History*, Madison: University of Wisconsin Press, 1969.

Roger Chartier, *On the Edge of the Cliff History, Language and Practices*, Baltimore and London: The Johns Hopkins University Press, 1997.

———, *The Order of Books Readers, Authors, and Libraries in Europe between the Fourteenth and Eighteenth Centuries*, Stanford: Stanford University Press, 1994.

Romila Thapar, *Cultural Transaction and Early India*, New Delhi: Oxford University Press, 1987.

———, 'Imagined Religious Communities? Ancient History and the Modern Search for a Hindu Identity', *Modern Asian Studies*, Vol. 23, No. 2, 1989, pp. 209–231.

Ronald Inden, *Imagining India*, London: Hurst and Company, 1990.

———, 'Orientalist Constructions of India', *Modern Asian Studies*, Vol. 20, No. 3, 1986, pp. 401–446.

Sabyasachi Bhattacharya, ed., *Approaches to History Essays in Indian Historiography*, New Delhi: Primus, 2011.

———, *The Contested Terrain Perspectives on Education in India*, New Delhi: Orient Longman, 1998.

Sajal Nag, 'Contesting Exclusion, Resisting Inclusion Contradictory Trends in Historical Research in North East India (1800–1900)', in Sabyasachi Bhattacharya (ed.), *Approaches to History Essays in Indian Historiography*, New Delhi: Primus, 2011.

———, *Pied Pipers in North-East India*, New Delhi: Manohar, 2003.

———, *Roots of Ethnic Conflict: Nationality Questions in North East India*, New Delhi: Manohar, 1990.

Sanghamitra Misra, *Becoming a Borderland: The Politics of Space and Identity in Colonial Northeastern India*, New Delhi: Routledge, 2011.

———, 'Changing Frontiers and Spaces: The Colonial State in Nineteenth-Century Goalpara', *Studies in History*, Vol. 21, No. 2, 2005, pp. 215–246.

———, *New Subjectivities: Writing Histories in Colonial Goalpara and Assam*, Lecture Series Publication, Lecture-XIV, Guwahati: ICHR North-East Regional Centre, 2007.

Sanjay Subrahmanyam, 'Connected Histories: Notes towards a Reconfiguration of Early Modern Eurasia', *Modern Asian Studies*, Vol. 31, No. 3, July 1997, pp. 735–762.

Sanjib Baruah, *Durable Disorder: Understanding the Politics of North East India*, New Delhi: Oxford University Press, 2005.

———, *India against Itself: Assam and the Politics of Identity*, New Delhi: Oxford University Press, 2001.

————, 'Post Frontier Blues toward a New Policy Framework for Northeast India', in *Policy Studies 33*, Washington: East-West Center.

Sarat Chandra Ghoshal, *A History of Cooch Behar*, Cooch Behar: State Press, 1942.

Shrutidev Goswami, *Aspects of Revenue Administration in Assam*, New Delhi: Mittal, 1987.

S.K. Bhuyan, *Anglo-Assamese Relations, 1771–1826*, Guwahati: Lawyer's Book Stall, 1974.

————, *Early British Relations with Assam*, Shillong: Assam Government Press, 1949.

————, ed., *Kamrupar Buranji*, Guwahati: DHAS, 1958.

————, *Studies in the Literature of Assam*, Guwahati: Lawyer's Book Stall, 1956.

S.N. Sarma, *The Neo-Vasinavite Movement and the Satra Institution of Assam*, Guwahati: Gauhati University, 1966.

Stuart Blackburn and Vasudha Dalmia, eds, *India's Literary History Essays on the Nineteenth Century*, Ranikhet: Permanent Black, 2004.

Sudipta Kaviraj, 'The Imaginary Institution of India', in Partha Chatterjee and David Arnold (eds), *Subaltern Studies*, Vol. VII, New Delhi: Oxford University Press, 1993.

Sugata Bose, *Agrarian Bengal: Economy, Social Structure and Politics*, Cambridge: Cambridge University Press, 1986.

Sumathi Ramaswami, *Passions of the Tongue: Language Devotion in Tamil India 1891–1970*, New Delhi: Munshiram Manoharlal, 1998.

Sumit Guha, 'Society and Economy in the Deccan, 1818–50', *IESHR*, Vol. 20, December 1983, pp. 389–413.

Sumit Sarkar, *Modern Times India 1880s–1950s Environment, Economy, Culture*, Ranikhet: Permanent Black, 2014.

————, *Writing Social History*, New Delhi: Oxford University Press, 1997.

Suniti Kumar Chatterjee, *The Place of Assam in the History and Civilization of India*, Bani Kanta Kakati Memorial Lectures, 1954, Guwahati: University of Gauhati, 1970.

Tapan Raychodhury, 'Permanent Settlement in Operation: Bakargang District, East Bengal', in Robert Eric Frykenburg (ed.), *Land Control and Social Structure in Indian History*, Madison: University of Wisconsin Press, 1969.

T.H. Eriksen, 'Ethnicity and Nationalism: Definitions and Critical Reflections', *Bulletin of Peace Proposals*, Vol. 23, No. 2, June 1992, pp. 219–224.

Thomas R. Metcalf, *Ideologies of the Raj*, New Delhi: Cambridge University Press, 1998.

Thomas R. Trautmann, *Aryans and British India*, New Delhi: Sage Publications India, 1997.

————, *Languages and Nations: The Dravidian Proof in Colonial Madras*, New Delhi: Yoda Press, 2006.

Tilottama Misra, *Literature and Society in Assam, 1826–1926*, New Delhi: Omsons, 1985.

————, 'Social Criticism in Nineteenth Century Assamese Writing: The Orunodoi', *Economic and Political Weekly*, Vol. 20, No. 37, 14 September 1985, pp. 1558–1566.

Udayon Misra, 'The Transformation of Assamese Identity: A Historical Survey', in *H.K. Barpujari Endowment Lecture (4)*, Shillong: The North East India History Association, 2001.

U. Goswami, *A Study on Kamrupi: A Dialect of Assamese*, Guwahati: DHAS, 1990.

Ulrike Stark, *An Empire of Books: The Naval Kishore Press and the Diffusion of the Printed in Colonial*, New Delhi: Orient Blackswan, 2009.

Upinder Singh, *The Discovery of India, Early Archaeologists and the Beginnings of Archaeology*, New Delhi: Permanent Black, 2004.

Vasudha Dalmia, 'The Locations of Hindi', *Economic and Political Weekly*, Vol. 38, No. 14, 5–11 April 2003, pp. 1377–1384.

————, *The Nationalization of Hindu Traditions Bharatendu Harishchandra and Nineteenth-Century Banaras*, New Delhi: Oxford University Press, 1997.

Veena Naregal, *Language, Politics, Elites, and the Public Sphere Western India under Colonialism*, New Delhi: Permanent Black, 2001.

Velcheru Narayana Rao, David Shulman and Sanjay Subrahmanyam, eds, *Textures of Time: Writing History in South India 1600–1800*, Ranikhet: Permanent Black, 2001.

Victor Hugo Sword, *Baptists in Assam: A Century of Missionary Service, 1836–1936*, Chicago, IL: Conference Press, 1935.

Willem Van Schendel, *Bengal Borderland beyond State and Nation in South Asia*, London: Anthem, 2005.

Yasmin Saikia, *Assam and India Fragmented Memories, Cultural Identity and the Tai-Ahom Identity*, Ranikhet: Permanent Black, 2005.

————, 'Religion, Nostalgia, and Memory: Making an Ancient and Recent Tai-Ahom Identity in Assam and Thailand', *The Journal of Asian Studies*, Vol. 65, No. 1, February 2006, pp. 33–60.

INDEX

Abors 19, 25, 92
Agarwalla, Chandrakumar 162
aggressive despotism 24
Ahoms 25, 50, 75, 79, 89–90,
    94–5, 101–2, 142, 159, 187, 189,
    193–4, 196, 198, 202, 218, 237–9;
    aristocracy 144; dynastic rule 189;
    elite 63; kings 22; language 159;
    legacy 39; monarchy 35, 98; rulers
    16, 24, 25, 78, 161
Alaler Ghorer Dulal 185
American Baptist Missionary Union 91
Ancient Geography of India 203, 204
Anderson, Benedict 1, 3
Anglo-vernacular schools 115, 119
Appadurai, Arjun 56
Arracan 21
Asamat Arya Basati 170
Asamiya Bhasa (Goswami) 168
Asiatic Journal and Monthly Register
    (vol. II) 145
Assam: acquisition of 31, 36–7,
    220; administration 20; Baptist
    missionaries in 24; benign state
    56–60; Brahmanical Hinduism
    in 219, 234; British rule in 37,
    39, 53, 56, 57; Burmese invasion
    and 22–3, 26; cadastral land
    survey in 48; colonial experience
    248; contending identities
    156–9; contending pasts 229–32;
    cultivation in 46, 47; economy of
    46, 55; education in 131, 133;
    ethnographic delusions 222–6;

evangelism and imperialism in 24;
frontier 16; government college
in 132–3; Hindu iconography
237–42; history of 184, 250;
integration, British Empire 29;
invoking traditions 38–45; landed
interests in 47–8; land revenue
measures 37; land tenure in
40; language policy in 79, 80;
literary works 86, 167; medium of
instruction, schools 87; monarchy
and nobility of 24; nationalist
turn 232–7; 'Northeast Frontier'
territory 22–3; paik system 39–43;
peasants in 49–54; plantation
economy 33; political history of
193; population of 99; revenue
assessment in 29; rude tribes
in 23–4; ryot 45–56; Singphos
24; survey of 19; temples in 56,
224; traditions, inventing 226–9;
traditions, violating 60–2; trajectory
24; Vasihnavism in 219–22
Assam Bandhu 169, 170, 175
Assam Buranji (Phukan, Kashinath
    Tamuli) 150
*Assam Buranji Arthat Assam Deshiya
    Itihas* (Phukkan, Haliram Dhekial)
145
Assam Deshar Itihas yani Buranji
183
Assamese dialect 85
Assamese language 78–9, 85, 87–8,
    92–3, 95, 97–8, 102, 155, 157–9,

273

161–2, 166–9, 171, 175, 197, 211; Carey's Bible 91, 92; debates 8, 251; laboratory of 102–5; lexical autonomy of 97; orthography of 88; Sadiya people 91; Sanskrit and 102; 'specifically different language' 84
Assamese literature 82, 157
Assamese people: autonomy of 84–5, 97; claims of 163, 168; community 155, 183, 193, 197, 200, 202, 250–1; intellectuals 133, 161, 163, 170, 175, 237; intimate histories of 183–214; middle class 143–4, 209, 237; middle-class politics 9–10, 249; nationalist agenda 188–92; peasantry 43, 56, 253; ryot 33, 63
Assamiya 8, 145
Assam Literary Society 158
Assam Proper 8, 48–9, 52, 55, 95, 115, 147, 210; syllogisms of 147
Assam Tenancy Act 55
Axomiya Bhaxar Byakaran (1859) 156
Axomiya Bhaxa Unnati Sadhini Sabha 162

Bamuni Konwar 170
Bandobast arrangement 30
Baptist Missionary Press 81
Barooah, Gunabhiram 198–202, 204
Barooah, Nirode K. 24, 29
Barth, Fredrik 3
Barua, Jaduram Deka 102–4
Baruah, Sanjib 43
Baruva, Hemchandra 156–7, 159
Baud, Michiel 6
Bengalee dialect 85
Bengali language 77–9, 83–4, 145, 167, 171–2, 183; standardization of 84
Bentinck, William 110
Bezbaroa, Lakshminath 146, 169, 171
Bhattachajee, Narayan 64–5
Bhavabhuti and His Place in Sanskrit Literature 157
Bhaxa 102, 147, 151

Bhutan, frontiers of 16
Bhutias 92
Bhuyan, Surya Kumar 150, 196
Blaquiere, W.C. 227
Borahs 35
Borooah, Anundoram 203
bounding speech, travesties of 152–6
British Assam 7; frontier 15
Bronson, Miles 98
Brown, Nathan 90, 94, 97, 102–4, 151, 152
Buchanan-Hamilton, Francis 223, 228
Burmese invasion 23
Burooahs 35
Butler, John 20

Cachar 21
Cacharese 75
Calcutta Gazette 16
Carey's Bible 97
caste–tribe dichotomy 18
Cederlof, Gunnel 17, 21, 22, 25
Chakrabarty, Dipesh 4–5
Chakraborty, Tarachand 145
Chatterjee, Indrani 25
Chatterjee, Partha 1, 188, 191
Chatterjee–Anderson debate 4
Chattopadhyay, Bankim Chandra 206
Chaudhury, Harakanta Sharma Barua 196
Chaudhury, Sonaram 205
colonial Assam 5, 8–9, 143, 183, 208
colonial educational policies 144; disability, rhetoric of 111–16; logic and desiring control 116–21; political economy, of education 121–4; privileges, reinforcing 124–33; village-level schools 114
colonialism 56, 143
colonial state's language policy 79–80, 247
communities, self-images of 4
Cornish, R. 86–7
Cornwallis system 30
Cossyah 21
Cotton, Henry 55, 132